The Political Economy of the Middle East

Series Editor
Ashraf Mishrif, Humanities Research Centre, Sultan Qaboos University, Muscat, Oman

This series explores the nature of Middle Eastern political regimes and their approaches to economic development. In light of the region's distinctive political, social and economic structures and the dramatic changes that took place in the wake of the Arab spring, this series puts forward a critical body of high-quality, research-based scholarship that reflects current political and economic transitions across the Middle East. It offers original research and new insights on the causes and consequences of the Arab uprisings; economic reforms and liberalization; political institutions and governance; regional and sub-regional integration arrangements; foreign trade and investment; political economy of energy, water and food security; finance and Islamic finance; and the politics of welfare, labor market and human development. Other themes of interest include the role of the private sector in economic development, economic diversification, entrepreneurship and innovation; state-business relationships; and the capacity of regimes and public institutions to lead the development process.

The book series is Scopus Indexed.

Ahmed Badran · Ashraf Mishrif
Editors

Shaping the Future of Development in the GCC

Artificial Intelligence Policies, Challenges and Opportunities

Gulf Research Centre Cambridge
Knowledge for All

palgrave
macmillan

Editors
Ahmed Badran
Department of International Affairs
Qatar University
Doha, Qatar

Ashraf Mishrif
Humanities Research Centre
Sultan Qaboos University
Muscat, Oman

ISSN 2522-8854 ISSN 2522-8862 (electronic)
The Political Economy of the Middle East
ISBN 978-981-96-7962-1 ISBN 978-981-96-7963-8 (eBook)
https://doi.org/10.1007/978-981-96-7963-8

This Palgrave Macmillan imprint is published by the registered company Springer Nature Singapore Pte Ltd.
The registered company address is: 152 Beach Road, #21-01/04 Gateway East, Singapore 189721, Singapore

Acknowledgements

The original research and valuable insights in this volume are the outcome of an extensive discussion in the workshop "Navigating the Future of Artificial Intelligences in the GCC: Challenges and Opportunities," which was organized by the Gulf Research Centre Cambridge and held in the University of Cambridge, UK, in July 2024.

The editors of this book would like to express their appreciation to all the participants for presenting the early version of their papers at the workshop and the more advanced version for publication in this book. They would also like to express their appreciation for the financial and logistical support provided by the Gulf Research Centre Cambridge during the organization of the workshop. The editor would also like to thank the anonymous peer reviewers for their thorough review, insightful views, and useful comments that contributed to the improvement of the book. We also thank the publisher and the production team for their outstanding efforts to produce this high-quality volume. Without their contribution this book would not have been published.

As we are rapidly engaging in the fourth industrial revolution, we hope that this book offers new insights and practical guidance to policymakers, practitioners, researchers, and students on the importance of artificial intelligence and its role in economic and social development.

Contents

Notes on Contributors

Hesham M. Al-Ammal is an assistant professor at the University of Bahrain and the University of London. His main research interests are in the analysis of algorithms, deep learning, and computer security. He served as Dean of the College of Information Technology at the University of Bahrain until 2017, and in 2020 established the Benefit Advanced AI Lab. He is a Senior Member of the Association for Computing Machinery (ACM).

Nasser Al-Azri is an associate professor in the Department of Mechanical and Industrial Engineering. His expertise lies in renewable energy systems, decarbonization, and process optimization, where he has made substantial contributions to both academic research and industrial applications. With interdisciplinary knowledge spanning mechanical, chemical, and industrial engineering, he plays a pivotal role in advancing sustainable energy solutions and improving industrial processes regionally and internationally. His work exemplifies the integration of engineering disciplines to address complex challenges in energy and process efficiency.

Nasr Al Hinai is an associate professor at Sultan Qaboos University with a Ph.D. in Industrial Engineering. He has received multiple international teaching and research awards. His research spans sustainable manufacturing, project management, and innovation. He has published widely in top journals and conferences and actively contributes to academic leadership and curriculum development.

Mahmoud Alsafy is a Ph.D. candidate in Industrial Engineering at Sultan Qaboos University, specializing in nanocomposite materials. He holds an M.Sc. with honors and a B.Sc. in Mechatronics Engineering. With 18 international publications, his research spans neural networks, additive manufacturing, sustainability, circular economy, and optimization. He previously served as a Lecturer Assistant at HTI, Egypt.

Mustafa Altıntaş graduated from Akdeniz University with a bachelor's degree in the department of international relations in 2015. He completed his master's degree in Gulf Studies at Qatar University in 2023. Currently, he is pursuing a Ph.D. in Gulf Studies at Qatar University.

Sanaa Ashour is a professor of Gulf Studies in the Center of Gulf Studies at Qatar University. Previously, she served as the director of the Sociology program at Al Ain University in the United Arab Emirates. She also served as a visiting professor at TU Dresden, DZHW, and FiBS in Germany. She has a Ph.D. in Development Studies from the Faculty of Arts at the University of Bonn, Germany, and a master's degree in social policy and planning from the London School of Economics and Political Science (LSE). Professor Sanaa Ashour has published her work in leading international journals on higher education institutional and policy dynamics, shedding light on the complex forces that shape higher education in rapidly developing contexts, particularly within the Gulf region. Her research bridges policy-oriented inquiries—including quality assurance, institutional development, and the evolution of private higher education systems, and digital transformation—with student-centered issues such as access, awareness, behaviors, and retention. By critically analyzing structural challenges like dropout phenomena and gender disparities, and exploring the cultural legacies that shape teaching evaluations, her scholarship offers valuable insights for policymakers and practitioners striving to improve educational quality in the region. She has also authored a book on ethnic politics and the policy-making process.

Mostafa Atia is a full professor and vice dean at the Arab Academy for Science and Technology and Maritime Transport, Cairo, Egypt. He received the degree of Doctor of Philosophy in 2002. His current research interests are in the areas related to manufacturing automation. He has published more than 50 papers in referred journals and conference proceedings. He accomplished a respected number of industrial projects in the field of design and manufacturing of heavy and special equipment.

Ahmed Badran is Associate Professor of Public Policy and former Department Head at Department of International Affairs College of Arts and Sciences, Qatar University. Dr. Badran holds a Ph.D. degree in Politics (Public Policy) from the University of Exeter, the United Kingdom. Dr Badran has extensive teaching and research experience in the field of Public Policy and Administration. Dr Badran has also worked as a Post-Doctoral Research Fellow at Aston Centre for Critical Infrastructure and Services (ACCIS), Aston Business School, Aston University, Birmingham, the UK. Dr. Badran's research interests extend to cover different areas of the AI regulatory governance and politics of regulation in liberalized public utilities including telecoms, water, and energy sectors particularly in transition and developing economies.

Sara Badran is currently undergoing an MPhil in Digital Humanities at the University of Cambridge. She is particularly interested in how colonial inherent biases perpetuate discriminative racial stereotypes in Generative AI software and facial recognition tools. She is also pursuing research into how AI intersects with political, economic, and social issues including democracy and freedom of speech. She holds a First-class BA (Hons) in Film & Television Studies from the University of Exeter, where she focused on intercultural conflict and postcolonialism using case study approaches through screen media. She currently has two upcoming publications focusing on how AI will affect labor markets (Qatar focused) and how AI will impact higher education. She has strong digital skills with confident abilities to use a range of editing software including Adobe Suite, with a general understanding of coding software such as NVivo. Previous work experience placements include: BBC Spotlight: News & Current Affairs Team, Channel 4 Skills Work Experience Program, Exmouth Journal (which included working with eight local newspapers and fifteen news-story publications), Optix Solutions (Digital marketing campaign focusing on Brand Strategy) & Bill Douglas Cinema Museum (curated a digital exhibition on Aboriginal Australian representation on-screen).

Zhaojin Chu serves as Computer Engineering intern at the School of Engineering, American University in Dubai. Known for his exceptional work ethic and commitment to research, Zhaojin specializes in Data Analytics and Deep Learning technologies. He is currently focused on a domain-specific Deep Learning acceleration project, where he applies his technical expertise to optimize neural network performance for specialized applications. His dedication to advancing AI technologies demonstrates his passion for innovation in the field. Zhaojin's research contributes to the growing body of knowledge in computational efficiency for deep learning models, positioning him as a promising talent in the computer engineering discipline.

Mohammadu Bello Danbatta is a researcher at Sultan Qaboos University, pioneering advancements in green energy and decarbonization through AI. His work enhances renewable energy systems using advanced data analysis and machine learning, providing critical insights for regional and global policymakers and supporting sustainable energy practices. His AI-driven methodologies offer scalable solutions for global energy transitions, aligning with net-zero targets. By integrating AI into environmental governance, Danbatta empowers governments to make informed decisions that support global sustainability goals. His contributions are pivotal in shaping the future of renewable energy and climate action strategies worldwide.

Rafael Hernández de Santiago is a senior research fellow at the Gulf Research Centre, Jeddah, Saudi Arabia.

Mohammed Faiz is a Ph.D. scholar in the Department of Remote Sensing and GIS Applications at Aligarh Muslim University. He holds an M.Sc. in Remote Sensing & GIS and a B.Tech in Civil Engineering. His work blends technical and spatial aspects of geospatial science. He has professional experience as a GPS/GIS Surveyor and Field Assistant on national projects. His research focuses on urban planning, LULC change, and natural hazard modeling. Faiz recently published a paper on landslide prediction in Uttarakhand using advanced geospatial techniques.

Rashid Aziz Faridi is a professor in the Department of Geography at Aligarh Muslim University. He has 24 years of teaching and research experience. His areas of interest are, Sustainable Urban Settlement Systems, Urban Development, Urban Modeling, and Urban Design, Migration, Diaspora, Population and Demographic Studies, Remote Sensing, Geographical Information Systems (GIS), and Geopolitics of Urban Systems. He has several publications in National and International journals. Dr. Faridi holds Ph.D., M. Phil, M.Sc., and B.Sc. (Hons.) degrees from Aligarh Muslim University and Certificate courses from the Indian Institute of Remote Sensing (IIRS, Dehradun). He has authored a book on Select Cities of North India.

Mohammad Osaid Farooq is currently in his final semester of Master of Architecture from Georgia Institute of Technology, USA. Along with his studies, he is working part time as Designer 1 with Brink Design in Atlanta. His professional work involves airport retrofits, along with designing residential, civic, and commercial spaces. His interests lie in educational, commercial, and civic spaces which merge human interaction with the built environment and create spaces that blur the lines between art and science. He is involved in researching urban systems that foster community, resilience, harmony, and growth.

Tahura Fatima is an architect currently working in the aviation sector with Assystem, India. Her professional work involves planning, design, and research of airport infrastructure. Her research interests lie at the intersection of architecture and emerging technologies, with a focus on the application of artificial intelligence in spatial planning and design. She is currently examining the feasibility and prospects of heliports within urban mobility systems.

Areeb Fazli is pursuing master's in Intelligent Interactive Systems from Pompeu Fabra University and a passionate and performance-driven Software Engineer with hands-on experience in web development and a strong foundation in AI and Machine Learning. With a background in Computer Applications and a track record of delivering scalable and user-centric digital solutions, he has contributed to both freelance and academic projects. Areeb brings expertise in Python, Flask, React Native, and a variety of data science tools and is committed to solving real-world problems through innovative tech solutions.

Rakshanda F. Fazli is a professor in the Department of West Asian Studies at Aligarh Muslim University. She holds an MA, M. Phil in Geography, and a Ph.D. in West Asian Studies from AMU. She received a Netherlands Fellowship in 2008 and multiple NNRMS Fellowships for training in Remote Sensing and GIS. Her research interests include migration, population, resource development, and geospatial studies. Dr. Fazli has published widely in reputed national and international journals. She has also led research clusters on migration, tourism, urbanization, and water resource management in Saudi Arabia and India-GCC relations.

Nejib Ben Hadj-Alouane joined AUD in 2022 as Professor of Computer Engineering after serving at Tunisia's ENIT and ENSI universities, where he modernized curricula and established graduate programs.

His industry experience includes developing control systems at Dow Chemical, creating traffic simulation software for FHWA/MDOT, and implementing ERP solutions in Tunisia. With over 90 publications, his research spans agile automation, security concepts, infrastructure optimization, and smart agriculture systems. He pioneered a genetic algorithm optimizing game server placement in cloud environments. As an entrepreneur, Dr. Alouane co-founded a software startup and architected HR management solutions for remote mining operations in Canada. He mentored over 20 graduate students.

Ashraf Mohamed Keshk is Director of the Strategic and International Studies Program and Editor-in-Chief of the Derasat Journal at the Bahrain Center for Strategic, International, and Energy Studies (Derasat). Previously I served as a mentor at the NATO Defense College in Rome during the Crisis Management Exercise from 2009 to 2018. the author of several notable works, including Maritime Security of the Arab Gulf States: Analysis of Current Threats, Confrontation Mechanisms, and Future Challenges (Springer, 2022); NATO and the Gulf Countries: An Analysis of the Fifteen Year Strategic Partnership (Springer Singapore, 2021); Security and Defense Policies of the Arabian Gulf Countries: Options, Crisis Management, and Challenges (Ethics Press, 2024).

Asharul Islam Khan is a seasoned academic and consultant currently affiliated with Sultan Qaboos University in the Sultanate of Oman. He holds a Ph.D. in Software Engineering and has been actively engaged in teaching, research, and academic development since 2010. Over the years, Dr. Khan has contributed significantly to the field through his scholarly work, with more than 30 research manuscripts published in reputable peer-reviewed journals and international conferences. Dr. Khan is particularly passionate about exploring how intelligent systems can transform urban environments to promote sustainability, efficiency, and improved quality of life for citizens. His work bridges theory and practice, offering insights valuable to both academia and real-world smart city initiatives across the GCC region and beyond.

Ashraf Mishrif is the founding director and chair of the Oman Chamber of Commerce and Industry Research Chair for Economic Studies, Sultan Qaboos University. Served as Industrial Development Advisor for UNIDO (Vienna), Lead Economic Consultant for the Ministry of Economy (Muscat), Cultural Advisor for the Egyptian Embassy

Cultural Bureau (London), and Managing Director of the London-based consulting firm EU-Med International. Graduate of King's College London, where he also served as Senior Research Fellow and Associate Professor, established the MA Political Economy of the Middle East Program, and supervised over 45 Ph.D. students. Established and led several research clusters and doctoral programs in economic development, political economy, and international business and finance in various British and Gulf universities. An investment expert with over 340 investment opportunities in various sectors worth US$5.5 billion. Managed several research projects with a budget of US$2.1 million and 32 research staff. Fellow of International Society for Development and Sustainability (Japan). Book Series Editor of the Scopus-indexed Palgrave Macmillan Political Economy of the Middle East (Singapore). Authored and edited more than 100 books, chapters, and papers, including two volumes on nationalization of labor markets and economic diversification in the GCC and UNIDO's Industrial Development Report 2024 https://www.unido.org/idr2024.

Vinod Pangracious is an associate professor and chairman of Electrical and Computer Engineering Department at the American University in Dubai, UAE. He holds a distinguished academic and industry background, having earned his degree from the prestigious Indian Institute of Technology Bombay (IITB) in 2001. Prior to his academic career, he held key technical roles as a Member of Technical Staff (Principal Development Engineer) at leading semiconductor companies, including Cypress Semiconductor Inc. (USA), Infineon Technologies GmbH (Germany), and Innovative Silicon SA (Switzerland). Before joining the American University in Dubai, Dr. Pangracious pursued his doctoral research at the University of Pierre and Marie Curie (Paris VI), France. His research expertise spans Three-Dimensional Integrated Circuits (3D ICs), Machine and Deep Learning, and Bioinformatics. With a strong publication record, he has authored or co-authored over 50 research papers and has been actively involved in the academic community as a reviewer, program chair, organizing committee member, and steering committee member for numerous international conferences. His contributions to both industry and academia highlight his deep technical knowledge and leadership in advanced computer engineering research.

Sujan Piya is currently working as Associate Professor in the Department of Industrial Engineering and Engineering Management, College of Engineering, University of Sharjah (UOS), UAE. Prior to joining UOS, he has an extensive experience working at Sultan Qaboos University (Oman) and Hiroshima University (Japan). He holds a Ph.D. degree in Industrial Engineering from the Department of Artificial Complex Systems Engineering, Hiroshima University. His major research interests are in Production planning and control, Supply chain management, and Process Optimization. He has authored several research papers published in reputable journals and conference proceedings. He serves as a regular reviewer of many international journals. He has also served as guest editors for reputable journals.

Raagav Ramakrishnan serves as a research intern at the School of Engineering, American University in Dubai, specializing in Electronics and Communication Engineering. With nine years of experience as both a debater and innovator, Raagav brings a unique perspective to engineering challenges. He excels at creating meaningful connections, valuing each interaction as an opportunity to enrich lives and generate value. His adaptive mindset and problem-solving abilities allow him to navigate complex situations with confidence. Passionate about creating tangible societal impact, Raagav leverages his expertise in innovation and marketing to drive positive changes in how people live, consistently seeking new learning experiences and growth opportunities.

Abdulla E. Subah is an assistant professor in the Computer Science Department at the College of Information Technology, University of Bahrain. He holds a Ph.D. in Computing and Information Sciences from the University of Bahrain and is a member of the management committee in the Benefit Advanced AI and Computing Lab. His research interests lie in HPC, Parallel Computing, and Machine Learning for Performance Optimization, with current involvement as a USER in the CMS Experiment at CERN focusing on HPC and GPU applications.

Muhammed Ali Topal is an undergraduate student in Finance at Qatar University. His research interests are tax revenue analysis, public investment optimization, and tax evasion detection.

Mustafa Selman Yaylalı is an MA graduate student in Gulf Studies at Qatar University, has a bachelor's degree in political science and public administration from Selcuk University, Türkiye. Previously, he studied at Nicholaus Copernicus University of Poland and worked as a research assistant at an NGO in the Netherlands as part of Erasmus+ Program. His research interests are cultural studies, soft power, and public diplomacy, aiming to contribute insightful perspectives specifically pertaining to the Arabian Gulf region.

Abbreviations

ANFIS	Adaptive Neuro-Fuzzy Inference System
ANN	Artificial Neural Network
AQI	The Air Quality Index
BA	Benchmarking Approach
BIPV	Building-Integrated Photovoltaic Systems
BP	Backpropagation
BP-NN	Backpropagation Neural Network
CERN	European Organization for Nuclear Research
CNN	Convolutional Neural Network
CRM	Customer Relationship Management Systems
CSRNet	Congested Scene Recognition Network
DMT	Desired Machining Time
EJA	Expert Judgment Approach
FF	Feedforward
FFANN	Function Fitting Artificial Neural Network Classifier
HPC	High-Performance Computing Centers
ILO	International Labour Organization
LLMs	Large Language Models
MENA	Middle East and North Africa Region
MLP	Multi-Layer Perceptron
MTO	Make-To-Order Production Model
NDMT	Normalized Desired Machining Time
RAA	Risk Analysis Approach
RBF-NN	Radial Basis Function Neural Network
SDGs	United Nations Sustainable Development Goals
STA	Software Tools Approach

SVM	Support Vector Machine
TMC	Total Manufacturing Cost
TMT	Total Manufacturing Time
TOMS	Total Ozone Mapping Spectrometer
WRF	Weather Research and Forecasting Models

List of Figures

List of Tables

CHAPTER 1

Navigating Artificial Intelligence in the GCC

Ashraf Mishrif and Ahmed Badran

1.1 Introduction

The Gulf Cooperation Council (GCC) countries are going through an important historical turning point because of the developments brought about by Industry 4.0 technologies, more specific Artificial Intelligence (AI) applications. The transformative impact of these technologies has affected various aspects of everyday life, from communications, work practice, social development, digitalization, manufacturing, smart home, education, healthcare, security, and cybersecurity. This means that AI is no longer just a technological innovation, but it has become a vital tool to develop smart homes and cities, healthcare and education systems, water management and food security, and protect our lives, and material and intellectual properties.

A. Mishrif (✉)
Humanities Research Centre, Sultan Qaboos University, Muscat, Oman
e-mail: ashraf.mishrif@gmail.com

A. Badran
Department of International Affairs, Qatar University, Doha, Qatar
e-mail: a.badran@qu.edu.qa

A. Badran and A. Mishrif (eds.), *Shaping the Future of Development in the GCC*, The Political Economy of the Middle East,
https://doi.org/10.1007/978-981-96-7963-8_1

The motive of the GCC countries to harness the power of the AI is to make them more socially connected, technologically efficient, economically productive, and culturally integrated. This also forced many of them to explore the application of this technology in achieving inclusive growth and sustainable development. Although the current state of AI adoption in the Gulf region is in its early stages, the estimated annual growth in the economic contribution of AI in gross domestic product (GDP) is expected to be between 20 and 34% per year across the region in the next twenty years, with the highest rates expected in the United Arab Emirates (UAE) and Saudi Arabia (Haider, 2023). The significance of the economic impact of AI was realized a decade earlier, with the UAE being the first GCC country to publish its AI national strategy in 2017, while Saudi Ariba incorporating AI in its Saudi Vision 2030.

There are also several driving forces that have accelerated AI adoption in the GCC region. The widespread effect of the COVID-19 pandemic pushed for technological advancement to contain the pandemic while continuing remotely business, economic and social activities. The effective use of technology in promoting remote work and education during the pandemic encouraged many countries to foster digitalization and invest in industry 4.0 technologies, including AI, machine learning, big data analytics, 3D printing, and cloud computing. A significant boost in AI adoption is also seen owing to the value of AI-powered automation, remote work, and a change in consumer habits. The closure of physical shops during the pandemic boosted e-commerce and online retail shopping opened a new venue for companies to sell their products while improving customer experience by collecting pools of customer data that resulted in the sector being one of the fastest sectors to opt for AI processes (Haider, 2023).

As AI has the potential to bring significant benefits to the economy and society in the GCC, this chapter aims to explore the emergence and rise of AI as a key driver for innovation and economic development in the region. It also aims to reflect on the use of AI in various aspects of human life, including healthcare, education, finance, and industry, as well as diverse economic and social policy sectors. The chapter also highlights the challenges and new opportunities that AI is providing to many industries, companies, and individuals, while underlining unique ethical, regulatory, and socio-economic challenges that GCC governments must deal with effectively when implementing AI technologies and applications.

This chapter also serves as an introduction to provide the main aims, objectives, and structure of the book.

1.2 Conceptualizing Artificial Intelligence and Its Role in Shaping Development

The concept of AI has emerged and developed over the past fifty years. The definition has gone beyond the function of computerizing or automating to deal with the ability to make informed judgments and decisions by responding to patterns in data. It is simply defined as a simulation by a machine of human behavior. Wang (2019) defines AI as "computer systems that are similar to the human mind in a certain sense, though a computer and a human mind cannot be identical in all aspects." This definition appears more complex than the simple information-processing system because it implies various aspects of human behavior, capabilities, intelligence, functions, and problem solving. The alignment of human behavior and machine learning has developed over the years. Sarmah (2019) argues that AI emerged from Artificial Narrow Intelligence (ANI), where a machine learning that specializes in one area to solve one problem at a time like recommending a product, a process that is close to replicating and sometimes surpassing how humans carry out tasks. The Artificial General Intelligence (AGI) is the next stage of development that has a human level of cognitive function. This system needs to connect thousands of ANI systems together to imitate human behavior. The Artificial Super Intelligence (ASI) is the highest level where AI can completely surpass any sort of human intelligence by being creative, making rational decisions, building relationships, and deciding on whether the function to be good or evil (Sarmah, 2019).

The advancement of ASI represents an extraordinary opportunity to shape the future of development in the global economic system. It differs from previous technologies in the way that technological advancement overcomes humans' capabilities, and that humans and companies are no longer controlling technology. Belk et al. (2023) argue that the adoption of AI is rapidly accelerating as customers embrace life in new technology-made environments. These advances are substantially expanding as the boundaries between human and technology become blurred. In addition, it has become apparent that most Industry 4.0 technologies incorporate disruptive analytical systems and hardware such as AI, autonomous robots, big data analytics, cloud computing, and Internet of Things. Many of these technologies are fast incorporated in business operations, with AI playing a crucial role in many industries including manufacturing, supply chains, education, healthcare, and services. The financial services are also expected to be totally automatized in the next decade, surpassing the level of automation in manufacturing (PwC, 2022).

Consequently, the utilization of AI is essential to our everyday life. In a rapidly growing digital world, AI plays a crucial role in defining cyber-attacks, identifying fraudulent transactions, and preventing unauthorized access to data. Sarmah (2019) argues AI helps in business process automation, where it can optimize the manual processes given its efficiency at handling routine tasks, improving interfaces, handling massive amounts of data, using robotics in factories, managing condition in product storage, processing payments, and registering customer requests.

In terms of its contribution to development, AI has significantly transformed the concept of a smart home from a science fiction idea to a present-day reality. Today, AI-powered devices and systems have become common fixtures in many homes, offering unprecedented levels of convenience, efficiency, and security. The integration of AI into our homes is a clear demonstration of how advanced technology is becoming an integral part of our everyday lives. For example, smart home devices with AI can learn from our behaviors, habits, and preferences to conduct automated routine tasks and make our homes more comfortable and efficient. This is apparent in a smart thermostat that can learn our schedule and adjust the temperature, accordingly, saving energy and reducing your utility bills.

Moreover, AI is transforming the healthcare sector, making it an essential tool to enhance patient care, streamline medical procedures, expedite research, and analyze vast amounts of data to identify patterns that humans might miss. This ability is transforming diagnostics and treatment plans, leading to more accurate diagnoses and personalized care. AI also plays an important role in medical research by speeding up the drug discovery process, analyzing the effectiveness of different treatments, and predicting disease outbreaks, hence enabling quicker responses to health crises.

In education, AI has transformed the way we teach and learn. Key functions include automating administrative tasks or grading systems, personalizing the learning experience for each student, and providing customized content and resources that cater to their specific needs. This level of personalization can enhance the learning process, making it more engaging and effective. Educators can also benefit from AI by analyzing students' interactions with the AI-powered platform to identify patterns and trends in the student's learning behavior and predict future learning outcomes, enabling them to intervene proactively and provide additional support where needed. In addition, AI is also revolutionizing the way educational content is delivered by adopting innovative learning tools such as virtual reality simulations and AI-powered educational games to make learning more engaging and fun, fostering a love for learning among students. The transformative impact of AI has made education more personalized, predictive, and immersive.

1.3 Navigating Artificial Intelligence in the GCC Countries

AI is developing at an accelerated pace in the GCC region. Today, AI applications are deployed in our homes, cars, and workplaces, with increasing use in finance, education, healthcare, manufacturing and supply chains, as explained above. The growing trend of AI adoption in the Gulf region and globally is largely attributed to the immense benefits of this technology in many critical applications (Baccour et al., 2022). Additionally, the topic of AI gains special importance for the GCC countries due to its intersection with many of the strategic social and economic goals, as well as its role in sustainable development, healthcare, education, labor market, and economic diversification policies in this region.

The presence of AI in many aspects of life in modern societies means that individuals and governments will struggle between its legal and ethical implications for some time (Al-Qadi et al., 2023). Hence, the rapid increase in AI applications in the GCC region raises fundamental questions about the potential impact of intelligent applications on the daily lives of humans. As time passes, AI technologies gain a foothold in new industries and become more immersed in our daily lives, and this trend appears to continue in the GCC for the foreseeable future (Al-Sulaiti, 2023). Despite the advantages of employing AI in various sectors, its activities and applications pose many socio-economic and security challenges to public policymakers in the GCC region. From a regulatory perspective, AI applications raise fundamental questions about the ethical, legal, and regulatory determinants that govern the use of these applications (Badran, 2021).

In this context, one has the right to wonder whether AI applications in the GCC countries will lead to a better life and more efficient use of available resources or negatively impact human activities. This discussion raises some concerns on whether the impact of AI disproportionately benefits higher-skilled workers, potentially exacerbating income and wealth inequality (Wright & Erbad, 2023). Some scholars are not sure of whether AI applications can be considered an absolute good or bad thing (Al-Ali et al., 2023). Rather, one can simply argue that AI technology provides us with many opportunities and, at the same time, creates many challenges. For the Gulf countries to be able to maximize the benefits and reduce the risks resulting from the expansion of the use of AI applications in their society, they should take advantage of the opportunities offered by this new field. They also need to develop policies and strategies that enable them to confront challenges in an effective and successful manner.

In terms of application, the COVID-19 pandemic offered the perfect opportunity for the GCC countries to introduce AI technology in the healthcare sector. The most significant use of AI applications was seen in detecting COVID-19 cases. Meanwhile, Saudi Arabia is using AI to diagnose and treat diabetic retinopathy. AI applications are also used in areas such as diagnosis, telemedicine, and drug discovery in the UAE. These applications are now widely used by healthcare and insurance companies by providing insurance for healthcare professionals and offering revenue cycle management tools for healthcare organizations with startups like Santechture and Klaim (Sarmah, 2019).

In the FinTech industry, several startup companies such as Sarwa have emerged in the UAE to help customers to easily trade stocks and ETFs, buy and sell cryptocurrencies, and invest money passively all in one place. The **AI-powered Sarwa startup has managed to raise close to US$25 million** as it continues to pave the way for financial technology.

In the labor market, the fear of job displacement due to automating some of the existing jobs has opened a whole new avenue of re-skilling and the chance for companies to attain high productivity and growth by equipping the workforce with the right skills as AI and automated processes are adopted. Although the concern over job loss is justifiable, one must stress that AI technologies and applications can create a whole new set of jobs that have not existed before, especially in innovation, creativity, data mining, and technology.

1.4 Aims and Structure of the Book

Considering the overall goal of the book, which is to explore the state of the art of AI in the Arabian Gulf region in terms of its reality and future, this book attempts to achieve the following goals:

- Exploring and assessing the current trends in the GCC countries regarding the adoption of AI applications and determining the impact of these applications on the various sectors in these countries.
- Analyzing the public risks associated with the expansion of the use of AI applications in the GCC countries and the impact of these potential risks on Gulf societies.
- Investigating the economics and social effects of artificial intelligence and automation on the job market (higher-skilled vs. lower-skilled workers), and the needed changes in curricula, training, and academic programs.
- Reviewing and evaluating the strategies and public policy frameworks developed by the Arab Gulf countries to face the challenges associated with the expansion of the use of AI applications.
- Analyzing case studies of some GCC countries that were able to develop an effective regulatory framework to deal with the challenges of AI.
- Bridging the gap between decision-makers and policymakers in the GCC countries and researchers interested in the field of AI, so that the policies and frameworks regulating this field are based on the evidence of their research.

This book comprises 15 chapters. Following this introductory chapter, in Chapter 2, Asharul Khan and Ashraf Mishrif investigate governance of AI in the oil and gas industry. They begin their analysis by underlining the exponential growth in the global oil and gas industry, which is expected to see a US$4.21 billion market for AI by 2028, growing at a compound annual growth rate of 12.09%. They offer real time case studies from ExxonMobil and Shell to stress that AI has the potential to revolutionize exploration and production techniques in the oil and gas industry by encompassing the analysis of satellite imagery, seismic data, well logs, and other geological data sets. AI benefits include the ability to analyze enormous datasets more quickly, which leads to more accurate information, forecasts, and predictions, as well as more individualized public services. However, several issues such as a dearth of transparency, unanticipated and unforeseen repercussions, mysterious decision-making, and governance are of great concern. AI also has significant ramifications for society, law, ethics, and organizations, as many organizations and service providers face difficulty in using AI governance to bridge the ethical divide in technology development. Thus, their chapter underscores the need to build regulatory guidelines, procedures, plans, governance processes, structures, and resources for ensuring the moral and responsible advancement of AI. It provides its analysis by investigating the successful application of AI governance in the oil and gas industry in the context of Oman. Using quantitative research methods, with 102 valid samples from the surveyed oil and gas companies operating in Oman, they found that AI is an emerging area in the oil and gas sector and that only 36% of the companies are using or have started using AI. Most companies that use AI are in upstream operation, where AI is used in predictive maintenance and machinery inspection (21%), material movement (21%), field services (11%), and quality control (10%). Furthermore, positive sentiments were expressed towards various AI governance modules, and most of them preferred to have an established committee to control responsible AI use. This study has some important implications for policy makers, mainly in the implementation and governance of emerging technologies such as AI and machine learning in the GCC region.

In Chapter 3, Hesham Al-Ammal and Abdulla Subah offer a conceptual framework for establishing an academic AI lab. They argue that AI and deep learning have revolutionized numerous disciplines. High-performance computing provides the necessary infrastructure to meet the computational demands of AI, allowing researchers to explore complex architectures and large-scale datasets. They focus their discussion on the design of the infrastructure that can handle such large AI models, including the hardware and software stacks. The latest advances in open-source HPC software and hardware have enabled small to medium sized organizations to build computing clusters using off-the-shelf hardware and software components. They present a case study in designing and implementing an advanced AI computing cluster within a GCC-based academic institution using open-source building blocks (software and hardware) to serve both research and training in AI. The adopted design principles for the lab include calculation of needed scalability, handling of big data, and cluster size. The model framework identifies the weight of each part of the design process, with phases that include design, operation and maintenance, training and knowledge transfer, and other cross-cutting factors within all phases. They ended by identifying challenges related to budgetary constraints, physical space and future expansion, user and operator skills in high-performance computing, and integration of open-source technologies and frameworks such as PyTorch, TensorFlow, LLMs, etc.

In Chapter 4, Sanaa Ashour evaluates the performance of ChatGPT-4 in summarizing academic texts by comparing AI-generated summaries with human-generated ones. To this end, using a sample of 12 self-authored academic articles, both ChatGPT- and human-generated summaries were first created and then evaluated by two independent evaluators based on accuracy, conciseness, coherence, comprehensiveness, and readability. She calculated Inter-rater reliability using Cohen's kappa coefficient and found that, while ChatGPT-4 exceled in producing concise and readable summaries, it frequently omitted nuanced details and supporting evidence, which resulted in moderate comprehensiveness. By contrast, human summaries were evaluated as more accurate, comprehensive, and capable of capturing critical counterarguments and detailed insights. Common issues with ChatGPT-4 summaries included abrupt transitions, occasional inaccuracies, and redundancies. However, despite these limitations, ChatGPT-4 effectively captured main arguments and conclusions, suggesting its utility for quick content overviews. Taken together, the results of the present study underscore the need for human oversight of AI-generated summarizations, along with further model training to enhance AI summarization capabilities in academic contexts. These findings provide valuable insights into the integration of AI tools in scholarly research and writing.

In Chapter 5, Ahmed Badran and Sara Badran examine the potential implications of AI for reshaping employment policies in Qatar. Their analysis focuses on the impact of integrating AI applications on employment policies, workforce dynamics, jobs structures and skills. They argue that labor markets in the GCC region are expected to witness major changes in all aspects to cease the opportunities of AI and to face the unprecedented challenges posed by smart technologies. They limit their analysis to the State of Qatar to examine whether the labor market can keep pace with the changes and face the challenges imposed by the application of AI technologies. They argue that the expansion of the application of AI technologies will entail restructuring labor markets in a way that reflects the importance of focusing on skilled and trained workers who possess the tools to employ these technologies in various sectors. Their study rejects the idea that the expansion of AI applications in various sectors will necessarily lead to machines replacing humans, at least in the foreseeable future. The primary findings underscore the necessity for Qatar to vigorously and strategically adopt an AI-centric future, as delineated in its AI Strategy. By leveraging its strengths in technological infrastructure and human capital, Qatar is well-positioned to harness the transformative potential of AI, driving innovation, economic diversification, and sustained growth.

In Chapter 6, Vinod Pangracious, Najib Ben Hadj-Alouane, Zhaojin Chu, and Raagav Ramakrishnan examine the impact and perception of generative AI and related automation tools in the Gulf region. They argue that generative AI can identify patterns across enormous sets of language-based data and generate new content. It has already caused 12 million occupational shifts globally and is even poised to cause more upheaval in future job markets. More than 50% of the recent occupational shifts are found in industries like food services, customer service, office support, design, and production. AI-enabled Machine Learning models are also being used to enhance the retail/consumer experience. This occupation displacement shall not be limited to low-wage labor, as the high-end job market shall be most affected by the use of AI. They limited their analysis to the impact of this global change on the job markets in the UAE, Bahrain, and KSA, where a strong e-government presence is already in place, and where the use of modern technologies is accepted and encouraged. These countries have integrated many AI technologies, such as face-recognition, 3D printing, augmented reality, industrial automation, and many others, into administrative and retail activities. They believe that both the government and the public would be receptive to the introduction of generative AI and autonomous robotics-based tools across different industries and service sectors.

In Chapter 7, Mustafa Altıntaş, Mustafa Yaylalı, and Muhammed Topal investigate people' attitudes and perceptions towards AI in Qatar, revealing generally optimistic views alongside significant concerns about privacy and security. They find that participants display a positive outlook on AI's potential for economic benefits, resource efficiency, and individual productivity. Participants with low interest in AI show significantly fewer positive attitudes while those with high interest show a more positive perception. Qataris are less concerned about AI's risks and security compared to non-Qataris. Low interest in AI correlates with decreased concern. Younger participants believe more in adequate AI regulation than older ones. Open-ended responses identify healthcare, education, and transportation as primary sectors benefiting from AI, with major concerns being privacy, job loss, over-dependence on AI, and regulatory gaps. They conclude by stressing that participants view AI as a tool for efficiency and improved decision-making but worry about reduced human skills and job opportunities.

In Chapter 8, Rafael Hernández de Santiago examines the ethics and the implication of AI for decision-making in the defense industry. He explores the intricate relationship between AI and ethics, particularly focusing on the ethical considerations arising from the integration of AI in defense. As AI capabilities are getting increasingly more sophisticated, concerns about their ethical implications in military applications have garnered attention from scholars, policymakers, and the public alike. He identifies three primary reasons for concern about ethical discrimination in AI systems: (1) automated decision-making systems will be increasingly applied across a wide variety of essential services, including defense; (2) without understanding these processes, it is challenging to discern whether, when, or how such systems discriminate against ethical principles affecting individuals or groups, challenging the concept of procedural fairness in decision-making; and (3) hasty implementation of AI risks undermining its benefits by eroding public trust in new technologies. His analysis stresses the need to balance between technological possibilities and ethical acceptability, as well as striking a delicate balance concerning decision-making in the defense industry. This involves analyzing economic expectations, gaps in the current regulatory system, and whether the creation of a responsible innovation and ethics organization would add value to balancing a world where stakeholders leverage data, potentially leading to new totalitarian regimes or unethical security and defense systems.

In Chapter 9, Ashraf Keshk explains the role of AI in enhancing security and defense capabilities of the GCC countries. He argues that many critical infrastructures in the GCC countries have been attacked by drones from armed militias in some neighboring countries, representing a qualitative development in the nature of the security threats facing the Gulf States. Meanwhile, the GCC countries have begun to focus on localizing military industries, which are evolving alongside the advancements in military technology. These two factors encouraged these countries to consider AI as potential tools to enhance their military capacities, especially after successfully implementing e-government and integrating AI into the economy. The chapter focuses also on identifying the main challenges these countries face and providing some suggestions for these countries to benefit from AI in security and military aspects, as these nations are located in a frequently unstable region where maintaining national security is of top importance.

In Chapter 10, Mohammed Faiz, Rashid Aziz Faridi, Rakshanda F Fazli, and Areeb Fazli assess solid waste management using geospatial techniques and AI in the UAE. They argue that the phenomenal rise in population across the globe due to economic growth, industrialization, urbanization, and population growth is correlated with waste production, which has led to inadmissible waste management in various countries, giving rise to multiple health issues and environmental pollution. Solid waste deposition in metropolitan areas has become a significant concern that can lead to environmental degradation and possibly endanger human health. Identifying a landfill location that poses the least amount of environmental damage is difficult since developing nations frequently have a variety of socio-economic, environmental, and legal restrictions. Potential sites must thus be maintained using tools and techniques that promote environmentally and socially sustainable communities. Thus, the main focus of this chapter is to analyze the existing solid waste disposal site and initially provide alternative sites in Dubai using Geographic Information Systems (GIS), Remote Sensing, weighted sum overlay, analytic hierarchy process (AHP) methods. Several criteria determine suitable locations for waste disposal. The chapter focuses on seven suitability indicators—slopes, proximity to built-up areas, airports, railways, existing dumpsites, land use land cover, and proximity to roads. For waste disposal sites, more trash recycling programs are recommended to minimize the quantity of waste and advance environmentally friendly waste monitoring techniques.

In Chapter 11, Ashraf Mishrif, Mahmoud Alsafy, and Mostafa Atia empirically investigate cost estimation using artificial neural network in industrial precision facilities in the Sultanate of Oman. They argue that the financial cost estimation of metal products in the machining sector is a significantly important aspect in industrial and equipment precision facilities. There are multiple methods for machining cost prediction before the products are manufactured, although each method has its own costs and varying levels of complexity and needs. However, the necessity for an economic approach to calculate the financial cost of machining a particular product has rapidly grown in recent years; this is particularly true when the product is manufactured in small numbers and limited financial resources.

They maintain that the current traditional approaches to calculate the cost of production in small industrial facilities proved complex and inaccurate due to the unlimited variety of workpieces in terms of features and dimensions. Calculating the manufacturing cost of a workpiece as a function of machining time is a standard approach, but determining the entire manufacturing time is an expensive and time-consuming procedure in and of itself. Machine learning techniques show a significant implication for predicting the production cost and time in different engineering sectors, which reduce the time consuming for estimating procedure that has a direct effect on the product price and the profit of enterprises.

Consequently, this chapter contributes to developing a parametric cost estimating technique using AI to predict total production cost and/or time more efficiently. The new approach requires a great deal of manufacturing knowledge, where the skilled human factor comes in which basically requires experts that provide accurate cost estimation of producing parts, particularly complex shapes. This approach takes into consideration the need for a substantial amount of learned knowledge that is susceptible to change as the expert accumulates more knowledge and expertise in the system. The study covers small and medium enterprises in different job shop facilities that mainly deal with the automotive sector and produce spare parts with small batch size in Oman. The data collected from different experts in Muscat provides an accurate parametric estimate of cost and time of production of spare parts. The result of this study is likely to produce an advanced estimator based on an artificial neural network that is designed to replace traditional approaches for estimating total manufacturing time and costs, which depended on either an expert engineer or a thorough operation sheet. The new model is expected to predict overall production time using training instances derived from real-world machining processes.

In Chapter 12, Mahmoud Alsafy, Nasr Al Hinai, Sujan Piya, and Ashraf Mishrif provide a comprehensive supply chain performance estimation with multi-output artificial neural networks. They argue that the success of supply chain companies hinges on cost effectiveness and customer satisfaction metrics. Integrating financial, product, and information flows across supply chain levels is vital for long-term success and productivity. In the manufacturing facilities, estimating component costs is crucial for pricing discussions and cost management along the supply chain performance. Artificial neural networks are commonly employed for procurement price estimation due to their ability to handle vast data quickly and efficiently.

They conduct their analysis by presenting a performance prediction model for Make-to-Order (MTO) supply chains based on the Supply Chain Operations Reference, incorporating multi-input and multi-output parameters. Utilizing real data from general manufacturing facilities located in Oman for repairing truck engines and machines, the model employs ANN technique to estimate total serving cost and order satisfaction time. Developed in MATLAB 2022b, the model's network topologies were selected via cross-validation, showing strong positive correlations between predicted and projected performance values. The integrated model offers potential to enhance supply chain operations by mitigating unexpected changes or failures. Practical implications include increased estimation accuracy, optimized inventory and production planning, improved supplier and transportation management, risk mitigation, and personalized client experiences. The outcome of this study contributes empirically to achieving the United Nations' Sustainable Development Goal 9 by promoting digitalization, infrastructure development, and sustainable supply chain performance in manufacturing facilities.

In Chapter 13, Mohammad Osaid Farooq and Tahura Fatima provide a comparative analysis of AI implementation in smart cities in the GCC countries. They believe that the idea of smart cities has emerged due to rapid technological advancements and that the effective use of technology and information can improve residents' quality of life while cutting expenses and resource consumption. AI integration can also prove advantageous in the sustainable sector to make smart cities greener. They provide a comparative analysis through multiple case studies of smart cities to understand the applications and benefits of the concepts and technologies classified as AI systems. For example, a comparative analysis between Singapore and Manama is conducted for their similarity in geographical location, dense population and high GDP. This examination could have practical implications for policy makers to consider the quality of life and resources efficiency when designing and constructing new smart cities in the region.

In Chapter 14, Mohammadu Bello Danbatta and Nasser Al-Azri explore AI-driven transformations in meteorology and solar radiation in the GCC region. They argue that the GCC region has become a focal point for research and innovation in the fields of meteorology and solar radiation, driven by the pressing need for sustainable solutions amidst rapid environmental changes. They begin their analysis by exploring the integration of AI techniques to address key challenges in these domains and underscoring the concerted effort to harness AI-driven methodologies for various applications, including weather prediction, air quality monitoring, electrical load forecasting, and solar radiation estimation. In the realm of meteorology, AI-driven approaches have demonstrated significant advancements in forecasting extreme weather events, analyzing the impact of weather variables on traffic congestion, and predicting rainfall patterns with high accuracy. Meanwhile, the integration of AI techniques in solar radiation estimation has emerged as a promising avenue for optimizing renewable energy systems. They highlight the recent advances in developing hybrid machine learning models to forecast solar radiation, utilizing numerical methods and historical weather data to improve prediction accuracy. These advancements have significant implications for the deployment of solar energy technologies and the transition towards sustainable energy sources in the GCC countries. The findings highlight the transformative potential of AI-driven approaches in meteorology and solar radiation estimation, offering insights into the development of innovative solutions to address environmental challenges and accelerate sustainable development in the GCC region.

Ahmed Badran and Ashraf Mishrif conclude this book in Chapter 15, where they underline the potential role of AI in transforming the economic outlook and landscape in the GCC region. They evaluate the various topics and case studies examined in the book to provide an educated assessment of the potential role that AI can play in shaping the future development in the Gulf region. They also discuss the key findings, insights, and lessons learned, while offering recommendations on how to address the challenges and develop a more effective AI transition in the GCC. It also offers some thoughts on new directions for future research on the topic.

1.5 Conclusion

This chapter provided a comprehensive analysis of the theoretical foundation and key concepts of AI and its applications. It explained the historical development of the technology that ranged from the ANI as an early stage of development to the AGI that are transforming almost all economic and social domains in our lives and the ASI, where machine intelligence surpasses human intelligence. The analysis reveals that the advancement of AI technology is highly like to make significant transformation in the global economy and human development. Our examination identified key sectors in the GCC countries that have already integrated AI into their activities, including healthcare, education, financial services, customer services, labor market, supply chains, manufacturing, the oil and gas sector, green energy, water management, and smart cities. The potential of adopting AI to improve social and economic development is significantly high in the GCC countries, with the UAE and Saudi Arabia are leading the way. Bahrain, Kuwait, Qatar, and Oman are also trying to catch up with the Emirates and Saudis by making substantial investments in AI technologies and applications, hoping that such investments could increase AI economic contribution to GDP from below 5% to above 10% in the next decade.

References

Al-Ali, S. Al-Amrani, & Al-Tawzani, M. (2023). The future of artificial intelligence: The metaverse model. *Journal of Law and Business,* (88), 256–278. Retrieved from http://search.mandumah.com/Record/1361491

Al-Qadi, R. N. G., & Al-Qudat, Y. A. S. (2023). *Civil liability for artificial intelligence robots: A comparative study* (Unpublished Master's Thesis). Middle East University. Retrieved from http://search.mandumah.com/Record/1366709

Al-Sulaiti, D. S. F. (2023). Artificial intelligence: Qatar's efforts and achievements as a model. *Culture and Development, 23* (190), 161–183. Retrieved from http://search.mandumah.com/Record/1404420

Baccour, E., Mhaisen, N., Abdellatif, A. A., Erbad, A., Mohamed, A., Hamdi, M., & Guizani, M. (2022). Pervasive AI for IoT applications: A survey on resource-efficient distributed artificial intelligence. *IEEE Communications Surveys & Tutorials.*

Badran, A. (2021). Thoughts and reflections on the case of Qatar: Should artificial intelligence be regulated? In E. Azar & A. N. Haddad (Eds.), *Artificial intelligence in the gulf* (pp. 69–92). Springer Singapore. https://doi.org/10.1007/978-981-16-0771-4_5

Belk, R. W., Belanche, D., & Flavián, C. (2023). Key concepts in artificial intelligence and technologies 4.0 in services. *Service Business, 17*, 1–9. https://doi.org/10.1007/s11628-023-00528-w

Haider, N. (2023). *The potential impact of AI in MENA*, MAGNiTT, April 27, 2023. https://magnitt.com/news/potential-impact-ai-mena-53905

PwC. (2022). *Sizing the prize What's the real value of AI for your business and how can you capitalise?* https://www.pwc.com/gx/en/issues/analytics/assets/pwc-ai-analysis-sizing-the-prize-report.pdf

Sarmah, S. S. (2019). Concept of Artificial Intelligence, its impact and emerging trends. *International Research Journal of Engineering and Technology, 6*(11), 2164–2168.

Wang, P. (2019). On defining Artificial Intelligence. *Journal of Artificial General Intelligence, 10*(2), 1–37. https://doi.org/10.2478/jagi-2019-0002A

Wright, S., & Erbad, A. (2023). *The strategic implications of AI: A roadmap for future engagement*. Global Institute for Strategic Research.

CHAPTER 2

Governance of Artificial Intelligence in the Oil and Gas Industry

Asharul Islam Khan and Ashraf Mishrif

2.1 Introduction

Artificial intelligence and/or machine learning (AI/ML) governance refers to the frameworks, policies, regulations, and ethical considerations put in place so that the AI systems are developed and deployed in the ethical and safe manner. Overall, AI governance aims to balance the benefits of AI technologies with the potential risks and ensure that AI/ML is developed and used in a way that aligns with societal values and priorities. AI governance is the process of managing access, implementing policies, enforcing regulations, and monitoring activities involving machine learning models. AI governance aims to responsible use of AI technologies within an organization. It consists of frameworks including practices and policies (Lazzeri & Robsky, 2024). It seeks to reconcile the benefits

A. I. Khan (✉) · A. Mishrif
HURC, Sultan Qaboos University, Muscat, Sultanate of Oman
e-mail: a.khan2@squ.edu.om

A. Mishrif
e-mail: ashraf.mishrif@gmail.com

A. Badran and A. Mishrif (eds.), *Shaping the Future of Development in the GCC*, The Political Economy of the Middle East,
https://doi.org/10.1007/978-981-96-7963-8_2

of AI with security and privacy concerns. It entails developing standards, protocols, and structures to manage access, enforce policies, and ensure transparency (Alsagheer et al., 2023a). In the oil and gas sector, AI is mainly used for operation, cost control, resource optimization, and work reform.

The assurance, ownership, life cycle management, and accountability are main components of AI governance framework developed by Chandrasekaran et al. (2021). The authors also highlighted the need for further research on risk interplay, inter-principal trust, and dataset cards to improve trust between ML principals. They also suggested that understanding the limitations of ML systems and enhancing explainability could complement their work on governance. According to Laato et al. (2022) within the technical layer of AI governance, there are three core components: data governance, model governance, and system governance. The aim of governance is to bring various stakeholders together in order to implement and execute policies aligned with the social and cultural norms (Sokalski et al., 2019).

The AI use is full of challenges such as lack of high-quality data, lack of expertise, and lack of collaboration. Chen (2023) highlights the challenges surrounding the governance of AI technology, despite its significant empowerment of human society. It notes that existing governance approaches have various flaws, both in theory and practice, including issues related to justice, security, and responsibilities. In addition, the responsibility and accountability of AI privacy and safety deals, social acceptance and trust in AI, workforce transformation and substitution, human interaction with machines, liability of AI-based defects, and data collection and usage laws. AI governance has garnered positive attention from scholars; it primarily focuses on the safety of technology, overlooking other ethical, legal, and social considerations (Nguyen, 2022).

Gill et al. (2022) underscores the widespread adoption of AI technologies across organizations and industries, highlighting the significant challenges and risks associated with their use. These risks encompass regulatory, compliance, reputational, user trust, financial, and societal aspects, emphasizing the need for responsible AI governance. Other researchers presented including Zhang et al. (2021) have raised concern on the AI use in the military combat. There is a need for regulations, governance frameworks, and international strategies in AI development. The current AI governance arrangements are fragmented and lack adequate oversight and accountability. Therefore, a balancing act is needed on the benefits and risks of using AI tools (Keen et al., 2021). Overall, Grace et al. (2018) highlighted the diverse perspectives within the AI research community regarding the societal implications of AI technologies and the role of researchers in addressing these issues.

Neghawi et al. (2023) proposes a multi-level governance approach to AI/ML ethics frameworks within organizations to ensure responsible AI/ML practices across all levels of their operations. It aims to address gaps in existing frameworks by providing a comprehensive and flexible framework that spans all levels of the organization's AI/ML systems. Nadler et al. (2019) proposes solutions to data governance, providing methods for increasing awareness among model developers regarding biases introduced by data governance policies and offering strategies to mitigate bias in Al/ML models. Thus, enhancing the transparency, fairness, and effectiveness of ML systems within the constraints of current data governance policies and privacy laws. As such the current study extracts the AI governance factors and empirically tests them considering the oil and gas industry in Oman. The factors under investigation are the developing trust in the AI systems, AI data, AI infrastructure, and close collaboration in implementation, cooperation on minimizing AI's risks, separation of responsibilities, knowledge management, documentation, and traceability.

The study aims to investigate the successful AI governance in the oil and gas industry. It poses questions on various governance modules and factors affecting the AI governance in general and oil and gas in particular. In addition, it identifies the AI applications in the oil and gas industry, specifically in Oman. This study has used quantitative research methods. Two research questions were designed to carry out this study, namely R1: What is the current state of AI in the oil and gas sector, and where do the oil and gas companies use AI? R 2: What is the purpose of using AI in the oil and gas sector, and how AI governance can be improved? A case study was conducted among the oil and gas companies operating in Oman. A total of 102 samples were used for the analysis.

There are six sections organized as follows. Section 2.2 describes the literature. Section 2.3 explains the research method. Section 2.4 presents data analysis. Section 2.5 presents the discussion. The last section summarizes the findings.

2.2 Literature Review

2.2.1 *Artificial Intelligence Overview*

AI is the simulation of human intellect to machines so to execute the human activities such as problem solving, learning, comprehension, pattern recognition, and decision-making. AI can be of two types: narrow AI and general AI. While the narrow AI is limited to single tasks such as image recognition systems and recommendation algorithms. On the other hand, General AI is capable of doing any intellectual activity similar to human. There are subcategories of AI such as machine learning, natural language processing, computer vision, robotics, expert systems, etc. They can be integrated into a variety of domains such as oil and gas, healthcare, banking, transportation, and entertainment, with the goal of boosting efficiency, productivity, and decision-making processes.

2.2.2 *Artificial Intelligence in the Oil and Gas Sector*

In the oil and gas AI can be used in up-stream, down-stream, and mid-stream operations (Hanga & Kovalchuk, 2019; Hussain et al., 2024; Patidar et al., 2024). The up-stream operations cover exploration, drilling, reservoir, and production. The production of fuels, lubricants, and plastics from crude oil refining is called down-stream operation while the mid-stream operations consist of transportation using pipelines, ships, and road vehicles. In addition to wider applications of AI in the oil and gas sector, the major functional areas where AI is used include predictive maintenance and machinery inspection, material movement, production planning, field services, and quality control. The AI predictive maintenance models, when used in the oil and gas industry lowers downtime by predicting equipment breakdowns ahead of time, thereby lowering the maintenance expenses and improving overall operational efficiency (Abbasi et al., 2019; Saputelli et al., 2022). The AI model analyses historical data, sensor readings, and machine performance indicators and then detects abnormalities suggesting possible issues thereby helping businesses to schedule maintenance tasks during planned downtime initiatives, avoiding expensive unscheduled time.

The use of AI models not only reduces the costs and improves productivity instead it is also environmentally sustainable since analysis of geological and seismic data allows precise and accurate pinpointing that uncovers probable oil and gas deposits. Moreover, AI-based predictive analytics enhances reservoir management through forecasting production, optimization of well spacing, and increasing recovery rates (Bahaloo et al., 2023; Castiñeira et al., 2020; D'Almeida et al., 2022). By spotting trends and anomalies in production data, AI can assist operators in increasing output while reducing downtime and operational expenses.

AI can improve supply chain operations by evaluating data from suppliers and logistics providers, estimating demand, optimizing inventories, improving the purchasing process, and increasing supply chain efficiency. AI algorithms can optimize inventory levels, reduce transportation costs, and improve scheduling and logistics planning to guarantee that equipment and materials are delivered on time to drilling sites (Abdelhamid et al., 2021; Helo & Hao, 2022; Lu et al., 2019). AI plays an important role in supply chain optimization. It optimizes logistics by considering a variety of elements such as transportation routes, weather conditions, and demand in the oil and gas business. Overall, AI in supply chain management can help oil and gas firms improve operating speed, efficiency, and sustainability.

Overall, the AI has the ability to improve quality control procedures in the oil and gas industry by automating inspection duties, predicting and preventing quality issues, optimizing operations, and assuring compliance with quality standards and laws (Khan et al., 2024; Heydari et al., 2024; Sattari et al., 2021). However, successful AI application in quality control necessitates careful integration with current systems, subject expertise, and continuous validation and optimization to assure reliable and accurate findings.

Alsagheer et al. (2023b) provided a thorough overview of ML governance in terms of observing activities, regulations and policies implementation. ML governance balances the benefits of ML along with security and privacy risks, ensuring responsible and secure usage of ML models. Nguyen (2022) highlights the ongoing debate surrounding AI/ML, with one side advocating for continued usage despite uncertainties and the other side expressing concerns about the dangers of technology. Given the widespread use and effectiveness of AI/ML, it's unrealistic to expect its usage to cease entirely. Thus, the governance of AI/ML is essential to ensure its reliability and safety.

2.3 Artificial Intelligence/ Machine Learning Governance

2.3.1 Separation of AI Governance Responsibilities

It is important to understand who should be responsible for AI governance: an individual or committees. Chen (2023) proposes an integrated AI/ML governance approach called "human-in-the-loop" ethics governance. This approach emphasizes the active involvement of multiple stakeholders in the governance process, placing humans at the center of decision-making and oversight. The "human-in-the-loop" approach is seen as advantageous because it allows for greater transparency, accountability, and ethical consideration in the development and deployment of AI technologies. By involving stakeholders from various sectors, including government, industry, academia, and civil society, it aims to address the complex ethical issues associated with AI in a more comprehensive and inclusive manner. However, the paper also acknowledges that there are future challenges and potential limitations associated with implementing this approach. These may include issues related to coordination, resource allocation, and the evolving nature of AI technology and its ethical implications. Alsagheer et al. (2023a) introduces the concept of decentralized AI/ML governance, emphasizing the need for a well-defined framework in response to the growing prevalence of AI/ML research and applications in various domains.

2.3.2 Developing a Reliable Environment for AI Systems, Data, and Digital Infrastructure

AI/ML governance should address ethical concerns such as fairness, transparency, and accountability. Managers must evaluate potential biases in data and models and take steps to mitigate them (Lazzeri & Robsky, 2024). AI governance involves addressing ethical questions such as fairness, accountability, transparency, and privacy in AI systems. This includes ensuring that AI algorithms do not discriminate against certain groups, are transparent in their decision-making processes, and respect user privacy (Gasser & Almeda, 2017). Grace et al. (2018) found ethical concerns about the potential negative impacts of AI, such as job displacement and biased decision-making.

Al/ML models rely heavily on data, so ensuring data quality, integrity, and security is crucial. Managers need to establish protocols for data collection, storage, and usage to maintain trust and compliance (Lazzeri & Robsky, 2024). The data-related AI/ML governance involves five core steps: data acquisition, cleaning, use/reuse, publishing, and preservation/destruction. The data auditing is crucial to avoid biases and ensure data quality (Laato et al., 2022). Keen et al. (2021) suggested that AI//ML tools have the potential to enhance decision-making by enabling deeper insights into datasets. However, this potential is limited by the poor quality of routine data and challenges in explaining methods and results to stakeholders. The current data governance policies and privacy laws regulate the use of personal and sensitive data, thus effecting data quality and volume available for training. This regulatory environment can lead to biases and inaccuracies in AI/ML models.

2.3.3 Documentation and Traceability

Laato et al. (2022) outlines the concept of organizational AI/ML governance, which involves a system of rules, practices, processes, and technological tools to ensure an organization's use of AI aligns with its strategies, objectives, values, legal requirements, and ethical principles. It highlights the multidimensional nature of AI/ML governance, encompassing social/ethical, legal, and technical elements. Zhang et al. (2021) researched the perceptions of AI/ML researchers on AI governance, based on the data of 524 researchers' publications. The Key findings include high trust in international and scientific organizations, moderate trust in Western tech companies, and low trust in national militaries, Chinese tech companies, and Facebook.

Alsagheer et al. (2023a) explores the concept of decentralized machine learning governance, focusing on its broad application in various aspects of computer systems, including management of finance, community, and value chain. It provides a comprehensive overview of the framework, research opportunities, challenges, and open problems, serving as a roadmap for its development. Keen et al. (2021) calls for greater oversight, transparency, and accountability to ensure that these tools are used responsibly and ethically. According to Gasser and Almeda (2017)AI governance occurs at different layers such as social, legal, ethical, and technical.

2.3.4 Close Collaboration in AI Implementation

Alsagheer et al. (2023b) discussed the community-driven approaches to decision-making in ML processes, fostering collaboration and consensus-building among stakeholders. The AI/ML researchers look at international organizations like the UN and EU for AI regulations, policies, and trust buildings. On the other hand, the American public have high level of trust in the US military regarding AI than the researchers of the country (Zhang et al., 2021). While most researchers support the idea that researchers should be encouraged to share all aspects of their research, there are nuanced views regarding what aspects must be shared every time. For example, a high percentage (84%) believe that high-level descriptions of methods should always be shared; however, when it comes to the trained model sharing only 22% accept it (Zhang et al., 2021).

2.3.5 Cooperation on Minimizing AI's Risks

Effective AI/ML governance requires collaboration between different departments, including IT, legal, compliance, and business units. Managers should foster communication and collaboration to align ML initiatives with organizational goals and values (Lazzeri & Robsky, 2024). Gill et al. (2022) proposed AI/ML governance framework to oversee the responsible use of AI/ML, aiming to prevent and mitigate risks while maximizing the value derived from AI projects. By establishing such a framework, organizations can navigate the complexities of AI applications and ensure consistency in their adoption across the organization. Given the global nature of AI technologies, AI governance also involves international cooperation and coordination. This can include sharing best practices, harmonizing regulations across jurisdictions, and addressing cross-border issues such as data sharing and cybersecurity (Gasser & Almeda, 2017).

The effective AI/ML governance requires comprehensive management of data, models, and systems, along with considerations for regulation, ethics, and transparency to address the challenges posed by AI technologies (Laato et al., 2022).

2.3.6 Knowledge Management

The AI/ML technologies development and deployment require governance under the control of governments and regulatory bodies. These regulations can cover issues such as data protection, algorithmic accountability, safety standards, and liability for AI-related incidents. Depending on the industry, there may be specific regulations governing the use of ML technologies. Managers need to stay informed about these regulations and ensure compliance within their organizations (Lazzeri & Robsky, 2024). Industry organizations and professional associations may develop voluntary standards and guidelines for the responsible development and use of AI/ML technologies. These standards can help ensure that AI systems meet certain criteria for safety, fairness, and transparency (Gasser & Almeda, 2017).

Legal challenges in AI governance are hindered by a lack of interdisciplinary work on law and AI. Therefore, there is a lag in how to handle the data and use it appropriately with regard to the laws of the land (Chandrasekaran et al., 2021). Grace et al. (2018) noticed some disagreement among researchers regarding the need for government regulation of AI technologies. Moreover, the researchers are supporting open access to research findings and datasets in the field of AI/ML.

2.4 Research Method

This study has used quantitative research methods. Two research questions were designed to carry out this study. RQ1: What is the current state of AI in the oil and gas sector, and where do the oil and gas companies use AI? RQ2: What is the purpose of using AI in the oil and gas sector, and how AI governance can be improved? A random sampling technique was used to collect the data through survey from oil and gas companies operating in Oman. The survey was developed using the identified key variables from academic and industrial literature.

The key variables are the gender, age, key concerns on AI governance, AI benefits, and responsible use of AI/ML. The other factors are developing trust in the AI/ML systems, data, infrastructure, collaboration, and cooperation on addressing the AI risks. The use of AI/ML can be in exploration and drilling (up-stream operations), shipping and transportation (mid-stream operations), and fuels and lubricant production (down-stream operations). A total of 104 samples were collected, which were cleaned, and then 102 were used in the final analysis. There are 28% female response while 72% male responses. The majority of the respondents fall in the age group of 20–25 years (32%). The survey was filled by employees holding various job titles such as admin, automation system engineer, consultant, data analyst, director, HR manager, IT manager, maintenance engineer, marketing manager, mechanical engineer, operational manager, process safety engineer, production operator, programmer/software engineer, quality assurance manager, supervisor, surveyor trainee, and well engineer. Table 2.1 shows the descriptive analysis.

Several companies participated in the study, including 3D (1.0%), A.C.S.C (2.0%), A.M.LLC (1.0%), A.O.G.SLLC (1.0%), A.O.T.C (1.0%), A.P.G (1.0%), ABC (1.0%), Al Thuraya Minning (1.0%), BP (6.1%), Beah (1.0%), CC Energy Development (1.0%), FOS Energy (1.0%), Haimo Technology (1.0%), Halliburton (1.0%), KC Dutac (1.0%), MED Energy (1.0%), Middle East Oilfield Services LLC (5.1%), OQ (OQ and OQ8) (9.2%), Oman Chlorine (3.1%), Oxy (2.0%), PDO (32.7%), Petrogas E&P (3.1%), Precision World National LLC (1.0%), RAFO (1.0%), Ray International (2.0%), S.O.S (4.1%), SLB (2.0%), SOMSCO (1.0%), STS (2.0%), Stomo Energ (1.0%), Target Oil field Services (1.0%), Truck Oman Group (5.1%), UTAS–Muscat (1.0%), United Engineering Services (1.0%). However, the higher share corresponds to few companies such as BP (6.1%), Middle East Oilfield Services LLC (5.1%), OQ (OQ and OQ8) (9.2%), Oman Chlorine (3.1%), Oxy (2.0%), PDO (32.7%), Petrogas E&P (3.1%), Ray International (2.0%), S.O.S (4.1%), and Truck Oman Group (5.1%),

2.5 Data Analysis and Results

R1: What is the current state of AI in the oil and gas sector, and where do the oil and gas companies use AI?

The companies were asked if they are using AI for the completion of various tasks. It was found that 36% are using or have started using it; however, 31% have not used it at all. Figure 2.1 shows the distribution of AI usage in oil and gas companies in Oman.

tFigure 2.2 shows the companies who are using AI in their operations.

Table 2.1 Descriptive analysis of the primary data

Gender	*% of Total*	*Cumulative %*	*Job title*	*% of Total*	*Cumulative %*
Female	28.0%	28.0%	Admin	7.5%	7.5%
Male	72.0%	100.0%	Automation system engineer	2.5%	10.0%
			Consultant	3.8%	13.8%
Age (Years)	**% of Total**	**Cumulative %**	Data analyst	16.3%	30.0%
20–25	32.4%	32.4%	Director	5.0%	35.0%
26–30	27.5%	59.8%	HR manager	1.3%	36.3%
31–35	20.6%	80.4%	IT manager	3.8%	40.0%
36–40	10.8%	91.2%	Maintenance engineer	5.0%	45.0%
Above 40	8.8%	100.0%	Marketing manager	5.0%	50.0%
			Mechanical engineer	11.3%	61.3%
Job experience (Years)	**% of Total**	**Cumulative %**	Operational manager	5.0%	66.3%
11–15 years	15.7%	15.7%	Process safety engineer	2.5%	68.8%
16–20 years	7.8%	23.5%	Production operator	1.3%	70.0%
5–10 years	29.4%	52.9%	Programmer/ software Engineer	7.5%	77.5%
Above 20 years	5.9%	58.8%	Quality assurance manager	3.8%	81.3%
Less than 5 years	41.2%	100.0%	Supervisor	5.0%	86.3%
			Surveyor	1.3%	87.5%
			Trainee	2.5%	90.0%
			Well engineer	10.0%	100.0%

Additionally, among the respondents who indicated they are not currently using AI, 42% reported having no plans to adopt it in the future, while 58% indicated that they are planning to implement it at a later stage. Notably, those with no intention of future adoption were primarily within the 31–40 age group (61%), followed by the 26–30 age group (31%), and the 20–25 age group (8%).

There are three major areas where the oil and gas companies are using AI. They are down-stream operations, mid-stream operations, and up-stream operations. The higher share of AI corresponds to up-stream

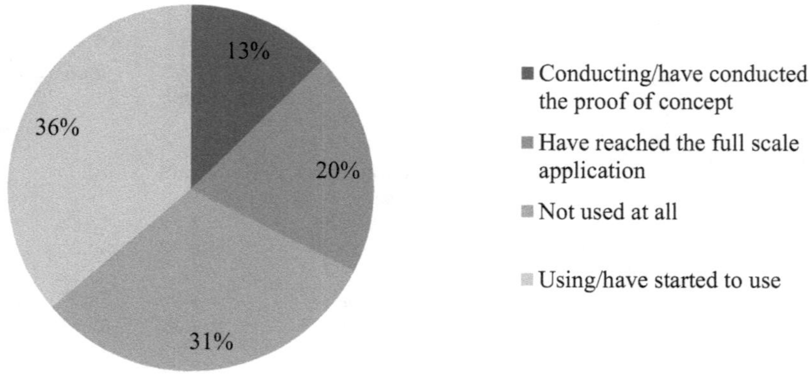

Fig. 2.1 AI usage in oil and gas sector in Oman

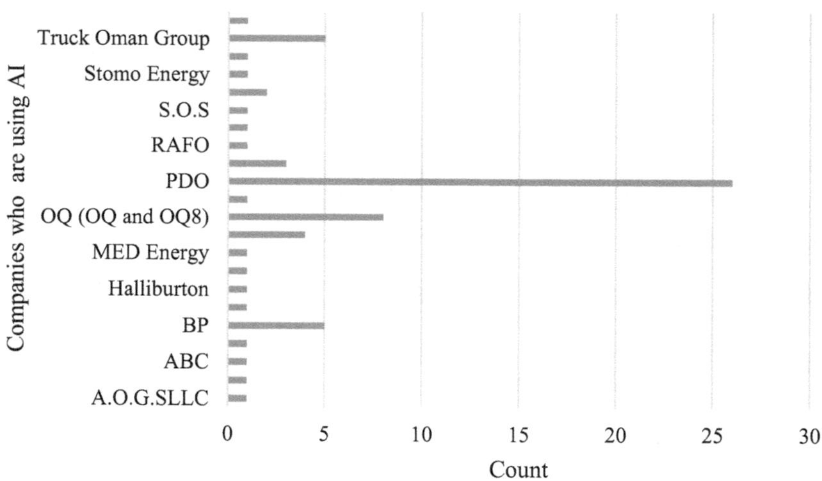

Fig. 2.2 Oil and gas companies who are using AI in their operations

operations (49%). Figure 2.3 shows the AI operational areas in the oil and gas sector.

R2: What is the purpose of using AI in the oil and gas sector, and how AI governance can be improved?

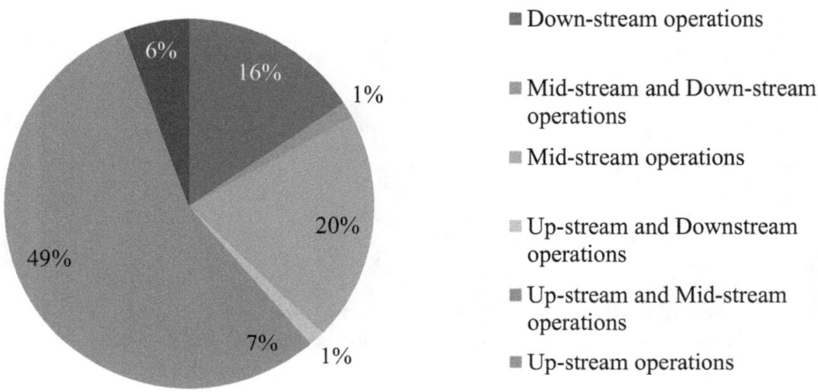

Fig. 2.3 AI operational areas in the oil and gas sector

In this research question the purpose and impact of AI in the oil and gas sector were investigated considering four variables: operational efficiency, cost reduction, creation of new business, and work reform. The mean and standard deviations are as follows: operational efficiency (*Mean* = 3.81, *SD* = 1.23), cost reduction (*Mean* = 3.9, *SD* = 1.16), creation of new business (*Mean* = 3.51, *SD* = 1.32), and work reform (*Mean* = 3.74, *SD* = 1.18). The respondents' response was coded into positive sentiment, neutral, and negative sentiment. The majority of the respondents expressed positive sentiments except for the creation of new businesses, where the negative opinion is higher than the neutral option and other variables. The positive sentiments towards operational efficiency (73%), cost reduction (73%), work reform (68%), and creation of new businesses (37%). The higher level of negative sentiments corresponds to creation of new businesses (24%), work reform (16%), operational efficiency (14%), and cost reduction (11%). Figure 2.4 shows the purpose of AI in the oil and gas sector.

The key issues examined in AI governance include challenges in establishing a trustworthy environment for AI systems, data, and digital infrastructure; difficulties in fostering close collaboration during implementation; obstacles in cooperating to minimize AI-related risks; unclear separation of responsibilities; and gaps in knowledge management, documentation, and traceability. The mean and standard deviations are as follows: designing a reliable AI systems (*Mean* = 3.74, *SD* = 1.24),

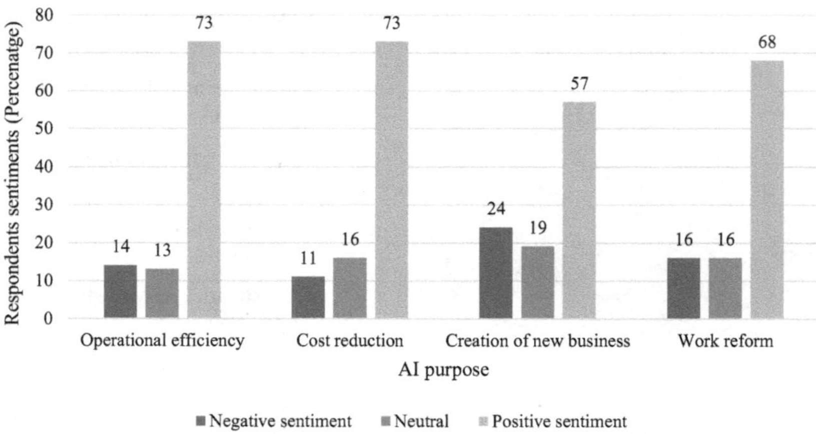

Fig. 2.4 AI purpose in oil and gas sector

designing a reliable environment for data (*Mean* = 3.79, *SD* = 1.15), designing reliable digital infrastructure (*Mean* = 3.97, *SD* = 1.19), close collaboration in implementation (*Mean* = 3.83, *SD* = 1.06), cooperation on minimizing AI's risks (*Mean* = 3.86, *SD* = 1.17), separation of responsibilities, (*Mean* = 3.67, *SD* = 1.27), knowledge management (*Mean* = 3.93, *SD* = 1.16), and documentation and traceability (*Mean* = 3.93, *SD* = 1.16).

The majority of the respondents expressed positive sentiments except for the separation of responsibilities. For instance, documentation traceability (75%), knowledge management (75%), cooperation in minimizing AI s risks (73%), close collaboration in AIs implementation (70%), designing a reliable digital infrastructure (71%), designing reliable data (67%), separation for responsibilities (65%), designing reliable AI system (63%). Figure 2.5 shows the AI governance factors in oil and gas sector.

Moreover, the respondents who are using AI were enquired if they are familiar with AI governance? 70% replied YES while 30% replied NO. The same respondents were asked about, the responsible use of AI, 66% expressed that committees should be created to take the responsibility while 34%put their opinion on individuals.

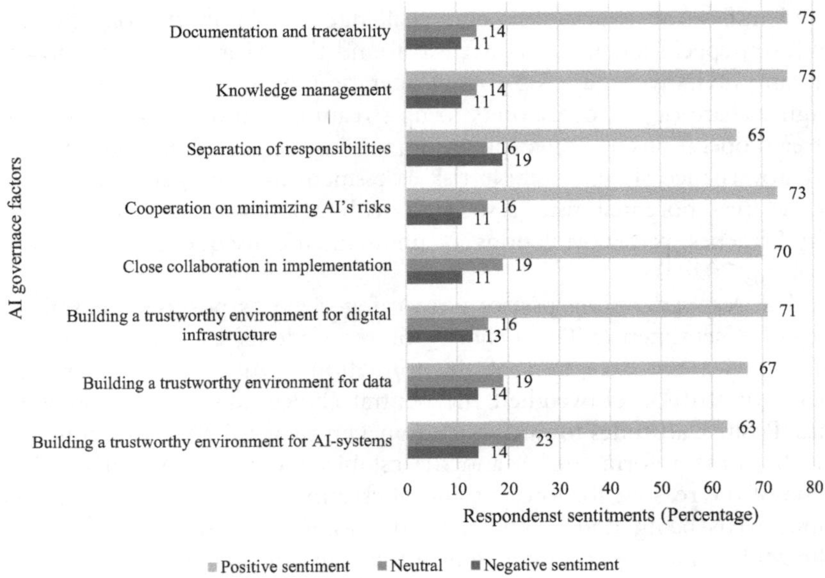

Fig. 2.5 AI governance factors in oil and gas sector

2.6 Discussion

The goal of AI is to bring competitiveness, save times, and customer satisfaction while the ethical concerns can be evaluated with transparency and trust. The issue of AI/ML includes lack of strategy, data risks, safety and security, hiring and retaining AI/ML talent, social, legal, ethical, and technical. This study provides the context for studying the AI/ML governance implications. Managers need to grasp the fundamentals of AI/ML, including its capabilities, limitations, and potential biases. ML governance is not a one-time task but an ongoing process. Managers should regularly review and update governance policies and procedures to adapt to changing technologies, regulations, and business needs (Lazzeri & Robsky, 2024). By implementing robust AI/ML governance practices, managers can ensure that their organizations derive maximum value from machine learning technologies while minimizing risks and promoting ethical and responsible use (Lazzeri & Robsky, 2024).

The study poses questions on various governance modules and factors affecting the AI governance in general and oil and gas. In addition, it identifies the applications and challenges of AI in the oil and gas industry specifically in Oman. It was found that AI is used in the down-stream, mid-stream, and up-stream operation in oil and gas sectors. The higher share of AI corresponds to up-stream operations (49%). The up-stream operations include exploration, drilling, reservoir, and production. AI governance should include risk assessment and mitigation strategies to address potential risks associated with ML projects, such as security breaches, privacy violations, or unintended consequences (Lazzeri & Robsky, 2024).

The respondents' responses were categorized as positive, neutral, or negative sentiments. The majority of respondents expressed favorable views, with the exception of the formation of new firms, where the negative attitude outweighed the neutral choice and other characteristics. Positive attitudes towards operational efficiency (73%), cost reduction (73%), work reform (68%), and the establishment of new firms (37%). One of the reasons for lowest value of creation of new businesses is that since AI is being undergoing rapid development in the west, however the Middle Eastern countries remain the consumers, and thus chances of creating new businesses is low.

On the responsible use of AI, 66% of respondents expressed that committees should be created to take responsibility while 34% put their opinion on individuals. While those who have not used AI, have also similar opinions. For instance, 56% of committees should be created to take responsibility while 44% put their opinion on individuals. Similarly, regarding the separation of responsibilities, the respondent expressed negative feelings. Centralized governance has issues such as a lack of transparency and vulnerability to security threats (Alsagheer et al., 2023b). Alsagheer et al. (2023a) developed insights and guidelines for the establishment of decentralized AI/ML governance frameworks. Such frameworks are essential for promoting transparency, accountability, and sustainability in the development and deployment of AI/ML technologies. The recent research indicates that user expectations for privacy may not align with the provided information, affecting governance. Trust in regulators, especially in authoritarian regimes, may be compromised, as data transfer is strictly governed by laws (Chandrasekaran et al., 2021). A significant majority (68%) of AI/ML researchers believe that AI safety should be prioritized more than it currently is. This underscores the importance researchers place on ensuring the safe and responsible development of AI technologies (Zhang et al., 2021).

Alsagheer et al. (2023b) studied how to assign the ownerships to ML assets, including datasets, models, and algorithms, through decentralized mechanisms. The study by Grace et al. in 2018 investigated the attitudes of AI/ML researchers towards the potential societal impacts of their work. Most respondents believe that AI researchers have at least some responsibilities to ensure their work benefits society. AI/ML governance involves establishing mechanisms to hold developers and users of AI/ML systems accountable for their actions. This may include requirements for auditing and testing AI systems, as well as mechanisms for addressing and remedying harm caused by AI technologies (Gasser & Almeda, 2017).

The main functional areas where AI is used include predictive maintenance and machinery inspection (21%), material movement (21%), field services (11%), and quality control (10%). The model governance focuses on testing and increasing transparency/explainability of AI/ML models (Laato et al., 2022). While AI/ML governance tools depend on data, AI/ML approaches, and the surrounding system, other factors like regulation and ethics also influence the technical layer. The AI/ML model developers may not have mechanisms to identify biases and inaccuracies introduced by data governance policies, thus hindering their ability to address these issues effectively. Furthermore, the existing mechanisms do not offer effective solutions for mitigating bias introduced by data governance policies, leaving model developers without adequate tools to improve model fairness (Nadler et al., 2019).

Moreover, it was found that 36% are using or have started using it; however, 31% have not used it at all. It was observed that, those who said they are not using it, 42% of them replied to "No plan to use in the future" while 58% of them replied to "Planning to use in the future" out of 32 responses. Those who do not plan to use in future were mainly in the age group of 31–40 years 61%, 26–30 years 31%, 20–25 years 8%. Those who have not used AI, 66% are familiar with AI governance and 34% are not familiar.

2.7 Conclusion

The oil and gas sectors are looking to use advanced technology such as AI technology in different areas. The AI is seen as a true enabler in the oil and gas industry. The AI is exhibiting its impact on the oil and gas industry from every stage of production and refining of oil and gas, understanding reservoirs, lowering maintenance costs, supply chain optimization that assures smooth operations to predictive maintenance and prioritize compliance and safety. The study highlights the potential consequences of unmonitored AI/ML, which may lead to undesirable results and significant adverse impacts on organizations. Therefore, it stresses the importance of proactively addressing risks associated with AI/ML technologies through effective governance frameworks. A random sampling technique was used to collect the data through surveys from oil and gas companies operating in Oman. The study found the need to develop AI governance frameworks for the oil and gas sector under the umbrella of committees rather than individuals. Further research and refinement are needed to address design, implementation, and effectiveness of the various AI governance modules.

2.7.1 Theoretical and Practical Implications

This study contributes to the growing body of knowledge on AI adoption and governance by highlighting the critical need for comprehensive AI governance frameworks within the oil and gas sector. It advances theoretical understanding of how AI technologies can be integrated responsibly to enhance operational efficiency while mitigating risks. The research emphasizes the role of collective governance—through committees rather than individuals—in managing AI systems, providing a conceptual foundation for future studies on governance models and risk management in AI deployment. Additionally, the findings pave the way for further exploration of design and implementation challenges, enriching academic discourse on AI governance in complex industrial contexts. From a practical standpoint, the study offers valuable insights for oil and gas companies seeking to leverage AI technologies effectively and safely. The identified need for robust governance frameworks supports industry leaders in developing strategies that ensure AI-driven transformation aligns with safety, compliance, and operational goals. The emphasis on committee-based governance can guide organizational structures to foster collaboration and accountability in AI implementation. Furthermore, policymakers and regulators can use these findings to formulate regulations and guidelines that promote responsible, risk-mitigated AI adoption, supporting sustainable growth in the sector across the GCC region and Oman.

References

Alsagheer, D., Diallo, N., Karanjai, R., Xu, L., & Shi, L. (2023a). Decentralized machine learning governance. In *2023 IEEE international conference on blockchain and cryptocurrency (ICBC)* (pp. 1–3). IEEE.

Alsagheer, D., Xu, L., & Shi, W. (2023b). Decentralized machine learning governance: Overview, opportunities, and challenges. *IEEE Access, 11,* 96718–96732.

Abdelhamid, K., Ammar, T. B., & Laid, K. (2021, January). Artificial intelligent in upstream oil and gas industry: A review of applications, challenges and perspectives. In *International conference on artificial intelligence and its applications* (pp. 262–271). Springer International Publishing.

Abbasi, T., Lim, K. H., & Yam, K. S. (2019, June). Predictive maintenance of oil and gas equipment using recurrent neural network. In *IOP conference series: Materials science and engineering* (Vol. 495, p. 012067). IOP Publishing.

Bahaloo, S., Mehrizadeh, M., & Najafi-Marghmaleki, A. (2023). Review of application of artificial intelligence techniques in petroleum operations. *Petroleum Research, 8*(2), 167–182.

Chandrasekaran, V., Jia, H., Thudi, A., Travers, A., Yaghini, M., & Papernot, N. (2021). *SoK: Machine learning governance. arXiv preprint* arXiv:2109.10870

Chen, X. (2023). *Ethical governance of AI: An Integrated approach via human-in-the-loop machine learning.* Paper presented at the Computer Sciences & Mathematics Forum.

Castiñeira, D., Darabi, H., Zhai, X., & Benhallam, W. (2020). Smart reservoir management in the oil and gas industry. In *Smart manufacturing* (pp. 107–141). Elsevier.

D'Almeida, A. L., Bergiante, N. C. R., de Souza Ferreira, G., Leta, F. R., de Campos Lima, C. B., & Lima, G. B. A. (2022). Digital transformation: A review on artificial intelligence techniques in drilling and production applications. *The International Journal of Advanced Manufacturing Technology, 119*(9), 5553–5582.

Gasser, U., & Almeida, V. A. F. (2017). A Layered Model for AI Governance. *IEEE Internet Computing, 21*(6), 58–62. https://doi.org/10.1109/MIC.2017.4180835

Grace, K., Salvatier, J., Dafoe, A., Zhang, B., & Evans, O. (2018). When will AI exceed human performance? Evidence from AI experts. *Journal of Artificial Intelligence Research, 62,* 729–754.

Gill, N., Mathur, A., & Conde, M. V. (2022). A brief overview of AI governance for Responsible Machine Learning Systems. *arXiv preprint* arXiv:2211.13130.

Hussain, M., Alamri, A., Zhang, T., & Jamil, I. (2024). Application of artificial intelligence in the oil and gas industry. In *Engineering applications of artificial intelligence* (pp. 341–373). Springer Nature Switzerland.

Hanga, K. M., & Kovalchuk, Y. (2019). Machine learning and multi-agent systems in oil and gas industry applications: A survey. *Computer Science Review, 34*, Article 100191.

Helo, P., & Hao, Y. (2022). Artificial intelligence in operations management and supply chain management: An exploratory case study. *Production Planning & Control, 33*(16), 1573–1590.

Heydari, M., Alinezhad, A., & Vahdani, B. (2024). A deep learning framework for quality control process in the motor oil industry. *Engineering Applications of Artificial Intelligence, 133*, Article 108554.

Keen, J., Ruddle, R., Palczewski, J., Aivaliotis, G., Palczewska, A., Megone, C., & Macnish, K. (2021). Machine learning, materiality and governance: A health and social care case study. *Information Polity, 26*(1), 57–69.

Khan, A., Al Busafi, M., Al Thuhli, A., & Siddiqui, S. (2024). Accident and incident analysis in the oil and gas sector using artificial intelligence and machine learning. *Procedia Computer Science, 251*, 295–302.

Lu, H., Guo, L., Azimi, M., & Huang, K. (2019). Oil and Gas 4.0 era: A systematic review and outlook. *Computers in Industry, 111*, 68–90.

Laato, S., Birkstedt, T., Mäantymäki, M., Minkkinen, M., & Mikkonen, T. (2022). *AI governance in the system development life cycle: Insights on responsible machine learning engineering*. Paper presented at the Proceedings of the 1st International Conference on AI Engineering: Software Engineering for AI.

Lazzeri, F., & Robsky, A. (2024). *Machine learning governance for managers*. Springer Nature.

Nadler, S., Raz, O., & Zalmanovici, M. (2019). *Governance and regulations implications on machine learning (brief announcement)*. Paper presented at the Cyber Security Cryptography and Machine Learning: Third International Symposium, CSCML 2019, Beer-Sheva, Israel, June 27–28, 2019, Proceedings 3.

Neghawi, E., Wang, Z., Huang, J., & Liu, Y. (2023). *Linking team-level and organization-level governance in machine learning operations through explainable AI and responsible AI connector*. Paper presented at the 2023 IEEE 47th Annual Computers, Software, and Applications Conference (COMPSAC).

Nguyen, T. (2022). The Contribution of Ethical Governance of Artificial Intelligence & Machine Learning in Healthcare.

Patidar, A. K., Agarwal, U., Das, U., & Choudhury, T. (2024). Understanding the oil and gas sector and its processes: Upstream, downstream. In *Understanding data analytics and predictive modelling in the oil and gas industry* (pp. 1–20). CRC Press.

Saputelli, L., Palacios, C., & Bravo, C. (2022). Case studies involving machine learning for predictive maintenance in oil and gas production operations.

In *Machine learning applications in subsurface energy resource management* (pp. 313–336). CRC Press.

Sattari, F., Macciotta, R., Kurian, D., & Lefsrud, L. (2021). Application of Bayesian network and artificial intelligence to reduce accident/incident rates in oil & gas companies. *Safety Science, 133*, Article 104981.

Sokalski, M., Klous, S., & Chandrasekaran, S. (2019). Controlling AI: The imperative for transparency and explainability. *KPMG*. https://advisory.kpmg.us/content/dam/advisory/en/pdfs/kpmg-controlling-ai.pdf

Zhang, B., Anderljung, M., Kahn, L., Dreksler, N., Horowitz, M. C., & Dafoe, A. (2021). Ethics and governance of artificial intelligence: Evidence from a survey of machine learning researchers. *Journal of Artificial Intelligence Research, 71*, 591–666.

CHAPTER 3

Establishing Academic AI Lab Infrastructures: Challenges and Lessons

Hesham M. Al-Ammal and Abdulla E. Subah

3.1 Introduction and Background

AI and deep learning have revolutionized numerous industries, including computer vision, natural language processing, and robotics. The effectiveness of these models heavily relies on their ability to learn intricate patterns and make accurate predictions, necessitating substantial computational power. High-performance computing provides the necessary infrastructure to meet the computational demands of AI, allowing researchers to explore complex architectures and large-scale datasets.

Why do we need HPC for AI? The close relationship between AI and HPC was not evident in the outset years of investigating AI techniques such as neural nets and other learning algorithms. This, however, changed drastically during the past decade. This section attempts to build the link

H. M. Al-Ammal (✉) · A. E. Subah
Department of Computer Science, University of Bahrain, Sakheer, Bahrain
e-mail: halammal@uob.edu.bh

A. E. Subah
e-mail: asubah@uob.edu.bh

A. Badran and A. Mishrif (eds.), *Shaping the Future of Development in the GCC*, The Political Economy of the Middle East,
https://doi.org/10.1007/978-981-96-7963-8_3

between these two fields and answers the question: why is HPC necessary for any meaningful AI or deep learning research or education?

Computational Power and Training Time: The success of deep learning models is closely tied to the availability of computational power for training. Several studies have demonstrated the correlation between model performance and the computational resources used during training. Goyal et al. (2017) showed that increasing the computational power by utilizing multiple GPUs significantly reduced the training time for large-scale models, such as ResNet and LSTM. Furthermore, Ginsburg et al. illustrated the substantial benefits of distributed training across multiple nodes, allowing for faster convergence and improved scalability (Ginsburg et al., 2019).

Scalability and Model Size: As AI models grow in size and complexity, the need for scalable computing resources becomes increasingly critical. Large-scale models, such as GPT-3 (Mann et al., 2020) and AlphaGo (Silver et al., 2017), have demonstrated unprecedented performance but require significant computational capabilities for both training and inference. HPC systems offer distributed computing architectures, allowing researchers to parallelize computations across multiple nodes and GPUs. By harnessing HPC, training time can be significantly reduced, enabling the exploration of more extensive model architecture.

Efficient Exploration of Hyperparameters: Deep learning models often require extensive hyperparameter tuning to achieve optimal performance. The search space for hyperparameter optimization can be vast, requiring numerous experiments to find the best configuration. By utilizing HPC resources, researchers can expedite the exploration of hyperparameter settings through parallel computing. Efficient hyperparameter tuning methods, such as Bayesian optimization (Snoek et al., 2012) and genetic algorithms (Real et al., 2019), can be further enhanced by leveraging HPC, resulting in faster convergence and improved model performance.

Handling Big Data and Complex Datasets: AI models often require vast amounts of labeled data for effective training. Processing and analyzing these large datasets can be computationally demanding. HPC systems excel at handling big data through distributed storage and processing frameworks, such as Apache Hadoop (White, 2012) and Apache Spark (Zaharia et al., 2010). These frameworks enable efficient data parallelism, allowing researchers to scale their experiments and analyze massive datasets with ease.

High-performance computing (HPC) plays a pivotal role in advancing AI and deep learning research. The increasing complexity of models, the need for scalable computing power, and the efficient exploration of hyperparameters necessitate the utilization of HPC resources. By leveraging distributed computing architectures and parallelization techniques, researchers can significantly reduce training time, handle complex datasets, and explore more extensive model architectures. As AI continues to evolve, HPC will remain a crucial component in enabling breakthroughs and driving innovation in the field.

3.2 Why Is HPC Needed for Academic Institutions?

Educational institutions serve as hubs for AI and deep learning research, where faculty and students engage in groundbreaking projects and contribute to scientific advancements. However, the computational demands of AI research require access to high-performance computing resources. This paper investigates the necessity of HPC in educational institutions, emphasizing its contributions to research capabilities, educational opportunities, and skill development.

Enabling Cutting-Edge Research: HPC infrastructure empowers educational institutions to conduct sophisticated AI research. High-performance clusters equipped with powerful CPUs and GPUs facilitate large-scale model training, simulation, and analysis. By leveraging HPC, researchers can explore complex AI architectures, process massive datasets, and achieve faster experimentation cycles. Access to HPC resources enables educational institutions to compete on a global scale and contribute to cutting-edge AI research.

Accelerating Model Development and Optimization: AI and deep learning models often require extensive experimentation and optimization. HPC systems provide the computational power necessary to train and fine-tune complex models efficiently. Parallel computing techniques, such as distributed training across multiple nodes, enable researchers to expedite model development, explore hyperparameter settings, and enhance the performance of AI algorithms. HPC empowers educational institutions to push the boundaries of AI capabilities and drive innovation.

Enhanced Educational Opportunities: HPC infrastructure in educational institutions opens a plethora of educational opportunities for students. By providing access to powerful computing resources, students can engage in hands-on AI and deep learning projects, gaining practical experience in developing and deploying advanced models. HPC facilitates collaborative research environments, enabling students to work on interdisciplinary projects, contribute to scientific publications, and foster innovation. Exposure to HPC systems equips students with invaluable skills and prepares them for careers in AI research and industry.

Bridging the Gap between Academia and Industry: HPC resources in educational institutions bridge the gap between academic research and industry applications. Collaborative projects involving academia, industry partners, and HPC centers enable the transfer of knowledge and technologies. Students and researchers can work on real-world AI challenges, tackle industry-relevant problems, and gain insights into industry practices. HPC empowers educational institutions to nurture industry-academia collaborations, fostering technology transfer and driving economic growth.

High-performance computing is a fundamental requirement for educational institutions engaging in AI and deep learning research. By providing computational power, scalability, and collaborative opportunities, HPC empowers researchers and students to tackle complex AI challenges, drive innovation, and bridge the gap between academia and industry. Embracing HPC in educational institutions is crucial for nurturing the next generation of AI professionals and advancing scientific frontiers.

3.3 Case Studies and Success Stories

Numerous educational institutions have embraced HPC and witnessed remarkable achievements in AI research. For example, the University of California, Berkeley, utilized HPC systems to train deep reinforcement learning models for autonomous driving, leading to breakthroughs in navigation and control. Similarly, Carnegie Mellon University leveraged HPC resources for natural language processing research, contributing to advancements in dialogue systems and machine translation. These following examples highlight the transformative impact of HPC in educational settings.

Texas Advanced Computing Center (TACC)—University of Texas at Austin, USA:

TACC operates several supercomputing systems, including Frontera, Stampede2, and Maverick2. As of my knowledge cutoff in September 2021, Frontera, TACC's flagship supercomputer, has a peak performance of 38.7 petaflops (quadrillions of floating-point operations per second). Stampede2, another system at TACC, has a peak performance of 18 petaflops. The exact number of servers and their configurations may vary, but these systems typically consist of thousands of compute nodes with powerful CPUs and GPUs.

Barcelona Supercomputing Center (BSC)—Universitat Politècnica de Catalunya, Spain:

BSC hosts MareNostrum, one of Europe's most powerful supercomputers. The latest iteration, MareNostrum 4, has a peak performance of around 13.7 petaflops. The system comprises thousands of servers, including Intel Xeon and IBM Power processors, as well as NVIDIA GPUs for acceleration.

National Center for Supercomputing Applications (NCSA)—University of Illinois at Urbana-Champaign, USA:

The NCSA operates Blue Waters, a supercomputer designed for sustained petascale computing. Blue Waters has a peak performance of approximately 13.3 petaflops. It consists of thousands of computational nodes, each equipped with powerful CPUs and accelerators like NVIDIA GPUs.

High-Performance Computing Center Stuttgart (HLRS)—University of Stuttgart, Germany:

HLRS operates several supercomputing systems, including Hawk and Hazel Hen. Hawk, the latest addition, has a peak performance of 26.8 petaflops. It is equipped with AMD EPYC processors and NVIDIA GPUs. Hazel Hen, an earlier system, has a peak performance of 7.4 petaflops. Both systems consist of thousands of compute nodes.

Pawsey Supercomputing Center—Various Australian Universities:

The Pawsey Supercomputing Center provides HPC resources to multiple Australian universities. While specific details about the number of servers and peak performance may vary based on the systems deployed, Pawsey's supercomputers, such as Magnus and Galaxy, have provided significant computational power for research projects. Magnus, for instance, has a peak performance of around 1.97 petaflops and comprises thousands of compute nodes equipped with Intel Xeon processors.

3.3.1 CERN HPC Center—Geneva, EU

For the purposes of the case study at hand, we will also describe in more detail the computing capabilities at CERN, the European Organization for Nuclear Research, which had a major influence in the design of the Benefit AI lab cluster. This is mainly due to the close cooperation between the University of Bahrain and CERN's Muon Collider. The open model adopted by CERN as well as the spirit of collaboration was the main force behind the knowledge transfer that was achieved in building the HPC cluster at UOB.

For the purposes of data collection CERN operates an HPC center known as the CERN Data Center. While the primary focus of the center is on processing and managing the massive amounts of data generated by the Large Hadron Collider (LHC) experiments, it also provides substantial computing resources for scientific research and analysis. The following are some statistics and information about the HPC center at CERN:

1. Worldwide LHC Computing Grid (WLCG): The CERN Data Center is a key component of the Worldwide LHC Computing Grid (WLCG), a global computing infrastructure that supports the processing and analysis of LHC data. The WLCG connects computing centers worldwide, enabling researchers from various institutions to collaborate and access shared resources.
2. Storage Capacity: The CERN Data Center houses an extensive storage infrastructure to handle the vast amounts of data generated by the LHC experiments. As of 2021, he centers stored more than 250 petabytes (250 million gigabytes) of data, making it one of the largest scientific data repositories in the world.

3. Computing Resources: The CERN Data Center provides significant computing resources for data processing, simulation, and analysis. It operates a large number of servers and clusters to support the diverse needs of the LHC experiments and other scientific projects. The exact number of servers and their specifications may vary over time due to upgrades and expansions.
4. Worldwide Data Distribution: CERN's HPC center plays a crucial role in distributing LHC data to research institutions worldwide. Through the WLCG, data is distributed to computing centers located across different countries, allowing scientists to access and analyze the data remotely. This global distribution of data enables collaborative research and ensures that the scientific community can effectively utilize the LHC datasets.
5. Computing Models: The CERN Data Center utilizes a combination of dedicated computing resources and opportunistic resources from various partner institutions to meet the computing demands. Opportunistic resources refer to the unused computing capacity of participating institutions that can be leveraged for data analysis when available. This approach optimizes the utilization of resources and enhances the overall computing capabilities of the center.
6. Collaboration and Open Science: CERN promotes collaboration and open science principles, making data and computing resources available to researchers worldwide. The center actively encourages sharing research code, tools, and methodologies, fostering a culture of scientific collaboration and innovation.

The HPC center at CERN plays a vital role in processing and managing the enormous volumes of data generated by the LHC experiments, enabling groundbreaking research in particle physics. The center's computing resources, and collaborative infrastructure support the scientific community in exploring the fundamental nature of matter and the universe.

Why Open Source?

The open-source movement has fostered collaboration, innovation, and knowledge sharing within the realm of software development. This section investigates the influence of the open-source movement on HPC for AI and deep learning, focusing on the benefits it has brought to the field. The utilization of open-source software in HPC has democratized access to advanced computing resources, facilitated the development of scalable AI models, and encouraged interdisciplinary research.

The Impact of the Open-Source Movement on HPC

The two movements were closely intertwined, and the following are the main impact points of the open-source movement on high-performance computing.

Collaborative Development and Knowledge Sharing

The open-source movement promotes collaboration and knowledge sharing among researchers, developers, and practitioners. Through open-source communities, HPC experts can share ideas, exchange code, and contribute to the improvement of software tools and libraries. This collaborative approach has accelerated the development of HPC frameworks and algorithms, enabling researchers to leverage shared resources and benefit from collective expertise.

Democratization of Access to HPC Resources

Open-source software has played a pivotal role in democratizing access to HPC resources. By eliminating proprietary barriers and licensing costs, open-source solutions have enabled a broader user base, including academic institutions, research organizations, and small-to-medium enterprises, to leverage powerful computing infrastructure. This accessibility has fostered a more inclusive and diverse HPC community, fueling innovation and driving advancements in AI and deep learning.

Examples of Open-Source Software for HPC in AI and Deep Learning

TensorFlow

TensorFlow, an open-source deep learning framework developed by Google, has emerged as a prominent tool for AI and deep learning research in HPC environments (Abadi et al., 2016). Its scalability, distributed computing capabilities, and support for GPUs have made it a go-to choice for training large-scale deep neural networks. TensorFlow's open-source nature has encouraged the development of extensive community-contributed libraries, models, and tools, further enhancing its usability and applicability.

PyTorch

PyTorch, an open-source deep learning framework developed by Facebook's AI Research lab, has gained significant popularity in HPC for AI and deep learning (Paszke et al., 2019). With its dynamic computational graph and intuitive programming interface, PyTorch provides flexibility and ease of use, particularly in research settings. Its strong integration with Python and support for distributed computing enable efficient utilization of HPC resources for training and inference tasks.

Horovod

Horovod, an open-source distributed training framework developed by Uber, has emerged as a crucial tool for scaling deep learning workloads on HPC clusters (Sergeev & Del Balso, 2018). By leveraging message passing interface (MPI) techniques, Horovod enables efficient parallelization of training across multiple compute nodes. Its compatibility with TensorFlow, PyTorch, and other popular deep learning frameworks makes it a versatile choice for distributed training in HPC environments (Abadi et al., 2016; Chollet, 2021; Jozefowicz et al., 2016).

3.4 Case Studies and Research Contributions

Numerous case studies and research contributions highlight the impact of open-source software on HPC for AI and deep learning. For example, the use of TensorFlow and PyTorch in large-scale distributed training has enabled breakthroughs in image recognition, natural language processing, and reinforcement learning. The availability of open-source software has empowered researchers to collaborate, reproduce results, and build upon existing work, fostering rapid progress in the field (Coulter et al., 2019).

The open-source movement and open-source software have revolutionized HPC for AI and deep learning in the past two decades. The collaborative development model, democratization of access to resources, and the availability of key open-source software tools like TensorFlow, PyTorch, and Horovod have significantly contributed to advancements in research, innovation, and practical applications. The ongoing evolution of the open-source ecosystem will continue to shape the future of HPC for AI and deep learning, facilitating interdisciplinary collaborations and accelerating scientific discoveries.

3.4.1 Design Process for the Benefit AI Lab

The main objective was the design and implementation of a mid-level AI HPC lab and its distributed cluster (see item number 2 below). According to the HPC-AI Leadership Organization (see https://hpcaileadership.org/), AI HPC clusters can be classified by the number of nodes as follows:

1. *Entry-level HPC-AI*, on individual systems or small clusters, 1–4 server nodes (or equivalent in cloud)
2. *Mid-range HPC-AI*, on moderate size clusters less than one full rack, 5–32 server nodes (or equivalent in cloud)
3. *High-end HPC-AI*, on full-rack or multi-rack systems, 33–128 server nodes (or equivalent in cloud)
4. *Supercomputing HPC-AI*, on systems of several racks, over 128 server nodes (or equivalent in cloud)

After waying in the available budget, physical location, and needs, a decision was made to initiate the project with a mid-range design with 8 computing nodes and 2 high-end GPU nodes.

Vision and Objectives

From the outset, the University of Bahrain was seeking the following high-level *vision* when creating an AI lab with HPC capabilities: *"A national center of excellence, national resource, and an inspiration for AI researchers, students, and entrepreneurs."*

The following were the main *objectives* of the project:

1. The lab would be created to strengthen the human and computing capacity for future technologies and enable students, researchers, and staff to conduct cutting-edge AI learning and research.
2. The high-performance computing facility is intended to satisfy the computing needs for UOB and other national research organizations for the coming decade.
3. The Advanced AI Lab will serve to strengthen AI research and innovation in areas such as machine learning, artificial intelligence, cybersecurity, big data, computing for particle physics, engineering applications, and climate change forecasting.

The proposal was then submitted to the board of the Benefit Bahrain Company, as a first phase. The board supported the proposal with a budget that would enable building a small cluster as a first phase. The proposal also included a two-year plan for further activities to strengthen engagement with the research community, such as an expert preparation program, an undergraduate students' AI hackathon, and two annual AI research prizes. All of the activities were generously supported by the Benefit Company board.

The *scope* (and estimated *workload*) of the project included using it for the following goals and areas.

- Teaching:
  - Undergraduate courses in machine learning, parallel processing, senior projects, etc. The number of students is estimated at 150 per semester.
  - MSc and PhD courses in machine learning, AI, cybersecurity, and HPC. Number of students is estimated at 35 per semester.
  - Short courses for the community especially in AI and machine learning.
- Research:

  PhD and MSc thesis work in AI and HPC.

  Faculty research from the College of IT, Engineering, and Science.

  Guest researchers from national and regional institutions.

The Design Process

Designing a small-scale HPC cluster for educational and research purposes involves several key steps. The following steps outline the process of designing such a cluster:

Define Requirements and Objectives:

Clearly define the requirements and objectives of the HPC cluster. Consider the specific needs of the educational institution or research project, such as the types of applications to be run, anticipated workloads, data storage requirements, budget constraints, and any specific hardware or software preferences.

Determine Cluster Size and Budget:

Assess the available resources, including space, power, and budget, to determine the cluster's size and capacity. Consider factors such as the number of computer nodes, storage capacity, network infrastructure, and cooling requirements. Balance the desired performance with the available resources to ensure an optimal configuration within the allocated budget.

Based on the objectives and scope listed above (to start with a mid-range 8 compute and 2 GPU nodes), the project team decided on the resources and architecture listed in Table 3.1 and Fig. 3.1.

Selecting the Hardware Components:

Choose the hardware components based on the defined requirements. Consider factors such as processors (CPUs), accelerators (such as GPUs or FPGAs), memory capacity, storage devices (hard drives or solid-state drives), and networking equipment. Ensure compatibility and scalability of the chosen components to support future expansion. Based on the available budget and the scope, the project team chose the hardware components shown in Table 3.1.

Design the Network Architecture:

Plan the network architecture of the cluster, including the interconnectivity between the compute nodes, storage devices, and management infrastructure. Determine the network topology (such as Ethernet or InfiniBand), network switches, and bandwidth requirements to ensure efficient communication and data transfer within the cluster.

Table 3.1 Overview of cluster design

	Description	*OS*	*Number*
Management nodes	Controller nodes with Infiniband switches	CentOS Stream	2 (for redundancy)
Compute nodes	Main compute nodes with low level GPU with 2 switches	CentOS Stream	8
GPU nodes	Main GPU with 2 Nvidia A100 GPUs each	CentOS Stream	2
Backup node	BeeGFS with storage	CentOS Stream	1

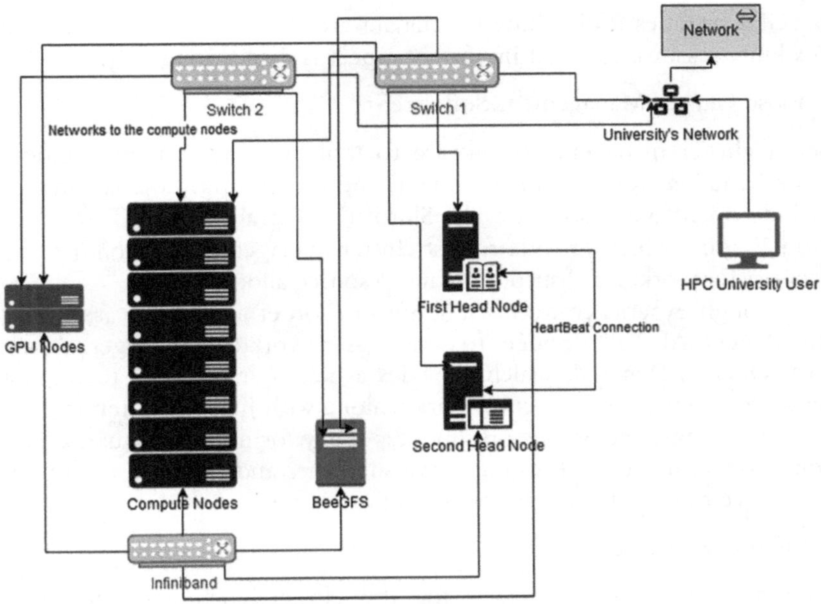

Fig. 3.1 A model framework for initiating and operating a mid-range AI HPC lab

As one of the intended objectives was big data and HPC, the team chose to use InfiniBand to connect the main compute and GPU nodes. This would guarantee enough network capacity for handling big data transfer among the nodes. This was not an easy choice, as the InfiniBand was one of the most expensive hardware components of the project.

Determine Storage Infrastructure:

Assess the storage requirements for the cluster, considering the anticipated data size, I/O performance, and data access patterns. Determine whether centralized or distributed storage architecture is more suitable. Consider options such as network-attached storage (NAS), storage area networks (SAN), or object storage systems. Select appropriate storage technologies and capacities based on the workload and budget. The chosen file system for the storage was BeeGFS, which is a parallel file system, developed and optimized for high-performance computing.

BeeGFS includes a distributed metadata architecture for scalability and flexibility reasons. Its most important aspect is data throughput.

Choose Cluster Management Software:

Select cluster management software to facilitate cluster administration, job scheduling, resource management, and monitoring. Popular options include open-source software like Slurm (Yoo et al., 2003), Torque, or Grid Engine, which provide robust cluster management capabilities and support for workload distribution and resource allocation.

Through experience from using Slurm (Yoo et al., 2003), at CERN, the Benefit AI Lab decided to use it as a workload manager. Along with OpenOnDemand, which provides a nice user interface to request resources from Slurm, the combination along with Juputer Notebook and the file manager seems to work fine, especially for non-Linux users. This combination made the learning curve smoother and offers more options for novice to expert users at the Benefit Lab.

Configure Software Stack:

Determine the software stack for the cluster, including the operating system, compilers, libraries, and parallel programming frameworks. Consider the requirements of the specific applications and research workloads to ensure compatibility and optimal performance. Popular software frameworks for HPC include MPI (Message Passing Interface) for parallel computing and frameworks like TensorFlow or PyTorch for deep learning workloads.

To manage the software stack, it was decided to use Spack (Gamblin et al., 2015) and Conda (Anaconda Software Distribution, 2020) for package management. These tools provide better means to maintain multiple versions of the same software package. It is important to do so in HPC environments to support the different users' requirements and the reproducibility of their work.

Implement and Test the Cluster:

Assemble the hardware components, configure the network, and install the software stack based on the design. Thoroughly test the cluster to ensure its stability, performance, and reliability. Validate the functionality of the networking, storage, and compute infrastructure, and verify the integration of the cluster management software.

Documentation and Training:

Document the cluster design, configuration, and management procedures for future reference and troubleshooting. Provide training to the cluster administrators and users on how to effectively utilize the cluster resources, submit jobs, and manage their workloads.

Ongoing Maintenance and Upgrades:

Plan for ongoing maintenance, monitoring, and periodic upgrades of the cluster. Stay updated with the latest software updates, security patches, and hardware advancements to optimize performance and address any potential vulnerabilities.

By following these steps, small to medium-scale educational institutions (such as the University of Bahrain with 32,000 students) can design a small-scale HPC cluster tailored to their specific needs, enabling enhanced computational capabilities for educational purposes, research endeavors, and scientific discovery.

Challenges

Building a small to medium-scale High-Performance Computing (HPC) cluster for universities presents various challenges. This paper explores the main challenges associated with the construction of such clusters and provides insights from relevant sources. The challenges include budget constraints, resource availability and space limitations, scalability and future growth, expertise and skills, software and application compatibility, data management and storage, user accessibility and training, and maintenance and upgrades. Understanding and addressing these challenges are crucial for universities aiming to deploy effective HPC clusters to support research and educational endeavors.

1. *Budget Constraints:* Budget limitations posed significant challenge when constructing HPC clusters for universities. Limited funding may restrict the acquisition of high-performance hardware components, networking infrastructure, and storage systems, potentially impacting the overall performance and scalability of the cluster (Lockwood et al., 2024). Furthermore, because of the specialized and costly nature of HPC labs, university administrations may find it hard to allocate the amount of budget needed for such a project. Although the partnership with the private sector (namely Benefit

Bahrain) alleviated this challenge, it was still quite challenging to fit all of the different needs for big data, parallel process, AI, etc. in a single small HPC cluster. Recently, and because of the research and teaching needs for advanced topics, HPC resources have become vital for higher education.

2. *Resource Availability and Space Constraints:* Universities commonly face constraints in terms of physical space, power supply, and cooling infrastructure. Designing and setting up an HPC cluster within the available resources can be challenging, particularly when considering the need for multiple compute nodes, storage devices, and network switches (Malla & Christensen, 2020). The project had to rely on the support of the university infrastructure development to build the power, cooling, and fire safety needs for the project's server room. Further support from the University of Bahrain was needed for the heavy power consumption of the lab, as operational cost.
3. *Scalability and Future Growth:* Planning for scalability and accommodating future growth are crucial when building an HPC cluster. Anticipating increasing demands for computational resources and storage capacity is challenging, as it requires predicting the future requirements of research projects and educational needs. Ensuring that the cluster design allows for easy expansion and upgrades is essential to support evolving workloads (Varrette et al., 2022). The project was established by both UOB and Benefit as a first phase. The maintenance and warranty is for 5 years from Dell, and we are hoping to expand the power of the cluster in the second phase of the project.
4. *Expertise and Skills:* Building and managing an HPC cluster requires specialized skills and expertise in areas such as system administration, cluster management, networking, parallel programming, and software optimization. Universities may face challenges in recruiting and retaining skilled personnel with HPC knowledge, potentially impacting the efficient operation of the cluster (Gamblin et al., 2015).

   This challenge was one of the hardest, but due to a partnership with CERN, the College of IT had a student training at this international research institute with massive HPC capabilities. This allowed significant knowledge transfer both in the design of the hardware and software stacks and in the operation phase. Considering the extensive costs of building an HPC Center, this challenge must be met as early as possible, as it could render all of the expensive servers and GPUs useless without proper utilization and support for the users.

5. *Software and Application Compatibility:* Ensuring software compatibility and support for diverse research applications can be challenging. Different research groups may have specific software requirements and dependencies. Compatibility issues, version mismatches, or lack of software support for specific hardware components can hinder the successful deployment and utilization of the cluster (Yoo et al., 2003). The Benefit AI Lab project relied on open-source software, which was quite mature in the HPC sector. Almost all of the designed software stack relied on open and free software such as Slurm, PyTorch, TensorFlow, etc.

   Even with the use of HPC package managers, managing the different packages on the system is not an easy task. For example, Spack (Gamblin et al., 2015) provides recipes to build optimized versions of major AI and HPC software packages. However, building these packages often takes a lot of time and the users usually require a faster solution to get the package, especially in early stages of experimentation and development. On the other hand, Conda provides a precompiled repository of AI and HPC packages, but the packages cannot be tuned or optimized for a specific environment. Moreover, Conda requires a much larger (Anaconda Software Distribution, 2020) storage space to maintain all the fat binaries.

6. *Data Management and Storage:* Efficient data management and storage solutions are critical for HPC clusters. Balancing the need for high-performance storage with cost considerations can be a challenge. Determining the most suitable storage architecture, addressing data security and integrity, and implementing effective backup and recovery strategies are important considerations that universities need to address (Allen et al., 2020).

   This is an important challenge, and the project alleviated it by determining the average data and storage needs for each group of users: undergrads, postgrads, and faculty. Another solution was to provide a dataset directory for the massive datasets used which is shared by all users on the BeeGFS storage server.

7. User Accessibility and Training: Providing easy access to the HPC cluster for users and ensuring proper training and support can be challenging. The cluster should have user-friendly interfaces,

job submission systems, and documentation to facilitate usage by researchers, students, and faculty members who may have varying levels of HPC expertise (Gamblin et al., 2015)).

The project also created a *GitHub* webpage and repository with documentation and FAQs regarding the main software components of the Benefit AI cluster (https://uob-ai.github.io/). The page has comprehensive guidance to new users for all aspects of the cluster, from requesting an account to controlling the HPC jobs. Further support was also offered through running short courses for the faculty and students.

8. *Maintenance and Upgrades:* Regular maintenance, software updates, and hardware upgrades are essential for the optimal functioning of an HPC cluster. However, managing maintenance activities while minimizing disruptions to ongoing research and educational activities can be challenging, requiring careful planning and coordination (Michalakes, 2020). The project demanded a warranty and hardware maintenance contract for 5 years and assigned a UOB technician to provide support to the system. Another system admin (second author) is also responsible for maintaining the software environments and upgrades.
9. *Collaboration and Resource Sharing:* Facilitating collaboration and resource sharing among different research groups or departments within the university can be a challenge. Implementing policies, access controls, and fair allocation mechanisms to ensure equitable usage of cluster resources among various stakeholders can be complex (Tate et al., 2014).

   The project team is planning on providing the resources of the Benefit AI lab to external national users such as private companies for a fee. This is considered as a lifeline for continuing to provide the HPC services both inside the educational institute and nationally.

Addressing these challenges requires careful planning, collaboration, and support from the university administration, IT departments, and researchers. By understanding and mitigating these challenges, universities can successfully build and maintain small to medium-scale HPC clusters that meet the computational needs of their academic and research communities. We have tried to briefly describe some of the mitigating actions taken by the project team in the above list of challenges.

A Design Framework

Based on design and user experience, Fig. 3.2 shows a suggested framework that encompasses all of the design issues and important decision points needed for the creation and maintenance of a small to mid-range HPC-AI laboratory at an academic/research institution.

The following are the elements of the framework suggested in Fig. 3.2.

1. ***Design and Establishment Phase (30%)***
    - ***Planning & Funding:*** *Focuses on budgeting, securing funding sources, andensuring financial sustainability.*
    - ***Infrastructure & Hardware:*** *Covers physical location, power, cooling, scalability, and redundancy.*
    - ***Software & Tools:*** *Selection of OS, AI frameworks, data management tools, containerization, and orchestration.*
    - ***Staffing & Training:*** *Hiring skilled personnel and providing continuous training and workshops.*
2. ***Operation, Management, and Upgrade Phase (50%)***
    - ***Operational Management:*** *Implementation of monitoring tools, regular maintenance schedules, and efficient resource allocation.*

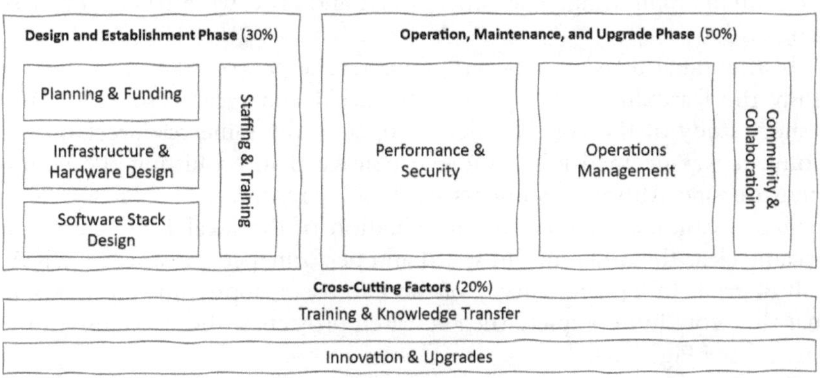

Fig. 3.2 A model framework for initiating and operating a mid-range AI HPC lab

- ***Performance& Security:*** *Optimization for high-performance computing, ensuring robust security measures, and managing data security.*
- ***Community & Collaboration:*** *Encouraging collaboration, forming partnerships, and engaging with the academic and research community.*
- ***Compliance & Cost:*** *Ensuring regulatory compliance, managing licensing costs, and overall cost management.*

3. *Cross-Cutting Factors (20%):*

- ***Innovation & Upgrades:*** *Staying current with technology upgrades, supporting R&D, and fostering innovation through special projects.*
- ***Training & Knowledge Transfer:*** *Focused on capacity building through workshops, courses, and training programs, as well as facilitating research output through publications and patents.*

3.5 Discussion

The University of Bahrain witnessed a big expansion in advanced post-graduate programs in the past three years. This included MSc programs in Big Data, Machine Learning, and Cybersecurity, as well as a PhD program in Computing. The benefit of AI and HPC were crucial for these programs.

In the initial phases of the program, several people asked the team to study the feasibility of using cloud-based AI and HPC resources. After a short study of the costs needed to operate the same resources on the cloud, it was deemed much more expensive than acquitting the equipment on site. Although students used cloud resources such as Google's Collab occasionally, after the full operation of the local HPC cluster, it became clear the difference in speed and performance that the Benefit AI Lab offered. In a recent survey of the Lab users, approximately 17% said that they couldn't complete their research projects without the use of the cluster (see Fig. 3.3).

The survey also indicates that the highest percentage of users are using it for machine learning and AI model training. However, there are students using it also for parallel processing and big data tasks (see Fig. 3.4).

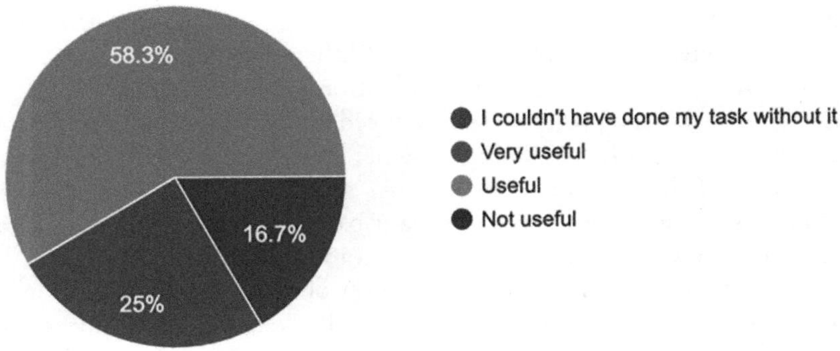

Fig. 3.3 User acceptance of the benefit AI cluster

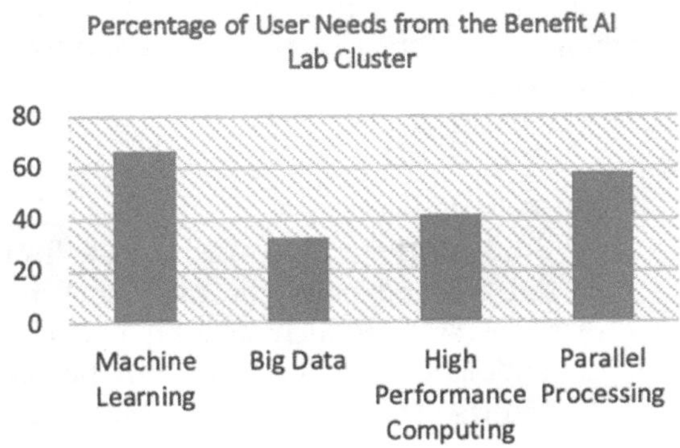

Fig. 3.4 Survey results for percentage of projects use cases

In conclusion, the use of High-Performance Computing (HPC) for AI education in higher education holds great promise for fostering advanced learning experiences and preparing students for the rapidly evolving field of artificial intelligence. This project explored the various challenges and opportunities of HPC in AI education, including enhanced computational power, accelerated training of deep learning models, and the ability to tackle complex AI problems.

By leveraging HPC resources, universities can offer students hands-on experience with cutting-edge technologies, enabling them to develop practical skills and gain insights into the real-world challenges of AI. The integration of HPC in AI education facilitates the exploration of large datasets, enabling students to work on high-dimensional problems and conduct sophisticated analysis that would otherwise be infeasible.

Moreover, HPC clusters provide a platform for collaborative research and interdisciplinary projects (as evidenced by collaboration among the three colleges at UOB), bringing together students and faculty members from diverse fields to address complex AI challenges. Through collaborative efforts, students can engage in team-based projects, fostering critical thinking, problem-solving, and effective communication skills.

However, the successful implementation of HPC for AI education in higher education is not without challenges. Universities must address the issues of funding and resource constraints, provide training and support to students and faculty members, ensure software compatibility and access to necessary tools, and overcome infrastructure limitations. These challenges require careful planning, coordination, and collaboration among stakeholders, including administrators, faculty members, IT departments, and researchers.

The following is a list of the main *challenges* faced by the HPC-AI lab:

1. *Data Availability:*

   Although the project hardware, software, and infrastructure can be sourced and built, the main challenge in AI-based projects is that they are extremely data-hungry. Utilizing the cluster depends on finding quality data that can be used in producing efficient AI models. This has been a challenge especially when it comes to finding localized data, due to concerns with privacy, security, and lack of open data. Growing awareness in this regard is essential in the GCC countries, as this is a vital component of any AI strategy.
2. *Budgeting and Monetization*:

   Many such projects require not just the budget to establish the infrastructure but also a sustainable means of income. Monetizing such projects is possible due to the high cost of cloud-based HPC solutions but requires a plethora of financial policies and regulations.
3. *Training and Knowledge Transfer:*

   Knowledge of building and running an HPC cluster for AI applications is necessary. Although depending on open-source software helps, the scale and infrastructure needed require experienced and capable engineers.
4. *Access to Upgrades (GPUs):*

With the looming war on GPUs between the US and China and the limits on accessing special GPUs by Nvidia, including the H100; it is vital to find a source for these powerful processors to maintain a working HPC cluster.

5. *Security*

   Securing access, usage, and data for the AI models is another important challenge. This again requires extensive experience and must be managed by capable engineers. Creating policies for access and usage is another challenge that can be ameliorated by partnerships with established HPC and AI centers.

6. *Utilization: Parallelism, and Concurrency.*

   Perhaps one of the biggest challenges is ensuring proper utilization of the AI cluster. The huge initial budget must be justified, especially with the availability of cloud solutions. Unfortunately, many programmers and HPC users lack the necessary experience to run their software in a manner that utilizes parallelism in code. This can lead to 100s of magnitude faster code and a noticeable increase in efficiency. This challenge can clearly be seen through the monitoring software, as most nodes will see a 100% utilization of a single core or one CPU, while the GPU and other cores stay dormant.

To overcome these challenges, universities should invest in HPC infrastructure, establish dedicated HPC centers or clusters, and provide adequate technical support and training programs for students and faculty members. Collaboration among universities and industry partners can also facilitate access to state-of-the-art HPC resources and promote knowledge exchange.

The following are some *opportunities* when managing an HPC for AI lab:

1. *Data Localization*

   Most AI models are quite biased toward the data used for training them. Using non-local data to train AI models presents several dangers, primarily related to relevance, privacy, and bias. Non-local data may not accurately reflect the specific conditions, behaviors, and nuances of the local context, leading to models that perform poorly or make incorrect predictions when applied locally. Privacy concerns also arise, as data sourced from different regions may have varying regulations and protections, risking violations of data protection laws and ethical standards. Additionally, non-local data can introduce biases, as it might contain inherent cultural, social, or demographic biases that do not align with the local population, potentially perpetuating or even exacerbating unfair outcomes and discrimination in AI applications. Ensuring data relevance, respecting privacy regulations, and mitigating bias are critical when sourcing and utilizing data for AI training.

This leads to an opportunity in providing local data that can be used to build local AI models. Building awareness and user need for such localized data is crucial by local AI labs. These applications include medical diagnosis, language models, culturally dependent models, etc. Importing international data will not help in building local applications, and thus the need for building local repositories for local needs by data scientists.

2. *Open-Source Software*

   Open-source software offers numerous opportunities for high-performance computing (HPC) and AI applications by providing cost-effective, flexible, and collaborative solutions. It allows institutions, including academic and research centers, to leverage cutting-edge technologies without the financial burden of proprietary software licenses. Open-source HPC frameworks, such as Apache Hadoop and Spark, facilitate large-scale data processing and parallel computing. AI applications benefit from robust frameworks like TensorFlow, PyTorch, and scikit-learn, which are continuously improved by a global community of developers. These tools are highly customizable, enabling tailored solutions for specific research needs. Additionally, open-source software promotes transparency and reproducibility in scientific research, fostering innovation and accelerating technological advancements through community-driven development and shared knowledge.

3. Open Learning

   Open learning platforms are crucial for knowledge transfer in AI, HPC, and data science, democratizing access to cutting-edge information and educational resources. They provide learners from diverse backgrounds with free or affordable access to high-quality courses, tutorials, and collaborative projects, breaking down traditional barriers to education. This inclusive fosters a global community of practitioners who can share knowledge, contribute to open-source projects, and stay abreast of rapid technological advancements. Open learning platforms also facilitate continuous learning and skill development, essential in these fast-evolving fields. By promoting widespread dissemination of knowledge and best practices, they accelerate innovation and enable a broader range of individuals to contribute to and benefit from advancements in AI, HPC, and data science. It is crucial that such AI labs in the GCC participate in growing the base of open learning platforms, especially for localized applications.

4. Software Repositories: GitHub

   Software repositories like GitHub are essential for building a robust AI and HPC lab, offering a collaborative environment that enhances code management, version control, and project tracking. These platforms provide a centralized space for storing, sharing, and documenting code, ensuring that projects are accessible and maintainable over time. Version control systems, such as Git, enable researchers and developers to track changes, collaborate efficiently, and revert to previous code states, if necessary, which is crucial for complex AI and HPC projects. GitHub's integration with various development tools and continuous integration/continuous deployment (CI/CD) pipelines facilitates automated testing, deployment, and scaling of applications. Additionally, the open-source nature of many repositories encourages community contributions, fostering innovation and allowing labs to leverage a vast pool of shared knowledge and resources. This collaborative ecosystem accelerates development cycles, enhances transparency, and supports the reproducibility of scientific research, making GitHub and similar platforms indispensable for modern AI and HPC labs. It is hoped that through such repositories experience in HPC can be shared among GCC academic institutions and worldwide.

3.6 Conclusions

In conclusion, the integration of HPC in AI education has the potential to revolutionize the learning experience, empower students with advanced computational capabilities, and foster innovation in the field of artificial intelligence. By addressing the challenges and seizing the opportunities presented by HPC, higher education institutions can equip the next generation of AI professionals with the skills and knowledge necessary to tackle complex problems and drive advancements in AI research and applications.

For the project team at UOB, the integration of HPC in AI education was a transformative step that can empower students, advance research, and contribute to the development of innovative solutions to real-world challenges. Acknowledgment and thanks should be given to our private sector partners at Benefit Bahrain, as more support and investment in HPC is needed throughout the GCC region.

References

Abadi, M., Barham, P., Chen, J., Chen, Z., Davis, A., Dean, J., Devin, M., Ghemawat, S., Irving, G., Isard, M., & Kudlur, M. (2016). TensorFlow: A system for Large-Scale machine learning. In *12th USENIX symposium on operating systems design and implementation (OSDI 16)* (pp. 265–283).

Allen, B. S., Ezell, M. A., Peltz, P., Jacobsen, D., Roman, E., Lueninghoener, C., & Wofford, J. L. (2020). *Modernizing the HPC system software stack. arXiv preprint* arXiv:2007.10290

Anaconda Software Distribution. (2020). *Anaconda documentation.* Anaconda Inc. Retrieved from https://docs.anaconda.com/

Chollet, F. (2021). *Deep learning with Python.* Simon and Schuster.

Coulter, J. E., Knepper, R., Reynolds, R., Sprouse, J., & Bird, S. (2019). Beyond campus bridging: A retrospective of cyberinfrastructure integration efforts. In *Proceedings of the practice and experience in advanced research computing on rise of the machines (learning)* (pp. 1–4).

Gamblin, T., LeGendre, M., Collette, M. R., Lee, G. L., Moody, A., De Supinski, B. R., & Futral, S. (2015, November). The Spack package manager: Bringing order to HPC software chaos. In *Proceedings of the international conference for high performance computing, networking, storage and analysis* (pp. 1–12).

Ginsburg, B., Castonguay, P., Hrinchuk, O., Kuchaiev, O., Lavrukhin, V., Leary, Li, J., Nguyen, H., Zhang. Y., & Cohen, J. M. (2019). *Stochastic gradient methods with layer-wise adaptive moments for training of deep networks. arXiv preprint* arXiv:1905.11286

Goyal, P., Dollár, P., Girshick, R., Noordhuis, P., Tulloch, L. W. A. K. A., & He, Y. J. K. *Accurate, Large Minibatch SGD: Training ImageNet in 1 Hour.* arXiv preprint arXiv:1706.02677

Jozefowicz, R., Vinyals, O., Schuster, M., Shazeer, N., & Wu, Y. (2016). *Exploring the limits of language modeling. arXiv preprint* arXiv:1602.02410

Lockwood, G. K., Hazen, D., Koziol, Q., Canon, R. S., Antypas, K., Balewski, J., Balthaser, N., Bhimji, W., Botts, J., Broughton, J., & Wright, N. J. (2024). *Storage 2020: A vision for the future of hpc storage.*

Malla, S., & Christensen, K. (2020). HPC in the cloud: Performance comparison of function as a service (FaaS) vs infrastructure as a service (IaaS). *Internet Technology Letters, 3*(1), Article e137.

Mann, B., Ryder, N., Subbiah, M., Kaplan, J., Dhariwal, P., Neelakantan, A., Shyam, P., Sastry, G., Askell, A., Agarwal, S., & Herbert-Voss, A. (2020). *Language models are few-shot learners. arXiv preprint* arXiv:2005.14165, 1.

Michalakes, J. (2020). Hpc for weather forecasting. *Parallel Algorithms in Computational Science and Engineering*, 297–323.

Paszke, A., Gross, S., Massa, F., Lerer, A., Bradbury, J., Chanan, G., Killeen, T., Lin, Z., Gimelshein, N., Antiga, L., & Desmaison, A. (2019). Pytorch: An imperative style, high-performance deep learning library. *Advances in neural information processing systems, 32.*

Real, E., Aggarwal, A., Huang, Y., & Le, Q. V. (2019, July). Regularized evolution for image classifier architecture search. In *Proceedings of the aaai conference on artificial intelligence* (Vol. 33, No. 01, pp. 4780–4789).

Sergeev, A., & Del Balso, M. (2018). *Horovod: Fast and easy distributed deep learning in TensorFlow. arXiv preprint* arXiv:1802.05799

Silver, D., Schrittwieser, J., Simonyan, K., Antonoglou, I., Huang, A., Guez, A., Hubert, T., Baker, L., Lai, M., Bolton, A., & Chen, Y. (2017). Mastering the game of go without human knowledge. *Nature, 550*(7676), 354–359.

Snoek, J., Larochelle, H., & Adams, R. P. (2012). Practical bayesian optimization of machine learning algorithms. *Advances in neural information processing systems, 25.*

Tate, A., Kamil, A., Dubey, A., Groblinger, A., Chamberlain, B., Goglin, B., Edwards, H. C., Newburn, C. J., Padua, D., Unat, D., & Leung, V. J. (2014). *Programming abstractions for data locality.* Office of Scientific and Technical Information (OSTI).

Varrette, S., Cartiaux, H., Peter, S., Kieffer, E., Valette, T., & Olloh, A. (2022, July). Management of an academic HPC & research computing facility: The ULHPC experience 2.0. In *Proceedings of the 2022 6th High Performance Computing and Cluster Technologies Conference* (pp. 14–24).

White, T. (2012). *Hadoop: The definitive guide.* O'Reilly Media, Inc.

Yoo, A. B., Jette, M. A., & Grondona, M. (2003, June). Slurm: Simple linux utility for resource management. In *Workshop on job scheduling strategies for parallel processing* (pp. 44–60). Springer Berlin Heidelberg.

Zaharia, M., Chowdhury, M., Franklin, M. J., Shenker, S., & Stoica, I. (2010). Spark: Cluster computing with working sets. In *2nd USENIX workshop on hot topics in cloud computing (HotCloud 10).*

CHAPTER 4

Evaluating ChatGPT-4's Performance in Summarizing Academic Texts: A Qualitative Analysis Using Self-Authored Publications

Sanaa Ashour

4.1 Introduction

The concept of "Generative AI" encompasses a wide array of tools spanning the disciplines of statistics, computer science, and engineering (Bail, 2024; Goodfellow et al., 2020). Recent years have witnessed a pivotal shift in AI's functions—from merely identifying patterns in datasets to actively generating complex content like text, images, and video. This evolution in machine learning technologies is fundamentally changing the landscape of various fields, including large language models (LLMs) (Mitchell & Krakauer, 2023).

S. Ashour (✉)
Gulf Studies Centre, College of Arts and Sciences (CAS), Qatar University, Doha, Qatar
e-mail: sashour@qu.edu.qa

A. Badran and A. Mishrif (eds.), *Shaping the Future of Development in the GCC*, The Political Economy of the Middle East,
https://doi.org/10.1007/978-981-96-7963-8_4

As argued by Grossmann et al. (2023), owing to the ability to generate, and interpret human language with accuracy and scale, large language models (LLMs) represent a significant methodological advancement in AI and thus transform social science research. Trained on vast datasets of text, LLMs are capable of performing a wide range of language-related tasks, including but not limited to translation, summarization, question answering, and content generation (Jin et al., 2024). Leveraging deep learning techniques, these models process and analyze large volumes of text, which makes them capable of capturing complex patterns and nuances in language usage.

Of note, however, the capabilities of LLMs extend beyond mere text analysis—specifically, LLMs are equally instrumental in simulating human-like dialogues, predicting linguistic outcomes based on contextual understanding, and uncovering social insights from unstructured text data (Tang et al., 2024). The advent of generative AI, including tools like ChatGPT, has sparked considerable scholarly interest across various fields, highlighting its potential to revolutionize present-day research practices. However, while the capacity of generative AI to produce realistic and creative outputs can enrich social science research (Bail, 2024), it also has several limitations, such as biases and the risk of misinformation. This underscores the importance of taking into account ethical considerations and the need for informed consent in research involving human participants (Solaiman, 2023).

One particularly salient area where AI tools have recently come into wide use is academic writing (Bail, 2024). Crafting a research paper demands considerable effort and time. In response to these demands, in recent years, several artificial intelligence (AI) tools—including but not limited to such tools as Paper Digest, Elicit, Scholarcy, QuillBot, and Grammarly, among several others—have emerged to aid scholars. Specific tasks where such tools have proved to be instrumental for academic researchers include summarizing academic papers (Hake et al., 2024), identifying key concepts, extracting information, rephrasing sentences, enhancing grammar, and refining the clarity and structure of academic writing (Lingard, 2023). While the aforementioned AI tools have been relatively non-problematically incorporated into academic practice, the widely used all-in-one tool ChatGPT has raised many questions about its potential for errors, inaccuracies, and ethical issues.

To date, generative AI has made significant strides into academic writing and content analysis. Seeking to analyze this trend, Lin (2023) outlined key principles and methods for integrating generative AI—and, more specifically, large language models (LLMs)—into academic practice to enhance both quality and productivity of academic writing. To this end, Lin (2023) presented a human-AI collaboration framework that conceptualizes the reasons (why), methods (how), and essence (what) of AI involvement in academic writing. The proposed framework identifies both immediate and long-term motivations for using AI, along with their mechanisms, such as cognitive offloading and imaginative stimulation. Capturing the role of AI throughout the writing process, Lin's (2023) framework is organized around a two-phase model of human-AI collaborative writing and categorizes the types and levels of AI assistance in writing. Based on this framework, the author discussed effective techniques for integrating AI into the writing process, such as outlining, drafting, and revising, on the one hand, and strategies for ensuring rigorous academic standards, compliance with journal policies, and avoiding excessive dependency on AI, on the other hand. Although Lin (2023) acknowledged the limitations of generative AI and its implications for ethical use, equality in education, the author concluded that a careful incorporation of AI into academic writing can effectively reduce the burden of communication, empower researchers, speed up discoveries, and enhance diversity in the scientific community.

One central area in academic writing where AI-based tools can be particularly valuable is academic text summarization (Hake et al., 2024). In simple terms, the goal of text summarization is to condense written content while preserving its key information. With the exponential growth of the volume of publicly accessible textual data, the importance of automated summarization methods can hardly be overestimated. Specifically, text summarization is central to systematic literature reviews and can facilitate the screening of articles.

Conventional summarization systems operate on an end-to-end, one-shot approach, producing summaries in a single action. In contrast, the human approach to writing, which involves repeated cycles of drafting and revising, is frequently evolutionary (Zhang et al., 2023).

Yet these one-shot, end-to-end systems face several issues. They are prone to "hallucinations," as well as to creating grammatically incorrect or factually inaccurate information (Kryscinski et al., 2020; Zhang et al., 2023). Furthermore, these summarization systems tend to be trained on imperfect reference summaries, and commonly used metrics like ROUGE may not fully capture the quality of the generated summaries. Another important limitation of conventional summarization systems is their lack of customization; they generate a single, standard summary based on the input text. Yet, in most practical applications, users frequently need summaries tailored to specific aspects or queries.

In this context, recent advancements in large language models (LLMs), such as ChatGPT, have opened up promising avenues for summarization technologies, and the corresponding models demonstrated robust capabilities in a variety of tasks without specific training. To date, cutting-edge developments in summarization technology based on neural networks and sophisticated pre-trained language models have yielded impressive improvements (Cheng & Lapata, 2016; Nallapati et al., 2016; Lewis et al., 2019; Liu & Lapata, 2019; Sorokina et al., 2024). For instance, Goyal et al. (2022) benchmarked GPT-3 against conventional fine-tuning approaches to find out that, even though GPT-3 might have received lower ROUGE scores, the summaries it produced were preferred by human reviewers. In another relevant study, Zhang et al. (2023) demonstrated that LLMs can generate news summaries that rival the quality of those written by humans. Likewise, Liu et al. (2023) showcased the effectiveness of LLMs like GPT-4 in evaluating natural language generation, arguing that it more closely aligns with human judgment in summarization tasks than prior methods that relied on references. What the evidence briefly reviewed above suggests is that the emergence of LLMs is carving out new paths for summarization, moving beyond the conventional single-step generation process.

In this context, the present study aims to test ChatGPT's summarization abilities, with a particular focus on self-authored academic texts. Our second goal is to compare ChatGPT's performance to that of human reviewers. The overarching objective is to determine the extent to which ChatGPT can accurately and effectively condense scholarly articles while maintaining integrity and significance of the original content. While previous studies, such as Goodrich et al. (2019), utilized quantitative methods like ROUGE, which is a set of metrics in natural language processing used to evaluate the quality of machine-generated summaries or translations by comparing them to reference texts and focusing on word sequences and word pairs, I use qualitative evaluation of summaries produced by ChatGPT's performance and then compare it to human-generated summaries. Furthermore, a complementary goal is to identify areas where ChatGPT excels or, alternatively, requires further enhancement. The results of this study provide meaningful insights into the possibilities of using ChatGPT as a tool for academic summarization, thereby contributing to the broader scholarly discussion on the role of AI in academic research and writing.

4.2 Literature Review

In this section, I briefly review extant research on evaluation of the performance of AI models—and, particularly, that of ChatGPT—in summarizing academic texts. The aim of this review is to provide a comprehensive understanding of the current state of research through a presentation of key findings, methodologies, and gaps in the field.

Recent studies on the effectiveness of AI models in text summarization have specifically focused on those models' accuracy, coherence, and ability to capture the main ideas of academic texts. In one of the relevant studies in this area, Sorokina et al. (2024) conducted an extensive evaluation of various AI models, including ChatGPT, comparing their summarization outcomes against human-generated summaries. The authors found that, while AI models frequently produce coherent summaries, they sometimes miss nuanced details critical in academic contexts (Sorokina et al., 2024).

In another relevant study, Hayawi and Shahriar (2024) analyzed the performance of ChatGPT in summarizing research articles from different scientific domains. The results of this investigation indicated that, although ChatGPT performs well in generating concise summaries, it does have some limitations with regard to domain-specific terminology and complex sentence structures (Hayawi & Shahriar, 2024). The findings highlight the importance of training AI models on diverse datasets to improve their summarization abilities across academic texts from various disciplines.

In terms of methodologies applied in previous studies to evaluate ChatGPT's performance in summarizing research articles, the dominant approach has been qualitative research. A qualitative approach to evaluating AI-generated summaries involves evaluating their readability, coherence, and informativeness. For instance, Liao et al. (2023) compared medical texts authored by human experts to those produced by ChatGPT, by constructing datasets of both types of texts and analyzing them for linguistic differences in vocabulary, parts of speech, dependency, sentiment, and perplexity. The study implemented machine learning techniques, specifically a transformers-based model, achieving an F1 score over 95% in detecting texts generated by ChatGPT. Liao et al.'s (2023) study indicated that while ChatGPT texts are fluent and logical, they lack the specific, contextual information found in human-written texts.

Similarly, Johnson et al. (2023) conducted a qualitative analysis of ChatGPT's performance in summarizing medical research papers. The authors found that, although the summaries produced using ChatGPT were generally rather accurate, they sometimes missed critical information needed for a comprehensive understanding of the presented research findings. Based on this evidence, the authors argued for the need to continuously improve AI models so as to enhance their ability to accurately summarize complex academic texts (Johnson et al., 2023).

A distinct body of work in qualitative studies on ChatGPT's performance in summarizing academic research comprises comparative studies analyzing ChatGPT against other state-of-the-art summarization models. One pertinent study in this respect is Arshad et al.'s (2023) comparison of ChatGPT against BERT and GPT-3. The authors evaluated the corresponding performance of three approaches on a standardized dataset of academic articles. Interestingly, the results revealed that, while ChatGPT and GPT-3 outperformed BERT in generating coherent summaries, GPT-3 had a slight edge over ChatGPT in terms of accuracy and detail inclusion (Arshad et al., 2023).

An approach to improving ChatGPT's summarization of academic texts—called SummIt—was proposed by Zhang and co-authors (2023). SummIt allows ChatGPT to iteratively refine its summaries based on feedback, thereby enhancing the final output. The system also leverages knowledge and topic extractors to retain crucial details from the original texts. Zhang et al.'s (2023) results demonstrated that SummIt reduces common mistakes such as adding incorrect information and omitting important points. Based on this evidence, the authors concluded that iterative refinement in text summarization can greatly improve the quality of summaries for academic purposes (Zhang et al., 2023).

The aforementioned recent advances in methods of abstractive text summarization have been propelled by the use of pre-trained language models. However, a key concern with these methods is their vulnerability to producing summaries that may not always align with the facts of the original text. In a relevant study, Luo et al. (2023) explored ChatGPT's performance as a factual inconsistency evaluator for abstractive summarization. Their findings demonstrated that, when fine-tuned by reframing questions and prompted correctly, ChatGPT can outperform existing state-of-the-art models in identifying factual inconsistencies, which is a common issue in abstractive summarization models. This capability is essential for maintaining the integrity of academic summaries where accuracy is of a paramount importance (Luo et al., 2023).

From a different perspective—namely, the one concerned with ethical considerations in using ChatGPT in academic settings—Jarrah et al. (2023) emphasized the need for proper citation practices to uphold scholarly integrity and deter plagiarism. Concurrently, ChatGPT's performance in summarization tasks was also put to test in cross-lingual settings where ChatGPT was demonstrated to be capable of balancing detail with conciseness, which is particularly useful in terms of producing summaries in various languages (Wang et al., 2023).

In summary, previous studies seeking to evaluate the performance of ChatGPT in summarizing tasks used a combination of automated evaluation metrics and human evaluations. Using innovative methodologies such as iterative refinement, aspect-based summarization, and factual consistency checks, previous studies validated the efficacy of AI tools, including ChatGPT, in academic settings. These methodologies provide a solid foundation for further research and offer meaningful insights into potential areas for improvement in AI-driven text summarization.

In this context, the present study uses a qualitative research design to evaluate ChatGPT's performance in summarizing academic texts as compared to human-generated summaries. This approach allows for an in-depth assessment of the tool's capabilities and limitations based on a detailed analysis and interpretation. By leveraging both AI-generated and human-generated summaries, our aim is to highlight the strengths and limitations of ChatGPT in summarizing academic texts, thus providing valuable insights into its potential applications and areas needing improvement.

4.3 Methods

In this section, we present the methodology used in the present study, including the data collection process, evaluation criteria used to analyze ChatGPTand human-generated summaries, and the subsequent data analysis.

4.3.1 *Data Collection*

The dataset of research papers used in the present study contained exclusively the author's own publications. The reason underlying this decision was two-fold. First, using self-authored works ensured that the analysis was strengthened by an in-depth understanding of the content, allowing for a more accurate evaluation of the summaries. Second, using self-authored studies eliminated any concerns about potential copyright issues. The selected publications ($N = 12$) varied in length, and complexity to provide a comprehensive assessment of ChatGPT's summarization capabilities across different contexts. However, this selection is limited by the dataset, which lacked a variety of fields and styles.

To generate summaries for each selected academic text, ChatGPT was queried. In order to ensure standardization, the following prompt was consistently used to generate a summary of each publication included in the sample:

> *I have attached a research article. Please provide a concise summary covering the key aspects of the study. Include the following elements in the summary:*
> *1. Title and Authors: Mention the title of the article and the authors' names.*
> *2. Objective: Clearly state the primary objective or research question of the study.*
> *3. Methods: Summarize the research methods used, including the study design, sample size, and data collection techniques.*
> *4. Findings: Highlight the main findings or results of the study.*
> *5. Conclusion: Summarize the conclusions drawn by the authors and any implications or recommendations provided.*
> *6. Significance: Comment on the significance of the study in its field.*
> *Please ensure the summary is concise, accurate, and written in straightforward, professional English. Avoid adding any interpretations or opinions that are not present in the original article.*

In order to provide a baseline for comparison, summaries produced by a human expert (the present author) were created and used as a control. This step ensured that the evaluation of ChatGPT's performance was based on a comparison with high-quality human-generated output.

4.3.2 *Evaluation Criteria*

Once produced, the summaries generated by both ChatGPT and the human expert were evaluated using the following five criteria.

1. *Accuracy:* The degree to which the summary accurately reflected the main points and key details of the original text.
2. *Conciseness:* The extent to which the summary condensed the original text without losing essential information.
3. *Coherence:* The logical flow and clarity of the summary.
4. *Comprehensiveness:* The completeness of the summary covering all major aspects of the original study.
5. *Readability:* The ease with which the summary could be read and understood.

4.3.3 *Data Analysis*

For data analysis, a qualitative content analysis of the summaries was conducted during which the evaluations of ChatGPT-generated and human-generated summaries on the five evaluation criteria were compared. The goal was to identify patterns, strengths, and weaknesses in AI-generated summaries.

During the data analysis process, particular attention was paid to recurring issues in both groups of summaries, such as common errors, omissions, or particularly well-summarized aspects.

Finally, to ensure reliability of the findings, two external anonymous evaluators independently evaluated both groups of summaries using the aforementioned evaluation criteria. Upon this evaluation, inter-rater reliability of these evaluations was computed using Cohen's Kappa Coefficient (Vieira et al., 2010). Cohen's Kappa coefficient is a statistical measure that evaluates the agreement between two raters, thereby assessing the consistency of categorical classifications (McHugh, 2012; Vieira et al., 2010). In order to ensure reliability of the evaluations, two independent evaluators evaluated the summaries using the five predefined evaluation criteria (accuracy, conciseness, coherence, comprehensiveness, and readability). The raters were not informed which summaries were human-generated or ChatGPT-generated. The raters evaluated each of the 24 summaries of the 12 articles included in the sample (12 human-generated and

12 ChatGPT-generated) on the five criteria using a 5-point scale from 1 (lowest) to 5 (highest). Next, consistency of their evaluations was measured through calculating inter-rater reliability using Cohen's kappa coefficient.

4.4 Results

In this section, we report the results of data analysis, with a particular focus on strengths and weaknesses of ChatGPT's summarization capabilities. A summary of the findings derived from the qualitative analysis of ChatGPT's performance in summarizing 12 self-authored academic articles is shown in Table 4.1.

In the remainder of this section, I provide further detail on the evaluation of ChatGPT-generated summaries based on five aforementioned criteria, as well as present the findings concerning the overall performance, comparison with human-generated summaries, recurring issues in ChatGPT summarization performance, and inter-rater reliability.

4.4.1 Accuracy

ChatGPT summaries were generally accurate in capturing the main points of the original texts. However, some nuances and specific details were occasionally omitted or misrepresented. By contrast, human summaries maintained a higher level of precision, ensuring that all critical aspects and intricate details of the articles were accurately reflected.

Example 1: In Article 3, ChatGPT accurately summarized the main argument but omitted a significant factor presented in the latter part of the text, which was included in the human summary (see Table 4.2).

Example 2: In Article 3, ChatGPT provided a good general overview of the findings, but failed to mention important factors highlighted by the authors, which were effectively captured in the human summary.

4.4.2 Conciseness

ChatGPT excelled in producing concise summaries, effectively condensing lengthy articles (6000–7500 words) into shorter texts (around 300 words) without excessive information loss. The ChatGPT-generated summaries were generally shorter than those produced by the human summarizer (300 words vs. 450 words, respectively), which

Table 4.1 Comparison of ChatGPT-generated and human-generated summaries

Evaluation criteria	*ChatGPT summary*	*Human summary*	*Examples*
Accuracy	Generally accurate, but misses nuances	Highly accurate with detailed precision	Article 3: Missed detailed information in the study concept (ChatGPT); Omitted important findings (ChatGPT)
Conciseness	Very concise, sometimes excessively so	Concise, but includes necessary detail	Article 1: Lacked time-frame of the systematic review (ChatGPT); Article 11: Omitted nuanced points (ChatGPT)
Coherence	High coherence, but sometimes abrupt transitions	Highly coherent and having smooth transitions	Article 6: Abrupt transitions (ChatGPT)
Comprehensiveness	Covers major points, but misses secondary details	Comprehensive with full coverage of content	Article 6: Missed supporting evidence (ChatGPT); Article 8: Omitted anecdotes (ChatGPT)
Readability	High readability, clear and straightforward	Readable, but uses more complex language	Article 12: Included technical jargon (Human)

sometimes resulted in overly condensed content that skipped essential context.

Example 1: In Article 1, the human-generated summary provided a more balanced and detailed account, while ChatGPT's summary was brief and lacked some necessary details.

Example 2: In Article 1, ChatGPT's summary omitted some nuanced discussion points to keep the summary short, whereas the human summary included these details, making it slightly longer, but more informative (see Table 4.3).

Table 4.2 Examples of comparison of accuracy between ChatGPT and human summaries

Examples	*ChatGPT summary*	*Human summary*	*Explanation*
Article 3, Design	Design: Conceptualized gender differentiation as an outcome of socialization processes and rational choice factors.	Although the study focuses on the university stage, the undergraduate student is the product of an educational process that begins at school age; therefore, some factors related to the schooling stage are also discussed.	Despite being thoroughly discussed in the article, the schooling factors were neglected in ChatGPT's summary.
Article 3, Findings	Findings: Differences are shaped by socialization at home and school, rational choice motivations, and non-cognitive traits.	It finds that socialization mechanisms at home and schools, rational choice motivations, and other factors such as socially constructed, non-cognitive traits of females shape these differences.	ChatGPT's summary neglected other factors that were thoroughly discussed in the article

4.4.3 *Coherence*

Overall, ChatGPT summaries were characterized by high coherence, with logical flow and clear sentence structure. However, there were instances where transitions between ideas were abrupt or connections between key points were weak. By contrast, human summaries tended to be more coherent, with smoother transitions and better-integrated concepts.

Example: In Article 6, ChatGPT's summary was clear, but had abrupt transitions between sections, whereas the human summary exhibited a more seamless flow (see Table 4.4).

4.4.4 *Comprehensiveness*

ChatGPT's summaries were found to be less comprehensive compared to human summaries. Despite effectively covering major points, ChatGPT's summaries frequently missed secondary arguments, examples, or supporting evidence that were present in human-generated summaries that consistently provided a fuller picture of the articles' content.

Table 4.3 Examples of comparison of conciseness between ChatGPT and human summaries

Examples	*ChatGPT summary*	*Human summary*	*Explanation*
Article 1, Methods (Ashour, 2022)	**Data Collection Techniques:** Searches were conducted in databases such as Scopus and Taylor and Francis archives, using key terms related to refugees, higher education, and Germany. The selection process followed the PRISMA guidelines to ensure transparency and minimize biases.	This systematic review of studies published on this topic between 2015 and 2020, ……	The period in which the literature was reviewed and the reasons for selecting this period are important for understanding the context. However, this important information was omitted by ChatGPT.
Article 1, Findings (Ashour, 2022)	These challenges are exacerbated by conflicting demands between the asylum system and educational requirements.	Refugee students in Germany face major barriers to higher education, mainly due to language challenges and accreditation issues. Conflicting asylum and educational requirements, financial insecurity, bureaucratic complications, social isolation, psychological trauma, and the need to work while studying hinder their progress and delay integration and program completion.	The statement by ChatGPT is very concise but unclear, while the human summary is explanatory.

Example: In Article 6, unlike the human-generated summary, ChatGPT's one did not capture all important details that were crucial for understanding (see Table 4.5).

Table 4.4 Examples of comparison of coherence between ChatGPT and human summaries

Example	*ChatGPT summary*	*Human summary*	*Explanation*
Article 6, Findings (Ashour, 2020)	**Challenges Identified:** The UAE faces significant challenges in aligning higher education outcomes with labor market needs. There is a mismatch between the skills of graduates and the requirements of a rapidly changing economy. Additional barriers include demographic issues, cultural attitudes towards education, insufficient research funding, and a heavy reliance on expatriate labor. **Institutional and Cultural Issues:** The study highlights the lack of synchronization between educational policies and economic demands, overemphasis on non-STEM fields, and the underrepresentation of Emiratis in the private sector.	The article uncovered challenges facing the UAE's higher education system. **Primarily**, there is a significant mismatch between the skills of graduates and the requirements of a rapidly changing economy. **This issue is compounded by** demographic challenges, cultural attitudes towards education, insufficient research funding, and a heavy reliance on expatriate labor.	Lack of transition between ideas was noted in the ChatGPT summary.

Table 4.5 Comparison of comprehensiveness of ChatGPT-generated and human summaries

Example	*ChatGPT summary*	*Human summary*	*Explanation*
Article 6, Findings (Ashour, 2020)	**Challenges Identified:** The UAE faces significant challenges in aligning higher education outcomes with labor market needs. There is a mismatch between the skills of graduates and the requirements of a rapidly changing economy. Additional barriers include demographic issues, cultural attitudes towards education, insufficient research funding, and a heavy reliance on expatriate labor. **Institutional and Cultural Issues:** The study highlights the lack of synchronization between educational policies and economic demands, overemphasis on non-STEM fields, and the underrepresentation of Emiratis in the private sector.	There is a clear mismatch between the skills of graduates and the needs of the labor market, largely due to a misalignment between educational offerings and economic demands. The system prioritizes four-year degrees over vocational training, resulting in an oversupply of graduates in some fields and a shortage of technical skills in others. Additionally, the reliance on a student-fee-based model limits funding for research and innovation. Gender disparities persist, with low female participation in the workforce. Culturally, there is a strong emphasis on obtaining credentials rather than acquiring practical knowledge and skills, leading to graduates who are poorly prepared for the job market. Traditional and patriarchal values influence educational and career choices, often limiting opportunities for women and discouraging participation in STEM fields. Furthermore, students often enter higher education without the necessary skills due to insufficient preparation at primary and secondary levels.	The human summary is more comprehensive.

4.4.5 *Readability*

ChatGPT-generated summaries were characterized by high readability, with clear and straightforward language that made them easy to understand. Human summaries were also readable, but frequently included more complex academic language and terminology.

Example: In Article 12, ChatGPT's summary was clear and concise, whereas the human summary included more technical jargon, making it slightly less accessible to non-experts (see Table 4.6).

4.4.6 *Overall Performance of ChatGPT*

In summary, one of the important strengths of ChatGPT's summarization performance identified in the qualitative analysis is the tool's strong capability in producing concise and readable summaries. In addition, ChatGPT-generated summaries maintained a high level of coherence and clarity, which made them more accessible to the general public and easy to read.

However, we observed weaknesses of ChatGPT's summarization performance in the areas of comprehensiveness and accuracy, where ChatGPT occasionally missed important details and context that were nonetheless captured by human-generated summaries. Another shortcoming of ChatGPT-generated summaries was a somewhat lower coherence of transitions between ideas.

4.4.7 *Comparison of ChatGPT- vs. Human-Generated Summaries*

Via providing a more detailed and nuanced reflection of the original texts, with smoother transitions and a more integrated presentation of ideas, human-generated summaries consistently outperformed ChatGPT in terms of accuracy, comprehensiveness, and coherence. However, ChatGPT's ability to produce concise and highly readable summaries demonstrates its potential as a valuable tool for initial summarization, especially for lay audiences requiring quick and clear overviews.

Overall, the findings suggest that, while ChatGPT is effective for generating quick and readable summaries, its use should be complemented by human oversight to ensure accuracy and comprehensiveness. In academic contexts that typically require detailed understanding and precise representation of information, human-generated summaries

Table 4.6 Examples of comparison of readability between ChatGPT and human summaries

Example	*ChatGPT summary*	*Human summary*	*Explanation*
Article 12, Theoretical Frame (Ashour & Kleimann, 2024)	Methods: The study employs a neo-institutionalist approach to analyze the private HE systems in Germany and the UAE. It juxtaposes the two systems by examining secondary data from government reports, policy documents, academic publications, and statistical records. The study uses a comparative analytical framework to highlight the similarities and differences influenced by national policies and global trends.	The study utilizes the early neo-institutionalist approach by DiMaggio and Powell (1983), focusing on isomorphism, which describes the process by which institutions become similar due to various pressures. Three Forms of Isomorphism: Coercive Isomorphism: Results from formal and informal pressures exerted by external actors such as the state, which enforces standardization and regulation. Mimetic Isomorphism: Occurs under conditions of uncertainty where institutions imitate models perceived as successful, driven by the need for legitimacy. Normative Isomorphism: Arises from professionalization and the establishment of norms through educational and professional networks, influencing institutions to adopt certain practices.	Human summary used jargon in the theoretical frame and explained it very well.

remain superior. Further development of AI summarization tools should focus on improving the accuracy and comprehensiveness of the generated content, as well as enhancing the logical flow and integration of ideas in ChatGPT-generated summaries.

4.4.8 Recurring Issues in ChatGPT-Generated Summaries

Table 4.7 provides an overview of recurring issues and notable aspects observed in the ChatGPT-generated summaries as compared to human-generated ones.

4.4.9 Inter-Rater Reliability

Table 4.8 summarizes inter-rater reliability values for each evaluation criterion for both human-generated and ChatGPT-generated summaries.

First, with regard to accuracy, both human-generated and ChatGPT-generated summaries yielded substantial agreement among evaluators, with Cohen's kappa coefficients of 0.80 and 0.76, respectively. Furthermore, the second criterion, conciseness, yielded moderate agreement for both human-generated (0.68) and ChatGPT-generated (0.63) summaries, indicating some variability in how evaluators perceived the balance between brevity and completeness. Third, with regard to coherence, the two independent evaluators demonstrate a substantial agreement for human-generated (0.75) and ChatGPT-generated (0.70) summaries, suggesting that the evaluators generally agreed on the logical flow and clarity of both types of summaries. The fourth criterion, comprehensiveness, yielded moderate agreement for both human-generated (0.70) and ChatGPT-generated (0.65) summaries among the evaluators, reflecting differences in their judgments on the completeness of summaries. Finally, the fifth criterion, readability, yielded high agreement between the two evaluators of human-generated and ChatGPT-generated summaries, with the corresponding Cohen's kappa coefficients of 0.82 and 0.78, respectively, indicating a strong consensus on the ease of understanding.

Taken together, these results highlight that, while there was a substantial agreement among the two evaluators on most criteria, the conciseness was slightly higher for human-generated summaries across all evaluated aspects.

Table 4.7 Recurring issues and notable aspects: ChatGPT vs. human summaries

Category	*Issue/aspect*	*Description*	*Example*
Common errors	Omission of nuanced details	Frequently omitted nuanced details and subtle points	Excluding minor but important procedural details in methodological descriptions (Article 2).
	Inaccuracies and misinterpretations	Produced summaries with inaccuracies or misinterpretations.	Misinterpreting statistical results or specific findings (Article 5).
	Abrupt transitions	Abrupt transitions between ideas, disrupting logical flow	Shifting between major points without adequate contextual linking (Article 6)
	Redundancies	Included redundant information or repeated points	Reiterating the same argument or result in different sections (Article 2)
Omissions	Supporting evidence	Left out supporting evidence and examples	Excluding anecdotal evidence used to illustrate key points (Article 9)
	Critical counterarguments	Missed critical counterarguments or limitations	Omitting sections discussing potential limitations or alternative interpretations (article 3)
Well-Summarized	Main arguments and conclusions	Accurately captured main arguments and conclusions	Effectively summarizing the central thesis and key findings
Aspects	Clarity and readability	Produced clear and easy-to-read summaries	Using straightforward language and clear sentence structures
	Conciseness	Excelled in generating concise summaries without extraneous information	Condensing lengthy discussions into brief, coherent summaries

Table 4.8 Inter-rater reliability for evaluation criteria

Evaluation criterion	*Human (Cohen's Kappa)*	*ChatGPT (Cohen's Kappa)*
Accuracy	0.80	0.76
Conciseness	0.68	0.63
Coherence	0.75	0.70
Comprehensiveness	0.70	0.65
Readability	0.82	0.78

4.5 Discussion

Our findings reported in the previous sections offer several important implications. First, with regard to strengths and utility of ChatGPT in summarizing academic texts, the high inter-rater agreement on readability and the moderate to high agreement on conciseness suggest that ChatGPT is effective in generating clear, concise summaries. The same conclusion was made in our analysis of the data. Based on this evidence, it can be concluded that ChatGPT is a valuable tool for quickly grasping the main points of lengthy academic texts, which is particularly useful in academic and professional contexts where time efficiency is crucial.

Second, our results emphasize the need for human oversight. Specifically, considering the substantial agreement between the two independent evaluators on accuracy, but moderate agreement on comprehensiveness, while ChatGPT can accurately capture the main ideas, it frequently misses critical details. This suggests that human oversight is essential to ensure the completeness and depth of the ChatGPT-based summaries, particularly for complex academic texts where nuances and detailed understanding are vital.

Third, variability in conciseness and comprehensiveness ratings suggests that ChatGPT may benefit from additional training on diverse and domain-specific datasets. More specifically, fine-tuning the model to handle specialized terminology and complex sentence structures could improve its performance in summarizing texts from various academic disciplines.

Fourth, the findings also suggest that iterative refinement processes, where AI-generated summaries are continuously updated based on feedback, could significantly enhance the accuracy and comprehensiveness of the outputs. Future research could explore the effectiveness of such methodologies in improving AI summarization capabilities.

Finally, further comparative studies that would involve a larger and more diverse sample of academic texts could provide deeper insights into the strengths and limitations of AI models like ChatGPT.

4.6 Conclusion

Taking together, the results of the present study demonstrate the promising performance of ChatGPT in producing readable and concise summaries, suggesting that ChatGPT has a strong potential as a supplementary tool in educational and research settings. As a complementary tool (albeit not as a complete substitute of human analysis), ChatGPT can aid students and researchers to quickly understand vast amounts of literature.

However, while ChatGPT demonstrates significant potential as a powerful summarization tool, its limitations in capturing detailed and nuanced information necessitate ongoing improvements and human oversight. Accordingly, the integration of AI in academic summarization should be approached with careful consideration of its strengths and limitations, ensuring that the use of the tool enhances, rather than detracts from the scholarly communication process.

More specifically, while the results of our qualitative analysis indicate that ChatGPT is a promising tool for summarizing academic texts, particularly in terms of conciseness and readability, it currently falls short in capturing the full depth and detail provided by human summaries. Accordingly, continued improvements in AI summarization technology could enhance its utility in academic and other professional contexts. On the condition that ChatGPT's capabilities are harnessed with an emphasis on accuracy, ethical use, and human oversight, its use can revolutionize academic research. However, for a successful integration of ChatGPT into academic workflows, ongoing research and development ensuring that the tool complements rather than supplants the human intellectual effort are essential.

Among other venues of improvement, future work should focus on fine-tuning AI models to better handle the complexities of academic texts, incorporating domain-specific knowledge, and developing robust evaluation metrics. Another area that needs close attention is addressing the ethical considerations associated with AI-generated content, such as ensuring proper citation and preventing misinformation.

A key insight that can be derived from the results of the present study is that ChatGPT's effectiveness is maximized when used in conjunction with human expertise. Human oversight is essential to address inaccuracies and enhance the quality of the summaries. Likewise, implementing iterative refinement processes, where AI-generated summaries would be continuously updated based on feedback, would also significantly enhance the accuracy and comprehensiveness of the AI-generated outputs.

References

Arshad, S., Yaqoob, M., & Mehmood, T. (2023). The performance of GPT-3.5 in summarizing scientific and news articles. In *The international conference on data science and emerging technologies* (pp. 49–61). Springer Nature Singapore.

Ashour, S., & Kleimann, B. (2024). Private higher education: A comparative study of Germany and the United Arab Emirates. *Research Papers in Education*, 1–17.

Ashour, S. (2020). Quality higher education is the foundation of a knowledge society: Where does the UAE stand? *Quality in Higher Education, 26*(2), 209–223.

Ashour, S. (2022). Access for Syrian refugees into higher education in Germany: A systematic literature review. *European Journal of Higher Education, 12*(1), 98–116.

Bail, C. A. (2024). Can generative AI improve social science? *Proceedings of the National Academy of Sciences, 121*(21), e2314021121.

Cheng, J., & Lapata, M. (2016). Neural summarization by extracting sentences and words. *Proceedings of the 54th annual meeting of the association for computational linguistics, 1*, 484–494.

Goodfellow, I., Pouget-Abadie, J., Mirza, M., Xu, B., Warde-Farley, D., Ozair, S., Courville, A., & Bengio, Y. (2020). Generative adversarial networks. *Communications of the ACM*, *63*(11), 139–144.

Goodrich, B., Rao, V., Liu, P. J., & Saleh, M. (2019). Assessing the factual accuracy of generated text. In *Proceedings of the 25th ACM SIGKDD international conference on knowledge discovery & data mining* (pp. 166–175).

Goyal, T., Li, J. J., & Durrett, G. (2022). *News summarization and evaluation in the era of GPT-3. arXiv preprint* arXiv:2209.12356

Grossmann, I., Feinberg, M., Parker, D. C., Christakis, N. A., Tetlock, P. E., & Cunningham, W. A. (2023). AI and the transformation of social science research. *Science, 380*(6650), 1108–1109.

Hake, J., Crowley, M., Coy, A., Shanks, D., Eoff, A., Kirmer-Voss, K., Dhanda, G., & Parente, D. J. (2024). Quality, accuracy, and bias in ChatGPT-based summarization of medical abstracts. *The Annals of Family Medicine, 22*(2), 113–120.

Hayawi, K., & Shahriar, S. (2024). A cross-domain performance report of OpenAI ChatGPT o1 model. [Preprint]. https://doi.org/10.20944/preprints202412.1930.v1

Jarrah, A. M., Wardat, Y., & Fidalgo, P. (2023). Using ChatGPT in academic writing is (not) a form of plagiarism: What does the literature say. *Online Journal of Communication and Media Technologies, 13*(4), Article e202346.

Jin, H., Zhang, Y., Meng, D., Wang, J., & Tan, J. (2024). *A comprehensive survey on process-oriented automatic text summarization with exploration of llm-based methods. arXiv preprint* arXiv:2403.02901

Johnson, D., Goodman, R., Patrinely, J., Stone, C., Zimmerman, E., Donald, R., Chang, S., et al. (2023). *Assessing the accuracy and reliability of AI-generated medical responses: an evaluation of the Chat-GPT model.* Research square.

Khlaif, Z. N., Mousa, A., Hattab, M. K., Itmazi, J., Hassan, A. A., Sanmugam, M., & Ayyoub, A. (2023). The potential and concerns of using AI in scientific research: ChatGPT performance evaluation. *JMIR Medical Education, 9*, e47049.

Kryscinski, W., McCann, B., Xiong, C., & Socher, R. (2020). Evaluating the factual consistency of abstractive text summarization. *Proceedings of the 2020 Conference on Empirical Methods in Natural Language Processing* (pp. 456–470).

Lewis, M., Liu, Y., Goyal, N., Ghazvininejad, M., Mohamed, A., Levy, O., Stoyanov, V., & Zettlemoyer, L. (2019). *BART: Denoising sequence-to-sequence pre-training for natural language generation, translation, and comprehension.* arXiv:1910.13461

Lin, Z. (2023). Why and how to embrace AI such as ChatGPT in your academic life. *Royal Society Open Science, 10*(8), Article 230658.

Liao, W., Liu, Z., Dai, H., Xu, S., Wu, Z., Zhang, Y., Huang, X., et al. (2023). Differentiating ChatGPT-generated and human-written medical texts: quantitative study. *JMIR Medical Education, 9*(1), e48904.

Lingard, L. (2023). Writing with ChatGPT: An illustration of its capacity, limitations & implications for academic writers. *Perspectives on medical education, 12*(1), 261.

Liu, Y., & Lapata, M. (2019). *Text summarization with pretrained encoders. arXiv preprint* arXiv:1908.08345

Luo, Z., Xie, Q., & Ananiadou, S. (2023). *Chatgpt as a factual inconsistency evaluator for abstractive text summarization. arXiv preprint* arXiv:2303.15621

McHugh, M. L. (2012). Interrater reliability: The kappa statistic. *Biochemia medica, 22*(3), 276–282.

Mitchell, M., & Krakauer, D. C. (2023). The debate over understanding in AI's large language models. *Proceedings of the National Academy of Sciences, 120*(13), Article e2215907120.

Nallapati, R., Zhou, B., Gulcehre, C., & Xiang, B. (2016). *Abstractive text summarization using sequence-to-sequence rnns and beyond. arXiv preprint* arXiv:1602.06023

Solaiman, I. (2023). The gradient of generative AI release: Methods and considerations. In *Proceedings of the 2023 ACM conference on fairness, accountability, and transparency* (pp. 111–122).

Sorokina, S. (2024). Exploring automated summarization: From extraction to abstraction. Vestnik Volgogradskogo Gosudarstvennogo Universiteta. Seriâ 2. *Âzykoznanie*, (5), Article 4. https://doi.org/10.15688/jvolsu2.2024.5.4

Tang, L., Shalyminov, I., Wong, A. W.-m., Burnsky, J., Vincent, J. W., Yang, Y., Singh, S., et al. (2024). *TofuEval: Evaluating hallucinations of LLMs on topic-focused dialogue summarization. arXiv preprint* arXiv:2402.13249

Vieira, S. M., Kaymak, U., & Sousa, J. M. C. (2010). Cohen's kappa coefficient as a performance measure for feature selection. In *International conference on fuzzy systems* (pp. 1–8). IEEE.

Wang, J., Liang, Y., Meng, F., Zou, B., Li, Z., Qu, J., & Zhou, J. (2023). Zero-shot cross-lingual summarization via large language models. *arXiv preprint*arXiv:2302.14229.

Zhang, H., Liu, X., & Zhang, J. (2023). *Summit: Iterative text summarization via chatgpt. arXiv preprint* arXiv:2305.14835

CHAPTER 5

Reshaping Employment Policies in Qatar: Potential Implications of Artificial Intelligence

Ahmed Badran and Sara Badran

5.1 Introduction

Technological progress can be considered a double-edged sword. On the one hand, many advantages can be gained from using new technologies to improve people's quality of life in various fields. On the other hand, recent technological developments, especially in the field of computing and robotics, have raised a fundamental question about the possibility of newly developed AI applications acting independently of human control and thus making their own decisions that may harm humanity. In this context, many scientists and technology experts have expressed concerns about the

A. Badran (✉)
Department of International Affairs, College of Arts & Sciences,
Qatar University, Doha, Qatar
e-mail: a.badran@qu.edu.qa

S. Badran
Digital Humanities, Faculty of English, Hughes Hall College,
University of Cambridge, Cambridge, UK
e-mail: samab2@cam.ac.uk

A. Badran and A. Mishrif (eds.), *Shaping the Future of Development in the GCC*, The Political Economy of the Middle East,
https://doi.org/10.1007/978-981-96-7963-8_5

potential threats posed by innovations in the field of AI in the absence of government oversight and regulations. From an economic standpoint, many economists share the fear that applications of AI, coupled with advances in computing and robotics, may lead to economic disruption and high unemployment rates, especially among low-skilled workers. Hence, AI applications are expected to lead to job losses in all fields including among blue and white collar as well as professional services. At the same time, many activists and intellectuals oppose the idea of developing autonomous weapons and killing machines that operate autonomously, free from human intervention, and may select and destroy their targets, leading to huge security risks.

The presence of AI in many aspects of life in modern societies means that individuals and governments will struggle between its legal and ethical implications for some time. Hence, the rapid increase in AI applications raises fundamental questions about the potential impact of intelligent applications on the daily lives of humans. As time passes, AI technologies gain a foothold in new industries and become more immersed in our daily lives, and this trend appears to continue for the foreseeable future. In this context, one has the right to wonder whether AI applications will lead to a better life and more efficient use of available resources, or will they negatively affect human activities?

At a time when the applications of AI are accelerating in various fields, questions and concerns are increasing about the repercussions of these applications on human lives. One of the most important areas receiving increasing attention from researchers and practitioners is related to the implications of integrating AI applications on employment policies, workforce dynamics, jobs structures and skills. Labour markets in the GCC region are expected to witness major changes in all aspects in order to seize the opportunities of AI and to face the unprecedented challenges posed by such new smart technologies. From this perspective, this paper attempts to answer a main research question: Can the labour market in the State of Qatar keep pace with the changes and face the challenges imposed by the application of AI technologies?

5.2 Literature Review

5.2.1 Artificial Intelligence Defined

The concept of AI and discussions about its pros and cons go back at least a few decades (Badran, 2021, 2023). The term AI was first coined by John McCarthy in 1955, and the field of AI began as a scientific field in 1956 (Calo, 2017). Additionally, the potential impact of robots on employment has been a concern in the United States since 1980, when the New York Times published an article titled 'A Robot Is after Your Job.'(Shaiken, 1980). Some may go further with regard to the debate surrounding AI to point to the debate about the impact of computers and new technological technologies in general on society as initial precursors to the emergence of this term. Regardless of the age of the debate around AI and the ways in which its applications influence societies, AI is becoming a reality and the debate around its impacts is attracting more attention from stakeholders in AI decision-making and policy circles. Perhaps one of the main reasons for this interest is that computing power and access to data have increased significantly over the years, which has resulted in more opportunities for machine self-learning (Erdelyi & Goldsmith, 2018). In addition, policymakers are now paying more attention to the issue of AI in response to calls from those involved in this field to develop the necessary regulatory frameworks and rules to govern its activities and applications. In fact, AI is a thought-provoking field where science fiction and reality are often mixed up. Despite the varying views on this topic, we can see different forms of AI applications in various aspects of our daily lives, from autonomous flight systems in passenger aircraft to virtual services and medical and nursing assistance. Hence, the applications of AI have expanded to include many fields, and humans have become more dependent than ever on robots and other smart applications in manufacturing, health care, and even in finding answers to their questions through electronic search engines.

Although AI innovations and applications are accelerating, the concept itself still lacks a clear definition. In other words, the term AI provides a broad umbrella that covers several concepts (Stone, 2016). The term AI can be viewed in general as 'a group of modern technologies that aim to approach some aspects of human cognition' in the way smart applications work and behave (Calo, 2017). In this sense, the cognitive element and the ability to learn in the way these applications are made through AI is what makes new technologies in this field different from all other types of technologies. AI can also be defined as 'technology that has the ability to apply the concept of intelligence to any task it undertakes, rather than following a set of pre-defined tasks.' (Etzioni, 2018; Russell & Norvig, 1994). The essence of AI from this perspective lies in making applications more intelligent in the sense that they can act responsibly and in an appropriate manner, without harming the human societies in which they operate. From this standpoint, AI can be conceptualized as an attempt to emulate human intelligence in the way applications work, so that these intelligent applications perform some tasks that require intelligence in its human sense.

AI is defined from a narrower perspective as 'the computerized analysis of large databases for the purpose of modelling reality.' In this sense, it includes tangible technological developments that are reflected in the components of smart programs and applications. Through these technological developments, computers can, through advanced software based on algorithms, process large amounts of data at tremendous speed, which enables AI applications to make decisions, reach conclusions, and most importantly, learn from experiences. In this context, the concept of learning, and in particular 'machine learning,' becomes one of the basic pillars of the concept of AI (Faggella, 2019). Using this type of learning, many AI applications, including Apple's Siri, Microsoft's Cortana, and Amazon's Alexa, are designed to learn from users' behaviour in order to serve them better. Compared to older AI concepts such as 'symbolic systems,' which viewed machine intelligence in terms of its ability to organize abstract symbols using logical rules, today's AI applications rely on 'a set of techniques known as machine learning.' (DATAx, 2019). The learning feature in the work of smart applications makes them behave in a manner similar to the way humans think and act (Burrell, 2016). This is done by providing machines with data and information in the form of observations and interactions in the real world. Such information increases machines' ability to learn on their own and improves the performance of their functions and their ability to make decisions.

In light of the above, and in the context of this study, AI will be viewed as a field that focuses on 'the development of a range of applications based on computational technologies inspired by the methods that humans use to learn and make decisions.' Comparing this definition with the definitions mentioned above, it is clear that it expands to accommodate different types of AI innovations. In addition, this definition emphasizes the practical and scientific nature that governs the development of the field of AI and helps demarcate its boundaries as an interdisciplinary field that benefits from, and builds on, cognitive, theoretical, and applied developments in diverse disciplines.

5.2.2 *Artificial Intelligence, Employment Policies and Labour Markets*

There is no one universal definition for Artificial Intelligence (AI), and thus, no universal understanding of how AI will impact the labour market, particularly because this technology is rapidly and continuously evolving and developing. The following focal points are indicative, although not exhaustive, of some the ways the labour market will be impacted by AI: Automation and job displacement, augmentation and new opportunities, transformation of work, and ethical and social considerations which will be explored throughout this literature review, and with particular focus on Qatar's labour market.

5.2.2.1 Automation and Job Displacement

Automation can be understood as 'a device or system that accomplishes (partially or fully) a function that was previously, or conceivably could be carried out (partially or fully) by a human operator' (Parasuraman et al., 2000). Understandings of what falls under the bracket of 'automation' have also developed as automation has expanded 'beyond its roots in manufacturing' to include applications in healthcare, security, transportation, agriculture, construction, energy, and many other areas (Goldberg, 2012). Similarly, Boy notes that automation has developed 'cognitive functions' that have been transferred from people to machines (2017). Thusly, AI can be understood as 'the latest tool in a toolkit of 'automation' technologies that perform tasks previously performed by humans, often more cheaply, faster, and better' (Tyson & Zysman, 2022). Although economic output benefits greatly from automation through efficiency and cost cuts, a rising concern is the risk of job displacement due to AI's capabilities. Firstly, it is important to establish what is meant by 'job displacement,' what jobs will be affected and whether this necessarily means a decline in available jobs, or simply a need for upskilling and retraining to work alongside the rapidly developing technology. Tyson and Zysam note that although AI applications remain narrow and task specific, recent breakthroughs are achieving human-comparable results through Machine Learning (ML). The topic of job displacement has been greatly contested over the last few years. Papers such Frey and Osborne's conclude that 'a substantial share of employment, across a wide range of occupations, are at risk in the near future' referring to the next 10 to 20 years (qtd in Bessen, 2018). Melyaptaki also note that primarily employees performing 'operator work' which can easily be automated are at higher risk of job loss (2019), whereas other labour markets, such as technology and particularly online labour markets (OLMs) have 'substantially grown in economic size and political relevance' (Brown et al., 2022). This expansion has led to a 'significantly higher demand for AI-related labour' to match the 65% market increase over the last four years (Brown et al., 2022). These statistics suggest a shift in labour demand, with the automation of some jobs, and the increased demand of others. Similarly, based on the World Economic Forum's (WEF) Future of Jobs report, 75% of surveyed companies are likely to incorporate AI in their workplaces, with 50% anticipating the creation of new jobs, and only 25% foreseeing potential job loss (Garcia, 2023). For this gap in the market to be bridged, Garcia indicates employers must undertake extensive reskilling and upskilling programs (2023) in order to adapt to the changing labour market. This chapter adopts the perspective that although job displacement is a risk, particularly for operational work, AI will also create and provide an array of new opportunities and jobs, some of which employ AI as a tool to enhance their work and make existing roles more efficient. This will result in a shift in employment practices and expectations, and require an adjustment period of 'upskilling,' but the labour market will not replace all human jobs with AI.

5.2.2.2 Augmentation and New Opportunities

Garcia notes that the impact of AI in the Middle East will be substantial with the region projected to generate $320 billion in economic value from AI by 2030. Although risk of job displacement in some sectors is likely, as discussed in Sect. 1.1, a range of promising new opportunities will also be apparent across AI sectors. New AI contributions are expected to increase Qatar's GDP to 8.2% by 2030 (Hamad Bin Khalifa University) which has many implications on the labour market across a range of different industries. Similarly, Helou notes that AI technology increases productivity and efficiency, freeing employees for strategic work, while posing opportunity for AI to assist in decision-making processes due to its ability and efficiency in analysing complex data. Helou also notes that AI engineers, data scientists and AI trainers in particular are all in high demand (2023). Although this potential of AI may sound daunting, the WEF predicts by 2022 AI and Machine Learning (ML) will create 133 million new jobs while displacing 75 million jobs (Tiwari,

2023). Tiwari also notes that the potential impact on employment opportunities also depends on the speed of technological advancement and the ability of workers to adapt to these changes (2022), indicating the necessity for upskilling to work parallel to technological advances in order to leverage the benefits of AI while minimizing job displacement due to inability to work with this technology. Autor states that although routine jobs are easily automated, and therefore their availability has decreased over time, non-routine tasks such as problem-solving and decision-making have increased (2015). This does not necessarily mean that non-routine industries are not impacted by developments within AI. Lane and Saint-Martin note that roles such as radiologists, lab technicians, engineers, and lawyers have increasingly been utilizing AI (2021). Furthermore, exposure to AI does not necessarily lead to job loss as 'humans outperform AI in creative and social intelligence, reasoning skills and dealing with uncertainty' (Lane & Saint-Martin, 2021) indicating that AI has the potential to create new opportunities within working industries, without automatically leading to job displacement, as Fig. 5.1 demonstrates. Additionally, as there is significant uncertainty regarding the impact of AI, and the risk of misuse, unemployment and dangers towards vulnerable individuals, opportunities within the regulation and monitoring of this software are increasingly becoming imperative. This process will not only be conducted on a national scale with the prediction of the introduction of standardized policies in the 'race to AI regulation' (Smuha, 2021), but also on a smaller scale, with each company

	(Webb, 2020[23])	(Felten, Raj and Seamans, 2019[24])	(Brynjolfsson, Mitchell and Rock, 2018[25])
Most exposed	- High-skilled occupations, including clinical lab technicians, optometrists and chemical engineers. - Production jobs involving inspection and quality control, which Webb describes as representing a small proportion of the low-skilled workforce	- White-collar occupations, such as chemical/civil/nuclear engineers, epidemiologists, actuaries, statisticians, credit analysts, accountants, computer programmers, operations research analysts.	- Concierges, mechanical drafters, credit authorisers, brokerage clerks, and morticians, undertakers, and funeral directors.
Least exposed	- High-skilled occupations requiring reasoning about novel situations (e.g. researchers). - Occupations requiring interpersonal skill (e.g. teachers and managers), including manual work such as baristas, food preparation workers or massage therapists.	- Physical occupations, including maids and cleaners, cafeteria attendants, dishwashers, hotel porters, slaughterers and meat packers, roofers and painters, massage therapists, fitness instructors.	- Massage therapists, animal scientists, archaeologists, public address system and other announcers, and plasterers and stucco masons.

Fig. 5.1 Occupations most and least exposed to AI

needing roles that adapt and adhere to these changes. As noted by Poba-Nzaou, due to the scale and speed of evolving technology, new roles in Human Resources (HR) may be needed, which will play a key role in the deployment of AI across various industries (2017).

The provided data evidence although concern surrounding job displacement is clear, many industries will benefit from AI exposure, as well as a range of new jobs and new opportunities arising to coexist with the rapidly changing technology. However, it is also clear that although new jobs will be available, there is a process of upskilling and transformation within working industries that will be inevitable, and completely necessary, in order to truly utilize and widely integrate AI technologies.

5.2.2.3 Transformation of Work (The 'Gig Economy' and Remote Work)

Sections 1.1 and 1.2 infer that there will be a somewhat considerable change within a considerable number of industries which are both directly, and indirectly, impacted by AI developments. Whether this change is positive, or negative is still widely disputed, and perhaps will not be proven until the impacts of AI become more apparent, but nonetheless, there is a universal acknowledgement of a transformation of work, and that there will be a transitional period to meet these changes. McKinsey Global Institute estimates that by 2030, 375 million workers (14% of the global workforce) may need to transition to new occupational categories as AI and machine learning automate many existing jobs (qtd in Talk, 2023). They also estimate that AI and machine learning have the potential to create 2.3 million new jobs by 2025. Brown et al. note that digital platforms, powered by the labour of millions of workers in addition to their digital interface creates what is considered a 'gig' or 'on-demand' economy providing workers with the flexibility traditionally associated with self-employment, but with far less managerial oversight due to the digital communication AI provides. Lobel however notes that 'modern employment law is based on the assumption of two worlds of work: you are either an employee or you are not, and if not, you have none of the protections afforded to employees' (2016). This acknowledgment of the gap in employment law indicates the transformation of labour markets that AI is creating but also signifies the need for the regulatory systems that protect labourers to evolve.

Besides from impacts on the physical industries, and 'gig economy' as discussed, another labour market that is significantly impacted, if not entirely created by, and wholly dependent on AI, is remote working.

Felstead notes that COVID-19 particularly spiked questions regarding where we work and how through the necessary shift towards 'remote working' to maintain workflow during periods of compulsory physical separation, lockdowns, and travel bans (2022). Many large companies such as Google, Twitter, Apple, Microsoft, and JP Morgan closed their offices so staff could work from home. This meant that digital and developing AI software was heavily relied upon to connect meetings, provide lines of communication and to allow the continuation of businesses to run. COVID-19 has significantly impacted societal structures globally, and the labour markets are still navigating how to best benefit from the technological adoption millions had to familiarize themselves with during a period of such rapid and unexpected working conditions. Notions of worker well-being cannot be divorced from, or considered in isolation from, technological developments impacting labour markets globally. There are many mixed opinions about the effectivity of remote working both on employers and employees, offering benefits to employees of increased working flexibility and comfortability and to employers through cost cuts of not renting office space which 'will save employers billions' (Thomas, 2021). Equally, there have been concerns about employee productivity and the difficulty of keeping home and work life separate, meaning jobs 'take over your life' (Harris, 2021). This significant change will only become more apparent with advancing technology making remote working more likely, efficient, and providing the resources to create high-quality work while minimising costs and time. Thusly, Cutter notes that more companies now envision a 'hybrid future' (2020) as AI is proving increasingly beneficial and efficient, for both employee and employer. The synergy of the mentioned focus areas allows for the benefits of AI to emerge, yet indicate a need for protection, for users within companies which adopt AI, and for those within the 'gig economy' to ensure this software is being used ethically, and vulnerable individuals are protected. Subsequently, questions surrounding ethical practice, data protection, accessibility, and income inequality are generated.

5.2.2.4 Ethical and Social Considerations

As history has proven, new developments within technology often prompt a variety of social and ethical considerations regarding its use, and potential misuse. AI has triggered similar questions suggesting the need for regulation, and for the divide within wealth inequality across nations to be considered. Firstly, it is important to acknowledge that the labour market globally will be impacted in different ways dependent on AI exposure, the extent of AI integration, and the financial accessibility to invest in, and utilize this technology. Banga and Velde note that in the short term, emerging markets and low-income countries may encounter fewer disruptions caused by AI in comparison to higher-income nations which will further the wealth inequality within nations 'widening the gap' through the 'polarization within income brackets' between high- and low-income nations even further (2020). Similarly, Dwivedi et al. note that one of the main shortcomings of the existing literature is that it primarily focuses on the impact of AI and machine learning on developed countries, which does not consider the implications on developing countries (2021). The impact of AI on the labour market in developed countries is already contested, as evidenced throughout this literature review, but the impact on underdeveloped countries is even more uncertain. This gap in research emphasizes the lack of geographic transferability when discussing this matter.

Furthermore, although AI has promise in increasing efficiency and productivity within a range of industries, the gains generated within organizations are disproportionate. Many scholars such as Manyikia et al. (2017) and Nedelkoska and Quintini (2018) acknowledge that AI exposure is not equally beneficial to all industries with highly skilled workers tending to benefit from the assistance of AI, whereas lower skilled workers can be supressed, or even replaced by AI, also furthering the income inequality and accentuating the inequalities in the redistribution of wealth (Makridakis, 2017) both nationally and internationally. Maniyka et al. provide a key example of this with the rate of potential automation for an industry welder at 90%, whereas it is only 30% for customer service representatives and only 25% for chief executive officers (2017). Although there are no guarantees which jobs will be replaced, there is a clear correlation between skilled workers benefiting from AI, and unskilled workers at a significantly greater risk of job displacement. This pattern further reinforces the existing disparity between accessibility to education, also intersecting with economic opportunity and class divides, which AI may only heighten. Although it is unlikely that there will be a universal strategy that nations adopt in working to bridge this gap, and to upskill employees to meet these rapid changes, Garcia suggests it is a governmental responsibility to 'create a better environment for AI implementations by developing supportive policies and regulations' (2023). The creation of this 'environment' involves education, and training incentives as well as sharing resources, expertise, and best practices (Garcia, 2023). The synergy of these elements will assist in bridging the skill gap for existing employees, as well as ensuring upcoming generations are better-trained and more familiar with how to utilize AI upon entry to the labour market. Similarly, Berg suggests a need for regulators to intervene and enforce adapted forms of labour conditions and social legislation (2016) to protect workers, as well as ensure AI technologies are not being misused and vulnerable individuals, such as children, are gradually introduced to AI in an educational manner to better equip them for the changing labour market so AI can be used ethically, and its potential benefits can be maximized. Other prominent user concerns focus on issues surrounding privacy, data security and potential biases in AI technologies which heavily impact user perception on how AI will affect labour markets, as well as influencing user willingness to incorporate AI into their workplaces. Scholars such as Golda et al. note that several approaches are being employed to address concerns surrounding privacy and security such as Privacy-Preserving Techniques (PPTs), Adversarial Defence Mechanisms, and Regulatory Measures and Policies (2024). These are necessary first steps in reassuring and protecting those which are willingly, or willingly, making the shift towards an AI-assisted workplace. The necessity of regulatory measures, and how they will impact each labour market will naturally fluctuate dependent on the workplace; however, it is clear some introductory efforts can be seen to address some of the prominent social and ethical considerations AI raises.

This literature review has exemplified a wide range of possibilities that AI can offer to existing and upcoming labour markets. Although most of the studies examined have been predication-based, there is a clear divide regarding whether the overall impact of AI will be positive or negative. There is a strong potential for AI to increase productivity and cut costs, making work more efficient for a variety of industries globally. However, there is also concern particularly regarding job displacement and the disproportionately negative effect on low-skilled work, and the potential economic inequality gap globally that AI can further heighten. On the other hand, AI has also acted as a bridge in times of global crises, such as COVID-19, where digital technologies were able to maintain workflow where it would have otherwise been extremely difficult, if not impossible. There is a consensus among most literature that infers AI will continue to develop over time, and therefore adapting to these changes and bridging the skill gap is one of the first steps towards the beneficial incorporation of AI among labour markets. However, there is also a clear uncertainty and anxiety regarding the misuse of this technology, suggesting the need for intervention and regulation, whether that be governmental or by other regulatory bodies. AI shows great positive potential and promise, but the need for regulation and navigation in the ways this technology can be utilized both nationally, and internationally, is increasingly becoming apparent.

5.3 Artificial Intelligence and Potential Impacts on the Labour Market in Qatar

The literature review has exemplified a wide range of possibilities that AI can offer to existing and upcoming labour markets. Although most of the studies examined have been predication-based, there is a clear divide regarding whether the overall impact of AI will be positive or negative. There is a strong potential for AI to increase productivity and cut costs, making work more efficient for a variety of industries globally. However, there is also concern particularly regarding job displacement and the disproportionately negative effect on low-skilled work, and the potential economic inequality gap that AI can further heighten worldwide. On the other hand, AI has also acted as a bridge in times of global crises, such as COVID-19 where digital technologies were able to maintain workflow where it would have otherwise been extremely difficult, if not impossible (El-Haddadeh et al., 2023). There is a consensus among most literature that infers AI will continue to develop over time, and therefore adapting to these changes and bridging the skill gap is one of the first steps towards the beneficial incorporation of AI among labour markets. However, there is also a clear uncertainty and anxiety regarding the misuse of this technology, suggesting the need for intervention and regulation, whether that be governmental or by other regulatory bodies. AI shows great positive potential and promise, but the need for regulation and navigation in the ways this technology can be utilized both nationally, and internationally, is increasingly becoming apparent (Badran, 2023).

5.3.1 The Qatari Labour Market: Policy and Regulatory Frameworks

One of the most important distinguishing features of the labour market in Qatar is its heavy reliance on expatriate workers from abroad. Over the past decades, Qatar has attracted a large number of expatriates to work there as a result of the expansion of the state's development plans. The discovery of large quantities of natural gas in Qatar increased the demand for skilled and unskilled labour to reach the state's development goals. This increase in demand for labour has not been matched by a corresponding increase in supply on the part of the national labour force. The Qatari government sought to fill the gap in labour demand by importing foreign labour from various parts of the world. With the presence of this huge number of expatriates, which in total exceeds the number of nationals by a ratio of 7 to 1, it has become necessary to develop appropriate policies and an effective regulatory framework to control the processes of recruiting and employing this large number of workers (Mohamed, 2021).

To regulate the conditions of expatriate workers, the State of Qatar has made many amendments to the legislation and rules regulating the conditions of workers. In this regard, the State of Qatar was ahead of other countries in the region (Davies, 2023). Amended Labour Law No. 19 of 2020 provides the legislative framework through which the Qatari government aims to restructure the labour market and address many of the problems that previously faced expatriate workers. At the forefront of the amendments introduced by the new labour law is the cancellation of prior permits for workers to travel abroad. In addition to this, the law grants workers the right to change the work for which they are employed without obtaining a no-objection certificate from the employer. These two changes are very important in that they abolish the foundations on which the restrictive sponsorship system 'kafala' was built and on which Qatar has relied for many years. It is worth noting that many Arab Gulf countries still implement the sponsorship system, which limits workers' freedom of movement outside the country and makes them lose the ability to move between different jobs within the same country. In addition to these amendments to the conditions of expatriate workers, the Qatari government was also keen to improve the conditions and living conditions of workers by adopting a policy of non-discrimination in wages among workers. The state was also keen to stress the need for employment agencies to provide suitable living conditions for workers brought in from abroad in accordance with international standards in force in this regard.

As part of its effort to regulate the labour market, the Qatari government also issued Law No. 17 of 2020, which stipulated setting the minimum wage at 1,000 Qatari riyals. The law affirms that the stipulated minimum wage is given to workers regardless of their nationality and is binding on all employers. Employers are also committed to providing workers with suitable housing and living conditions. In the event that housing is not provided directly by the employer, the law forces companies to give appropriate allowances for housing and food to workers. The law also guarantees workers' rights by stipulating procedures by which contracts are cancelled and jobs are terminated. In this context, the law emphasizes the necessity of giving the worker a written notice one month before terminating his/her contract if the period of employment is less than two years. If the employment period exceeds two years, the employing entity should give the worker a written notice two months before terminating his contract.

Taken together, these amendments would improve the conditions of workers in the State of Qatar and guarantee a decent life for them and their families, whether inside or outside Qatar. It is also expected that these amendments will help the State of Qatar in its quest to shift towards a knowledge-based economy by giving workers greater flexibility to move between different jobs and obtain better job opportunities that match their skills. From the point of view of employers, the amendments introduced to the Labour Law would reduce the costs of recruitment and appointment processes. Employers can search for skilled workers locally and attract them without the need to recruit from outside the country, which increases the cost of recruitment and recruitment processes.

An important element of Qatar's labour policies is the policy of replacing foreign workers with nationals, known as Qatarization policies. The primary goal of Qatarization policies is to build a national workforce and rely on employing Qatari citizens in strategic sectors in the country, including the energy and finance sectors and key government jobs. This trend, which Qatar shares with many other Gulf countries, is expected to be affected, like other aspects of the Qatari labour market, by developments in the field of artificial intelligence. Although it is too early to talk about the form and size of the impact that artificial intelligence will have on Qatarization policies, it is possible to point out some of the challenges that the adoption of artificial intelligence applications will pose to the state's approach to replacing foreign workers with Qataris. With regard to the demand side for labour, it is expected that the expansion of artificial intelligence applications will reduce the demand for expatriate workers, most of whom used to occupy routine administrative jobs that can be efficiently performed by artificial intelligence. This decrease in demand for expatriate workers may open up new job opportunities for Qataris, provided that they are trained in the new requirements for dealing with artificial intelligence applications. From this perspective, Qatarization policies can focus on training Qatari national workers on the skills required in labour markets dominated by AI applications and smart technology. Perhaps focusing on this important aspect within Qatarization policies will help the state build a national workforce armed with the skills required to fill future jobs and make the Qatari workforce more competitive in global labour markets. In addition, with the expected economic growth resulting from the expansion of AI applications, the Qatari labour market will provide more jobs for Qataris to fill, especially creative jobs related to leadership and decision-making, which are not expected to be significantly affected by the spread of AI applications.

5.3.2 *The Qatari Labour Market: Key Indicators*

Focusing on the Qatari Labour market, it can be noted that the labour market in Qatar has some distinctive features due to its rapid economic growth and strategic government policies. The first distinctive feature of the labour market in the State of Qatar is the high rate of participation in economic activity. Statistics in this regard indicate that 87.8% of the population over the age of fifteen are active in the Qatari labour market (Mohamed, 2021). It is also noted in this context that men's participation clearly exceeds women's participation. The second feature of the labour market in Qatar is the dominance of foreign labour in the market compared to the size of the national labour force. As noted by the Qatar Computing Research Institute, in Qatar, 95% of the workforce is made up of an expatriate population that has a high turnover rate (Qatar Computing Research Institute, 2023). Regarding unemployment rates, it can be noted that Qatar has been able to maintain low unemployment rates, as the percentage of unemployed people did not exceed 0.1%. The composition of the labour market also reflects the prevalence of fixed-wage contract types among workers, with an average wage ranging between 12,390 Qatari riyals for female workers and 11,486 Qatari riyals for two-year men. Another feature that distinguishes the Qatari labour market is the Qatari government's keenness to continue economic development policies and increase economic growth rates. In the period following the Corona epidemic, the government was interested in intervening through financial and monetary tools, with the aim of maintaining high levels of spending by citizens and residents (El-Haddadeh et al., 2023). This intervention by the government helped limit the negative effects of the pandemic on the Qatari economy. In general, the labour market in the State of Qatar during the post-pandemic period showed a high level of dynamism in many sectors, as the flexibility of the market helped maintain high employment rates.

5.3.3 *The Qatari Labour Market: Potential Impacts of AI*

The State of Qatar is considered one of the leading countries in investing in technological infrastructure and AI (Araz, 2020). The government aims to transform the country into an information and communications technology centre in the region. To this end, Qatar has witnessed a growing trend towards applying modern technologies, including AI. Such a trend is one of the country's priorities in its journey towards the digital economy. In this context, several initiatives and programs have been launched to promote AI in Qatar, such as the Qatar Computing Research Institute (QCRI) and the Qatar Foundation for Scientific Computing (QSC). There are also several government and private initiatives aimed at promoting the use of modern technology and AI in vital sectors such as health, education, transportation and trade. The State of Qatar launched its Artificial Intelligence Strategy in 2019 (Ministry Of Communication & Information Technology, 2019). Through this strategy, the Qatari government aims to create an AI-augmented labour market and seeks to employ this major shift in the field of automation to create new jobs and enhance existing ones. This move towards employing AI technologies in the Qatari labour market will help the State of Qatar achieve its national vision and shift towards a knowledge-based economy. Additionally, the creation of AI-augmented workplace will support the process of diversifying the national economy.

The impact of AI on jobs varies greatly and depends on the industry and economic sector in question (Al-Sharq, 2023). For example, AI can lead to increased productivity and efficiency in some industries, increasing demand for labour, while it may lead to job cuts in some other industries. It is expected that the rapid development in technology and AI will lead to fundamental changes in the way work and production are done. These changes may lead to the reduction of some jobs and the modernization of many of them. However, the rapid development in technology and AI will lead to the creation of new job opportunities in emerging and advanced industries in addition to fundamental changes to current functions. Some analysts believe that there is no direct harm to the use of AI on the labour market in Qatar. Nevertheless, at the same time, they do not rule out the existence of indirect harm in the sense that humans have become more dependent on AI to the point of relying on the computer to think and make decisions on their behalf. This is evident in the recent hype caused by 'GPT Chat' and the great demand for it to perform some tasks (D'Arcy et al., 2024). This is considered the other side of AI, which may make humans more 'dependent' on it in the future and limit their way of thinking and human intelligence. It is true that AI may replace humans in some jobs, but at the same time, it will create new job opportunities, especially to a greater extent in the field of technology. For example, if we use a 'robot doctor,' the robot cannot be produced and designed without consulting the human doctor to benefit from his experience and knowledge in his specialty. This in turn creates more jobs, and does not directly replace humans (Qatar Tribune, 2024).

It is clear from the previous discussion of that there is an expansion in the employment of AI techniques and applications in various fields. In the Qatari case in particular, this expansion raises many important questions related to its repercussions on the labour market. As international reports indicate, about 300 million jobs are expected to be affected globally by the expansion of in the use of AI technologies by various bodies and institutions (PricewaterhouseCoopers, 2023). In this context, the main question becomes: Which jobs will be more likely to be affected by these changes? Will the increase of the use of AI lead to increased unemployment rates? Will AI create new job opportunities? These are all legitimate questions given the uncertainty created by the growth of AI applications.

In general, it is expected that the labour market in Qatar will be affected by AI such that its applications will replace many jobs. Nevertheless, these smart applications can also help create new job opportunities and improve existing ones. For example, AI can be used in many industries in Qatar such as oil and gas, retail, finance, and logistics (AL-Dosari et al., 2024). Therefore, the expansion of AI applications can improve work efficiency and improve economic performance in the country. As such, AI may contribute to improving economic performance and strengthening the labour market in Qatar. However, this requires providing appropriate training and qualifications to current and future workers, so that they can adapt to AI technologies and benefit from the new job opportunities it can create.

Outside the armed forces and police, the Qatari national workforce is concentrated in government jobs in the state's administrative apparatus. These jobs, known as white-collar jobs, are among the types of jobs that are expected to be most affected by the application of AI in the business environment (Mohamed, 2021). These jobs are routine in nature and can be performed by AI applications much faster and more efficiently than the human element. In other words, the majority of jobs held by Qataris in the government apparatus are vulnerable to being replaced by various AI applications. In this context, one of the statistical studies conducted on the impact of AI on the labour market in the State of Qatar indicated that about 50% of the current jobs are vulnerable to being replaced by AI. From this, we can conclude that the jobs held by most Qataris will be affected in the near future by the entry of AI applications into the labour market, including administrative jobs, those related to financial analysis, and also jobs related to decision-making. This observation requires rapid intervention by decision-makers in the state to retrain and qualify Qatari employees to deal with this change in the workplace (QCAI, 2020).

In terms of the opportunities that AI will create in global economies and labour markets, it can be noted that as per 2018 estimates, AI will contribute up to US$15.7 trillion to the global economy in 2030, of which the Middle East region is expected to accrue US$320 billion in growth. AI's contribution to the GDP of Qatar is expected to be 8.2% by 2030 (PricewaterhouseCoopers, 2023). Hence, while some jobs may be affected by the application of AI technologies, such as repetitive, regular and low-skilled jobs, such as administrative and accounting work and industrial products that use manual labour, AI can also lead to the creation of new jobs. These new jobs include areas such as programming, graphic analysis, robotics, design and development, and thus could boost the labour market in Qatar (QCAI, 2020).

5.3.4 *AI and the Future Landscape of Employment in Qatar*

Following on from the above discussion the key question now is how the State of Qatar can face the challenges of AI and its potential impact on the Labour market. The answer to this question requires fundamental changes in the current educational and training system in the country. It also calls for a comprehensive rethinking and reconsideration of the way we deal with information and data in Qatar (Aboulnaga et al., 2021). With regard to education and training, in order for Qatar to be able to benefit from the AI revolution in developing the labour market, an appropriate ecosystem should be created that helps achieve this goal. In other words, to face the future challenges of applying AI to employment in the Qatari labour market, radical transformations should be made in the existing educational system at its various levels to prepare the new generation of the future workforce (Qatar Tribune, 2024b). To reach this goal, the topic of AI should be integrated into various educational curricula, starting from the primary education and ending with education at the university level (Garcia, 2023). In the initial stages of education, children can be trained on how to deal with the outputs of AI applications and how to evaluate these outputs in terms of the extent to which they are consistent with or differ from the cultural and social reality of the country. This type of training would develop the critical mentality of these students and help them distinguish between the bad and the valuable in the outputs of AI applications. At a more advanced educational stage, curricula can provide students with guidelines on how to ethically deal with AI applications and the risks that some applications may pose to society, such as violating privacy. At the university level, colleges specialized in the field of technology and computers should equip their graduates with the AI skills that enable them to benefit from the AI revolution and make them more prepared for the changes that the Qatari labour market will witness in the coming years. In this context, AI is expected to influence students' undergraduate choices. For example, there is great interest from the state and students to study cybersecurity. This specialization has become greatly in demand in the labour market. In addition, AI has become a major or sub-specialization taught in some universities 'AI is the future' (Qatar Tribune, 2023).

This trend towards integrating AI into the various stages of education would build a national workforce that has the skills and capabilities to enter a different labour market in terms of the type of jobs required as well as the skills that qualify graduates to join those jobs (Global Studies Institute, 2023). In addition to preparing the future workforce in Qatar to adapt to the potential effects of AI, the skills of current employees in various sectors should also be developed. This aspect can be achieved by preparing intensive training courses for state employees through which they can learn about the impact of AI on the jobs they perform and how to benefit from it in developing their performance and improving the quality of activities and operations provided by their organizations. This form of transformative training will develop the skills of the current workforce and help them deal positively with the consequences of implementing AI in their organization. In addition to building the workforce by relying on national competencies, Qatar can also attract skilled and creative people in the field of AI globally by offering some job benefits and better conditions of employment and residency in the country.

Access and share information is paramount in facing future challenges of AI. In the age of AI, information is the 'new oil,' meaning that it has become the primary source of nations' wealth and progress. In this way, access to information and the freedom to exchange it between different organizations and within one organization between different levels becomes vital for proper planning and setting strategic directions for the future of the labour market (Fatima et al., 2020). In general, the prevailing organizational culture in many organizations, especially government organizations, does not encourage the sharing of information. The reason behind this is one of two things. The first is the fear of competition between organizations, which makes some of them reluctant to share the information they have with other organizations. The other reason is the fear that sharing information with various parties will result in a violation of the right to privacy of the owners of this information. This mentality makes organizations seem like silos isolated from each other and encourages a culture of information retention among employees. To remedy this matter, we should rely on building an effective information governance system within the country that specifies the rules for collecting, organizing and storing this information, in addition to how it is shared with other parties (McKinsey, 2023). In this regard, the law on data privacy protection recently issued by the Qatari government is a good point to start building the information governance system in the country. It is worth noting in this regard that freedom of access to information and sharing of data between different parties within Qatar is vital for developing local solutions to the problems that may face the labour market in the coming period because of the expansion of the application of AI. Among the comparative advantages that the State of Qatar enjoys in this regard is its small size and the interconnectedness of its administrative apparatus. This enables Qatar to build joint databases among various state agencies and connect these databases in a way that can maximize the benefits from AI applications (Fatima et al., 2020).

To thrive in an AI-centric landscape, nations should excel in three critical areas: data management, technological infrastructure, and human capital. While nations can regulate and harness data within their borders, achieving and maintaining superiority in infrastructure and talent presents a more complex challenge (Qatar Tribune, 2023). Qatar has historically prioritized investment in cutting-edge technological infrastructure; however, its substantial focus on developing a premier higher education and research ecosystem is even more significant. The World Economic Forum (WEF) has acknowledged Qatar as a leader among MENA countries in two crucial areas for fostering AI-based automation: the quality of its education systems and the ease of sourcing skilled employees. Consequently, Qatar holds a competitive edge in the MENA region to capitalize on the advancements of the AI revolution (Qatar Computing Research Institute, 2023).

5.4 Conclusions and Policy Recommendations

With the entry of AI applications into our contemporary life, the form of many activities has changed, and we have become dependent on smart technologies to perform many of the functions that humans used to do. In this paper, we tried to shed light on the potential changes of AI applications on the labour market in the State of Qatar. It is clear from the discussion that the Qatari labour market is not very different from global labour markets with regard to the potential effects of AI. At a time when AI opens the door to many opportunities in terms of productivity and economic efficiency of various activities, there are many challenges that should be faced in order to achieve the maximum benefit from the entry of this new variable into the labour markets (Qatar Tribune, 2024b).

In general, Qatar is a good place to invest in AI and develop projects that benefit from it. Qatar has a strong technology infrastructure and a clear strategy to transform the country into the ICT hub of the region. AI is one of the most common modern technologies in the digital world, and is characterized by great importance in various fields, whether at the level of individuals, societies, or countries. First, individuals can use AI to improve their lives, increase their productivity, manage time, and improve personal productivity. Using AI algorithms, data can be analysed, making it useful for individuals in making the right decisions. Second, communities can benefit from AI in multiple areas, such as improving public health, helping to develop renewable energy, and managing waste in a more effective way. AI can also be used to develop smart cities and improve public government services. Third, countries can benefit from AI to enhance economic development, improve national security, and manage crises and disasters. AI can also be used in military fields, such as developing air defines systems and identifying potential targets.

To maximize the benefits of AI applications and minimize the potential negative impacts on the labour market in Qatar, decision-makers should take a set of measures, most notably changing the prevailing organizational culture that encourages the hording of information and not sharing it between different parties. This traditional culture should be replaced by another work culture that is more open and more flexible in dealing with data and information. This new organizational culture revolves around the good use of available information and data to support decision-making processes in various sectors of the state. Hence, the good use of data helps make the public policy-making process data-driven and evidence-based, which is consistent with the nature of the next stage in light of AI. To achieve this goal, organizations should first evaluate their current situations in terms of data availability and identify the gaps that may exist in the available data and information, as well as work to address these gaps by providing missing information and data from other sources. All of this should be done while calculating the opportunity cost of information and data.

At the educational level, Qatar should cultivate a culture of lifelong learning within its institutions, society, and economy to adapt to an AI-driven future. This involves fostering cultural acceptance of continuous education and skill development. The existing workforce needs ongoing upskilling to thrive in AI-enhanced environments. Educational curricula at all levels should emphasize the significance of AI, preparing the next generation of Qatari citizens to be proficient with intelligent systems. Furthermore, the roles of family and societal structures will need to evolve to support this shift towards an AI-integrated lifestyle.

At the sectoral level, analyses show that there are specific sectors in the Qatari economy that must receive the attention of decision-makers and be the starting point for bringing about the required change in the labour market. At the forefront of these sectors are the government sector, the financial sector, and insurance activities, in addition to the information and communications sector, the education sector, the healthcare sector, and the energy sector. These sectors are expected to be among the most affected economic sectors by AI in the coming period. Therefore, the government must intervene through transformational training programs to help workers in these sectors deal with the new reality in light of AI applications.

To fully capitalize on the potential of AI, workers in both government and private sectors in Qatar must enhance their skill sets to effectively engage with AI technologies. This involves a multi-faceted approach: first, understanding fundamental AI concepts and their applications in the workplace is crucial. Staying abreast of the latest tools and technologies in AI is also necessary. Additionally, workers should invest in foundational skills, such as computer literacy, programming, and creative thinking. Effective time management and the ability to balance new technological skills with traditional ones are key to increasing productivity. Building positive interactions with AI systems and enhancing human–machine collaboration will further support this integration. Moreover, developing innovative solutions to leverage AI features and technological advancements is essential. Finally, a commitment to continuous learning and skill development is vital to remain current with ongoing AI advancements. Through these efforts, workers can ensure they are well-prepared to thrive in an AI-enhanced environment, thereby boosting productivity and maintaining job relevance in an increasingly digital landscape.

While it is true that AI will lead to the displacement of some jobs, it is equally important to recognize that it will also create new job opportunities. The initial resistance to AI is similar to the reactions witnessed when digital technology first replaced traditional 'pen and paper' systems. Initially, people struggled to accept this technological shift, but over time, they adapted to and embraced the new methods. This pattern of initial resistance followed by eventual acceptance is common with significant technological changes. The same scenario is likely to play out with AI, as society gradually adjusts and learns to leverage the benefits it brings, ultimately leading to new opportunities and advancements in various fields. Hence, to maximize the benefits of AI, workers in both the government and private sectors should not view AI as a 'competition' between humans and machines but rather as a collaborative partnership. This teamwork approach can harness the strengths of both humans and AI, leading to greater efficiency and innovation. Relying solely on AI could lead to limitations due to its lack of human-like thinking, while complete reliance on humans can be physically demanding for tasks better suited for robots. It is crucial for humans to accept AI, cooperate with it, and work together as one team to enhance productivity and keep pace with technological advancements.

References

Aboulnaga, A., Chawla, S., Elmagarmid, A., & Al-Mannai, M. (2021). *An AI-enabled future for Qatar and the region*. https://cacm.acm.org/magazines/2021/4/251345-an-ai-enabled-future-for-qatar-and-the-region/abstract

AL-Dosari, K., Fetais, N., & Kucukvar, M. (2024). Artificial intelligence and cyber defense system for banking industry: A qualitative study of AI applications and challenges. *Cybernetics and Systems*, *55*(2), 302–330. https://doi.org/10.1080/01969722.2022.2112539

Al-Sharq. (2023, April 30). *The rise of AI: How Qatar's job market is adapting to the fourth industrial revolution*. What's Goin On Qatar. https://wgoqatar.com/198526

Araz, S. (2020). *Qatar plots its AI future*. Middle East Institute. https://www.mei.edu/publications/qatar-plots-its-ai-future

Badran, A. (2021). Thoughts and reflections on the case of Qatar: Should artificial intelligence be regulated? In E. Azar & A. N. Haddad (Eds.), *Artificial intelligence in the Gulf* (pp. 69–92). Springer Singapore. https://doi.org/10.1007/978-981-16-0771-4_5

Badran, A. (2023). *Artificial intelligence between government and self-regulation policies: A theoretical approach*. جكامة. https://doi.org/10.31430/IJZH4708

Bessen, J. (2018). *AI and Jobs: The role of demand* (w24235; p. w24235). National Bureau of Economic Research. https://doi.org/10.3386/w24235

Brown, S., Francis, M., Hnida, N., Peracchio, W., Rosales, V., Simons, K., & Trujillo, A. (n.d.). Protecting workers' rights in the gig economy: AI and digital labour platforms. *Lehigh University and University of San Francisco de Quito, Global Village in Collaboration with the International Labour Organisation*, 1–11.

Burrell, J. (2016). How the machine 'thinks': Understanding opacity in machine learning algorithms. *Big Data & Society*, 1–12.

Calo, R. (2017). *Artificial intelligence policy: A primer and roadmap*.

D'Arcy, C., Song, D., Chalker, F., Stagman, M., & Malek, R. (2024). *Regulating Generative AI | Global Counsel*. https://www.global-counsel.com/insights/report/regulating-generative-ai

DATAx. (2019). *Guide to AI and machine learning trends in 2019*. File:///D:/Users/ab16495/Downloads/Ebook_____DATAx_Guide_To_AI_and_Machine_Learning_Trends_in_2019__1_.pdf.

Davies, Z. (2023, June 29). *Artificial labour markets in the Gulf.* Near East Policy Forum. https://nepf.org.au/index.php/artificial-labour-markets-in-the-gulf/

El-Haddadeh, R., Fadlalla, A., & Hindi, N. M. (2023). Is there a place for responsible artificial intelligence in pandemics? A tale of two countries. *Information Systems Frontiers, 25*(6), 2221–2237. https://doi.org/10.1007/s10796-021-10140-w

Erdelyi, O., & Goldsmith, J. (2018). *Regulating Artificial Intelligence Proposal for a Global Solution.* Association for the Advancement of Artificial. http://www.aies-conference.com/wp-content/papers/main/AIES_2018_paper_13.pdf

Etzioni, O. (2018). Should AI technology be regulated? Yes, and Here's How. *Communications of the ACM*, 30–32.

Faggella, D. (2019). *What is machine learning?* https://emerj.com/ai-glossary-terms/what-is-machine-learning/

Fatima, S., Desouza, K. C., & Dawson, G. S. (2020). National strategic artificial intelligence plans: A multi-dimensional analysis. *Economic Analysis and Policy, 67*, 178–194. https://doi.org/10.1016/j.eap.2020.07.008

Garcia, A. (2023, April 8). *The impact of AI on the job market in the region.* Economy Middle East. https://economymiddleeast.com/news/impact-of-ai/

Global Studies Institute. (2023, August 6). *Embracing the AI revolution: How artificial intelligence and machine learning are reshaping the job market.* Global Studies Institute—Qatar. https://gsi.edu.qa/ar/embracing-the-ai-revolution-how-artificial-intelligence-and-machine-learning-are-reshaping-the-job-market/

Goldberg, K. (2012). What is automation? *IEEE Transactions on Automation Science and Engineering, 9*(1), 1–2. https://doi.org/10.1109/TASE.2011.2178910

Harris, J. (2021, July 3). Homeworking sounds good—Until your job takes over your life. *The Guardian.*

Lane, M., & Saint-Martin, A. (2021). *The impact of Artificial Intelligence on the labour market: What do we know so far?* (OECD Social, Employment and Migration Working Papers 256; OECD Social, Employment and Migration Working Papers, Vol. 256, pp. 1–60). https://doi.org/10.1787/7c895724-en

Makridakis, S. (2017). The forthcoming Artificial Intelligence (AI) revolution: Its impact on society and firms. *Futures, 90*, 46–60. https://doi.org/10.1016/j.futures.2017.03.006

McKinsey. (2023). *Governance and regulation as generative AI advances.* https://www.mckinsey.com/capabilities/risk-and-resilience/our-insights/as-gen-ai-advances-regulators-and-risk-functions-rush-to-keep-pace/

Ministry Of Communication and Information Technology. (2019). *National artificial intelligence strategy for Qatar*. https://www.mcit.gov.qa/sites/default/files/national_artificial_intelligence_strategy_for_qatar_0.pdf

Mohamed, H. (2021). The labor market in Qatar: Qataris, Non-Qataris, and youth in the workforce. *International Journal of Creativity and Innovation in Humanities and Education*, *4*(2).

Parasuraman, R., Sheridan, T. B., & Wickens, C. D. (2000). A model for types and levels of human interaction with automation. *IEEE Transactions on Systems, Man, and Cybernetics—Part A: Systems and Humans, 30*(3), 286–297. https://doi.org/10.1109/3468.844354

PricewaterhouseCoopers. (2023, June 20). *PwC Middle East workforce hopes and fears survey 2023*. PwC. https://www.pwc.com/m1/en/media-centre/articles/hopes-fears-employees-across-qatar-2023.html

Qatar Computing Research Institute. (2023). *Impact of artificial intelligence on Qatar's labor market*. https://qcai-blog.qcri.org/wp-content/uploads/2020/11/The-Impact-of-Artificial-Intelligence.pdf

Qatar Tribune. (2023, November 24). *Qatar harnessing AI to improve labour market data: Dr Marri*. Qatar Tribune. https://www.qatar-tribune.com/article/94356/nation/qatar-harnessing-ai-to-improve-labour-market-data-dr-marri

Qatar Tribune. (2024a). *Qatar's Labour ministry unveils groundbreaking AI initiative at global forum in New York*. https://www.zawya.com/en/world/middle-east/qatars-labour-ministry-unveils-groundbreaking-ai-initiative-at-global-forum-in-new-york-haiavayh

Qatar Tribune. (2024b, February 12). *Preparing workforce ready for future challenges focus of Qatar's National Development Strategy: Labour minister*. Qatar Tribune. https://www.qatar-tribune.com/article/107532/nation/preparing-workforce-ready-for-future-challenges-focus-of-qatars-national-development-strategy-labour-minister

QCAI. (2020, December 29). *AI impact on Qatar's labor market: An assessment*. https://www.hbku.edu.qa/en/news/ai-impact-qatar

Russell, S., & Norvig, P. (1994). *Artificial intelligence a modern approach*. Prentice Hall.

Shaiken, H. (1980). A robot is after your job: New technology isn't a panacea. *N. Y. TIMES, 1980*.

Smuha, N. A. (2021). From a 'race to AI' to a 'race to AI regulation': Regulatory competition for artificial intelligence. *Law, Innovation and Technology, 13*(1), 57–84. https://doi.org/10.1080/17579961.2021.1898300

Stone, P. (2016). *Artificial intelligence and life in 2030: One hundred year study on artificial intelligence*.

Thomas, H. (2021, August 4). Offices: Homeworking will save employers billions. *Finanical Times*.

Tiwari, R. (2023). The impact of AI and machine learning on job displacement and employment opportunities. *International Journal of Scientific Research in Engineering and Management, 7*(1), 1–8. https://doi.org/10.55041/IJSREM17506

Tyson, L. D., & Zysman, J. (2022). Automation, AI & Work. *Daedalus, 151*(2), 256–271. https://doi.org/10.1162/daed_a_01914

Walk the Talk. (2023, April 14). The future of work: Balancing the promise and peril of AI. *Medium*. https://medium.com/@WalktheTalk/the-future-of-work-balancing-the-promise-and-peril-of-ai-b4d1e62018a3

CHAPTER 6

Impact and Perception of Generative AI and Related Automation Tools in the Gulf Region

Vinod Pangracious, Nejib Ben Hadj-Alouane, Zhaojin Chu, and Raagav Ramakrishnan

6.1 Introduction

The Gen-AI technologies are expected to transform the traditional industries in an unprecedented pace and movement, characterized by new technology like AI/Generative AI, Robotics, the Meta-verse, and other such platforms—they are poised to change how we conduct business and live our lives (Gan et al., 2023). Generative AI comes as the most recent addition to this collection of these modern new technology tools; it can be automated to identify patterns across enormous sets of language-based data and generate new content (Ellingrud et al., 2023). The emergence of Generative AI is the beginning of a new era in the domain of content generation like images, music, videos etc. According to a recent, widely referenced, analysis report from a reputed firm (Ellingrud et al., 2023).

V. Pangracious (✉) · N. B. Hadj-Alouane · Z. Chu · R. Ramakrishnan
School of Engineering, American University, Dubai, United Arab Emirates
e-mail: vpangracious@aud.edu

A. Badran and A. Mishrif (eds.), *Shaping the Future of Development in the GCC*, The Political Economy of the Middle East,
https://doi.org/10.1007/978-981-96-7963-8_6

Generative AI has already caused 12 million occupational shifts worldwide and is even poised to cause more upheaval in future job markets. More than 50\% of the recent occupational shifts are found in industries like food services, customer service, office support, and production (Ellingrud et al., 2023). We see industry-wide disruption, with many companies making use of such AI technologies and autonomous robotics (including cars): Amazon is putting robots in its warehouses (Shen et al., 2023) and is promoting robots for home care (Shen et al., 2023). AI-enabled Machine Learning models are also being used to enhance the retail/ consumer experience (find sources for this). This occupation displacement shall not be limited to low-wage labor, however. A recent economics study by a prominent Stanford economist (Panigrahi et al., 2023), has found that the high-end job market shall be most affected by using AI. The public and private owned institutions in the Middle Eastern countries and especially United Arab Emirates (UAE) have an interest not only on how the new or old generation cope with the advanced AI Technologies but also on how prepared people are to act in shorter or longer distance futures.

In this paper we propose to examine the impact of this global change on the job markets in the Middle East region, in countries like the UAE, Bahrain, and KSA, where a strong E-Government presence is already in place (Kim et al., 2019), and where the use of modern technologies is accepted and encouraged. These countries have integrated many AI technologies, such as face-recognition, 3D Printing, Augmented Reality, and many others, into administrative and retail activities (Ali et al., 2022). We believe that both the Government and the General Public would be receptive to the introduction of Generative AI and autonomous robotics-based tools across different industry and service sectors. We are most interested in determining the general public's preparedness and perception of these Generative AI and automation tools. In fact, we conducted a survey targeting multiple segments of the populations in the Gulf region, for the purpose of finding answers linked to the understanding, perception, and readiness of the populations to the upcoming job market change. The results are analyzed based on a methodology with two main components; the first is a survey, and the second is a statistical model used to analyze the survey results (aus dem Moore et al., 2018).

This paper is structured as follows. After the introduction, the second section gives a literature survey. The third section explores the current job market, overviews the main AI/Gen-AI tools, and a discussion of their impact on industries such as Information Technology (IT), healthcare, finance, and Government services and trade. The fourth section gives a brief overview of structural equations modelling, a formal tool for developing the statistical model used to analyze the results of our survey. The next section lays out our methodology and research design. This is followed by a section exposing and analyzing our results. The last section provides a conclusion and some future perspectives.

6.2 Literature Review (State of the Art)

The introduction of AI/Generative AI into our world today has marked significant changes in multiple industries, changing the fabric of society. It has affected the way we interact with the world around us. The rapid progression of such programs, focused on the ability of computers to perform subtle, non-routine, cognitive tasks, has the potential to affect the workforce and labor markets around the world. Despite such progress, the implementation of any potential use cases with AI has remained abstract; until the rise of Generative Pre-trained Transformers (GPTs)—Interfaces that connect Generative AI Models with the end-user (Webb, 2020). We look at John Keynes and his work on technological unemployment (Petropoulos, 2018). In previous industrial revolutions, advancements in technology led to widespread job loss. However, it also led to significant increases in productivity, along with the creation of new jobs and new industries, which far outweigh the associated disadvantages. We now stand at a similar juncture with the rise in AI/Generative AI.

Looking at workers with varying degrees of experience in different jobs, we see a complex perception (Ogbolu et al., 2020) of the incoming changes—despite acknowledging their capabilities to adapt and adopt new technologies, there is some uncertainty and concern surrounding the extent to which AI will change the labor market (Manyika et al., 2017). The European perception of Generative AI study shows a positive correlation between AI's anticipated impact on the way of life in the next 20 years and the perceived displacement of jobs caused by AI technology and automation (Budeanu et al., 2023). The "Bristow's" 2018 report on Artificial Intelligence: Public perception, attitude, and trust (Holder et al., 2018) shows the public understanding of Generative AI is broad, but not deep, expectations are very high, and young people are more confident and optimistic about the use of AI/Generative AI in work as well as life.

6.2.1 Impacts of AI and Generative AI on Jobs

We should briefly introduce AI and Gen-AI, compare both and give examples of new applications, and then distinguish major studies about their impact on job markets across the world. AI refers to the simulation of the human intelligence processes by machines and computer systems. These processes encompass a range of activities such as learning, reasoning, problem-solving, and generalizing. Gen-AI is a sub-field of AI capable of generating new data, content, or outputs via derivations from input data, or so-called prompts. Unlike traditional AI systems, which primarily analyze and interpret data, Generative AI systems can create and produce new data (and thus Generate data,) such as texts, images, and videos.

There have been significant advancements in Gen-AI, with the adaptation of the technology skyrocketing due to releases of majorly popular software such as Bard, DALL-E, GPT-4 and Sora that allow the generation of content with almost indistinguishable authenticity to a human (Feuerriegel et al., 2023). For example, GPT-4 provides users with the ability to input both images and texts as prompts, using a multi-modal model "exhibiting human-level performance on various professional and academic benchmarks" (OpenAI, March 2023). Another model, Sora, is capable of producing high quality videos from multiple different camera angles as well as video manipulations, which could have major effects on not just film and movie industries, but on any jobs in any fields involving video production (Brooks et al., 2024). The ease of access, accuracy, and performance of recent developments of Gen-AI are often shockingly surprising to the public and have led to both doubts and praise for the future of AI.

The effects of Gen-AI are often described as either augmentation or automation. Augmentation refers to the collaboration between humans and machines, while automation is the act of substituting machines for humans in tasks. Although these are not completely perfect indicators and measurements for the impact of Generative AI (Raisch & Krakowski, 2021), we believe they are sufficient characterizations, for the purposes of this paper. According to a paper published by the International Labour Organization (ILO) (Gmyrek et al., 2023), clerical support workers are at the highest risk for automation. These types of jobs include repetitive tasks and often follow a specific set of rules, guidelines, and patterns, allowing AI to be programmed to execute these tasks efficiently, and without human guidance. Such effects can already be seen from the increased usage of ChatGPT and the GPT models from OpenAI, with tasks such as summarizing, formatting, and organizing becoming significantly simplified. On the other hand, the analysis from the ILO also concludes that jobs fields such as technicians, professionals, associate professionals, and service/sales workers have a high potential for augmentation due to the intrinsically routine and repetitive tasks which do exist in such fields. This presents an area where AI could excel at and freeing up human workers to focus on higher-value tasks which require more problem-solving, creativity, and critical thinking.

For example, ADNOC fuel stations in the United Arab Emirates are launching and testing a robotic arm to refuel vehicles, which could replace a sizable number of human workers and staff (Web Desk et al., 2024). The company states that "Fuel stations will use the robot to support the existing staff, boost productivity, and reduce wait time", suggesting future augmentation for the occupation of fuel station attendants. Although it may be able to completely make human staff redundant at refueling vehicles, processes such as customer service and safety checks are still far from being automated. Few government offices in the UAE use Gen-AI based agents to provide policies and procedures of their customers, which were previously done by service providers. This is also an indication that the impact and challenges of AI/Gen-AI are not only on the job market/displacement but also on the business-to-business (B2B) type business models.

6.2.2 *Background on Structural Equation Modelling (SEM)*

SEM is a comprehensive statistical technique. SEM combines multiple regression equations and factor analysis to analyze the structural relationship between measured variables and latent constructs. The overview on SEM given in this section is based on Kline et al. (2015) and Meshcheryakov et al. (2021). SEM is a statistical technique used for modelling and analyzing complex relationships between numerous variables. It is used for testing and estimating causal relationships using a combination of statistical data and qualitative causal assumptions. It is also a multivariate method that combines factor analysis and multiple regression analysis to analyze the structural relationship between "observed" or measured variables and latent constructs. In this method each of the survey questions, for example, is "observed" variables, which is directly measured by the data provided by the survey's respondents. The observed variables have a direct effect on the so-called latent variables. The latent variables are those that we are interested in measuring but cannot actually measure directly.

SEM works with a model that has two components, the measurement model and the structural model. These two models work together to assess both the relationships between observed variables and latent constructs (measurement model) and the relationships between those latent constructs themselves (structural model). The measurement model specifies how latent variables are related to the observed variables. Essentially, it defines the part of the model that describes the relationships between the observable indicators (measured variables) and their underlying latent variables. The measurement model is based on the idea that the observed variables are influenced by underlying factors that are not directly observed. Without going into the mathematical details, under this model the latent variables are linked to the observed variables in a linearly using so-called constant loading factors and error terms. The purpose of the measurement model is to confirm that the observed variables are reliable indicators of their respective latent variables. This is often assessed using Confirmatory Factor Analysis (CFA), where the model's fit is evaluated to see if the data supports the hypothesized measurement structure.

The structural model specifies the relationships among the latent variables themselves. While the measurement model deals with how well the observed variables represent the latent constructs, the structural model focuses on the direct and indirect relationships between these constructs. The structural model is where the causal relationships are tested. The following are key concepts for the structural model:

- Endogenous Variables: The latent variables that are influenced by other latent variables within the model. They are dependent variables within the context of the structural model.
- Exogenous Variables: The latent variables that are not influenced by other variables in the model. They act as independent variables in the structural model.
- Path Coefficients: The coefficients describe the strength and direction of the relationships between latent variables in the structural model. They are like regression coefficients.
- Direct and Indirect Effects: Direct effects refer to the influence of one latent variable on another without mediation, while indirect

effects involve mediating variables through which the influence is transmitted.

- Disturbances or Structural Errors: Associated with the endogenous variables in the structural model, representing unmeasured influences on the latent variables.

Again, without going to mathematical details, the endogenous and exogenous latent variables are linearly related through coefficients and disturbances/errors (of course there is a recursive relationship since endogenous variables may be related to endogenous and exogenous variables). The structural model tests the hypothesized causal relationships between the latent variables. It evaluates whether the proposed model of how the variables influence each other and fits the data. The fit of the structural model is assessed using various fit indices, like those used in the measurement model.

The following five step process is in general used to access the goodness of an SEM model:

- Specify the Model: Define both the measurement and structural models based on theory or prior research.
- Estimate the Model: Use statistical software to estimate the parameters (factor loadings, path coefficients, etc.).
- Assess Model Fit: Evaluate the fit of both the measurement and structural models using fit indices.
- Refine the Model: If necessary, modify the model based on modification indices or theoretical considerations and reassess fit.
- Interpret Results: Once the model fits well, interpret the relationships between the latent variables (structural model) and the relationships between latent and observed variables (measurement model).

In general, examining the fit of a constructed SEM model to a given data may be complex as it involves a number of measures and techniques. The easiest method, however, involves reading and interpreting the fit of an SEM model obtained from some software tool, such as AMOS, LISREL, "Mplus", R packages like "lavaan", or SEMOPY (the last one is the one used in this paper). Most SEM software will generate a variety of fit indices, parameter estimates, and diagnostic information that you can use to assess the model's fitness. Fit indices are the most crucial indicators to examine, however. After "executing" the SEM model (the hypothesis) with the given data, the software (in our case SEMOPY) outputs a set of fit indices: the so-called path coefficients with their associated p-values. They are a good indication for the strength of the relationships between variables in the model.

Path coefficients represent the strength and direction of the relationships between variables in your model. They are analogous to regression coefficients in standard regression analysis. Path coefficients typically range from −1 to +1. A positive coefficient indicates a positive relationship between the variables (as the predictor variable increases, the outcome variable also increases). A negative coefficient indicates a negative relationship between the variables (as the predictor variable increases, the outcome variable decreases). The closer the coefficient is to −1 or + 1, the stronger the relationship. A coefficient close to 0 suggests a weak or no relationship. The *p*-value indicates the statistical significance of the path coefficient. It tests the null hypothesis that the coefficient is equal to zero (i.e., no relationship). Typically, there is a threshold used to evaluate the significance of the relationship. In this paper we use 0.15, that is, if $p < 0.15$, the coefficient is statistically significant, meaning there is strong evidence against the null hypothesis, and the relationship is likely not due to chance.

6.3 Methodology and Research Design

This study's methodology is based on two tools, a survey and a model for analyzing the survey results. To measure the impact and perception of AI and Generative AI, we have employed a survey of 14 questions, which are used as a basis for our experiment and research. These questions were asked of 100 participants, all of whom reside in Gulf countries, since our research is also limited to Gulf countries. Furthermore, the study targeted participants who are either students and/or currently active in the job market, since those represent the segments of the population most interested in our study. Our model for analyzing the survey results is based on the structural equation modelling (SEM) approach (Hair et al., 2011; Sarstedt et al., 2019).

Our SEM approach consists of three steps. In the first step a model is built relating the measurable variables to the latent variables. The second step involves conducting the survey and accumulating the results for the measurable variable. The third step involves computing various correlations of these variables using multiple regression techniques. The results and values of these correlations provide a basis for validating the constructed model and give directions for the desired research analysis.

The observed variables of our study, i.e., the survey questions, are given in Table 6.1. Questions are numbered 1 through 12. They consist of both qualitative and quantitative questions. Questions 5 and 8 are qualitative questions, as they do not ask the participant for a number reflecting appreciation but a rank of some choices. The results of the qualitative questions cannot be integrated directly and needed to be quantified using well-known techniques (Sandelowski et al., 2009), before being integrated into our SEM model computation. Quantizing involves essentially decomposing a question into multiple variables.

Table 6.1 Survey questions or observed variables

Observed Variables	*Question*
Q1	On a scale from 1 (not familiar) to 5 (very familiar), rate your knowledge of Generative AI or AI technologies
Q2	On a scale from 1 (negative) to 5 (very positive), how do you perceive the impact of Generative AI on your work?
Q3	On a scale from 1 (negative) to 5 (very positive), how do you perceive concerns about the impact of AI on your work?
Q4	On a scale from 1 (unlikely) to 5 (very likely), how likely are you to use Generative AI or AI in your work?
Q5	Rank the following according to your concerns about Generative AI
Q6	On a scale from 1 (strongly disagree) to 5 (strongly agree), do you believe Generative AI or AI will creates new job opportunities?
Q7	On a scale from 1 (not prepared) to 5 (very prepared), how prepared is your work domain for integrating Generative AI?
Q8	Rank the following skills from most necessary to least necessary for enabling effective work with Generative AI or AI?
Q9	Do you think you possess the skills needed to work with Generative AI or AI?
Q10	If you think you don't have above skills, how willing are you to learn necessary skills, from 1 (unlikely) to 5 (very likely)?
Q11	On a scale from 1 (strongly disagree) to 5 (strongly agree), rate the effectiveness of public institutions in up-skilling programs to assist individuals to better adapt to AI integration with the Labor Market
Q12	Rate the depth of introduction of Generative AI and AI in your geographical area from 1 (no introduction) to 5 (deep introduction)

Table 6.2 gives our hypothesis, i.e., how our latent variables, which are the target of our study, are linked to the survey question. Table 6.2 shows that we are measuring three variables. The first latent variable shows the extent of support by public institutions given to the introduction of AI in various departments in a way to improve productivity of job replacement. This variable, according to our hypothesis, is supported by Questions 11 and 12 (see Table 6.1). The second latent variable deals with how the public perceive AI or Generative AI tools and their impacts, positively or negatively. This variable is supported by Questions 2, 3, 6 and quantified versions, a and b of Question 5. The third and last latent variable deals with how the public is prepared for dealing with AI/Generative AI tools and impacts. This variable is supported by Questions 1, 4, 7, 9 and quantified versions, a, b, c, and d of Question 8.

A graphical representation of our SEM model is given in Fig. 6.1. As discussed above, it shows our first three hypotheses, indicating how our measured variables, derived from the question results, link to the latent variables. It also shows two other hypotheses. Our fourth hypothesis postulates that the first latent variable, indicating support from public institutions, has an impact on the second latent variable, public perception. The fifth hypothesis states that perception is also impacted by preparedness.

Table 6.2 Latent variables or measured variables

Latent Variables	*Definition*	*Corresponding Questions*
Government Support	The effectiveness of government policies and actions related to the introduction AI	Q11 + Q12
Perception	The public perception of AI and Generative AI	Q2 + Q3 + Q6 + Q5a + Q5b
Preparedness	The public's view on their own preparedness to utilize and deploy Generative AI	Q1 + Q4 + Q5c + Q7 + Q8a + Q8b + Q8c + Q8d + Q9 + Q10

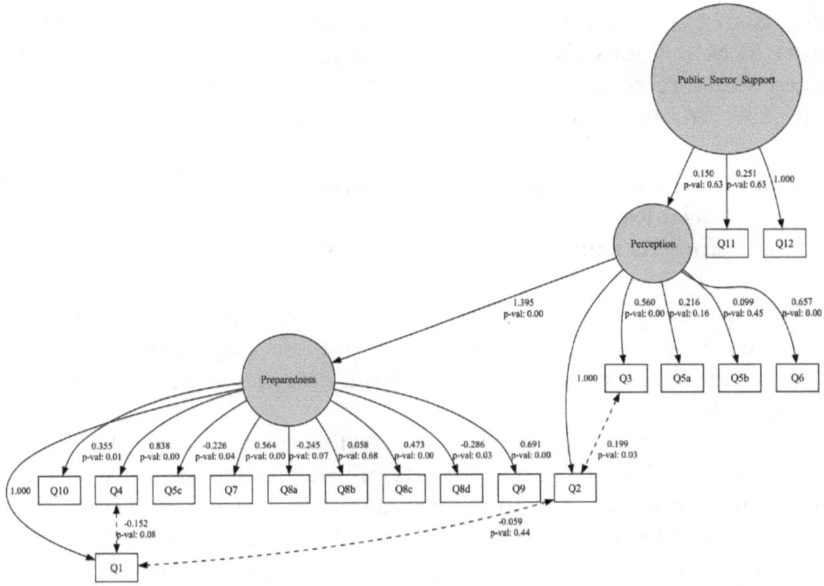

Fig. 6.1 Graphical representation SEM model, that shows the relationships between latent variables and questions raised in the survey

6.4 Results and Discussion

This section gives the results of the survey and interprets and analyses them. However, it starts with commenting on the validity of the hypotheses we stated in the previous section. This validity is important since it shows the importance of the survey questions, we asked for in measuring our target latent variables or questions. The validity or lack of it is based on the correlation provided by the computations made based on the SEM model (Meshcheryakov et al., 2021).

The following results were obtained using SEMOPY, Python-based library used for generating and analyzing SEM models (Meshcheryakov et al., 2021). This is a covariance-based SEM (CB-SEM) which focuses on understanding and measuring the relationships between variables and how they change regarding one another. CB-SEM is often used for testing and validating a hypothesis. Another notable method of SEM includes partial least squares SEM (PLS-SEM), which is more practical and prediction oriented. This is employed in exploratory studies, where the primary goal is to generate predictions rather than theory testing. Numerous other SEM methods also exist such as Bayesian, two-stage, and generalized structure component analysis SEM, but are outside the scope of this paper. In our SEM, we have the following:

H_0: There is no significant correlation between the two latent variables....
H_1: There is significant between the two latent variables....

We are testing at a significant level of 15%, that is, results with p-values below 0.15 will reject the null hypothesis, suggesting that there is sufficient evidence to indicate significant correlation between the two test variables.

Initially, we must analyze Fig. 6.1, before moving onto Table 6.3. Within Fig. 6.1, there are a multitude of variables interlinked with each other, and between each there are causal or directional relationships (single-headed arrow) or covariances (double-headed arrow). The single-headed arrows indicate the direction of the effect of one variable to another and indicate direct effects from the change of one variable to another. Covariances, depicted by double-headed arrows, represent the relationship between two variables without implying a causal relationship. It measures the degree to which two variables change together and is used in SEM to express the shared variance between pairs of variables. In the context of SEM, covariances between exogenous variables are often estimated to account for their interrelationships (Hair et al., 2011).

A major point of discussion is the general public's opinion regarding AI. From Table 6.2, we can see that perception has been dealt with in our survey using several questions. Q5 and Q8 were the questions that had significance, with p-values less than 0.15. The positive path coefficient of Q8 suggests a strong correlation between better perceptions and

Table 6.3 Structural equation modelling results

Standardized paths	*Path coefficients*	p-*Value*	*Conclusion*
Perception  Preparedness	1.395	0.00	Supported
Public Sector Support Perception	0.150	0.63	Not Supported

the belief that Gen-AI or AI will create new job opportunities due to the advanced technologies and tools that being developed in AI/Generative, automation, and healthcare. We can infer from this that people generally have very strong opinions on the impacts of AI on jobs depending on their stance and perception of AI, and that the topic of job modifications may be a large concern for people. Q5 solidifies the fact that people perceive the impacts of AI on their work depending on their perception.

The extremely strong correlation between Perception and Preparedness displays one of the core reasons for people's perceptions on AI. People who have a better perception are almost certain to be more prepared to utilize AI in work and improve productivity. This shows that with more knowledge regarding AI and how it works, people tend to have more positive views and are less pessimistic regarding its effects. This is a strong indicator that concerns about AI and Gen-AI stem somewhat from a lack of preparedness to face the challenges imposed by these new technologies. Looking at Table 6.3, we see that "Public Sector Support" has no correlation to "Perception", and most likely has no significant correlation to "Preparedness" either. One reason for this could be the relative freshness of the adaptation by the public sector of AI-based technologies. Although there are some efforts in the public sector related to educating and spreading awareness of the benefits and negatives of AI, it seems that most people still don't recognize these attempts and campaigns as noteworthy or useful to them. To the public, ethical issues are one of the biggest concerns that people have. Surprisingly, the concerns regarding the efficiency and accuracy of work done have no correlations to "Perception".

We can also, from our rankings question, Q10, relates to "Preparedness", that technical AI knowledge and knowledge about programming, produce higher indicators of less preparation due to the negative path coefficient of −0.286 and −0.245, respectively. This is correct as there is no need to have an in-depth technical knowledge about AI or programming to use these tools. However, it is important to note that the path coefficient is relatively low compared to other variables, which indicates that knowledge of AI and Gen-AI technologies and how they work is necessary to some and needs to be extended to the public, to take advantage of it. This can suggest that there is a weaker correlation, perhaps demonstrating that some segments of the general public are categorized as being prepared, but don't necessarily understand what is mostly needed to effectively utilize Gen-AI and AI. This highlights a potential lack of comprehensive knowledge of these fields, at least from an experienced user perspective. When people develop a better perception, alongside a good degree of preparedness, they would be better positioned to deal with upcoming AI/Gen-AI impacts on jobs and society. Q11 and Q12 are great indicators of whether people are willing to learn and adapt to the changes.

6.5 Conclusion

We are most interested in determining the general public's preparedness and perception of these Generative AI and automation tools. Our study targets multiple segments of the populations in the Gulf region, for the purpose of finding answers linked to the understanding, perception, and readiness of the populations to the upcoming job market change. The results are analyzed using appropriate formal methods. Since AI/Generative AI is continuously evolving technology, the challenges are to study its impact on people's perception and preparedness. Our study revealed that the human perception of the impact and future of AI/Generative AI technology in people's work and lives mostly depend on their understanding of how it works, and many of them believe an in-depth understand not required. Given the accelerated development of AI/Generative AI, it is very likely that tools and technologies will increase their presence in work and day-to-day life, and people's attitude toward preparation is expected to change. The questions we asked in the study about preparedness include technical AI knowledge and knowledge about programming as well. The study results show people are less prepared since most of the institutions and industries in the field of design, architecture, manufacturing, healthcare, and sports are not directly involved in the design and development of AI/Generative AI tools, rather than end users only. This leads us to make new proposals to introduce new courses or programs at school and university level that will benefit society to be better prepared to face the challenges and impact of AI in work and life. We expect the large-scale IT and manufacturing industries in the UAE to come forward to fund the research and development activities in the AI/Generative AI is one way to increase the awareness in the design and development of AI/Generative AI technologies in the UAE.

References

Ali, A. F., Zowayed, S. I., Showaiter, D. A., Khder, M. A., Ali, B. J. A. (2022). *Artificial intelligence's potential on Bahrain's Labour Market*. ASU International Conference in Emerging Technologies for Sustainability and Intelligent Systems (ICETSIS).

aus dem Moore, J. P., Chandran, V., & Schubert, J. (2018, January). *The future of jobs in the middle East*. World Government Summit, in collaboration with McKinsey and Company.

Brooks, Peebles, et al. (2024). *Video generation models as world simulators*, 2024. https://openai.com/research/video-generation-models-as-world-simulators

Budeanu, A. -M., Ţurcanu, D., & Rosner, D. (2023). *European perceptions of artificial intelligence and their social variability. An exploratory study*. 24th International Conference on Control Systems and Computer Science (CSCS), Bucharest, Romania (pp. 436–443). https://doi.org/10.1109/CSCS59211.2023.00075

Ellingrud, K., Sanghvi, S., Dandona, G. S., Madgavkar, A., Chui, M., White, O., Hasebe, P., & Renaud, L. (2023, July). *Generative AI and the future of work in America*. McKinsey Center for Government, McKinsey Global Institute.

Feuerriegel, S., Hartmann, J., Janiesch, C., & Zschech, P. (2023, September). Generative AI. *Business and Information Systems Engineering, 66*.

Gan, W., Ye, Z., Wan, S., & Yu, P. S. (2023, April). *Web 3.0: The Future of Internet*. Jinan University, Guangdong University of Technology, University of Illinois at Chicago, ACM Web Conference (WWW) in USA.

Gmyrek, P., Berg, J., & Bescond, D. (2023). *Generative AI and jobs: A global analysis of potential effects on job quantity and quality* (International Labor Organization Working Paper 96).

Hair, J. F., Ringle, C. M., & Sarstedt, M. (2011). PLS-SEM: Indeed, a silver bullet. *Journal of Marketing Theory and Practice, 19*.

Holder, C., & Khurana, V. (2018). *Artificial Intelligence: Public perception, attitude and trust* (report available on "www.bristows.com").

Kim, J., Mishra, A. K., Limosani, R., Scafuro, M., Cauli, N., Santos-Victor, J., Mazzolai, B., & Cavallo, F. (2019, July–August). Control strategies for cleaning robots in domestic applications: A comprehensive review. *International Journal of Advanced Robotic Systems*.

Kline, R. B. (2015). *Principles and practice of structural equation modelling* (4th ed.). Guilford Press.

Manyika, J., et al. (2017, January). *A future that works: Automation, employment, and productivity*. McKinsey Global Institute.

Meshcheryakov, G., Igolkina, A. A., Samsonova, M. G. (2021, June). *SEMOPY-2: A structural equation modelling package with random effects in Python*. arXiv preprint arXiv:2106.01140

Ogbolu, A. N., Sukidjo. (2020, November). The future of jobs amidst the rise of artificial intelligence: How ready are Asian undergraduates? *Journal of Robotics and Control (JRC), 1*(6).

Openai. (2023, March). *GPT-4 Technical Report* (available on "https://arxiv.org/pdf/2303.08774.pdf").

Panigrahi, S., Al Ghafri, K. K., Al Alyani, W. R., Ali Khan, M. W., Al Madhagy, T., & Khan, A. (2023). Lean manufacturing practices for operational and business performance: A PLS-SEM modelling analysis. *International Journal of Engineering Business Management, 15*, 1–16.

Petropoulos, G. (2018). *The Impact of artificial intelligence on employment*. Work in the Digital Age.

Raisch, S., & Krakowski, S. (2021). Artificial intelligence and management: The automation–augmentation paradox. *Academy of Management Review, 46*(1).

Sandelowski, M., Voils, C. I., & Knafl, G. (2009). On quantitizing. *Journal of Mixed Methods Research, 3*, 208–222.

Sarstedt, M., Hair, J. F. Jr., Cheah, J. -H., Becker, J.-M., & Ringle, C. M. (2019). How to specify, estimate, and validate higher-order constructs in PLS-SEM. *Australian Marketing Journal, 27*.

Shen, Y., McClosky, B., Durham, J. W., Zavlanos, M. M. (2023). *Multi-agent reinforcement learning for resource allocation in large-scale robotic warehouse sortation centers*. Amazon Science—Robotics Division, IEEE CDC.

Web Desk. (2024). *Watch: Soon, robot arm will refuel your vehicle tanks in Abu Dhabi*. Khaleej Times (available on "https://www.khaleejtimes.com/business/tech/watch-soon-robot-arm-will-refuel-your-vehicle-tanks-in-abu-dhabi") (accessed 21 March 2024).

Webb, M. (2020). *The Impact of Artificial Intelligence on the Labor Market*. Stanford.

CHAPTER 7

People's Attitudes and Perceptions in Qatar Towards Artificial Intelligence Technologies

Mustafa Altıntaş, Mustafa Selman Yaylalı, and Muhammed Ali Topal

7.1 Introduction

Artificial intelligence (AI) is gaining significance and exerting a growing impact across every aspect of life. AI is used in most of the systems, gadgets, and technology that we use on a daily basis (Schepman & Rodway, 2020). Examples of industries that benefit from AI include healthcare, retail, manufacturing, infrastructure, finance, banking, and education (Azar & Haddad, 2021). While social scientists usually examine the government policies related to adopting AI, in the last times, studies searching people's perception and attitude have shown an increase. Given

M. Altıntaş (✉) · M. S. Yaylalı · M. A. Topal
Qatar University, Doha, Qatar
e-mail: ma2010358@qu.edu.qa

M. S. Yaylalı
e-mail: my2201014@qu.edu.qa

M. A. Topal
e-mail: mt2112446@qu.edu.qa

A. Badran and A. Mishrif (eds.), *Shaping the Future of Development in the GCC*, The Political Economy of the Middle East,
https://doi.org/10.1007/978-981-96-7963-8_7

the widespread adoption and ongoing advancements of AI, it is nearly impracticable to avoid its influence. Therefore, it is crucial to examine people's attitudes and perception regarding this technology. Allport (1935) defined attitude as a cognitive or neurological state that is formed by past experiences and has a guiding or influential effect on an individual's reactions to all things and events that are connected to it. When someone's attitudes are referred to, it is meant to explain the behavior of this person. Attitudes encompass a multifaceted mixture of personality traits, beliefs, values, behaviors, and motivations (Pickens, 2005).

Accordingly, attitudes have a significant impact on individuals' willingness to accept and embrace new technologies, as well as the extent to which these tools become broadly adopted in society (Bergdahl et al., 2023). On the other hand, perception is referred as a cognitive process by which living organisms evaluate and arrange information from their senses in order to generate a coherent and significant understanding of the surrounding environment (Lindsay & Norman, 2014). In other words, when an individual is faced with a scenario or stimulus, the individual translates the stimuli into something that has meaning for them based on previous experiences (Pickens, 2005). In this study, attitude has been defined as gained knowledge, in a word, it is consciously a preference. Perception has been also defined as sensory information, in other word, it is unconsciously preference. Perceptions of AI exhibit significant diversity. There are concerns about the security of applications and programs that use AI. People are worried that AI may replace human workers and perhaps take control of human societies (Challen et al., 2019; Lichtenthaler, 2019).

Simultaneously, the potential of AI captivates individuals and provokes inquisitiveness. Gaining a deeper comprehension of diverse perspectives on AI can result in more effective deployment and utilization of these technologies. Moreover, studies have demonstrated that sentiments towards artificial intelligence diverge from the adoption of traditional technologies whose use is decided by people. In other words, unlike traditional technologies, Artificial Intelligence can be integrated and applied to individuals' everyday life without having their consents, mostly based on the decisions made by governments or large companies (Bergdahl et al., 2023; Kelly et al., 2023; Schepman & Rodway, 2020). Therefore, the end user does not consistently possess the option to select how to incorporate AI into their daily life, making the understanding of perception and attitudes of people even more important in this regard.

In the Gulf countries, artificial intelligence has been promoted as a means of expanding economic activities in an economy mostly reliant on oil income or investments. The anticipation of higher capital returns is one of the main reasons in support of Gulf countries' decision to invest a sizable portion of their domestic revenue in AI development. In Qatar, the Ministry of Communications and Information Technology established the Artificial Intelligence Committee in 2021. According to the ministry's TASMU program, the artificial intelligence industry in Qatar was anticipated to be worth US $31 million in 2022 and is projected to expand by 17.4% yearly to reach US $58.8 million in 2026 (QF, 2023). Analytical projections indicate that the application of AI technology and associated expenditures will boost the GDP of the region (Potesta, 2021). Similarly, AI has been recognized as a facilitator for achieving many long-term economic, social, human, and environmental policy objectives outlined in the Qatar National Vision (QNV) 2030, as noted by Badran (2021). Although the GCC countries have expressed a desire to utilize AI applications in various industries, there has been no previous study on the attitudes and perceptions of people towards AI in either the other GCC countries or Qatar. Existing literature predominantly focuses on the policies of governments and strategies of relevant companies regarding AI, leaving a critical overlook to the personal attitudes and perceptions. This shortage creates a critical gap for studies that explore AI's integration into society. Understanding individual perceptions within this context is important, as public opinion can significantly influence the successful adoption and implementation of AI technologies.

Therefore, this research aims to fill this gap by focusing on people's attitudes and perceptions of AI in Qatar, which is essential for developing more effective policies and strategies for AI integration that are aligned with public sentiment and understanding. Within this context, this study has four main objectives: First, it aims to determine the level of interest about AI among individuals in Qatar. Second, it intends to analyze how socio-cultural factors and educational background have impact on people's opinion towards AI. The third objective of the study is to explore how demographic variables such as age and gender shape general perception towards AI. Finally, this research aims to explore concerns and expectations of people in Qatar towards AI. Within these four specific goals, our research aims to establish a solid fieldwork that will contribute to the existing literature providing a comprehensive understanding of the people's perception of AI in Qatar. To achieve these objectives, this study will employ a quantitative research methodology using surveys, intending to grasp overall approach of the population in Qatar.

7.2 Literature Review

People's attitudes towards artificial intelligence vary widely. Researchers have examined the impact of demographic, personality, anxiety, and trust factors on views towards AI. There is considerable enthusiasm regarding the potential of AI to enhance the quality of life of the people, particularly in hazardous occupations that pose risks to human workers. However, there are concerns among individuals that AI may lead to job displacement, and they express apprehension about AI taking over decision-making from humans. The factors that impact people's perception and attitudes towards AI have been studied from different dimensions in literature. Multiple studies have consistently found that men exhibit a greater inclination towards embracing AI technology, as evidenced by their more favorable sentiments towards it (Park & Woo, 2022; Schepman & Rodway, 2020, 2023). Many scholarly works assert that a younger age is correlated with more favorable sentiments towards artificial intelligence. Additionally, having education or knowledge about AI can potentially change people's perceptions and attitudes towards AI. Those who are knowledgeable about technology and its developments may be more willing to accept AI usage compared to those who lack such knowledge (Gillespie et al., 2021; Schepman & Rodway, 2023; Zhang & Dafoe, 2019). In this regard, Kim and Lee (2023) found that among 1,677 middle school students in South Korea, those with AI education or programming experience showed significantly more positive attitudes towards AI. Also, they found that students who faced challenges due to socio-cultural factors also exhibited a more positive attitude towards AI if they had received AI instruction. This study suggests that knowledge and experience with AI can lead to willingness or acceptance to use AI, regardless of socio-cultural differences and challenges.

The existing literature also investigates specific characteristics that influence the adoption of artificial intelligence. Kelly et al. (2023) conducted a comprehensive analysis aimed at identifying the factors that influence the adoption of artificial intelligence. Study findings indicate that behavioral intention, willingness, and use of AI can be predicted by perceived usefulness, performance expectancy, and effort expectancy. Moreover, trust and attitudes are seen as equally significant factors in the development of user acceptance (Gillespie et al., 2021). Park and Woo (2022) examined the impact of psychological and technological aspects on the adoption of AI-based applications. The researchers found that specific psychological characteristics, such as intrinsic drive, self-assurance, willingness, and anticipated achievements, were associated with the acceptance and use of AI apps. In addition, the adoption of AI-based applications was found to be influenced by technological characteristics such as functionality, accessibility, technological complexity, and comparative advantage (Park & Woo, 2022).

Existing literature also investigates public opinion about the possible benefits and drawbacks of integrating AI into people's private and public lives. The global perspective is first analyzed in a media analysis study conducted by Fast and Horvitz (2017), who analyzed three decades (1986–2016) of New York Times articles to track the trajectory of public sentiment towards AI. It is observed that there has been a significant surge in the discourse surrounding artificial intelligence since 2009, with a consistent preference for optimism over pessimism. Furthermore, Neudert et al. (2020) conducted an international study aiming to identify people's attitudes and perceptions towards AI, utilizing a sample of 154,195 respondents in 142 countries. The research reveals three significant outcomes: First, China leads the world in enthusiasm and optimism on the application of AI to decision-making (91%). Second, public opinion on AI-driven automated decision-making varies between Eastern and Western regions, with 47% of North American and 49% of Latin American respondents viewing AI as potentially harmful, compared to just 25% in Southeast Asia and 11% in East Asia. Lastly, while 44% of professionals and 47% of business and government executives are enthusiastic about AI, only 35% of manufacturing and service industry workers believe it will benefit society significantly. Luca Liehner et al. (2023) investigated German citizens' views, beliefs, and levels of trust regarding artificial intelligence, revealing the fact that respondents generally saw AI as a tool that can function on its own, adapt, and support people in their day-to-day activities.

In a different study, Albarrán Lozano et al. (2021) analyzed the perception of artificial intelligence by individuals in Spain and the factors associated with it, utilizing binary logit and probit models to investigate Spanish attitudes towards AI and robotics. The literature demonstrates that many of the people follow a similar pattern in their attitudes towards AI. Positive attitudes towards AI stem from the belief that AI benefits society by performing hazardous jobs, providing general services that facilitate daily life, and raising expectations in healthcare and education. Conversely, negative attitudes towards AI arise from concerns about difficulties in adapting to innovations, the potential loss of control over AI, ethical implications, misuse, lack of trust, job losses, diminished face-to-face communication, and the impact of AI and robots on employment (Albarrán Lozano et al., 2021; Fast & Horvitz, 2017; Gao et al., 2020; Luca Liehner et al., 2023; Shin, 2021; Zhang et al., 2022).

The literature in the Gulf Cooperation Council (GCC) countries on artificial intelligence includes case studies and applications of AI projects in a variety of industries, including healthcare, banking, and economics (Ashfaq & Ayub, 2021; Mogielnicki, 2021; Sharfi, 2021; Sulthan et al., 2023). Even though these studies explain the recent development in AI in the GCC states within multiple sectors, still there is an important knowledge gap about people's general perception and attitudes towards artificial intelligence in these countries. This study aims to fill this gap in the literature by providing a field study, taking Qatar as a case for the research.

7.3 Methodology

7.3.1 *Survey Creating Procedure*

The survey questions in this study were prepared based on the relevant literature. Before the main study, two pilot studies were conducted to test the reliability and validity of the survey. The number of participants for the pilot study varied between 15 and 20.

7.3.2 *Data Collection Procedure*

The population of this study is the capital of Qatar, Doha. A random stratified sampling method was used in this study. The population was divided into different locations, and face-to-face surveys were conducted in public places within each location, such as malls, parks, shops, and cafes, to reach the people. Data was collected by the authors of the study between March 17, 2024, and May 17, 2024. To test the participation of individuals from each stratum in the survey, the professions of the relevant participants were asked in the survey. These professions are displayed in the word cloud below (Fig. 7.1).

Fig. 7.1 Professions of participants

Participants in the professions indicated in larger font sizes show a higher number of participants in that profession. Some participants chose not to disclose their professions in the survey. Still, the word cloud reveals that individuals from various sectors participated in the survey. Additionally, the survey included participants ranging in age range from 18 to 61, ensuring a wide demographic representation. Therefore, it can be said that the survey achieved the desired randomness. Finally, ethical clearance for this study was obtained from Qatar University. The relevant document is provided in Appendix A.

7.3.3 Sampling Procedure

According to the Planning and Statistics Authority of Qatar (2020), the population of Doha is 1,186,023. Figure 7.2 shows the age distribution of this population.

In this study, the following formula was used to calculate the sample size:

$$\text{Formula} > \text{n} = \frac{\text{N}.\text{t}^2.p.q}{d^2(N-1)+t^2p.q}$$

n = Sample size

N = Population size (1,186,023).

t = Z-score for the desired confidence level (1.96 for 95%).

p = Estimated proportion (0.5 for maximum variability).

q = Proportion of the population without the attribute (1 - p).

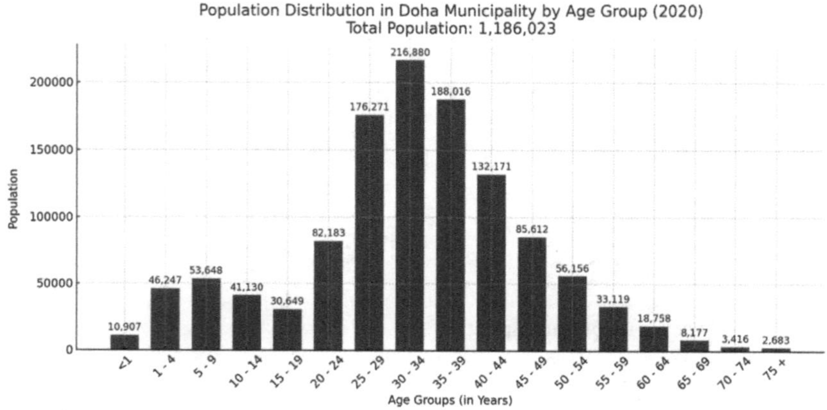

Fig. 7.2 Population distribution in Doha Municipality by age group

d = Margin of error (0.05)

$$= \frac{1,186,023.1,96^2.0,5.0,5}{0,05^2(1,186,023-1)+1,96^2.0,5.0,5} = 384,04$$

7.3.4 Analyzing Procedure

A total of 424 survey responses were collected, and 39 erroneous surveys were excluded. The relevant data were analyzed using the SPSS data processing program, and Fig. 7.3 was also created by using ChatGPT-4o. The data were analyzed using the Generalized Regression method.

7.4 Results

Table 7.1 presents the descriptive information of the sample. In the gender distribution, the numbers of males and females are nearly equal. The nationality distribution shows mostly non-Qatari individuals. In terms of education level, most participants have a university degree, followed by high school graduates, individuals with a master's degree, and those with a Ph.D. The age distribution indicates that the largest group is in the 18–24 age range, followed by the 31–40 and 25–30 age groups. The income distribution reveals that many participants earn

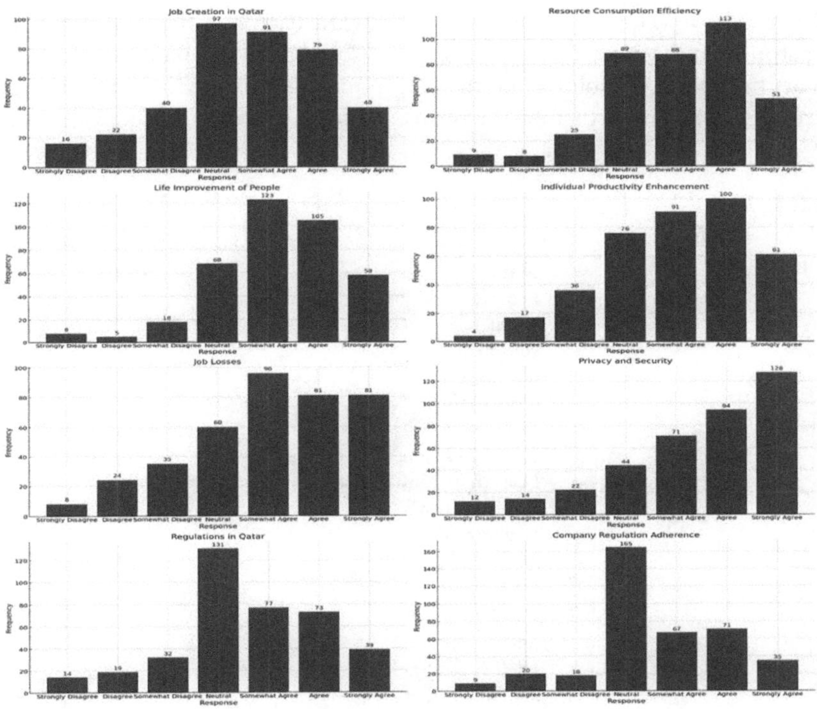

Fig. 7.3 Frequency distribution among items

less than 5,000 QAR. Regarding interest levels, most participants show medium interest.

This Fig. 7.3 presents descriptive information on the participants' responses to various factors. In job creation, most participants have positive opinions. Similarly, in resource consumption efficiency, life improvement, and individual productivity enhancement, most participants also have positive views. However, there are concerns regarding job losses, privacy, and security. For regulations in Qatar and company regulation adherence, participants' opinions are more neutral. Overall, the data indicates generally positive perceptions of some areas of concern.

Table 7.2 shows that the scale consists of 8 items with a Cronbach's Alpha value of 0.743, indicating good internal consistency. Additionally, factor analysis shows that items are most strongly associated with each factor. The first four items are associated with Factor 1, the next two with Factor 2, and the last two with Factor 3. Cronbach's Alpha value indicates that the scale is reliable, while the factor analysis reveals that the items are grouped into distinct sub-dimensions. Factor 1 is coded as Economic and

Table 7.1 Demographic information

Gender	
Male	187
Female	198
Total	385
Nationality	
Qatari	63
Non-Qatari	322
Total	385
Education Level	
Less than high school	3
High school	138
University	173
Master	53
Ph.D	18
Total	385
Age	
18–24	129
25–30	93
31–40	121
41–50	32
51–61	10
Total	385
Income (QAR)	
< 5,000	192
5,001–10,000	64
10,001–15,000	47
15,001–20,000	23
20,001–25,000	20
25,001–30,000	21
> 30,000	18
Total	385
Interest Level	
Low Interest	19
Medium Interest	221
High Interest	145
Total	385

Productivity Benefit, Factor 2 is coded as Risks and Security Concerns, and Factor 3 is coded as Regulation.

Table 7.3 presents the generalized regression analysis (GRA) results for three factors: Economic and Productivity Benefit, Risks and Security Concerns, and Regulation. For Economic and Productivity Benefit, only the interest level has a significant impact with a sig value of 0.001. Regarding Risks and Security Concerns, gender shows a significant impact with a sig value of 0.007, and nationality is also significant with a sig value of 0.043. Additionally, the interest level impacts this factor significantly, with a sig value of 0.017. For the Regulation factor, gender has a significant impact with a sig value of 0.037, and age is significant with a sig value of 0.033. These results highlight the significance of different demographic variables on the three identified factors.

Table 7.4 shows the significant variables in Table 7.2. In the Economic and Productivity Benefits factor, it is observed that as people's interest in artificial intelligence decreases, their attitudes become less positive. Specifically, participants with low interest in AI show significantly fewer positive attitudes compared to those with a high interest, as indicated by the negative B value of −1.187 and a significant p-value of 0.000. Participants with medium values also show a slightly less positive attitude, but this result is not statistically significant (B = −0.206, Sig. = 0.099).

In the Risks and Security Concerns Factor, males are significantly less concerned about risks and security compared to females. Qatari people

Table 7.2 Reliability and factor analysis

Reliability Analysis			
Scale	*Items*	*Cronbach's Alpha*	*Number of Items*
All Items	8	0.743	8
Factor Analysis			
Item	Factor 1	Factor 2	Factor 3
Job Creation in Qatar	0.767		
Resource Consumption Efficiency	0.797		
Life Improvement of People	0.804		
Individual Productivity Enhancement	0.854		
Job Losses		0.852	
Privacy and Security		0.836	
Regulation in Qatar			−0.912
Company Regulation Adherence			−0.870

Table 7.3 Model effects and Wald statistics

Test of Model Effects			
		Type III	
Source	Wald Square	df	Sig
Factor 1			
Intercept	528.16525	1	0
Gender	0.000746	1	0.978
Nationality	0.287413	1	0.591
Education Level	1.013414	4	0.907
Age	4.076892	4	0.395
Income	8.878516	6	0.180
Interest Level	17.014023	2	0,001
Factor 2			
Intercept	475.817	1	0
Gender	7.388	1	0.007
nationality	4.079	1	0.043
Education	4.143	4	0.387
Age	4.19	4	0.381
Income	3.547	6	0.738
Interest Level	8.205	2	0.017
Factor 3			
Intercept	479.434	1	0
Gender	4.36	1	0.037
Nationality	0.682	1	0.409
Education	6.97	4	0.137
Age	10.473	4	0.033
Income	5.104	6	0.531
Interest Level	0.491	2	0.782

are also less concerned about risks and security compared to non-Qataris, with a B value of −0.423 and a sig value of 0.043. Lastly, having low interest in AI significantly decreases concerns about risks and security, as indicated by a B value of −0.955 and a sig value of 0.004. These findings indicate that gender, nationality, and interest level in AI significantly influence concerns about risks and security. Specifically, males and Qataris exhibit lower concern levels, and those with low interest in AI are also less concerned about risks and security.

Under the factor Regulation, males are less likely to agree that there is sufficient regulation and oversight of AI in Qatar compared to females. This finding contradicts the second factor, Risks and Security Concerns, where males also showed less concern. Younger age groups (25–50) are

Table 7.4 Parameter estimates for factors

Parameter	*B*	*Std. Error*	*Sig*
Factor 1			
(Intercept)	4.564	0.4507	0.000
Low Interest	−1.187	0.2903	0.000
Medium Interest	−0.206	0.1248	0.099
High Interest	0[a]	–	
(Scale)	1.296b	0.0934	
Factor 2			
(Intercept)	5.907	0.5178	0
Male	−0.38	0.1399	0.007
Female	0[a]		
Qatari	−0.423	0.2093	0.043
Non-Qatari	0[a]		
Low Interest	−0.955	0.3335	0.004
Medium Interest	−0.126	0.1434	0.378
High Interest	0[a]		
(Scale)	1.711[b]	0.1233	
Factor 3			
(Intercept)	3.501	0.48	0
Male	−0.271	0.1297	0.037
Female	0[a]		
Age 18/24	0.633	0.461	0.17
Age 25/30	1.057	0.4517	0.019
Age 31/40	0.963	0.4377	0.028
Age 41/50	1.019	0.4702	0.03
Age 51/61	0[a]		
(Scale)	1.470[b]	0.106	

Dependent Variable: Economic and Productivity Impact, Risks and Security Concerns, and Regulation. (top/down)
Model: (Intercept), Gender, Nationality, Education, Age, Income, Interest Average
a. Set to zero because this parameter is redundant
b. Maximum likelihood estimate

more likely to agree that there is sufficient regulation and oversight of AI in Qatar, and that companies adhere to AI regulations, compared to the older age group (51–61). This indicates that older individuals are more likely to think that there is insufficient regulation or that regulations are not as comprehensive as perceived by younger individuals.

Looking at the open-ended questions, it is seen that the participants identified healthcare, education, and transportation as the primary sectors that would benefit from AI advancements. Their major concerns regarding AI include privacy, job losses due to automation, over-dependence on AI, and the lack of comprehensive regulations to govern AI use. They regard AI as a tool to increase efficiency and improve decision-making by automating routine tasks, allowing humans to focus on more creative and strategic work. While this can enhance the quality of work and time management, there are worries about over-dependence on AI, which could lead to a reduction in human skills and job opportunities. Additionally, it is generally observed that the business sectors expressed by the participants are closely related to their own professions. This alignment suggests that participants' perspectives on AI are significantly influenced by their direct experiences and professional contexts, underlining the importance of sector-specific approaches in AI policy and implementation.

7.5 Discussion

This research was conducted to investigate the attitudes and perceptions towards artificial intelligence (AI) in Qatar. The results show an optimistic view in general while containing some concerns about privacy and security, which correlates with the existing literature. The study specifically evaluated these attitudes and perception across three factors, including Economic and Productivity Benefits, Concerns and Negative Attitudes and Perceptions, and Regulatory Perspectives.

7.5.1 Attitudes and Perceptions Towards Economic and Productivity Benefits

On the one hand, the data indicates a positive approach towards resource consumption efficiency, individual production enhancement, and life improvement of people. The overwhelming majority of the participants have positive opinions, especially regarding the more efficient use of resources. This positive outlook aligns with the general trend in countries that develop natural resources, such as the Gulf countries, where AI is perceived as a catalyst for economic growth and diversity (Potesta, 2021). AI's potential to enhance productivity and economic efficiency is seen as a significant benefit contributing to the broader acceptance and positive perception of AI technologies in Qatar.

On the other hand, people's interest regarding artificial intelligence decreases, and their attitudes become less positive. This trend could be related to the level of exposure and familiarity with AI technologies. Individuals with higher interest in AI are likely more exposed to its applications, leading to a better understanding of its benefits and risks. This increased exposure may foster a more positive perspective, where the potential benefits of AI are weighed against the associated risks. Conversely, those with lower interest in AI might rely on generalized knowledge or perceptions, which could be influenced by negative portrayals of AI in media or lack of experience. This discrepancy in exposure and understanding could account for the variance in attitudes observed in this study. Specifically, participants with low interest in AI show significantly fewer positive attitudes compared to those with high interest. This finding is consistent with Albarrán Lozano et al.'s (2021) study on the perception of AI in Spain, which found that people have a negative attitude if they are not interested in scientific discoveries and technological developments.

7.5.2 Concerns and Negative Perceptions and Attitudes

Despite the general positive approach, participants expressed some concerns about privacy and security. This reflects AI-related concerns already existing in the literature (Challen et al., 2019; Lichtenthaler, 2019). The results clearly showed that non-Qatari people are much more concerned about AI. *This divergence in concerns between Qataris and non-Qataris could also be reflective of underlying socio-economic dynamics. For instance, non-Qatari residents, who make up a significant portion of the population, may have different job security and privacy concerns compared to citizens, given their potentially more precarious employment conditions and legal status. This sense of vulnerability might heighten their concerns about AI, particularly in areas related to surveillance and job displacement. Moreover, the variation in concerns based on gender and nationality points to the complex interplay between demographic factors and perceptions of AI.* This finding aligns with existing literature that suggests concepts such as citizenship influence people's approach to artificial intelligence (Kim & Lee, 2023; Schepman & Rodway, 2020). Non-Qatari residents may feel more vulnerable to the implications of AI, particularly regarding job security and privacy. Individuals with a low interest in AI also demonstrated less concern about risks and security. These findings indicate that gender, nationality, and interest level in AI significantly influence concerns about risks and security. Specifically, males and Qataris exhibit lower concern levels, and those with low interest in AI are similarly less concerned about these risks.

7.5.3 *Regulations*

The gender differences observed in attitudes towards AI regulation may be rooted in broader societal norms and expectations. Women, who are often more concerned about safety and security in various domains, might perceive AI regulation as a necessary safeguard to protect against potential harms. In this study, female participants are tended to show more positive approach compared to male, when it comes to regulation.

Furthermore, the age-related differences in trust towards AI, as highlighted in this study, indicate that younger individuals, who are often more adaptable to new technologies, are more likely to embrace AI with less skepticism. In contrast, older individuals, who may have grown up in an era with different technological paradigms, might view AI with more caution. This generational divide in trust underscores the importance of inclusive dialogue and education on AI, which addresses the specific concerns and expectations of different age groups.

7.6 Conclusion

This study aimed to investigate the attitudes and perceptions of people in Qatar towards artificial intelligence (AI). The findings reveal a generally optimistic view towards AI, particularly regarding its potential for economic growth and resource efficiency, which overlaps Qatar's national objectives of economic diversification and technological advancement. However, this optimism is tempered by significant concerns related to privacy and security, which mirror global worry about the integration of AI into various societal domains. The research underscores the importance of interest and familiarity with AI as key determinants of positive attitudes. Participants who demonstrated a higher level of interest in AI were more likely to recognize its benefits, suggesting that increased exposure to AI technologies can foster more favorable perceptions. Conversely, those with lower interests exhibited fewer positive attitudes, indicating a potential gap in understanding that could be addressed through targeted educational initiatives. Moreover, the study highlights the complex interplay of demographic factors such as nationality, gender, and age in shaping AI-related perceptions. Non-Qatari residents, for example, expressed more concerns about AI, high possibly due to their riskier socio-economic position in Qatar and vulnerability to job displacement and privacy problems. Similarly, gender differences were observed in attitudes towards AI regulation, with women showing greater support for regulatory measures, likely reflecting societal norms around safety and security. Age also emerged as a significant factor, with younger individuals exhibiting more trust in AI, while older participants approached AI with greater caution. These findings may have important implications for policymakers and stakeholders involved in the development and deployment of AI technologies in Qatar. To ensure the successful adoption of AI, it is crucial to address the public's concerns, particularly those related to privacy, security, and regulation. By creating a system that emphasizes both the benefits and risks of AI, policymakers can be built on an environment that supports innovation while be compatible with public opinion and societal values. Furthermore, the study puts forth that efforts to increase public interest and understanding of AI could play a vital role in enhancing positive attitudes towards AI technologies. This could be achieved through educational programs and public awareness events that engage various demographic groups, ensuring that the implementation of AI is both equitable and reflective of the diverse perspectives within Qatari society. In conclusion, while the future of AI in Qatar appears promising, its success will depend largely on the extent to which public concerns are addressed and how well the benefits of AI are communicated and realized. As Qatar continues to embrace AI as a cornerstone of its economic strategy, fostering public trust and ensuring that AI development is being compatible with societal values will be essential for achieving sustainable and inclusive growth.

7.6.1 Limitation of Study

Although the research included a diverse group of participants, the sample size of 385 may not fully capture the entire population's views in Qatar. The study was conducted in Doha, the capital of Qatar. This urban-centric focus may not represent the views of individuals living in rural or less developed areas of the country, potentially limiting the generalizability of the findings. The study focused on general attitudes and perceptions without examining deeply into specific applications of AI across different sectors. Future research could benefit from a more detailed analysis of attitudes towards AI in various contexts, such as healthcare, education, and finance.

References

Albarrán Lozano, I., Molina, J. M., & Gijón, C. (2021). Perception of artificial intelligence in Spain. *Telematics and Informatics, 63*, Article 101672. https://doi.org/10.1016/j.tele.2021.101672

Allport, G. W. (1935). Attitudes. In C. Murchison (Ed.), *Handbook of social psychology*. Clark University Press.

Ashfaq, M., & Ayub, U. (2021). Knowledge, attitude, and perceptions of financial industry employees towards AI in the GCC region. In E. Azar & A. N. Haddad (Eds.), *Artificial intelligence in the Gulf* (pp. 95–115). Springer Singapore. https://doi.org/10.1007/978-981-16-0771-4_6

Azar, E., & Haddad, A. N. (2021). An Introduction to AI in the GCC. In E. Azar & A. N. Haddad (Eds.), *Artificial Intelligence in the Gulf* (pp. 3–8). Springer Singapore. https://doi.org/10.1007/978-981-16-0771-4_1

Badran, A. (2021). Thoughts and reflections on the case of Qatar: Should artificial intelligence be regulated? In E. Azar & A. N. Haddad (Eds.), *Artificial intelligence in the Gulf* (pp. 69–92). Springer Singapore. https://doi.org/10.1007/978-981-16-0771-4_5

Bergdahl, J., Latikka, R., Celuch, M., Savolainen, I., Soares Mantere, E., Savela, N., & Oksanen, A. (2023). Self-determination and attitudes toward artificial intelligence: Cross-national and longitudinal perspectives. *Telematics and Informatics, 82*, Article 102013. https://doi.org/10.1016/j.tele.2023.102013

Challen, R., Denny, J., Pitt, M., Gompels, L., Edwards, T., & Tsaneva-Atanasova, K. (2019). Artificial intelligence, bias and clinical safety. *BMJ Quality & Safety, 28*(3), 231–237. https://doi.org/10.1136/bmjqs-2018-008370

Fast, E., & Horvitz, E. (2017). Long-term trends in the public perception of artificial intelligence. *Proceedings of the AAAI Conference on Artificial Intelligence, 31*(1). https://doi.org/10.1609/aaai.v31i1.10635

Gao, S., He, L., Chen, Y., Li, D., & Lai, K. (2020). Public perception of artificial intelligence in medical care: Content analysis of social media. *Journal of Medical Internet Research, 22*(7), Article e16649. https://doi.org/10.2196/16649

Gillespie, N., Lockey, S., & Curtis, C. (2021). *Trust in artificial Intelligence: A five country study*. The University of Queensland and KPMG. https://doi.org/10.14264/e34bfa3

Kelly, S., Kaye, S.-A., & Oviedo-Trespalacios, O. (2023). What factors contribute to the acceptance of artificial intelligence? *A Systematic Review. Telematics and Informatics, 77*, Article 101925. https://doi.org/10.1016/j.tele.2022.101925

Kim, S.-W., & Lee, Y. (2023). Investigation into the influence of socio-cultural factors on attitudes toward artificial intelligence. *Education and Information Technologies*. https://doi.org/10.1007/s10639-023-12172-y

Lichtenthaler, U. (2019). Extremes of acceptance: Employee attitudes toward artificial intelligence. *Journal of Business Strategy, 41*(5), 39–45. https://doi.org/10.1108/JBS-12-2018-0204

Lindsay, P. H., & Norman, D. A. (2014). *Human information processing: An introduction to psychology*. Elsevier Science.

Luca Liehner, G., Hick, A., Biermann, H., Brauner, P., & Ziefle, M. (2023). *Perceptions, attitudes and trust toward artificial intelligence—An assessment of the public opinion*. 14th International Conference on Applied Human Factors and Ergonomics (AHFE 2023). https://doi.org/10.54941/ahfe1003271

Mogielnicki, R. (2021). Free zones in Dubai: Accelerators for artificial intelligence in the Gulf. In E. Azar & A. N. Haddad (Eds.), *Artificial intelligence in the Gulf* (pp. 141–159). Springer Singapore. https://doi.org/10.1007/978-981-16-0771-4_8

Neudert, L.-M., Knuutila, A., & Howard, P. N. (2020). *Global attitudes towards AI, machine learning & automated decision making implications for involving artificial intelligence in public service and good governance*. University of Oxford. https://www.oii.ox.ac.uk/news-events/reports/global-attitudes-towards-ai-machine-learning-automated-decision-making-implications-for-involving-artificial-intelligence-in-public-service-and-good-governance

Park, J., & Woo, S. E. (2022). Who likes artificial intelligence? personality predictors of attitudes toward artificial intelligence. *The Journal of Psychology, 156*(1), 68–94. https://doi.org/10.1080/00223980.2021.2012109

Planning and Statistics Authority of Qatar. (2020). Qatar Census 2020. https://www.psa.gov.qa/en/statistics1/StatisticsSite/Census/Census2020/results/pages/result.aspx?rpttitle=p1_c1

Pickens, J. (2005). Attitudes and perceptions. *Organizational behavior in health care*.

Potesta, G. (2021). Sustainable development of Arabian Gulf cities: Is artificial intelligence conducive to equitable well-being for users? *The International Journal of Social Sustainability in Economic, Social, and Cultural Context*, *17*(2), 99–113. https://doi.org/10.18848/2325-1115/CGP/v17i02/99-113

QF. (2023). *Artificial intelligence: What do you know about the technology that will change the world?* https://www.qf.org.qa/stories/artificial-intelligence-what-do-you-know-about-the-technology-that-will

Schepman, A., & Rodway, P. (2020). Initial validation of the general attitudes towards Artificial Intelligence Scale. *Computers in Human Behavior Reports, 1*, Article 100014. https://doi.org/10.1016/j.chbr.2020.100014

Schepman, A., & Rodway, P. (2023). The General Attitudes towards Artificial Intelligence Scale (GAAIS): Confirmatory validation and associations with personality, corporate distrust, and general trust. *International Journal of Human-Computer Interaction, 39*(13), 2724–2741. https://doi.org/10.1080/10447318.2022.2085400

Sharfi, M. (2021). The GCC and global health diplomacy: The new drive towards artificial intelligence. In E. Azar & A. N. Haddad (Eds.), *Artificial intelligence in the Gulf* (pp. 117–139). Springer Singapore. https://doi.org/10.1007/978-981-16-0771-4_7

Shin, D. (2021). The effects of explainability and causability on perception, trust, and acceptance: Implications for explainable AI. *International Journal of Human-Computer Studies, 146*, Article 102551. https://doi.org/10.1016/j.ijhcs.2020.102551

Sulthan, N., AlGahtani, F., Mahjoub, M., Al-Surf, M., & Navas, S. (2023). Physician entrepreneurs and AI technology: An In-depth study of knowledge, competence, adoption, and sustainability in the GCC Region. *Emirati Journal of Business, Economics, & Social Studies, 2*(2), 28–38. https://doi.org/10.54878/9edwjx71

Zhang, B., & Dafoe, A. (2019). Artificial intelligence: American attitudes and trends. *SSRN Electronic Journal*. https://doi.org/10.2139/ssrn.3312874

Zhang, Z., Chen, Z., & Xu, L. (2022). Artificial intelligence and moral dilemmas: Perception of ethical decision-making in AI. *Journal of Experimental Social Psychology, 101*, Article 104327. https://doi.org/10.1016/j.jesp.2022.104327

CHAPTER 8

Ethics and the Implication of Artificial Intelligence for Decision-Making in the Defence Industry

Rafael Hernández de Santiago

8.1 Introduction

In a world not too distant from our own, a new era is beginning to unfold time heralded by a force known as Artificial Intelligence (AI). This remarkable technology is no longer a mere whisper in the corridors of academia; it is now a powerful driver of what historians will call the Fourth Industrial Revolution. As this new age dawns, AI promises to reshape the global landscape in ways never before imagined. Within the next decade, it is prophesied that AI will contribute an astonishing 40 percent to the world's Gross Domestic Product (GDP), a testament to its transformative power. But with great power comes not just opportunities, but challenges. The rapid advancements in AI bring with them a whirlwind of change that threatens to disrupt the very fabric of societies and economies.

R. H. de Santiago (✉)
GRC, Riyadh, Saudi Arabia
e-mail: rhernandezdesantiago@gmail.com

A. Badran and A. Mishrif (eds.), *Shaping the Future of Development in the GCC*, The Political Economy of the Middle East,
https://doi.org/10.1007/978-981-96-7963-8_8

From social interactions to government policies and economic systems, AI's influence is profound. Yet, this transformative force is not without its shadows. The advent of AI poses risks that are as significant as its benefits—risks of exclusion, discrimination, privacy breaches, loss of skills, and threats to the security of critical infrastructure. The interconnected web of the global economy means that these challenges are not confined to any one nation but are shared across the globe. In this moment of uncertainty, institutions find themselves at a crossroads. The journey ahead is one of developing new structures, policies, and relationships guided by ethical principles. The challenge is to navigate this uncharted territory with wisdom and foresight, balancing innovation with responsibility.

As the world enters this new technological era, the geopolitical landscape begins to shift. The global economy is no longer a unified entity but a mosaic of competing blocs. Firms and investors face a new reality where geopolitical considerations heavily influence decisions about resource allocation. This transformation is akin to a grand puzzle, with pieces shifting and realigning in ways that could alter the economic and political balance of power. Amidst this shifting terrain, there is an "elephant in the room" that could not be ignored: the need to reconcile the burgeoning data economy with fundamental values and human rights. It is a call to harmonize the rapid advances in technology with the ethical standards and societal norms that had long guided human progress.

As AI continues its relentless advance, it begins to weave itself into various sectors, with the defence industry being one of the most notable. The integration of AI into military operations promises a new era of enhanced decision-making and operational efficiency. Autonomous systems can execute tasks with precision and speed, transforming the nature of defence missions. Yet, with these advancements come a host of ethical considerations. The potential for AI to control autonomous weapons, conduct surveillance, and make critical decisions in conflict situations raises profound questions about morality and accountability. The very essence of warfare and security is being redefined, and the implications are vast and complex.

AI is emerging as a general-purpose technology, its influence spreading across diverse industries. However, history has shown that the path of technological innovation is fraught with pitfalls. The early 2000s dot-com bubble has demonstrated the dangers of unchecked enthusiasm, leading to significant failures and setbacks. As AI continues to evolve, there is a need for caution and thoughtful consideration to avoid repeating past mistakes. In this unfolding tale of AI, the stakes are high. The promise of a new technological age is intertwined with the responsibility to navigate its challenges with ethical integrity and foresight. The journey is just beginning, and how humanity chooses to steer this course will determine the future of both technology and society.

8.2 The Quest for Ethical AI: A Journey Through Time and Innovation

Imagine a grand quest, a journey through the realms of wisdom and technology, where the quest is not for gold or glory but for something far more elusive: ethical harmony in the age of Artificial Intelligence (AI). As our world embraces the dawn of this new technological era, the defence sector stands at a pivotal crossroads. Here, AI's formidable capabilities—like a double-edged sword—promise remarkable advancements but also raise profound ethical dilemmas.

In this unfolding saga, we find ourselves in need of a coalitional fellowship of diverse minds including policymakers, ethicists, technologists, and the general public. Together, they must forge a path that ensures AI in defence is not only powerful but also principled. This alliance must navigate a complex landscape of guidelines, regulations, and education, each player bringing unique strengths to the table to craft an ethical framework that can guide AI's development and deployment. To understand the quest for ethical AI, we must first journey back through the corridors of history, where different strands of ethical thought have woven the fabric of human morality. Ethics, the ancient art of understanding right and wrong, has long guided humanity in making choices that shape our world.

In ancient Greece, philosophers like Aristotle envisioned ethics as a quest for virtue and happiness. Aristotle's vision painted a world where the ultimate good was achieved through virtuous living, a life balanced by wisdom and character. Epicureanism, another ancient philosophy, suggested that happiness comes from the pursuit of pleasure and the avoidance of pain—a more hedonistic approach to the ethical quest. Further along our journey, we encounter the stoics, who championed virtue and self-discipline as the keys to true happiness. They taught that inner strength and resilience were the ultimate measures of a well-lived life. In contrast, Utilitarianism, a theory from the eighteenth century, shifted the focus to maximizing happiness for the greatest number, an idea that would later influence debates on AI's role in creating better outcomes for humanity.

Deontological ethics, as introduced by Immanuel Kant, offered a different perspective, emphasizing the importance of duty and adherence to moral rules, irrespective of the consequences. This approach raises poignant questions about the morality of AI systems in warfare—machines making decisions without human oversight. Virtue ethics, as further developed by philosophers like Alasdair MacIntyre, focused on the character of individuals, advocating for moral integrity in the creation and use of AI technologies. It calls for the virtues of courage, justice, and prudence to guide the development of AI systems.

8.2.1 Crafting the Ethical Blueprint

With these philosophical foundations as our guide, we embark on the task of building a robust ethical framework for AI in defence. This framework must be dynamic, encompassing principles that can adapt to the evolving landscape of technology while staying rooted in timeless values.

The first principle is Privacy and Data Protection. AI must respect the sanctity of individual privacy, guarding against misuse of personal data. This means individuals should retain control over their data, with clear consent required for any use or modification. Next, we have Accountability. Just as a knight is accountable for his actions, so too must those who design and implement AI systems be held accountable. Clear mechanisms must be placed to ensure that every decision made by an AI system can be traced back to responsible human agents. Safety and Security follow closely behind. AI systems must be shielded against cyber threats, safeguarding the well-being of both individuals and society at large. This involves not only preventing attacks but also having robust defences in place to respond effectively to any breaches. Transparency and Explainability are also crucial. Just as a map guides explorers through unknown lands, transparency in AI systems ensures that their algorithms, data sources, and decision-making processes are clear and understandable to all stakeholders. When AI makes decisions, individuals should be notified and able to understand how and why those decisions were made. The principle of Fairness ensures that AI systems minimize bias and operate inclusively, providing equitable outcomes for all. This involves designing systems that are free from discriminatory practices and actively managing risks associated with bias. Human Control of Technology emphasizes that despite AI's growing capabilities, humans must remain in charge. Automated decisions should always be reviewable, and individuals must have the option to override AI decisions if necessary. Professional Responsibility speaks to the importance of multistakeholder collaboration and maintaining the integrity of AI solutions. Developers, researchers, and policymakers must work together to ensure that AI technologies are accurate and ethically sound. Lastly, Promotion of Human Values underscores the importance of keeping AI human centric. AI should enhance human values and contribute positively to society, aligning with the core principles that guide our collective morality.

8.2.2 The Future of Ethical AI

As we move forward in this epic quest, the establishment of governance frameworks will be essential. These frameworks must incorporate these ethical principles into practical guidelines and policies, ensuring that AI's impact on defence and beyond is both beneficial and just. Countries and international organizations are already setting the stage for this new era, crafting models and frameworks that highlight these common ethical principles. From Australia to the United States, and from the European Commission to the World Economic Forum, the global community is engaged in shaping a future where AI advances are aligned with our deepest values and principles.

The path to ethical AI is a collaborative adventure. By drawing on historical wisdom and embracing innovative governance, humanity can ensure that AI serves as a force for good, guiding us through the complexities of the modern world with integrity and respect for our shared values.

8.3 Artificial Intelligence in the Defence Sector: A New Frontier in Warfare

8.3.1 The Shadows of Conflict

Imagine a world where artificial intelligence (AI) is no longer just a feature of your smartphone but a transformative force reshaping the very fabric of defence. By 2025, AI is poised to cross a pivotal threshold, blending with robotics and augmented reality to create a new era of military technology. This convergence promises a deeper, more immersive experience, fundamentally altering how wars are fought and won. In this evolving landscape, geopolitical shifts will cast long shadows over defence sectors. As political fragmentation influences trade and technology access, defence companies and investors will navigate a maze where geopolitical considerations increasingly dictate resource allocation. The defence industry's operational environment will be shaped by new political realities, where technology and power intermingle in complex ways.

8.3.2 *The Dual Edges of AI*

To grasp the full impact of AI on defence, we must explore its influence on some of humanity's most challenging aspects: war, conflict, and violence. Today, warfare extends beyond traditional battlefields into the digital realm, space, and the electromagnetic spectrum. This transformation demands a comprehensive understanding of how AI is redefining conflict and security. As private entities and cyber threats join state actors on the battlefield, the need to comprehend and manage AI's role in warfare becomes ever more urgent.

At the heart of this technological evolution lie pressing ethical dilemmas. AI's role in military decision-making raises fundamental questions about responsibility and transparency. Imagine AI systems making critical decisions in high-stakes scenarios. How do we ensure these systems act impartially and that their decisions are transparent and understandable to humans? The challenge is to design AI systems that are not only efficient but also accountable, maintaining human oversight even as technology advances.

Moreover, AI introduces significant concerns about privacy and human rights. Picture automated surveillance systems with the power to monitor individuals on a massive scale, potentially infringing on personal privacy without consent. The risk of AI systems being hacked or manipulated by malicious actors adds another layer of complexity, with serious implications for national security.

8.3.3 *The Ethical Labyrinth*

In the realm of cybersecurity, the distinction between prevention and response is crucial. Cybersecurity involves safeguarding digital systems from potential attacks through measures like firewalls and encryption. In contrast, cyber defence focuses on detecting and mitigating attacks that have bypassed these defences. Both aspects are vital for protecting electronic systems, networks, and data in today's digital age. Addressing these ethical and security challenges requires defence companies and governments to adopt robust policies and regulations. This includes establishing ethics committees to oversee AI development, ensuring adherence to international humanitarian law, and promoting transparency and accountability. Rigorous ethical reviews and safeguards must be integral to AI development and deployment to protect human rights and privacy.

On the global stage, initiatives such as NATO's strategic activities and China's ambitious plans for military modernization highlight the international dimension of AI in defence. NATO's efforts to understand AI's military impact and maintain technological superiority contrast with China's goal of achieving a fully automated and computerized military by 2027. In an era where military spending has surged to unprecedented levels, the influence of AI on arms innovation and security challenges is a topic of intense scrutiny. For nearly a decade, the United Nations has examined the risks posed by emerging technologies, particularly in relation to international humanitarian law (IHL) and human rights.

One of the central ethical issues is the principle of distinction, ensuring AI systems can differentiate between combatants and non-combatants. Current technology struggles with this due to limitations in algorithms, which lack the nuanced understanding of human judgment and emotions. This underscores the ongoing debate and development needed in autonomous weapons technology.

As AI continues to advance, it is essential that its integration into defence is guided by ethical principles from the start. Researchers, policymakers, and military leaders must collaborate to create guidelines that emphasize transparency, fairness, and accountability. By prioritizing these values, we can harness AI's potential to enhance defence while safeguarding human dignity and upholding the highest ethical standards.

https://www.ft.com/content/3744cad3-52ac-40d7-b97d-e085aec1a23e

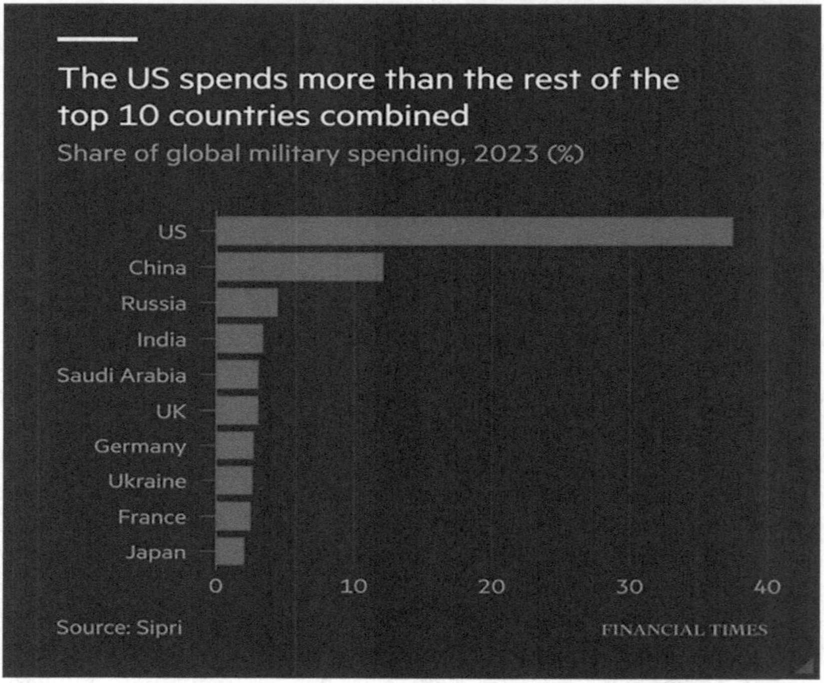

In 2023, the world witnessed a staggering surge in military spending, which skyrocketed by nearly 7% to a record \$2.4 trillion. This unprecedented increase marked the steepest annual rise in fifteen years, driven by rapid advancements in technology and a mounting arms race. As nations scramble to secure their strategic positions, the influence of cutting-edge technologies on weapons innovation and the resulting security challenges have become more pressing than ever. The United Nations, long a guardian of international peace and security, has been grappling with the implications of robotics and emerging technologies for almost a decade. The organization has been sounding alarm about the potential threats these advancements pose to global stability, compliance with international humanitarian law (IHL), and the protection of human rights.

8.3.4 *The Uncharted Territory of Autonomous Weapons*

One of the most contentious issues in this debate is the principle of distinction—the obligation to differentiate between combatants and civilians. Modern weapon systems, despite their sophistication, face significant challenges in this area. Current algorithms governing robotic weapons often fall short in making nuanced, context-sensitive judgments. Unlike humans, these systems lack the ability to perceive emotions or make ethical decisions based on complex scenarios. They can only operate within the limits of their predefined parameters, often resulting in crude or overly simplistic target identification. This means they might fail to recognize when a target has surrendered or when civilians are present, raising profound ethical concerns.

The debate over autonomous weapons systems is at the crossroads of technology, law, and ethics. The core issue is the intersection of technical capabilities and moral responsibilities. The development and deployment of these systems highlight a circular argument about the nature of autonomy and human control. While technology advances, the ethical questions remain deeply intertwined with technical limitations, fueling ongoing discussions about how to balance innovation with human dignity.

Accountability is a central ethical concern in the realm of AI-driven defence systems. The ability of autonomous machines to make decisions without direct human intervention raises critical questions about responsibility. Who is held accountable when an AI system makes a mistake or causes unintended harm? To address these concerns, it is essential to ensure transparency in the decision-making processes of AI systems. This involves implementing stringent oversight mechanisms and establishing clear guidelines to maintain accountability and uphold human rights in military operations.

8.3.5 *The Path Forward*

The ethical use of AI in warfare necessitates adherence to principles such as distinction, proportionality, and necessity. AI systems must be meticulously designed to distinguish between combatants and non-combatants, to avoid excessive force, and to ensure that military actions are strictly necessary to achieve legitimate objectives. These principles are particularly crucial in conflict zones like the Middle East, where the presence of irregular combatants and civilian populations complicates the application of these standards.

As we venture into this new era of AI in defence, it is imperative that ethical considerations guide every step of development. Researchers, developers, and policymakers must work together to establish robust guidelines and best practices that prioritize transparency, fairness, and accountability. Only through a collaborative and ethical approach can we navigate the complexities of AI in defence and ensure that technological advancements serve to enhance security without compromising human values.

8.4 The Cyber Frontier: AI in the Middle East's Digital Battleground

Around the globe, there is a rising, albeit gradual, effort to establish a legal framework to combat crimes involving AI. On July 18, 2023, the UN Security Council convened to discuss "Artificial Intelligence: Opportunities and Risks for International Peace and Security." UN Secretary-General Antonio Guterres proposed leveraging the 2018–2019 guidelines on lethal autonomous weapons alongside UNESCO's 2021 recommendations on AI ethics. He also endorsed the creation of a UN body dedicated to managing AI technology, highlighting the urgent need for a structured approach to these emerging threats.

The conversation about AI ethics is gaining traction across international and regional organizations, which are setting guidelines for member states. For example, the Gulf Cooperation Council, in partnership with the International Center for AI Research and Ethics in Saudi Arabia, hosted a workshop in January 2024 titled "Ethical Tools for Artificial Intelligence." This workshop, focused on AI ethics and UNESCO principles, underscored the growing importance of establishing ethical standards in AI development.

Yet, despite these advancements, universal support for AI ethics principles remains elusive. Countries like China, the UAE, and various EU members are making strides, but achieving global consensus is proving as challenging as the protracted negotiations that led to the United Nations Convention on the Law of the Sea. Addressing these global challenges demands concerted efforts from official bodies, civil society, and research centers to elevate awareness about the risks and foster a unified approach.

The distinction between cybersecurity and cyber defence remains crucial, though countries often face both simultaneously. Bahrain, for instance, countered approximately 8 million cyberattacks in 2023, including phishing and malware threats. The nation also grappled with a significant ransomware attack in 2017 that disrupted operations at Khalifa Bin Salman Port. This dual focus on prevention and response highlights the complex landscape of modern cyber threats. The critical issue of autonomous systems making decisions without human oversight was a focal point at the 2019 conference held by the Bahrain Center for Strategic, International, and Energy Studies (Derasat). While these systems can enhance efficiency, such as identifying smuggling risks or speeding up decision-making, they also introduce new risks. The use of underwater drones by Houthi militias to target ships is a stark example of how autonomous technologies can be weaponized.

For smaller and medium-sized countries, particularly those in the Gulf, discussing AI ethics in the military context is essential to offset their smaller armies. An international collaboration is necessary to set standards, akin to the U.S. partnership with five countries, including Bahrain, in 2024 to explore AI frameworks in military industries. The ongoing cyber warfare between Iran and Israel offers a vivid illustration of the stakes involved. Since October 7, 2023, there have been around 800 cyberattacks between the two nations. Iran is investing in technological education to bolster its cyber capabilities, while Israel has developed a cyber dome to defend against attacks. Additionally, Saudi Arabia's 2030 vision includes localizing military industries, marking a significant step in enhancing its defence infrastructure.

In the vast and turbulent arena of the Middle East, where conflicts have long defined the region's landscape, a new battlefield has emerged, cyberspace. Here, the clash extends beyond traditional warfare into the realm of digital skirmishes. In this new era, cyber threats have risen to prominence, posing significant risk to critical infrastructure, government institutions, military organizations, and media networks. This shift has highlighted the dual role of Artificial Intelligence (AI), which both fuels sophisticated cyberattacks and fortifies defences against them. Imagine a world where the digital realm is not just a backdrop but the very stage of conflict. In this environment, malicious actors wield AI to create increasingly sophisticated and personalized malware. This digital arsenal can bypass conventional defences, turning cyberspace into a treacherous battleground. Yet, AI's role isn't limited to offense; it's also a key player in cybersecurity. AI-driven systems, equipped with advanced intrusion detection capabilities, work tirelessly to shield against these sophisticated threats.

In this grey zone of cyber warfare, where traditional lines blur, we face a unified cyberspace, one that serves both defensive and offensive purposes. The four critical elements of a cyberattack: vulnerability, detection capability, exploitation, and operational capacity reveal the urgent need for an ethical framework in AI's deployment. The balance between security and ethics becomes paramount, emphasizing that AI, whether in defence or offense, carries profound ethical responsibilities. Consider the implications: AI systems designed for cybersecurity must integrate robust security measures to prevent exploitation. Meanwhile, AI's dual use in both detecting and launching cyberattacks raises ethical concerns, particularly regarding the boundaries of its application and the transparency of its decision-making processes.

8.4.1 The Middle Eastern AI Arms Race

In the Middle East, countries like Iran and Israel have harnessed AI to enhance their cyber capabilities. These nations have developed advanced tools for espionage, disrupting critical infrastructure, and gathering intelligence. However, with such power comes a host of ethical dilemmas. The use of AI in cyber warfare raises concerns about collateral damage and the challenge of accurately attributing attacks to their perpetrators. The region's response has been to bolster defensive measures with AI. Machine learning algorithms now play a critical role in real-time detection and mitigation of cyber threats, safeguarding national security and critical infrastructure. Yet, this reliance on AI brings its own set of ethical challenges. The balance between enhancing security and protecting privacy is delicate, with pre-emptive defence measures posing questions about their justification and scope.

As the ethical challenges of AI in defence grow, international collaboration becomes essential. Nations must unite to develop and enforce global norms and regulations governing AI's use in military operations. Treaties and agreements tailored to address the unique challenges posed by AI technologies in warfare are crucial for maintaining ethical standards. In the Middle East, where longstanding conflicts and political instability shape the landscape, the introduction of AI into defence operations could exacerbate existing tensions. Autonomous weapons systems, for example, may ignite an arms race, with nations racing to acquire advanced technologies to gain a strategic edge.

The deployment of AI in military operations carries significant implications for civilian populations. AI-driven surveillance and autonomous weapons systems could lead to increased civilian casualties and displacement if not carefully regulated. Adhering to international humanitarian law principles such as distinction and proportionality is essential to mitigate these risks. International treaties like the Geneva Conventions and the Convention on Certain Conventional Weapons (CCW) offer frameworks for the ethical use of AI in warfare. However, the rapid pace of AI advancement necessitates ongoing updates and adaptations to these legal instruments. At the national level, countries must establish comprehensive policies and doctrines to guide the ethical use of AI in defence. These guidelines should address accountability, transparency, and oversight, ensuring that AI systems are deployed in alignment with ethical principles and international standards. In the Middle East's complex and evolving cyber landscape, AI is both a tool and a challenge. As nations navigate this new frontier, the path forward must be guided by a commitment to ethical principles and international cooperation. By balancing innovation with responsibility, the region can harness AI's potential while safeguarding the values that define its future.

8.4.2 The Role of AI in Israeli Defence and Its Implications in the Conflict with Gaza

In the heart of the Middle East, where the echoes of conflict reverberate across borders, Israel's embrace of Artificial Intelligence (AI) has reshaped the landscape of defence. This advanced technology, a double-edged sword, serves to fortify national security while casting a spotlight on ethical dilemmas. Israel's defence strategy has always leaned heavily on technological superiority, and AI is now a cornerstone of this approach. The country's military operations are powered by AI innovations that transform modern warfare. Picture a battlefield where AI algorithms process enormous data streams from satellites, social media, and intercepted communications, weaving them into a tapestry of actionable intelligence. This capability allows the Israeli Defence Forces (IDF) to act with unprecedented precision, often neutralizing threats before they escalate into full-blown attacks.

One of the most compelling examples of AI's role is in Israel's unmanned aerial vehicles (UAVs), or drones. These drones, equipped with advanced AI, carry out both surveillance and targeted strikes against militant groups. They navigate the skies with minimal human intervention, their AI systems enhancing operational efficiency and accuracy. The evolution of autonomous weapons represents a significant shift in warfare, emphasizing how AI is pushing the boundaries of traditional combat. In the conflict with Gaza, AI's impact is vividly illustrated by Israel's Iron Dome defence system. This cutting-edge missile defence system leverages AI to identify, track, and intercept incoming rockets and missiles. Imagine the Iron Dome as a sentinel, distinguishing between projectiles that threaten populated areas and those that will land harmlessly. Its precision not only protects lives but also preserves the rhythm of daily life in Israeli communities.

Yet, the deployment of AI in such a high-stakes environment is fraught with controversy. The conflict with Gaza highlights a stark asymmetry: Israel's advanced technological capabilities vastly overshadow those of Hamas and other militant groups. This imbalance raises ethical questions about the use of AI and the potential for disproportionate harm to civilians in Gaza. The reliance on AI in military operations can lead to a loss of human oversight, where decisions made by algorithms might not fully account for the complexities of human life and suffering. Critics argue that as AI systems take on more decision-making roles, they risk eroding accountability. The prospect of autonomous systems making life-or-death decisions without human intervention is a chilling one. Moreover, the integration of AI can create a dehumanizing effect, reducing the brutal realities of war to mere data points and algorithms. This shift can desensitize decision-makers, making it easier to overlook the human cost of conflict.

For Israel, a leader in AI technology, addressing these ethical concerns is paramount. Ensuring that AI systems comply with international humanitarian law and incorporating robust oversight mechanisms are crucial steps in maintaining accountability. Transparency in AI operations and engaging in open dialogue with the international community will be essential for building trust and preventing misuse. AI has undeniably enhanced Israel's defence capabilities, offering significant advantages in intelligence, precision, and missile defence. However, as this powerful technology continues to evolve, its application in the conflict with Gaza demands a careful balance. The challenge lies in harnessing AI's potential while upholding ethical standards, a task that is as strategically necessary as it is morally imperative.

8.4.3 *AI in Counterterrorism: The Transformative Impact on Iran, Iraq, and Syria*

In the rugged landscapes of Iran, Iraq, and Syria, where shadows of conflict and terrorism loom large, Artificial Intelligence (AI) has emerged as a beacon of hope—and a source of profound ethical dilemmas. As these nations grapple with the menace of extremist groups, AI technologies have become indispensable in counterterrorism operations, offering a powerful edge in intelligence gathering and precision strikes. Yet, the very tools that disrupt terrorist networks also raise critical questions about the impact on civilian lives and the adherence to international humanitarian laws.

Imagine the vast deserts and urban sprawls of the Middle East, where terrorist cells weave their intricate webs of secrecy. In this high-stakes environment, AI operates as a vigilant guardian, tirelessly analyzing torrents of data from social media, intercepted communications, and satellite feeds. This sophisticated technology uncovers hidden links, tracks suspect movements, and anticipates threats with a level of accuracy that was once beyond human reach. For intelligence agencies in Iran, Iraq, and Syria, AI has become a vital ally in the fight against terrorism.

In the war-torn terrains of Iraq and Syria, AI-driven drones patrol the skies, their sensors casting a watchful eye over sprawling regions. These drones, equipped with cutting-edge AI, provide real-time intelligence that guides military and intelligence operations. The ability to survey vast areas continuously and to distinguish between genuine threats and benign activity has proven invaluable in targeting and neutralizing terrorist activities. AI's reach extends beyond the battlefield into the realm of online warfare. Extremist groups, adept at using the internet to spread their ideology and recruit new members, are countered by AI's capability to monitor and analyze digital content. Algorithms scour social media platforms, identifying extremist rhetoric and flagging potential threats. By detecting patterns of radicalization, AI helps pre-empt the spread of extremist ideologies and enables timely interventions to disrupt recruitment efforts.

In the cyber domain, Iran faces a unique set of challenges. The country's strategic emphasis on cyber warfare and espionage means that defending against digital threats is a top priority. Here, AI plays a crucial role in cybersecurity, detecting anomalies in network traffic and thwarting potential cyber-attacks with speed and precision that surpasses human capabilities. This digital fortification is essential for safeguarding critical infrastructure and maintaining the integrity of counterterrorism efforts.

However, the integration of AI into counterterrorism operations is not without its dark side. The use of autonomous systems in conflict zones raises ethical and legal concerns, especially when these systems make decisions with life-or-death consequences. Ensuring that AI applications comply with international humanitarian laws and respect human rights is imperative. Moreover, there is the risk of algorithmic bias, where AI systems might inadvertently target specific groups, leading to unintended harm and escalating tensions. It is essential to establish robust ethical guidelines and regulatory frameworks for AI in counterterrorism. International cooperation and transparency are critical to ensuring responsible and effective use of AI technologies. Nations must collaborate to share best practices, develop standards, and create frameworks that align with ethical principles and human rights.

In summary, AI has the potential to revolutionize counterterrorism efforts in Iran, Iraq, and Syria, enhancing intelligence capabilities, operational precision, and the fight against extremist propaganda. Yet, as we harness this powerful technology, we must tread carefully, balancing its advantages with a steadfast commitment to ethical standards and the protection of civilian lives. The challenge lies in leveraging AI's capabilities while upholding the values that define our humanity in the face of conflict.

8.4.4 The GCC and Saudi Arabia's Bold AI Journey

In the arid expanses of the Gulf Cooperation Council (GCC) region, a technological revolution is unfolding, with Artificial Intelligence (AI) leading the charge. Among these forward-thinking nations, Saudi Arabia is blazing a trail, harnessing AI to reshape its future, diversify its economy, and elevate its status as a global tech powerhouse. The GCC countries, driven by the potential of AI to transform their economies and societies, have embarked on ambitious journeys to embed AI into their national frameworks. This transformation is more than just a technological shift; it's a quest to redefine their futures. For Saudi Arabia, this means advancing towards the goals outlined in Vision 2030, the UAE's Centennial 2071, and Kuwait's Vision 2035—each a blueprint for leveraging AI to drive progress.

At the heart of Saudi Arabia's AI ambition is its Vision 2030, a landmark initiative aimed at reducing the kingdom's reliance on oil and fostering a dynamic, knowledge-based economy. Central to this vision is the National Strategy for Data and Artificial Intelligence (NSDAI), a roadmap designed to catapult Saudi Arabia into the top 15 AI nations globally by 2030. This strategy is focused on nurturing innovation, developing a skilled AI workforce, and creating an environment conducive to AI growth. The Saudi Data and Artificial Intelligence Authority (SDAIA) stands as a cornerstone of this effort. With initiatives like the National Center for Artificial Intelligence (NCAI) and the National Data Management Office (NDMO), SDAIA is at the helm of Saudi Arabia's AI revolution. These institutions are orchestrating the development of AI solutions across various sectors, driving the kingdom's technological advancement.

In the realm of defence, the GCC is leveraging AI to bolster its security and maintain stability in an era marked by rapid technological change. Saudi Arabia, in particular, is integrating AI into its defence strategy, aligning it with the broader Vision 2030 objectives to build a sophisticated defence infrastructure capable of meeting modern and future threats. A key element of Saudi Arabia's AI-driven defence strategy is the development of autonomous systems. Drones, equipped with AI, are becoming essential tools for surveillance, reconnaissance, and precision strikes. These AI-powered UAVs are not only extending the reach of Saudi Arabia's military capabilities but also enhancing operational efficiency while minimizing risks to human personnel.

Cybersecurity is another critical area where Saudi Arabia is making strides. As cyber threats evolve, the kingdom is investing in AI-driven defence capable of detecting and countering cyber-attacks in real time. AI systems are analyzing patterns, predicting vulnerabilities, and safeguarding critical infrastructure against sophisticated digital threats. Saudi Arabia's AI initiatives extend to intelligence analysis and decision-making. By processing vast amounts of data from sources like satellite imagery, social media, and intercepted communications, AI algorithms provide critical insights that inform strategic decisions. This capability enhances the speed and accuracy of intelligence operations, allowing for more effective responses to security challenges.

Border security and surveillance are also seeing significant improvements through AI. Advanced AI systems are deployed to monitor borders, detect unauthorized crossings, and prevent smuggling. These technologies are crucial for maintaining territorial integrity and ensuring the safety of citizens. In addition to aerial and cybersecurity advancements, AI is revolutionizing ground and naval operations. Autonomous vehicles, both on land and sea, are performing reconnaissance, logistics, and combat support roles. These AI-driven platforms offer tactical advantages and operational flexibility, reducing reliance on human-operated systems and enhancing military effectiveness.

The AI initiatives of the GCC and Saudi Arabia are reshaping the landscape of defence and security, positioning these nations as leaders in technological innovation. As they forge ahead with AI, it is essential to balance technological advancements with ethical considerations, ensuring that AI serves as a force for good in securing a prosperous and stable future for the region.

8.5 Crafting a Future for Ethical AI in Defence

In the evolving world of defence, where AI is increasingly pivotal, it's crucial to guide its development and deployment with ethical foresight. To navigate this complex terrain, several foundational steps can help ensure that AI serves as a force for good while upholding human values.

8.5.1 Forging International Norms

Imagine a global summit where leaders, diplomats, and experts gather to shape the future of AI in defence. The task at hand: to create a set of international norms and standards that will govern AI applications in military contexts. These norms would address critical issues such as the development of autonomous weapons, the ethical use of AI in surveillance, and responsible AI-driven decision-making processes. Picture the United Nations and the International Committee of the Red Cross as key architects in this endeavor, facilitating dialogues, forging agreements, and establishing guidelines that will steer nations towards ethical AI practices. This collective effort would ensure that AI's potential is harnessed responsibly on a global scale.

8.5.2 Establishing National AI Ethics Committees

Visualize a team of diverse experts coming together to form a National AI Ethics Committee. This team includes ethicists, legal scholars, military professionals, and civil society representatives. Their mission: to oversee the integration of AI technologies into the defence sector with an unwavering commitment to ethical standards. Their role involves reviewing AI projects for ethical compliance, offering guidance on best practices, and ensuring transparency and accountability in AI applications. Through their rigorous oversight, they would help create a robust framework that aligns AI developments with ethical principles and human rights.

8.5.3 Infusing AI Ethics into Education and Training

Envision a training program where future AI developers and military personnel engage in a curriculum designed to instill a strong ethical foundation. This education would encompass international humanitarian law, the ethical implications of AI technologies, and the necessity of transparency and accountability. By embedding these principles into their training from the outset, we can cultivate a generation of professionals who prioritize ethical considerations in their work. This approach would foster a culture of responsibility and ethical awareness within the defence sector, ensuring that AI technologies are developed and used in ways that respect human dignity and rights.

8.5.4 Championing Ethical AI Research

Picture a research landscape where funding agencies and institutions prioritize projects focused on the ethical dimensions of AI. Researchers are exploring how to create AI systems that are explainable, fair, and free from biases. They are investigating ways to address the limitations of AI technologies and ensure their equitable application. By supporting such research, we can integrate ethical considerations into every stage of AI development and deployment. This commitment to ethical AI research ensures that technological advancements are not only innovative but also aligned with fundamental values of fairness and justice.

Together, these recommendations create a roadmap for integrating AI into defence in a manner that is both innovative and ethical. By developing international norms, establishing national ethics committees, prioritizing ethics in education, and championing ethical research, we can navigate the complexities of AI in defence with integrity and foresight. As we embark on this journey, it is essential to balance technological advancement with a steadfast commitment to ethical principles, ensuring that AI serves as a positive force in shaping a secure and just future.

8.6 Conclusion: Navigating the Ethical Frontier of AI in Defence

In the vast and evolving landscape of modern defence, the integration of AI stands as both a beacon of promise and a harbinger of complex challenges. As AI technologies carve new paths in military operations, offering unprecedented enhancements in decision-making, efficiency, and accuracy, they simultaneously raise profound ethical concerns that demand our vigilant attention. Imagine a world where AI transforms the battlefield, where autonomous weapons systems, sophisticated surveillance technologies, and AI-driven decision support systems become integral to national security. These innovations promise to elevate military operations to new heights, providing capabilities previously unimaginable. Yet, this very potential underscores the necessity of embedding robust ethical frameworks into their development and deployment.

To manage this dual-edged frontier, we must forge comprehensive regulatory and policy frameworks that govern the use of AI in defence. Picture an international assembly where nations collaborate to establish norms and agreements, crafting guidelines that ensure AI technologies are employed responsibly. Envision national oversight bodies, empowered to enforce these standards, working together with ethicists and policymakers to safeguard ethical integrity. The establishment of such frameworks is essential to address the ethical quandaries associated with AI in defence, ensuring that technological advancements do not come at the expense of human rights and moral principles.

In regions like the Middle East, where ongoing conflicts and geopolitical complexities abound, the ethical implications of AI in defence are especially pressing. The deployment of AI in these tumultuous environments requires rigorous scrutiny to ensure adherence to international humanitarian law and the protection of civilian lives. Consider a scenario where international agreements and national policies are meticulously crafted to uphold accountability, transparency, and ethical deployment of AI technologies, even in the most challenging contexts.

Addressing these challenges calls for a collective effort from researchers, policymakers, military leaders, and ethicists. Visualize a dynamic team of diverse experts working together, blending their insights to create a culture of accountability and ethical responsibility. Through their collaboration, we can harness AI's potential to bolster national security while remaining steadfast in our commitment to ethical standards and human rights.

In the end, the journey towards integrating AI into defence is one of balancing innovation with ethics. As we chart this course, it is imperative to ensure that our strides in technological advancement are matched by a dedication to ethical principles. By prioritizing transparency, accountability, and the protection of human dignity, we can navigate the complex landscape of AI in defence, leveraging its benefits while upholding the highest standards of moral integrity.

References

Arquilla, J., & Ronfeldt, D. (1993). Cyberwar is coming! *Rand Corporation*. https://www.rand.org/pubs/reprints/RP223.html

Bentham, J. (1780). *An introduction to the principles of morals and legislation*. T. Payne.

Coeckelbergh, M. (2020). *AI ethics*. MIT Press.

Deeks, A., Lubell, N., & Murray, D. (2019). Machine learning, artificial intelligence, and the use of force by states. *Journal of National Security Law & Policy, 10*(1), 1.

De Haro, G., & Recuenco, J. G. (2022). *El pequeño libro de la filosofía estoica*. Alienta Ed.

Giles, K. (2016). *Handbook of Russian information warfare*. NATO Defence College. https://www.ndc.nato.int/download/downloads.php?icode=506

HBO. (2020). *The perfect weapon*. https://dk.hbonordic.com/movies/theperfect-weapon/1fl0ced-0133acb2763

Iniguez, S. (2023). *Philosophy Inc.: Applying wisdom to everyday management*. Palgrave Macmillan.

Jonsson, O. (2020). Putting modern war in perspective. In O. Jonsson (Ed.), *Modern warfare: New technologies and enduring concepts* (pp. 9–19). https://frivarld.se/bocker/modern-warfare-new-technologies-andenduring-concepts/

Kant, I. (1785). *Groundwork of the metaphysics of morals*. Harttnoch.

Kofman, M. (2016). Hybrid warfare and other dark arts. *War on the Rocks*. https://warontherocks.com/2016/03/russian-hybrid-warfare-and-other-dark-arts/

LaPointe, C., & Levin, P. L. (2016). Automated war: How to think about intelligent autonomous systems in the military. *Foreign Affairs*. https://www.foreignaffairs.com/articles/2016-09-05/automated-war

MacIntyre, A. (1981). *After virtue* (2nd ed.). University of Notre Dame Press.

McKinsey & Company. (2023). Notes from the AI frontier: Modeling the impact of AI on the world economy. https://www.mckinsey.com/featured-insights/artificial-intelligence/notes-from-the-ai-frontier-modeling-the-impact-of-ai-on-the-world-economy

Mill, J. S. (1863). *Utilitarianism*. Parker, Son, and Burne.

Netflix. (2020). *The great hack*. https://www.netflix.com/title/80117542

Netflix. (2020). *The social dilemma*. https://www.netflix.com/search?q=the%20social%20dilemma&jbv=8125

Pernik, P. (2018). The early days of cyberattacks: The cases of Estonia, Georgia, and Ukraine. In N. Popescu & S. Secreriu (Eds.), *Hacks, leaks, and disruptions: Russian cyber strategies* (pp. 53–64). EUISS. https://www.iss.europa.eu/sites/default/files/EUISSFiles/CP_148.pdf

Villas Olmeda, M., & Camacho Ibáñez, J. (2022). *Manual de ética aplicada en inteligencia artificial*. Anaya.

Vinci, A. (2020). The coming revolution in intelligence affairs: How artificial intelligence and autonomous systems will transform espionage. *Foreign Affairs*. https://www.foreignaffairs.com/articles/north-america/2020-08-31/coming-revolution-intelligence-affairs

World Economy Fracturing, Not Deglobalizing. (2023). *Chatham House*. https://www.chathamhouse.org/2023/02/world-economy-fracturing-not-deglobalizing?utm_source=linkedin.com&utm_medium=organic-social&utm_campaign=economy&utm_content=deglobalization

CHAPTER 9

The Role of Artificial Intelligence in Enhancing the Security and Defense Capabilities of the GCC States

Ashraf Mohamed Keshk

9.1 Introduction

This chapter aims to discuss the efforts of the Arab Gulf States in the use of artificial intelligence (AI) technologies in the security and military fields, especially over the past few years for three reasons. First, some Gulf States have already succeeded in employing AI in the field of security, albeit limited. Second, some critical infrastructure in the Arab Gulf countries have been attacked by drones from armed militias in neighboring countries, which the Arab Gulf States have identified as an enormous security challenge. Third, the Arab Gulf States have also started prioritizing the development of local military industries, which continue to evolve alongside advancements in military technology. The main idea of this chapter is to analyze how these countries use AI to address ongoing

A. M. Keshk (✉)
Bahrain Center for Strategic, International, and Energy Studies, Derasat, Awali, Bahrain
e-mail: akishk@derasat.org.bh

A. Badran and A. Mishrif (eds.), *Shaping the Future of Development in the GCC*, The Political Economy of the Middle East,
https://doi.org/10.1007/978-981-96-7963-8_9

security threats, given their location in a volatile region. The discussion will explore how AI is reshaping the concept of security and what this means for Gulf States, which are classified as small and medium-sized states facing significant security challenges. It will also assess their efforts in using AI to strengthen security and military capabilities, identify key challenges, and propose recommendations for maximizing AI's potential in these sectors.

9.2 Methodology

This paper employs a comparative analytical approach. It examines previous literature on the use of artificial intelligence in various sectors within Arab Gulf States, though studies specifically addressing security and military applications remain limited. Additionally, the paper compares the efforts of different Gulf States in these two fields to identify the most effective model, offering insights and lessons that could benefit other countries in the region.

9.3 Literature Review

In their study titled "Towards a Gulf Vision for Military Technological Challenges: An Analytical Study in Light of International Humanitarian Law," published in the University of Sharjah Journal of Legal Sciences (2023), Yusuf Salem Al-Zaabi and Wael Ahmed Alam discussed the importance of Gulf States employing technological advancements in the military field, particularly following the 2019 drone attacks on Saudi oil facilities. The study argues that the risks facing the Gulf States are not only security-related but also involve the difficulty of determining responsibility for the misuse of these technologies. The study proposes an international humanitarian legal framework to bind Gulf States when using such weapons. Meanwhile, Ahmed Majid, in his study titled "Artificial Intelligence in the United Arab Emirates," published by the Ministry of Economy (2018), focused on the factors explaining the UAE's interest in AI, most notably achieving leadership in various fields, especially in service sectors. The study highlights the UAE's emphasis on developing the education system to align with AI advancements and includes mechanisms for enhancing AI through increasing the efficiency of employees in government institutions and launching various AI projects. It also covers the UAE's AI Strategy for 2017.

Kholoud Al-Lenjawi's study titled "Artificial Intelligence Technology in Police Work in the United Arab Emirates," published by Naif Arab University for Security Sciences (2023), aimed to analyze and understand AI capabilities and behaviors in the security and technology sectors generally. The study explores the history and significance of AI technology in enhancing police operations in various UAE departments and examines the challenges faced by AI systems, alongside the experience of the UAE Ministry of Interior in AI technologies. As for Dr. Saad Muflih Al-Sowailih, in his study "The Role of AI Systems in Combating Electronic Rumors," published in the Arab Journal of Security Studies by Naif Arab University for Security Sciences (2023), proposed that rumors have become a form of fifth-generation warfare through social media platforms. He suggests combating them through machine learning, neural networks, algorithms, and information analysis, as well as developing security media agencies within security institutions.

Finally, the book "Military Technology in the Middle East," published by the Bahrain Center for Strategic, International, and Energy Studies (Derasat, 2019), includes a presentation of a conference organized by the center that year. It discussed several important issues for Gulf States, including the impact of military technology amidst current security challenges such as cyber terrorism conducted by non-state armed groups under the concept of "asymmetric warfare.“ These groups aim to target vital facilities in various countries. The book also discussed the global trend of integrating modern AI applications into military forces, developing combat simulation models using AI, and analyzing the requirements for localizing military technology.

This paper will analyze and discuss the impact of technological advancements on the security of Arab Gulf States. Traditionally, these states faced conventional threats such as border disputes that led to security crises, Iranian threats, and maritime security challenges. However, modern technology has intensified these threats, creating significant security challenges for the region. At the same time, Gulf States rely on advanced technology as part of their broader development strategies. This discussion also examines the current efforts of Gulf States in integrating AI into their security and military sectors, as well as the key challenges they face in this process.

While these studies provide significant academic background on this issue, none of them detail the extent of the Gulf States' success in employing AI technologies in the security and military fields amidst the impact of technological advancements on the concept of national security. This paper seeks to address this gap.

9.4 The Impact of Technological Advancements on National Security and Military Aspects

Technological advancements have significantly influenced the security and military landscape of Arab Gulf States. On the security front, the region hosts numerous global corporations and institutions, making it a prime target for cybercrime. The financial, oil, and military sectors are among the most vulnerable to cyberattacks. For instance, the UAE Cybersecurity Council, in collaboration with other national entities, successfully countered over 71 million cyberattacks from February 2023 to the third quarter of the same year. These attacks primarily targeted strategic sectors, including banking, finance, healthcare, and oil and gas.

Additionally, Kuwait, Saudi Arabia, and the UAE were the most targeted Gulf States between March 1, 2022, and February 28, 2023, with cyberattacks primarily affecting public administration, e-commerce, and information services. The most common cyber threats included ransomware, advanced persistent threats (APTs), and phishing attacks. These evolving cyber threats highlight the growing security challenges facing Gulf States as they continue to integrate technology into their critical sectors (Zaman & Ayyada, 2024).

Secondly, from the military field, the impact of the development of artificial intelligence technology on the work of armies must be taken into consideration, especially since the Gulf countries do not have large armies. This underscores the importance of drones, which are more suitable for the battlefield and act as a safety valve for deploying soldiers behind enemy lines. These drones can be equipped with advanced AI technologies to independently identify and respond to threats. Notably, the drones that Gulf countries are keen to purchase function mainly in intelligence, surveillance, and reconnaissance, contributing to improved battlefield awareness and meeting various military applications. On the regional level, the Gulf States face threats, particularly with Iran's keen investment in this field and its supply of such systems to non-state actors. (Abdel Wahab et al., 2018).

9.4.1 Security Threats Facing the Arab Gulf States Through the Misuse of Artificial Intelligence Technologies

If the AI revolution has transformed the concept of national security for states, this impact is even more pronounced for the Gulf countries, which are classified as small and medium-sized states. These countries exist in various regions of the world and face a security dilemma in how to achieve the concept of "balance of power" with their regional neighbors. While this concept is a requirement of national security for all countries, it is the essence of national security for small and medium-sized states. The balance of power in international politics is achieved "when no state or group of states in a certain area possesses enough power to dominate and force other states in that area to submit to its will." (Robinson, 2009).

Achieving this concept has been a concern for the Gulf Arab states throughout history. These states have adopted three options to achieve it. The first option is enhancing self-security, but this option has limitations, such as the inability of small states to continue buying weapons indefinitely and the challenge of establishing a large army due to the limited population. The second option is neutrality in regional crises, but neutrality does not last as long as regional parties do not respect it. The third option is regional and international alliances, but this option is also closely linked to the conditions and objectives of these alliances (Keshk, 2015).

While these are the options for small states, the remarkable development in military technology has added a new dilemma for these states. The issue is no longer just about self-armament, purchasing conventional weapons, or even establishing regional and international partnerships but also about the extent of technological advancement they possess. In other words, military technology has fundamentally changed not only the concept of balance of power but also concepts such as power, security, conflict, and wars. The Arab Gulf States have faced numerous threats related to modern technological threats, including but not limited to:

1. The cyberattack that targeted the computers of Saudi Aramco, the oil company in Saudi Arabia, on August 15, 2012, aimed to stop the flow of oil and gas to global markets. According to the official spokesperson for the Saudi Ministry of Foreign Affairs, Major General Mansour Al-Turki, "the cyberattack affected 30,000 computers in the company" and "an organized group from outside

the Kingdom was involved in the attack." (Al-Raya Newspaper Website, 2012)

2. The delivery of goods and containers at Khalifa Bin Salman Port in the Kingdom of Bahrain was disrupted for several days in June 2017. Goods were delivered manually due to APM Terminals, the port operator's IT systems, being hit by global ransomware attacks, which caused disruptions in many ports (Al-Bilad Newspaper Website, 2017). This is the only port in Bahrain and was established in 1962.
3. Two oil facilities in Abqaiq and Khurais, owned by Saudi Aramco, were targeted by drones on September 14, 2019. Although the Saudi Ministry of Interior's statement on the incident did not specify the source of the drones, the military spokesperson for the Houthi group said in a statement, "The Air Force carried out a large-scale operation with ten drones targeting the Abqaiq and Khurais refineries in eastern Saudi Arabia." Notably, this attack on Aramco was the second of its kind, as the Houthis had carried out an attack a month earlier, causing a fire at an Aramco gas facility in the Shaybah field in southeast Saudi Arabia without causing injuries (Agence France-Presse Website, 2019). Regarding the impact of this attack, Saudi Oil Minister Abdulaziz bin Salman said, "The strikes reduced the Kingdom's crude oil production by 5.7 million barrels per day, equivalent to half of the Kingdom's oil production." (BBC Arabic Website, 2019)
4. On January 17, 2022, drones targeted the new construction area at Abu Dhabi Airport and the Abu Dhabi National Oil Company (ADNOC) in the United Arab Emirates, resulting in the deaths of three people and injuries to six. The fire at the company was controlled, and the attack did not affect flight operations at the airport. The Houthi group confirmed they were behind the attack (Al Arabiya Website, 2020).
5. On September 25, 2023, the Bahrain Defence Force announced that Houthi drones targeted the Bahraini Task Force positions stationed in the southern border area of Saudi Arabia, resulting in the death of two soldiers and the injury of several others (Bahrain News Agency, 2023). Notably, by September 29 of the same year, the number of Bahraini casualties had risen to four (Russian News Agency Website, 2023).

These five incidents reflect three observations:

1. Utilization of Modern Technology in Conflicts: The effectiveness of traditional military capabilities has been rendered obsolete, necessitating a re-evaluation of the means employed in warfare.
2. Misuse of Technology: The targeting of critical infrastructure in Gulf countries, such as oil companies and airports, highlights the potential impact on the national security of these states.
3. Confrontation Between States and Non-State Actors: Non-state actors have gained the ability to leverage modern technology to threaten the security of states in unprecedented ways.

9.5 Efforts of Gulf Countries to Employ Artificial Intelligence in the Field of Security

The Gulf countries' interest in employing artificial intelligence in security fields is based on three main foundations. Firstly, the Gulf countries possess an advanced digital infrastructure, ranking highly in electronic performance metrics. Secondly, digital transformation plays a crucial role in achieving sustainable development goals in the Gulf. For example, in a statement, Bahrain's Minister of Sustainable Development, Mrs. Noor bint Ali Al Khulaif, said, "Bahrain's initiatives and support for the digital economy align with the Economic Vision 2030, achieving sustainable development goals.“ (Bahrain News Agency, 2024) Thirdly, the Gulf countries have achieved advanced positions in international cybersecurity indicators. This was highlighted by Jasem Al-Budaiwi, Secretary-General of the GCC, during the second ministerial meeting of the GCC Cybersecurity Committee on November 9, 2023 (Gulf Cooperation Council, 2023).

The Gulf countries have managed to employ artificial intelligence in the security field, even if to a limited extent. In the United Arab Emirates, AI has been used to reduce road accidents and during the COVID-19 pandemic to collect digital information, which enhanced the efficiency of preventive and security measures (Ihsan, 2022). Additionally, AI has been employed to simulate terrorist attacks and train security personnel to make collective decisions in response to these attacks. Smart police cars equipped with modern technologies and cameras attached to military uniforms are also in use. These technologies have led to the analysis of large amounts of data, facial recognition, and data processing, which have increased the effectiveness of security agencies (Al-Lenjawi, 2023). The added value of using these technologies is that the UAE, like other Gulf countries, hosts a large number of expatriate workers, and thus AI technologies contribute to the collection and accuracy of evidence and facilitate the arrest of suspects.

Despite its importance, the more significant development is the issuance of the "Charter for the Development and Use of Artificial Intelligence" by the UAE government in July 2024. The preamble of this charter states that it aligns with the goals of the UAE's Artificial Intelligence Strategy. The charter includes 12 principles: strengthening human–machine ties, safety, algorithmic bias, data privacy, transparency, human oversight, governance and accountability, technological excellence, human commitment, peaceful coexistence with AI for an inclusive future, promoting AI awareness for an inclusive future adherence to regulations, and commitment to treaties and applicable laws (UAE Government, 2024). There is no doubt that the issuance of this charter reflects the UAE government's recognition of the importance of regulating the uses of this modern technological revolution in a way that aligns with achieving the country's developmental goals while ensuring societal security.

In Saudi Arabia, the General Authority of Civil Aviation has adopted AI security screening technology for operational use in the Kingdom's airports after signing a partnership contract with Smiths Detection Group Ltd a global leader in the application, management, and manufacture of world-class security technologies for aviation, ports, borders, and military sectors. The use of this technology has enhanced operational efficiency in the Kingdom's airports, accelerating screening processes with high efficiency, providing additional security control over baggage flow, and boosting civil aviation capabilities. It encourages innovation in civil aviation, enhances security quality, and reduces human interaction. AI technologies were also employed in managing the 2023 Hajj pilgrimage, ensuring the smooth and easy movement of pilgrims between holy sites through the Guest of God Service Program, one of the Saudi Vision 2030 programs aimed at transforming the Hajj experience. This program increased the accuracy of monitoring security phenomena at pilgrimage sites, developed proactive security plans for crowd management, and transmitted data to decision-makers in the operations and control Centre for appropriate decision-making (Saudi Ministry of Interior website, 2023).

In Oman, there is a keen interest in employing artificial intelligence in epidemic and disaster management. In July 2022, Sultan Qaboos University organized an international forum with participation from academics and experts from 25 countries. The forum focused on employing AI in remote sensing for managing epidemics and natural disasters, in collaboration with several regional and global academic institutions and entities. The significance of the conference lies in its timing, following the COVID-19 pandemic and the impact of cyclones on Oman due to climate change. The recommendations resulting from the conference are undoubtedly valuable for the Sultanate in facing these challenges, especially since Sultan Qaboos University has a remote sensing research center. This center focuses on research in the field, coordinates between relevant government entities, and provides technical support and advice for disaster prediction (Al-Ashoul, 2022).

As for Qatar, it has a strategy for AI in various fields, including security. This strategy encompasses two main areas. The first is food security, a priority where AI technologies can be used in food, water, and energy sectors by leveraging experiences from countries like the Netherlands in vertical farming. This involves implementing plans that include the use of water and fertilizers to increase production while being environmentally friendly. Additionally, AI technologies are employed to implement emergency plans to secure food supplies during regional disturbances and threats. The second area is cybersecurity threats. AI technologies can be used to prepare warnings about cybersecurity threats through local solutions. Additionally, AI can monitor signals on modern social media platforms to predict future security events (Hamad Bin Khalifa University, 2019).

In Kuwait, there is significant interest in digital transformation with the goal of achieving a "Smart Kuwait." Fahad Al-Shula, the Minister of State for Municipal Affairs and Minister of State for Communications, stated that "Kuwait has been able to establish fruitful and effective partnerships with global information companies and local companies to accelerate the transition to a digital economy." This statement followed the signing of an agreement with Google Cloud in this field, which Kuwaiti officials describe as bringing security, economic, and political benefits to the country (Jassim, 2023).

In the Kingdom of Bahrain, an AI Academy has been established at Bahrain Polytechnic (Bahrain, n.d.), and the Sheikh Nasser Center for Research and Development in AI plays a crucial role in enhancing AI utilization efforts in various fields. Bahrain also hosts numerous AI conferences. On the legislative side, the Shura Council passed the first legislation aimed at regulating AI on April 29, 2024. The law aims to "regulate the use of AI technologies to achieve public interest and prevent misuse, such as manipulation, alteration, or falsification of images, data, and political statements, avoiding misinformation, defamation, and political, social, and economic crises." It includes various penalties for misuse of technology (Al-Ayam, 2024).

Despite the importance of these efforts, they do not reflect a unified comprehensive strategic vision for the Gulf countries. For example, the GCC has not issued a unified law like the EU's Artificial Intelligence Act of May 2024. Strategic integration among Gulf countries in this field is essential, given various integration projects like electronic linkage, as these countries are part of the GCC. The use of AI in security varies according to each country's priorities. Saudi Arabia focuses on airport security and Hajj crowd management, while other countries employ these technologies differently. Moreover, there are no announced plans from Gulf countries regarding AI use in security, and there is still a heavy reliance on international partnerships compared to local companies' efforts. There is also a gap among Gulf countries in establishing AI institutions or enacting related legislation.

In November 2024, the Gulf Cooperation Council (GCC) launched the "Gulf Cybersecurity Strategy" during the Ministerial Committee for Cybersecurity meeting in Doha. While limited details about the strategy have been disclosed, it is known to include a platform for sharing cyber threat intelligence among GCC countries and joint cybersecurity exercises. During the opening remarks of the meeting, Eng. Abdulrahman bin Ali Al-Farahid Al-Maliki, President of Qatar's National Cybersecurity Agency, highlighted that the greatest challenge lies in balancing AI technologies to serve the best interests of states and institutions. He emphasized that this can be achieved by identifying and addressing risks while strengthening cooperation at both regional and international levels (Al-Awsat, 2024).

9.6 Critical Analysis: Gulf Countries' Use of AI in the Military

The unique nature of Gulf States, regional dynamics, and evolving security threats necessitate the adoption of AI in the military. As small states, Gulf countries cannot build large armies, making advanced technology essential. Regionally, Iran, Turkey, and Israel have advanced AI use in military sectors. In terms of the concept of security threats, non-state groups have been able to acquire technological techniques and use them in a harmful manner to target vital installations in the Arab Gulf states, which means the emergence of new rules of war based on the quality of weapons, not their quantity. Therefore, the question is, have the Gulf States been able to employ these technologies in the military field?

The answer to this question is closely related to the Gulf countries' ability to develop military industries, as the Gulf countries have relied on importing weapons from abroad over the past decades. According to the 2023 report from the Stockholm International Peace Research Institute (SIPRI), Saudi Arabia ranked first in the Middle East and fifth globally in military spending, with an increase of 4.3% to approximately $75.8 billion. The UAE exported $28.1 million worth of weapons in 2022. Kuwait ranked third with military expenditures of $7.8 billion, 4.9% of GDP. Oman ranked fourth in the Arab world with military expenditures of $5.9 billion, 5.4% of GDP. Qatar's arms imports increased by 396% from 2019 to 2023 compared to the previous four years, with the United States being Qatar's largest arms supplier at 45% (SIPRI, 2024).

This is why there have not been significant efforts to localize these industries due to factors not related to the Gulf countries themselves, including the dominance of American companies in the global arms market. The United States is home to 12 out of the top 25 best arms manufacturing companies in the world (Dudley, 2020). Additionally, challenges to military manufacturing in the Gulf were summarized by Major General Pilot Ishaq Al-Balushi, Head of the Executive Directorate for Industries and Development of Defense Capabilities at the Ministry of Defense of the UAE, at the Middle East Military Technology Conference in Bahrain, October 29–30, 2019. He stated that, despite the goal of developing local military industries to acquire modern technologies, profit, improve the skills of armed forces personnel, and build and strengthen capacities with allies, the delay in starting local military manufacturing in the region is due to the need for a strong defense industry infrastructure, funding issues, legislative framework, and the inability of local producers to export military industries outside their countries in the presence of market monopolies (Derasat, 2019). Additionally, the economic feasibility between spending on local military manufacturing, which also requires allocating large budgets to cover scientific and logistical requirements of such manufacturing, and the impact of technological development on the feasibility of local manufacturing itself.

Despite the previous efforts, there have been attempts by the Gulf countries, although limited, to develop military industries, with some targeting the use of artificial intelligence in the military sector. For example, in the Kingdom of Bahrain, Royal Decree No. 23 of 2022 was issued to establish the Military Institution for the Development of Warfare Industries in the Bahrain Defence Force. The decree includes seven articles aimed at enhancing the kingdom's self-defense capabilities. Notably, Articles Two and Three stand out among the provisions. Article Two states that "The Military Institution for the Development of Warfare Industries aims to establish and organize war industry activities within the Bahrain Defence Force, including designing, developing, and modifying defense and security systems using modern technology." Article Three stipulates that "The Military Institution for the Development of Warfare Industries may establish factories for weapons, ammunition, and military equipment, manufacture modern technologies, and trade in them, as well as license any related economic activities within the Kingdom of Bahrain." (Bahrain News Agency, 2022).

In addition to Bahrain's efforts to learn from the experiences of other countries by organizing conferences on military technology, including artificial intelligence, the Bahrain Center for Strategic, International, and Energy Studies "Derasat" organized the Military Technology Conference in the Middle East on October 29–30, in conjunction with the Second Bahrain International Defence Exhibition. The conference included several sessions: a forward-looking view of military technology, cybersecurity strategies, the impact of artificial intelligence development on armed forces, developing models for future combat simulations, and the future of defense procurement in the Middle East: procurement strategy and local production. Additionally, the Royal Bahraini Air Force hosted the 5th Manama Air Power Symposium on November 12, 2024, with the participation of senior air force officials from the United States and European countries. During the event, Major General Sheikh Hamad bin Abdullah Al Khalifa, Commander of the Royal Bahraini Air Force, emphasized that modernizing defense doctrine is essential to address emerging threats. He highlighted the importance of advanced technologies, including AI, in military decision-making. He further stated that the advancement of military aircraft, such as the F-16 Block 70, significantly strengthens the armed forces in Bahrain and the broader Gulf region. (Bahrain News Agency, 2024).

On a global level, Bahrain was selected during an international conference in the United States in March 2024, along with Canada, Portugal, Austria, and the United States, to be part of a working group led by the United States. This group will engage in a year-long international effort to explore frameworks for using artificial intelligence in military industries, in addition to incorporating artificial intelligence into the military partnership between Bahrain and the United States. In an interview with Al-Watan newspaper on October 19, 2022, General Michael Kurilla, Commander of the U.S. Central Command, confirmed that "significant progress has been made with the Royal Bahraini Navy in integrating artificial intelligence systems and unmanned systems into U.S. Fifth Fleet operations through the establishment of Task Force 59. A variety of advanced unmanned surface ships, aerial platforms, and artificial intelligence systems are being used alongside regional forces, including the Kingdom of Bahrain." He noted that the United States has "a fleet of 100 unmanned surface and subsurface vessels operating in the Arabian Gulf through an interconnected network of sensors." (Sabri, 2022).

In the United Arab Emirates, one of the foundations for leveraging this technology is local military manufacturing efforts. In 2014, 16 small companies were integrated into the Emirates Defence Industries Company (EDIC), which is the largest weapons manufacturer in the UAE. This is complemented by specialized educational institutions and legislative frameworks. In the military sector, Gulf States have increasingly integrated AI into defense capabilities. For example, in 2023, the UAE's Tawazun Council and the U.S.-based L3Harris Defense Systems established BAZ (Intelligence Software Center), a specialized hub for machine learning and AI development for the UAE Armed Forces. The center aims to enhance cyber defense capabilities in the region and explore future applications in robotics. Additionally, EDGE Group, the UAE's national defense conglomerate, introduced 14 new defense products in 2023, including 11 autonomous systems such as drones and smart weapons. In January 2024, EDGE's subsidiary, Milrem Robotics, a European leader in autonomous systems, secured a contract to supply the UAE Ministry of

Defense with 20 tracked combat vehicles and 40 unmanned ground vehicles. EDGE described this deal as the largest combat robotics program of its kind globally. (Nasr, 2025).

In Kuwait, international partnerships in this field, particularly with the United States, are of great importance. On August 31, 2023, Paul Dean, Principal Deputy Assistant Secretary of State for the Bureau of Arms Control, Verification, and Compliance, visited Kuwait and held significant meetings with Kuwaiti government officials regarding the possibility of joining the international effort for responsible AI use in the military, especially in the weapons sector. In this regard, Jim Holtsnider, Chargé d'Affaires at the U.S. Embassy in Kuwait, said, "Kuwait is a key partner for the United States in artificial intelligence, particularly in the weapons field," and added, "One of the concerns that prompted the United States to engage in discussions with Kuwait on this matter is the scenario of terrorist groups breaching AI technology. (Al-Jarida, 2023).

In Oman, a significant development was the establishment of the Oman Munition Production Company in May 2018. The company aims to meet the needs of the Sultan's Armed Forces and the military and security agencies in the Sultanate for light ammunition. It is directly funded by the Sultanate's military and security funds, with an estimated capital of approximately $200 million. The company produces light ammunition in calibers of 5.56 mm, 7.62 mm, and 9 mm, with a production capacity of 750,000 rounds daily and about 250 million rounds annually (Al-Ittihad, 2019). In Qatar, Barzan Holding plays a significant role in the efforts to localize military technology. The company is wholly owned by the Qatari Ministry of Defence and focuses on three main areas: first, investing in defense technology both domestically and internationally; second, supporting the Qatari Ministry of Defence; and third, building local defense capabilities. The company has signed a cooperation agreement with the Saudi Arabian Military Industries (SAMI), which includes several provisions such as joint investment in security and defense sectors (Al-Zayani, 2024).

In Saudi Arabia, the kingdom's strategy for employing artificial intelligence in the military sector is linked to plans for localizing military industries. In 2017, the kingdom announced a strategy to localize 50% of military industries by 2030. To implement this vision, the Public Investment Fund of Saudi Arabia announced the establishment of a new national military industries company in 2017, known as the Saudi Arabian Military Industries (SAMI), which is a key component of the Vision

2030 initiative in defense. During the second World Defence Exhibition held in Riyadh from February 4–8, 2024, the Governor of the General Authority for Military Industries, Engineer Ahmed Al-Ohali, noted that "the Kingdom has already begun to reap the benefits of its strategy to develop military industrial capabilities, with the localization percentage rising from 4% to 13.6% by the end of 2022." He added, "The number of establishments permits and licenses reached 477, covering 265 companies operating in the military industries sector, in addition to announcing 74 investment opportunities for localizing supply chains." (Keshk, 2024).

9.7 The UAE Experience and Lessons for Other Gulf States

Among Gulf Arab states, the UAE stands out as a pioneering model in integrating AI into security and defense. Its approach offers several key lessons for other Gulf nations:

- The UAE understood early on that AI is not just a technological issue but a fundamental element of national power. As a result, it took significant steps to build the necessary infrastructure and institutions, including the UAE National AI Strategy 2031, the appointment of a Minister of AI in 2017, the establishment of Mohamed bin Zayed University of AI in 2019, and the introduction of the UAE AI Development and Usage Charter in July 2024.
- AI is projected to play a major role in the UAE's economy, prompting the government to invest heavily in education and research to prepare graduates for AI-related jobs. (Ibrahim, 2023)
- The UAE aims to be a world leader in AI and has allocated massive funding to AI research. In February 2025, it announced an investment of €30–50 billion to establish Europe's largest AI data center in France.
- The UAE has strategically linked AI to national security, as seen in the establishment of G42 in 2018, chaired by Sheikh Tahnoun bin Zayed Al Nahyan, Dubai's Deputy Ruler and National Security Advisor. The company focuses on AI infrastructure, big data analytics, and cloud computing, serving both the public and private sectors.

- Despite its small size, the UAE has leveraged AI, economic diversification, and advanced technologies to enhance its political, military, and economic influence in the region. Its rapid development and modernization have played a key role in strengthening its regional and global standing. (Nasr, 2025)

9.8 Challenges Facing Gulf Countries in Employing Artificial Intelligence in Security and Defense

1. The absence of sufficient legislation regarding the uses of artificial intelligence and investment in it represents a significant issue, as it would ensure protection for the private sector, especially considering the importance of funding in this field (Al-Asoomi, 2024).
2. There is a gap between threats and the use of AI to address them; this includes for example, maritime security threats. These threats are no longer limited to traditional issues such as piracy and the threat of blocking sea lanes but now involve non-state actors using technology to threaten maritime security in unprecedented ways. On February 19, 2024, Houthi rebels in Yemen launched an attack on ships in the Red Sea using an unmanned underwater vehicle for the first time. This attack was thwarted by U.S. forces present in the region (Al Arabiya Net, 2024).
3. Despite the Importance of International Partnerships for GCC countries in enhancing their technological capabilities, the localization of military technology still faces three challenges identified by Ahmed Al-Ohali, Governor of the General Authority for Military Industries in Saudi Arabia. The first challenge is the difficulty of long-term planning amidst the global technological race in military industries. The second challenge is acquiring the modern military technologies needed to develop local military industries. The third challenge is developing Saudi human resources capable of managing these industries. (Al-Fayfi, 2022).
4. The lack of comprehensive plans or strategies regarding the deployment of artificial intelligence technologies in the military sector through integrated national strategies means that reliance is still on external contracts with leading international companies in this field, or organizing conferences (Keshk, 2023).

5. The challenge of research and innovation is that the reality of education and skills in Gulf countries still does not meet the needs of these countries concerning the utilization of these technologies. Therefore, there should be a focus on educational programs centered around AI technology and ways to achieve cybersecurity, especially in developing national capabilities capable of addressing a comprehensive cyberattack on vital facilities in the Arab Gulf countries. Additionally, there is a need for research in the field of developing modern weapon manufacturing. Gulf countries still need to localize these industries, which is a goal that can only be achieved by localizing military research itself (Bayawi, 2024).

9.9 Conclusion and Recommendations

Arab Gulf countries face significant security risks due to technological advancements and the misuse of these technologies to threaten their critical infrastructure by non-state actors. Additionally, regional competition for acquiring such technologies has diminished the advantage of Gulf countries as the highest arms purchasers in the world and the Middle East. Technological developments have also challenged traditional concepts of Gulf security, such as balance of power and deterrence. Despite Gulf countries' efforts to employ AI in security, progress remains uneven depending on each country's priorities. Some have plans in place, while others have limited capabilities in this area. In the military domain, the use of AI by Gulf countries remains constrained by challenges in localizing military industries due to global arms market monopolies and structural issues related to the inability to localize military production. Furthermore, Gulf countries continue to view AI technologies from a technical rather than a security perspective. This indicates that Gulf countries have a long way to go in leveraging AI for security and military purposes. Addressing these challenges requires the development of comprehensive, realistic, and actionable strategies.

Based on the aforementioned, the most significant recommendations for Arab Gulf countries regarding the deployment of AI in security and defense are as follows:

1. Seek scholarships from major countries with distinguished AI experience in engineering and mathematics. This will enable Gulf countries to build a skilled workforce capable of handling advanced generations of AI.
2. Formulate comprehensive national strategies for AI that go beyond technical aspects and focus on security and military dimensions. These strategies should include security concepts, opportunities, challenges, and approaches for both the short and long term.
3. As Gulf countries continue to rely on importing weapons, the focus should be on military technology within these acquisitions. Purchase agreements should include clauses for the long-term localization of technology.
4. Facilitate the exchange of expertise between Gulf countries in the use of AI for security and military purposes. Since Gulf countries face similar security threats and are part of a regional organization, the GCC, establishing a coordinating body in this field could be beneficial.
5. Given the vulnerability of vital infrastructure to drone attacks, including airports and oil and civil facilities, there is a need to secure these facilities using AI technologies.

References

Abdel Wehab, S., Al-Ghaitani, I., Yahia, S., & Khalifa, E. (Eds.). (2018). *Opportunities and threats of artificial intelligence in the next decade*. Accessed May 23, 2024. https://futureuae.com/media/AI_e1c8632a-07ce-466e-a55f-a24de3daf190.pdf.

Abdul Majid, W. (2024). *Military use of artificial intelligence: Where to?* February 14. Accessed May 23, 2024. https://www.alarabiya.net/politics/2024/02/15/%D8%A7%D9%84%D8%A7%D8%B3%D8%AA%D8%AE%D8%AF%D8%A7%D9%85-%D8%A7%D9%84%D8%B9%D8%B3%D9%83%D8%B1%D9%8A-%D9%84%D9%84%D8%B0%D9%83%D8%A7%D8%A1-%D8%A7%D9%84%D8%A7%D8%B5%D8%B7%D9%86%D8%A7%D8%B9%D9%8A-%D8%A7%D9%84%D9%89.

Abu Mansour, H. Y. (2020). *Artificial intelligence and its security dimensions*. October 1. Accessed May 17, 2024. https://spp.nauss.edu.sa/index.php/spp/article/view/23.

Agence France-Presse. (2019). *Saudi Arabia: Houthi rebels claim drone attacks on two Aramco oil facilities*. September 14. Accessed May 17, 2024. https://www.france24.com/ar/20190914-%D8%AD%D8%B1%D9%8A%D9%82-%D8%B4%D8%B1%D9%83%D8%A9-%D8%A3%D8%B1%D8%A7%D9%85%D9%83%D9%88-%D8%A7%D9%84%D8%B3%D8%B9%D9%88%D8%AF%D9%8A%D8%A9-%D8%B7%D8%A7%D8%A6%D8%B1%D8%A7%D8%AA-%D9%85%D8%B3%D9%8A%D8%B1%D8%A9-%D8%AF%D8%B1%D9%8A%D8%A9.

Al Arabiya Net. (2024). *Details of American strikes against underwater drones used by the Houthis for the first time to target ships*. Accessed May 24, 2024. https://www.alarabiya.net/arab-and-world/yemen/2024/02/19/%D8%AA%D9%81%D8%A7%D8%B5%D9%8A%D9%84-%D8%B6%D8%B1%D8%A8%D8%A7%D8%AA-%D8%A3%D9%85%D9%8A%D8%B1%D9%83%D9%8A%D8%A9-%D8%B6%D9%8A%D8%AF-%D9%85%D8%B3%D9%8A%D8%B1%D8%A9-%D8%AA%D8%AD%D8%AA-%D8%A7%D9%84%D9%85%D8%A7%D8%A1.

Al Arabiya. (2020). *Abu Dhabi: 3 deaths and 6 injuries in fuel tank explosion*. January 17. Accessed May 17, 2024. https://www.alarabiya.net/arab-and-world/gulf/2022/01/17/%D8%B4%D8%B1%D8%B7%D8%A9-%D8%A3%D8%A8%D9%88-%D8%B8%D8%A8%D9%8A-%D8%A7%D9%86%D9%81%D8%AC%D8%A7%D8%B1-%D9%81%D9%8A-3-%D8%B5%D9%87%D8%A7%D8%B1%D9%8A%D8%AC-%D9%84%D9%84%D9%85%D8%AD%D8%B1%D9%88%D9%82%D8%A7%D8%AA.

Al-Ashoul, I. (2022). *Employing artificial intelligence in managing pandemics and disasters: An academic discussion at Sultan Qaboos University*. July 7. Accessed May 23, 2024. https://www.al-fanarmedia.org/ar/2022/07/%D8%AA%D9%88%D8%B8%D9%8A%D9%81-%D8%A7%D9%84%D8%B0%D9%83%D8%A7%D8%A1-%D8%A7%D9%84%D8%A7%D8%B5%D8%B7%D9%86%D8%A7%D8%B9%D9%8A-%D9%81%D9%8A-%D8%A5%D8%AF%D8%A7%D8%B1%D8%A9-%D8%A7%D9%84%D8%A3%D9%88%D8%A8.

Al-Assoumi, M. (2024). *The Gulf and the challenges of artificial intelligence*. *Al-Ittihad*. https://www.aletihad.ae/opinion/4474059/%D8%A7%D9%84%D8%AE%D9%84%D9%8A%D8%AC-%D9%88%D8%AA%D8%AD%D8%AF%D9%8A%D8%A7%D8%AA-%D8%A7%D9%84%D8%B0%D9%83%D8%A7%D8%A1-%D8%A7%D9%84%D8%A7%D8%B5%D8%B7%D9%86%D8%A7%D8%B9%D9%8A.

Al-Ayam. (2024). *Shura Council approves first law regulating artificial intelligence use and refers it to the government*. April 29. Accessed May 24, 2024. https://www.alayam.com/alayam/local/1053441/News.html#:~:text=%D9%88%D9%8A%D9%87%D8%AF%D9%81%20%D8%A7%D9%84%D9%82%D8%A7%D9%86%D9%88%D9%86%20%D8%A5%D9%84%D9%89%20%D8%AA%D9%86%D8%B8%D9%8A%D9%85%20%D8%A7%D8%B3%D8%AA%D8%AE%D8%AF%D8%A7%D9%85,%D9%88%D8%AD%D8%AF.

Al-Bilad. (2017). *Ransomware virus disrupts delivery of goods at Khalifa Port*. June 30. Accessed May 25, 2024. https://www.albiladpress.com/news/2017/3181/finance/434236.html.

Al-Fayfi, Z. (2022). *The Top 3 Challenges Facing Saudi Military Manufacturing*" July 18. Accessed May 24, 2024. https://www.independentarabia.com/node/352801/%D8%B3%D9%8A%D8%A7%D8%B3%D8%A9/%D8%AD%D9%88%D8%A7%D8%B1%D8%A7%D8%AA/%D8%A3%D8%A8%D8%B1%D8%B2-3-%D8%AA%D8%AD%D8%AF%D9%8A%D8%A7%D8%AA-%D8%AA%D9%88%D8%A7%D8%AC%D9%87-%D8%A7%D9%84%D8%AA%D8%B5%D9%86%D9%8A%D8%B9-%D8%A7%D9%لافتراضي%.

Alhurra. (2024). *5 countries leading global efforts to achieve "safer military artificial intelligence"*. Alhurra. https://www.alhurra.com/arabic-and-international/2024/03/29/5-%D8%AF%D9%88%D9%84-%D8%AA%D9%82%D9%88%D8%AF-%D8%A7%D9%84%D8%AC%D9%87%D9%88%D8%AF-%D8%A7%D9%84%D8%B9%D8%A7%D9%84%D9%85%D9%8A%D8%A9-%D9%84%D9%84%D9%88%D8%B5%D9%88%D9%84-%D8%B0%D9%83%D8%A7%D8%A1

Al-Ittihad. (2019). *Omani Ammunition Production: Local industry according to the latest technologies and standards*. https://www.aletihad.ae/article/11436/2019/%C2%AB%D8%A7%D9%84%D8%B9%D9%85%D8%A7%D9%86%D9%8A%D8%A9-%D9%84%D8%A5%D9%86%D8%AA%D8%A7%D8%AC-%D8%A7%D9%84%D8%B0%D8%AE%D8%A7%D8%A6%D8%B1%C2%BB-%D8%B5%D9%86%D8%A7%D8%B9%D8%A9-%D9%85%D8%AD%D9%84%D9%8A%D8%A9-%D9%88%D9%81%D9%82-%D8%A3%D8%AD%D8%AF%D8%AB-%D8%A7%D9%84%D8%AA%D9%82%D9%86%D9%8A%D8%A7%D8%AA-%D9%88%D8%A7%D9%84%D9%85%D8%B9%D8%A7%D9%8A%D9%8A%D8%B1.

Al-Jarida. (2023). *Paul Dean: Kuwait is a strong partner in developing military artificial intelligence applications. Al-Jarida*. https://www.aljarida.com/article/36905.

Al-Lenjawi, Khulood Mohammed. (2023). *Artificial intelligence technology in police work in the United Arab Emirates*. August 19. Accessed May 23, 2024. https://www.droitetentreprise.com/%D8%AA%D9%82%D9%86%D9%8A%D8%A9-%D8%A7%D9%84%D8%B0%D9%83%D8%A7%D8%A1-%D8%A7%D9%84%D8%A7%D8%B5%D8%B7%D9%86%D8%A7%D8%B9%D9%8A-%D9%81%D9%8A-%D8%A7%D9%84%D8%B9%D9%85%D9%84-%D8%A7%D9%84%D8%B4%D8%B1%D8%B7%D9%8A-%D9%81%D9%8A-%D8%AF%D9%88%D9%84%D8%A9-%D8%A7%D9%84%D8%A5%D9%85%D8%A7%D8%B1%D8%A7%D8%AA-%D8%A7%D9%84%D8%B9%D8%B1%D8%A8%D9%8A%D8%A9-%D8%A7%D9%84%D9%85%D8%AA%D8%AD%D8%AF%D8%A9.

Al-Raya Newspaper. (2012). *30,000 Devices disrupted in Aramco network breach*. December 10. Accessed May 16, 2024. https://www.raya.com/2012/12/10/%D8%AA%D8%B9%D8%B7%D9%84-30-%D8%A3%D9%84%D9%81-%D8%AC%D9%87%D8%A7%D8%B2-%D9%81%D9%8A-%D8%A7%D8%AE%D8%AA%D8%B1%D8%A7%D9%82-%D8%B4%D8%A8%D9%83%D8%A9-%D8%A3%D8%B1%D8%A7%D9%85%D9%83%D9%88.

Al-Zayani, Mosaed. (2024). *CEO of Barzan Holdings: We aim to localize and attract defense industries in Qatar*. https://aawsat.com/%D8%A7%D9%84%D8%A7%D9%82%D8%AA%D8%B5%D8%A7%D8%AF/4842261-%D8%A7%D9%84%D8%B1%D8%A6%D9%8A%D8%B3-%D8%A7%D9%84%D8%AA%D9%86%D9%81%D9%8A%D8%B2%D9%8A-%D9%84%D9%80%D8%A8%D8%B1%D8%B2%D9%86-%D8%A7%D9%84%D9%82%D8%A7%D8%A8%D8%B6%D8%A9-%D9%86%.

Asharq Al-Awsat. (2024). *GCC announces cybersecurity strategy*. https://aawsat.com/.../5077718-إعلان-استراتيجية-خليجية-للأمن-السيبراني..

Bahrain Center for Strategic, International, and Energy Studies. (2019). *Military technology in the Middle East*. Bahrain Center for Strategic, International, and Energy Studies.

Bahrain News Agency. (2022). *His Majesty the King issues royal decree to establish a military institution for the development of war production in the Bahrain Defense Force*. July 3. Accessed May 21, 2024. https://www.bna.bh/en/HMKingestablishesMilitaryInstitutionfortheDevelopmentofWarfareIndustriesatBDF.aspx?cms=q8FmFJgiscL2fwIzON1%2BDn3lLnDrle62orgjtBRrm7w%3D.

Bahrain News Agency. (2023). *Bahrain Defense Force mourns a number of its brave personnel*. September 25. Accessed May 17, 2024. https://www.bna.bh/.aspx?cms=q8FmFJgiscL2fwIzON1%2BDkAR19QcnBkEF5Q4gBJvJLQ%3D.

Bahrain News Agency. (2024). *Minister of Sustainable Development: Commitment to digital transformation supporting sustainable development goals*. February 4. Accessed May 25, 2024. https://www.bna.bh/.aspx?cms=q8FmFJgiscL2fwIzON1%2BDmpz3VrKy2H7VhcLO9sA%2B%2Fw%3D.

Bahrain News Agency. (2024). *Participants in the Manama Air Power Symposium emphasize the importance of keeping up with rapid technological advances and AI applications in air forces*. Retrieved from https://2cm.es/VAuW.

Bayawi, J. (2024). *Artificial Intelligence in the Arab Gulf: 'Transformations and Aspirations'*. May 11. Accessed May 24, 2024. https://elbadilabc-ar.dz/2024/05/11/%D8%A7%D9%84%D8%B0%D9%83%D8%A7%D8%A1-%D8%A7%D9%84%D8%A7%D8%B5%D8%B7%D9%86%D8%A7%D8%B9%D9%8A-%D9%81%D9%8A-%D8%A7%D9%84%D8%AE%D9%84%D9%8A%D8%AC-%D8%A7%D9%84%D8%B9%D8%B1%D8%A8%D9%8A-%D8%AA%D8%AD%D9%88/#:~:text=%D8%A7%D9%84.

BBC Arabic. (2019). *Attack on Abqaiq and Khurais: Saudi oil production cut in half after drone attacks*. September 14. Accessed May 17, 2024. https://www.bbc.com/arabic/middleeast-4969944.

Dudley, D. (2020). *Middle East starts to make a name for itself as a seller, not just a buyer, of arms*. December 8. Accessed May 17, 2024. https://www.forbes.com/sites/dominicdudley/2020/12/08/middle-east-starts-to-make-a-name-for-itself-as-a-seller-not-just-a-buyer-of-arms/.

Government of Bahrain. (n.d.). *Artificial intelligence*. Accessed May 21, 2024. https://www.bahrain.bh/wps/portal/ar/BNP/AboutTheKingdom/EmergingTechnologies/atkdetails/!ut/p/z1/jZJPU8IwEMW_Sjj0SrYgf8ZblXFAGVGxiLkwadmmwZAtIYDDpzeMJxgFcnuZ39vdvCwXfMqFlVutpNdkpQn6U7Rn8aAF_e49QP_5pQftUb_baXTumqNJk38cA_F7CvA6GSRvo4deDDcxF9f44Z-TwHX-M4A4X.

Gulf Cooperation Council. (2023). *Secretary-General of the GCC: The Council's countries have advanced positions in international cybersecurity indicators*. November 9. Accessed May 25, 2024. https://www.gcc-sg.org/ar-sa/MediaCenter/NewsCooperation/News/Pages/news2023-11-9-3.aspx.

Hamad Bin Khalifa University, Ministry of Communications and Transportation. (n.d.). *Qatar National Artificial Intelligence Strategy*. Accessed May 19, 2024. https://qcai-blog.qcri.org/wp-content/uploads/2020/04/QCRI-Artificial-Intelligence-Strategy-2019-AR.pdf.

Ibrahim, H. T. (2023). *AI in the UAE: A Leading Experience in the Arab World.*, *10*(2), 97–98.

Ihsan, B. A. (2022). *The importance of artificial intelligence in crisis management during COVID-19: The case of the United Arab Emirates*. December 31. Accessed May 19, 2024. file:///C:/Users/dcrsamk/Downloads/%D8%A7%D9%87%D9%85%D9%8A%D8%A9-%D8%A7%D9%84%D8%B0%D9%83%D8%A7%D8%A1-%D8%A7%D9%84%D8%A7%D8%B5%D8%B7%D9%86%D8%A7%D8%B9%D9%8A-%D9%81%D9%8A-%D8%A7%D8%AF%D8%A7%D8%B1%D8%A9-%D8%A7%D9%84%D8%A7%D8%B2%D9%85%D8%A7%D8%AA-%D9%81%D9%8A-%D8%B8%D9%84-%D9%83%D9%88%D9%81%D8%AF-19-%D8%AA%D8%AC%D8%B1%D8%A8%D8%A9-%D8%AF%D9%88%D9%84%D8%A9-%D8%A7%D9%84%D8%A5%D9%85%D8%A7%D8%B1%D8%A7%D8%AA-%D8%A7%D9%84%D8%B9%D8%B1%D8%A8%D9%8A%D8%A9-%D8%A7%D9%84%D9%85%D8%AA%D8%AD%D8%AF%D8%A9.pdf.

Jassim, M. (2023). *Kuwait Smart Nation Strategy*. Al-Watan. May 24. Accessed May 17, 2024. https://www.aljarida.com/article/25516.

Keshk, A. M. (2015). *The evolution of regional security since 2003: A study on the impact of NATO's strategy*. Center for Arab Unity Studies.

Keshk, A. M., & Al-Resais, M. S. (2022). *The impact of technological advancements on military doctrines of armies*. Derasat.

Keshk, A. M. (2023). *Challenges of localizing military technology in the Arabian Gulf*. Akhbar Al-Khaleej. https://akhbar-alkhaleej.com/news/article/1339038.

Keshk, A. M. (2024). "*Achieving Self-Security Through Military Industries*". Accessed May 23, 2024. Araa Magazine. https://araa.sa/index.php?option=com_content&view=article&id=6925:2024-02-29-07-50-02&catid=4750&Itemid=172.

Ministry of Interior, Saudi Arabia. (2023). *Ministry of Interior employs artificial intelligence for crowd management during Hajj season 1444 AH*. December 9. Accessed May 21, 2024. https://www.moi.gov.sa/wps/portal/Home/sectors/moidiwan/regions/contents/!ut/p/z1/rVNNc5swEP0r7oGjrAWJr97kOjVxcVzi2g66eEAoQGuQg4lp-usrkmk7_YhpJ9VBI-28fW_faoU5vsG8Tk5lnrSlqpO9vsfc2cElpYFJrXcwn0yBRTRcTh1G4D3F20fAmxkLqBsCeOHMhksWrK_9iBBgBPO_yYdnFoOh_A3mmIu6P.

Nasr, S. (2025). *What is the UAE seeking to achieve in AI?* BBC Arabia. Retrieved from https://www.bbc.com/arabic/articles/cvglyp7zgy7o.

Osoba, O. A., & Welser, W. IV. (2017). *The risks of artificial intelligence to security and the future of work*. December 6. Accessed May 17, 2024. https://www.rand.org/pubs/perspectives/PE237.html.

Robinson, P. (2009). *International security dictionary*. Abu Dhabi: Emirates Center for Strategic Studies and Research.

Russia Today. (2023). *Fourth Bahraini soldier dies from injuries sustained in attack near Yemen-Saudi border*. September 29. Accessed May 17, 2024. https://arabic.rt.com/middle_east/1499376-%D9%88%D9%81%D8%A7%D8%A9-%D8%AC%D9%86%D8%AF%D9%8A-%D8%A8%D8%AD%D8%B1%D9%8A%D9%86%D9%8A-%D8%B1%D8%A7%D8%A8%D8%B9-%D8%A5%D8%AB%D8%B1-%D8%A5%D8%B5%D8%A7%D8%A8%D8%AA%D9%87-%D9%81%D9%8A-%D9%87%D8%AC%D9%88%D9%85-%D8%AD%D8%AF%D9%88%D8%AF-%D9%8A%D9%85%D9%86-%D8%B3%D8%B9%D9%88%D8%AF%D9%8A.

Sabri, W. (2022). *U.S. Central Command Commander to Al-Watan: Bahrain Defense Force is professional and a partner in enhancing regional stability*. Al-Watan. https://alwatannews.net/Bahrain/article/1032628/%D9%82%D8%A7%D9%8A%D8%AF-%D8%A7%D9%84%D9%82%D9%8A%D8%A7%D8%AF%D8%A9-%D8%A7%D9%84%D9%85%D8%B1%D9%83%D8%B2%D9%8A%D8%A9-%D8%A7%D9%84%D8%A3%D9%85%D8%B1%D9%8A%D9%83%D9%8A%D8%A9-%D9%84%D8%A7%D9%84%D9%88%D8%B7%D9%8

Salem, N. (2024). *The impact of employing artificial intelligence techniques militarily: A study on the variables of wars and conflicts*. April 2. Accessed May 23, 2024. https://www.researchgate.net/publication/379459295_athr_twzyf_tqnyat_aldhka_alastnay_skrya_drast_fy_mtghyry_alhrwb_walnzaat_The_impact_of_employing_artificial_intelligence_techniques_militarily_a_study_of_the_variables_of_wars_and_conflicts.

SIPRI. (2024). *Military expenditure in 2023.* Stockholm International Peace Research Institute. https://www.sipri.org/sites/default/files/2024-04/2404_fs_milex_2023.pdf.

UAE Government. (2024). *Charter for the Development and Use of Artificial Intelligence.* Retrieved from https://ai.gov.ae/wp-content/uploads/2024/07/UAEAI-Methaq-EN2-3.pdf.

United Nations. (2023). *Secretary-General: We need a race to develop artificial intelligence for the public good*. July 18. Accessed May 24, 2024. https://news.un.org/ar/story/2023/07/1122052#:~:text=%D9%82%D8%A7%D9%84%20%D8%A7%D9%84%D8%A3%D9%85%D9%8A%D9%86%20%D8%A7%D9%84%D8%B9%D8%A7%D9%85%20%D9%84%D9%84%D8%A3%D9%85%D9%85%20%D8%A7%D9%84%D9%85%D8%AA%D8%AD%D8%AF%D8%A9,%D8%AE%D8%B5%D8%B5%D9%87%D8%A7%20.

Zaman, S. A. K., & Ayyada, A. A. (2024). *Cybersecurity challenges and their impact on institutions and organizations in the GCC.* Center for Kuwaiti and Arabian Gulf Studies. http://cgaps.ku.edu.kw/wp-content/uploads/2024/07/R36LL.pdf.

CHAPTER 10

Assessment of Solid Waste Management Using Geospatial Techniques and Artificial Intelligence—A Case Study of the United Arab Emirates

Mohammed Faiz, Rashid Aziz Faridi, Rakshanda F. Fazli, and Areeb Fazli

10.1 Introduction

Waste or waste released from human activity seriously endangers the environment and public health (Singh, 2019). It comprises various items, including dead animals, paper, textiles, food scraps, leaves, and bones (Ebistu & Minale, 2013). By 2050, waste output will reach 2.8 billion metric tons globally (Szpilko et al., 2023). The Africa Sub-Saharan area

M. Faiz (✉)
Interdisciplinary Department of Remote Sensing and GIS Applications, Aligarh Muslim University, Aligarh, India
e-mail: faiz5225@gmail.com

R. A. Faridi
Department of Geography, Aligarh Muslim University, Aligarh, India
e-mail: rashid.faridi@gmail.com

R. F. Fazli
Department of West Asian Studies and North African Studies, Aligarh Muslim University, Aligarh, India

A. Badran and A. Mishrif (eds.), *Shaping the Future of Development in the GCC*, The Political Economy of the Middle East,
https://doi.org/10.1007/978-981-96-7963-8_10

produces over 62 million of tons of trash yearly (Szpilko et al., 2023), which puts significant financial limitations on collection, landfills, and recycling. Intelligent waste management must be developed to foster true innovation in waste management, utilizing the Internet of Things (IoT) and Artificial intelligent technologies. Combining AI and GIS enhances the efficiency of waste management systems by *Dynamic Route Optimization:* AI analyzes real-time traffic data and waste levels in bins (via IoT sensors). GIS maps out the most efficient collection routes, reducing fuel and time costs. *Waste Generation Forecasting & Planning:* AI models analyze historical waste data and predict future waste trends. GIS visualizes these trends geographically for better resource allocation. *Illegal Dumping Detection:* AI-powered cameras detect and report illegal dumping sites. GIS maps show hotspot locations for better enforcement strategies. *Landfill Management & Environmental Monitoring:* AI processes satellite/drone imagery to track landfill growth. GIS maps overlay pollution data to assess environmental impact.

The Sub-Saharan Africa area is predicted to produce around 62 million tons of trash yearly, with the worldwide population forecast to expand to 9.75 billion by 2050 [a 22.5% rise from the 7.96 billion-person population in 2022 (Barré, 2014; Kalisha & Munthali, 2024)]. Solid waste mishandling and mismanagement of the wood, mining, and urban areas among other worldwide difficulties, significant concerns require combined assessments, comprehensive solutions for environmental pollution, social inclusion, and financial sustainability (Cacciuttolo & Atencio, 2022; de Souza Pinho et al., 2023; Ferronato & Torretta, 2019; Pheakdey et al., 2022; Szpilko et al., 2023; Turcott Cervantes et al., 2021). When it comes to garbage management, cities (Szpilko et al., 2023) and many countries throughout the world—Brazil (de Souza Pinho et al., 2023), India (Ferronato & Torretta, 2019), Cambodia (Pheakdey et al., 2022), and Chile (Cacciuttolo & Atencio, 2022), among others—face substantial financial obstacles.

e-mail: rffazli@gmail.com

A. Fazli
Department of Engineering, Pompeu Fabra University, Barcelona, Spain
e-mail: areebfazli123@gmail.com

These challenges include inappropriate disposal (open landfill) (Pheakdey et al., 2022), absence of worldwide consent related to Executive management and governance techniques (Cacciuttolo & Atencio, 2022), confined economic resources, insufficient technology, and absence of a framework for policies (Pheakdey et al., 2022). Additional obstacles are lack of interconnection between various types of data and cloud data that can be represented to multiple parties involved, an absence of the environmental consciousness from the perspective of citizens, and adoption of technology for reverse logistics, recycling, and the creation of environmental legislation. (Szpilko et al., 2023).

The UAE's growing population and consistent economic expansion are reflected in the country's rising chemical consumption and waste production rates. The nation produced one of the world's most significant amounts of municipal solid waste per capita, at 2.1 kg/day, until it began to decline to roughly 1.8 kg/day. (UAE n.d.)

It is still a major concern despite the amazing efforts made by the relevant UAE agencies to reduce this rate and limit the negative effects of waste and chemicals. The UAE government is striving toward its ambitious target of eliminating 75% of municipal solid waste from landfills by 2021 under the auspices of the National Agenda—UAE Vision 2021.

Raising awareness and developing creative ideas and technology are necessary to achieve this. By concentrating on the growth of the recycling sector and converting waste into energy, MOCCAE strives to accomplish this goal by fortifying collaborations between the public and private sectors to initiate projects that aim to turn waste from an environmental burden into an economic resource.

As waste management directly and substantially influences the environment and human health, it is regarded as one of the most severe environmental concerns and one of the significant difficulties confronting the nation. Over the previous 20 years, there has been a notable rise in the amount of garbage generated, its components and composition have also changed. To maintain sustainable development through environmental preservation and the attainment of a balance between social and economic advancement, the Ministry of Climate Change and Environment collaborates with its partners to improve safe and sustainable waste collection practices that are compliant with type and classification as well as Federal Law (No. 12 of 2018) related integrated waste management.

To guarantee that waste is managed sustainably, benefiting the environment, society, and economy, the Ministry also promotes waste treatment practices that align with environmental initiatives and investments to turn waste into a resource for locating primary or secondary materials or as a source of energy-related to four waste treatment plants and the 54 disposal sites in the United Arab Emirates out which, Dubai has six landfill Sites (Emirates n.d.)

A geographic information system (GIS) helps with practical planning for waste monitoring by gathering, storing, analyzing, organizing, displaying information related to the places. (Mohammedshum et al., 2014). Because it can store, retrieve, and analyze enormous data storage from several sources, it is a potential method for understanding complex phenomena. Applications of GIS in the environment include determining the impact of forest fires and evaluating water contamination. Additionally, it also applied to enhance management of municipal solid waste by identifying landfill site regions, improving collection and transportation, and predicting generation and composition trends. (Nascimento et al., 2017).

Developed by Saaty in the 1970s, one of the MCDA technique's planning-related components is the analytical hierarchy process (AHP) (Nascimento et al., 2017). Breaking down decisions involving multiple variables into pair comparisons and creating arbitrary priorities depending on user assessment creates a hierarchical structure (Ng'ang'a, et al., 2014). Since it allows for a consistent rating of possible landfill regions and simple data processing, combining GIS and AHP is vital for choosing landfill sites. (Ghazifard et al., 2016).

10.2 Study Area

With 4,114 square kilometres, or around 5% of the UAE, when islands are excluded, Dubai is the second-largest Emirate in the UAE. The area of Dubai's oldest district is 1,500 square meters. Because of its rich history and tradition, Dubai is called the "Jewel of the World" and the "Pearl of the Gulf". As of 2021, 3,478,300 people are expected to live in the Dubai emirate, with 1,078,200 women and 2,400,100 men. (Affairs n.d.) (Fig. 10.1).

The emirate is situated on the eastern coast of the Arabian Peninsula, at the southwest corner of the Arabian Gulf. Its borders are shared with Sharjah and Abu Dhabi in the northeast and south respectively. In the southeast, it borders the Oman's Sultanate internationally, about 16 meters, or 52 feet, above sea level in Dubai at 25°15′47″N 55°17′50″E.

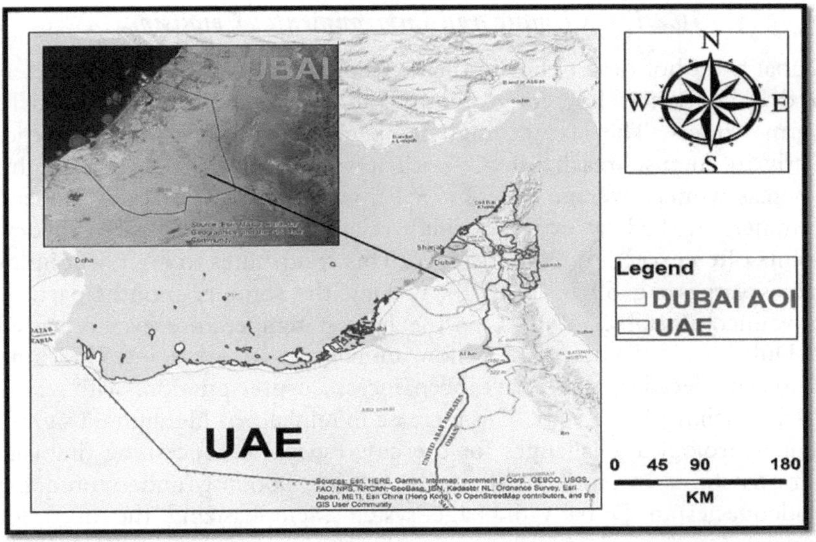

Fig. 10.1 Study area map

The emirate's capital is Dubai City. It is eminent by the ancient watercourse that divides the city in half. Deira is up north and south of Bur Dubai. The emirate was divided into 14 districts in 2016 to implement a new addressing system. Dubai has a lot of sandy beaches on its western shore, a mangrove at the creek's eastern end, lots of deserts in its interior and west, and wadis in the Hatta region.

Dubai Creek is the natural harbour of Dubai, initially facilitated its growth as a fishing, pearling, and sea trade Centre, leading to its development as a thriving port city by the early twentieth century. The discovery of oil in 1966 and the subsequent exports in 1969 spurred rapid development, shaping Dubai into a modern society. Currently, commerce, services, and finance account for the majority of Dubai's diverse economy, which has a thriving business community, and a GDP projected to reach AED 307.5 billion in the first nine months of 2022.

10.2.1 Climate and Environmental Conditions

Dubai has a hot desert climate that is tropical (Köppen BWh), characterized by extremely hot, long, windy, and humid summers and mild to warm winters. The average high temperatures during summer, particularly in August, reach 40 °C, with lows of about 30 °C Overnight, whereas winters average 24 °C (75°F), with lows of 14 °C in January. Summers marked by extremely high relative humidity levels, with dew points often exceeding 30 °C (86°F). This contributes to high heat index values surpassing 60 °C (140°F), making the summer months particularly uncomfortable. 49.0 °C is the hottest temperature ever recorded in Dubai. It is characterized by low annual rainfall, averaging 79.2 mm. In recent decades, there have been increased precipitation, with yearly totals reaching 110.7 mm. This increase in rainfall has highlighted significant hydrological challenges for the city, especially concerning drainage infrastructure. In April 2024, record-setting flooding underscored the inadequacies in Dubai's drainage systems, emphasizing the need for improved infrastructure to cope with the increasing rainfall and the broader impacts of climate change.

10.3 Methodology

This study determined the optimal Locations for a waste landfill area in Dubai Region by integrating spatial and non-spatial data using Geographical techniques. Various input map layers and attributes were generated for this purpose. An assessment of the maps of the two strategies showed that both techniques yielded similar results. Ground truthing using Google Earth Pro met the chosen criteria. This strategy includes a procedure or method that explains the different stages or steps of collecting information or data.

10.3.1 Goal

The primary objective is identifying and selecting the most suitable location for a dump site. This goal drives the entire process, ensuring all subsequent steps are aligned to achieve this objective.

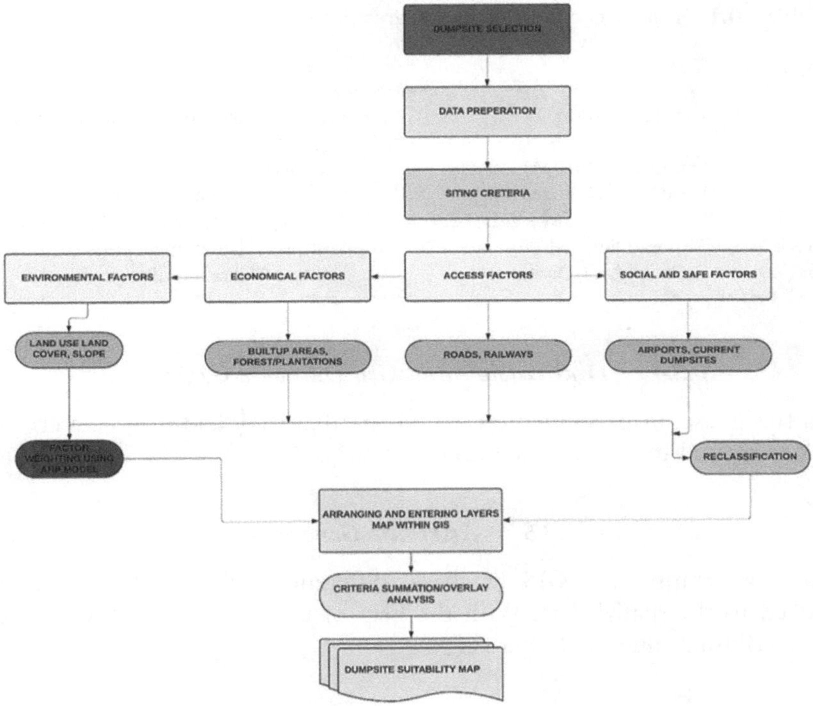

Fig. 10.2 Flow chart of methodology

10.3.2 Data Preparation from Various Sources

This step involves collecting and preparing data from multiple sources. These data sources include spatial data (maps and satellite imagery) and non-spatial data (demographic and economic data). Proper data preparation is crucial for accurate analysis and includes steps like data cleaning, formatting, and integration (Fig. 10.2).

10.3.3 GIS Data Collection

This section collects various spatial and non-spatial data from ministries (Ministry of Waste and Chemicals and other relevant departments) (Table 10.1).

Table 10.1 Data sets employed in research

S No	*Data*	*Sources*
1	Landfill location	GoogleEarth, https://www.moccae.gov.ae/
2	Sentinel 2A (10 M)	Copernicus
3	Road map Digitized	https://data.humdata.org
4	Slope map SRTM - DEM (30 m)	https://portal.opentopography.org
5	Airport Digitized	https://data.humdata.org
6	Built-up Area Digitized	https://data.humdata.org

10.3.4 Digitization and Geo Database Generation

In this phase, maps are georeferenced and digitized, and map data errors are corrected to prepare the GIS database.

10.3.5 Attribute Generation

After generating the GIS database, different attribute information is linked to the spatial data. With the help of GIS data, proximity can be created using multiple buffer rings.

10.3.6 Sitting Criteria

The sitting criteria are the specific factors that were considered in evaluating potential dumpsite locations. These criteria are derived from regulatory requirements, environmental considerations, and practical constraints. The criteria are grouped into four main categories:

- **Environmental Factors** These include land slopes, rivers, soil types, and wetlands. These factors are critical as they impact the environmental sustainability of the dumpsite.
- **Economic Factors** These consider the economic impact of the dumpsite location, such as proximity to built-up areas and forests/plantations. The goal is to minimize negative economic impacts.
- **Access Factors** These include the proximity to roads and railways, which are essential for transportation and accessibility.
- **Social and Safe Factors** These consider the safety and social implications, including proximity to airports and existing dumpsites.

10.3.7 *Buffer Analysis*

Buffer analysis is conducted to create buffer zones around certain features (e.g., roads, railways, airports, built-up areas, Current Dumpsites etc.) to either include or exclude areas within a specific distance. This helps in refining the potential sites by eliminating locations that fall within these buffer zones.

10.3.8 *Factor Weighting Using the AHP Model*

Each criterion is given a weight using the Analytical Hierarchy Process (AHP). AHP is a systematic strategy based on both psychology and mathematics that helps with complicated decision-making. It entails breaking down the decision problem into a hierarchy of simpler subproblems that may be studied separately and are all easily understood. The relative importance of each criterion is determined through pairwise comparisons, and weights are assigned accordingly.

10.3.9 *Reclassification*

Once the criteria are weighed, the data layers are reclassified. Reclassification involves categorizing the data into different classes based on their suitability. This step simplifies the data, making it easier to integrate and analyze.

10.3.10 *Arranging and Entering Layers Map Within GIS*

The reclassified data layers are then arranged and entered a GIS platform. GIS is used to perform spatial analysis and to manage and visualize the data layers effectively.

10.3.11 *Criteria Summation/Overlay Analysis*

Overlay analysis is performed to combine the multiple weighted criteria layers. This step involves summing the reclassified layers based on their assigned weights. The overlay analysis integrates the different criteria into a single composite layer, highlighting areas that best meet the combined suitability criteria.

10.3.12 Dumpsite Suitability Map

The final output of the process is the dumpsite suitability map. This map visually represents the most appropriate locations as a dumpsite according to the comprehensive assessment of the various factors and criteria. The suitability map helps decision-makers to identify and select the optimal site for a dump site.

10.3.13 Fuzzy Overlay Analysis

Overlay analysis helps to determine the areas that meet all the set criteria and that do not. A landfill site must be located and designed to prevent soil, groundwater, or surface water contamination and ensure effective leachate collection. Choosing an appropriate fuzzy function is essential for criteria standardization. In this section, an association function was determined for each criterion. The standardization process is described as a relative score belonging to a fuzzy set. This allows the integration of different spatial layers using Boolean Operation and index overlay to select suitable or unsuitable locations for landfill site selection. All criteria were represented by thematic maps of appropriateness, which were then superimposed to create a final suitability map.

10.3.14 Multi-Criteria Decision Analysis

Multi-criteria decision analysis (MCDA) consists of a collection of consecutive steps designed to analyze complex problems by breaking them down into minor, more manageable parts, examining every part, and then logically integrating them to arrive at an expressive and pertinent solution (J, 1997). The most widely used MCDA method is the AHP, developed by Saaty in 1980 (TL, 1980). AHP is a method for supporting and analyzing decisions with conflicting and numerous objectives, providing various alternatives. This process breaks a challenging decision problem into more simple issues, forming a hierarchy regarding choices. (Erkut & Moran, 1991). Reaching the top of the hierarchy is the goal of decision-making; the hierarchy gets increasingly specialized from broad to particular until the level of characteristics is attained. AHP combines the decision-makers subjective judgments with true data to facilitate and achieve the ideal options (Chabuk et al., 2017).

10.3.15 Evaluation Criteria

Evaluation criteria encompassing attributes and objectives should be established for optimal site selection (Keeney & Raiffa, 1976). These criteria should comply with existing government rules while minimizing the costs to the economy, environment, health, and society (Siddiqui et al., 1996).

Considering the environmental characteristics of the United Arab Emirates, seven criteria were selected for the AHP exercise. These criteria were chosen based on recent studies (Moeinaddini et al., 2010; Siddiqui et al., 1996; Özkan et al., 2019; Sisay et al., 2021; Asefi et al., 2020; Abu Samah et al., 2006). The criteria are divided into limitations and selection standards. The criteria consist of land use, land cover, slope, while the criteria consist of Distance to roads, airports, railways, built-up and Current Landfill sites. AHP toolbox in ArcGIS software (www.esri.com) used for this study. AHP helps to guarantee the validity of the assessment standards and lessens decision-making bias (Abu Samah et al., 2006; Sisay et al., 2021). To ensure that the results were reliable, the AHP consistency ratio was utilized.

10.3.16 Ranking Method

Every criterion was standardized for appropriateness and ranked according to the decision-makers' preferences, expert thoughts, and Literature. The alternatives' scores were assessed to establish their rankings, and weights were assigned. Every criterion was divided into five groups, with 1 denoting the least preference and 5 the most preference, ranging from 1 to 5 (Tables 10.2, 10.3, and 10.4).

Table 10.2 Criteria and buffer distances

Criteria	*Buffer distance*	*References*
Built-up Area	1000	Chabuk et al. (2016)
Road	700	Jerie (2017)
Rail	500	Chabuk et al. (2016)
Airport	3000	Ngwijabagabo et al., (2020)
Current Dump Site	1000	Dolui and Sarkar (2021)
Slope	< 12°	Chabuk et al. (2016)

Table 10.3 Indicators and score value

	Suitability class	*Score value*
Built-up area distance (m)		
0–250	Very Low	1
250–500	Low	2
500–750	Moderately	3
750–1000	Highly	4
> 1000	Very High	5
Road distance		
0–150	Very Low	1
250–300	Low	2
300–450	Moderately	3
450–600	Highly	4
> 600	Very High	5
Railway distance		
0–150	Very Low	1
150–300	Low	2
300–450	Moderately	3
450–600	Highly	4
> 600	Very High	5
Airport distance		
0–500	Very Low	1
500–1000	Low	2
1000–2000	Moderately	3
2000–3000	Highly	4
> 3000	Very High	5
Current landfills		
0–250	Very Low	1
250–500	Low	2
500–750	Moderately	3
750–1000	Highly	4
> 1000	Very Highly	5
Slope (degree)		
0°–12°	Very High	5
12°–16°	High	4
16°–20°	Moderate	3
20°–30°	Low	2
> 30°	Very Low	1
LULC		
Bare Land	Very High	1
Shrubs	High	2
Vegetation	Moderate	3
Water	Low	4
Built-up	Very Low	5

Table 10.4 Suitability score

Score	*Suitability*
1	Very low
2	Low
3	Moderate
4	High
5	Very high

10.4 Result

This study used various parameters: land use land cover, proximity to the built-up area, slope, and proximity to roads, railways, and airports, and proximity to the current dumpsite to evaluate the appropriateness of the Present dumpsite in Dubai to explore the possibility of potential landfill places in the Dubai Region. A range of spatial analysis tools in GIS, including multiple buffers, clipping the shapefile to the area of interest extent, extracting the raster layers, overlaying layers, reclassifying to give fixed classes, and proximity from the Centre of the criterion, were employed to create map layers. Suitability scores, relative weights were given from the literature relative to importance in decision-making (Sisay et al., 2021; Amy Richter, 2019; Nadali Alavi, 2012; Mipun 2015) and (ii) local conditions. Example, the criteria for land usage was given the most weight and given to the built-up area, LULC, and roads. On the contrary, railroads, airports, Dump sites, and slopes were viewed as less imperative because they can be broadened and altered if required by a given undertaking.

10.4.1 Proximity to Land Use and Land Cover

A region's pattern of land usage results from the interaction between both socio-economic and natural variables and their use by people throughout space and time (Karthiheyan & Yeshodha, 2016). Landfill sites often prefer arid and less suitable agricultural areas (Bahram Abediniangerabi, 2016). Landfills should not be located near built-up and vegetated areas to avoid negatively influencing future development and the value of land to minimize current and future environmental risks (Clark & Lee, 1976). This study consists of five land use classes: water bodies, built-up areas,

Table 10.5 Proximity to land use land cover

S. No	*Class*	*Area %*
1	Water Body	0.85
2	Agriculture	1.44
3	Built-up	21.04
4	Bare Land	41.51
5	Shrubs	36.05

vegetation, Bare land, and Shrubs. Water bodies, built-up areas, and vegetation class with the lowest suitability score. Bare Land and shrubs were considered the most suitable for landfill sites and assigned the highest suitability score, as shown below in Table 10.5 and Fig. 10.3.

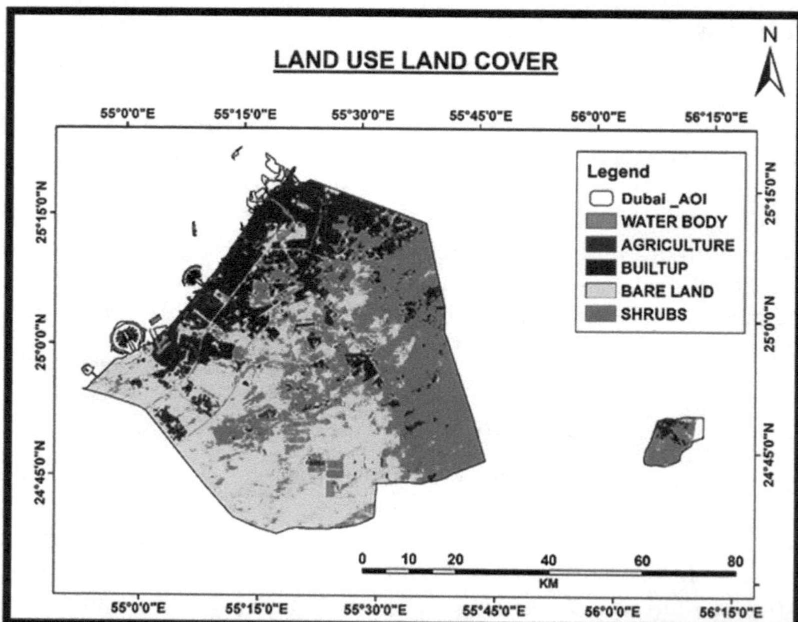

Fig. 10.3 Proximity to land use land cover

Table 10.6 Proximity to built-up

S. No	*Distance*	*Area %*
1	250	50.75
2	500	13.31
3	750	11.04
4	1000	9.56
5	1500	15.34

10.4.2 Proximity to Built-Up Area

Minimize adverse impacts dumpsites should be placed at a suitable distance from cities, commercial buildings, and other populated places in order to minimize negative effects on human health and society, such as unpleasant smells, illnesses, and flies. Approximately 64% of the entire region is inappropriate for the disposal of solid garbage. Additionally, 11.04% is somewhat appropriate, while 9.56% and 15.34% (buffer distance of greater than 1000 meters) are highly and very appropriate respectively, as shown below in Table 10.6 and Fig. 10.4.

10.4.3 Proximity to Road

When choosing a location, the distance from roadways is an important economic consideration. (Gbanie et al., 2013; Gunko & Medvedev, 2016Bahram Abediniangerabi, 2016). To cut construction costs, landfill sites should be located adjacent to major highways and roads (MA, 1993; Lin & Kao, 1999). Roads were to be kept at least 100 meters away from solid waste-laden trucks to minimize disruption to main traffic. We avoided going more than one kilometre from major thoroughfares and freeways. (Allen A 2.15), as well as the possibility of using other all-weather routes to access waste sites. The proximity zone that has the highest appropriateness score is between 150 and 600 meters, meaning that landfills are not situated within 150 meters of busy roads, city streets, or other transit routes (CHEEPO, 2016) as shown below in Table 10.7 and Fig. 10.5.

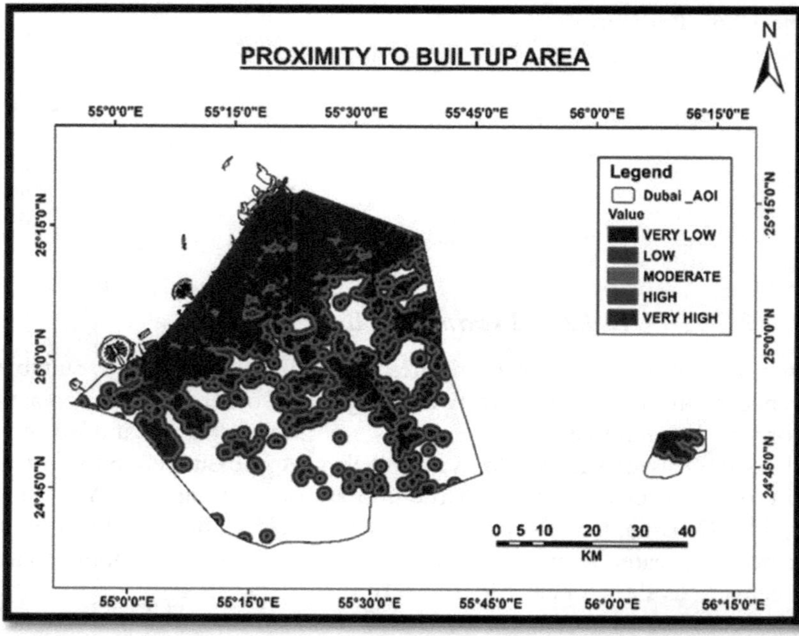

Fig. 10.4 Proximity to built-up area

Table 10.7 Proximity to road

S. No	*Distance*	*Area %*
1	150	26.99
2	300	68.71
3	450	14.76
4	600	12.59
5	1000	27.06

10.4.4 Proximity to Slope

The slope layer is created from the SRTM DEM. (NASA NASA Shuttle Radar Topography Mission (SRTM) (2013))GIS environment. The location of the trash disposal facility ought to be on a reasonable slope. The region is judged better by the inclining region with high topography.

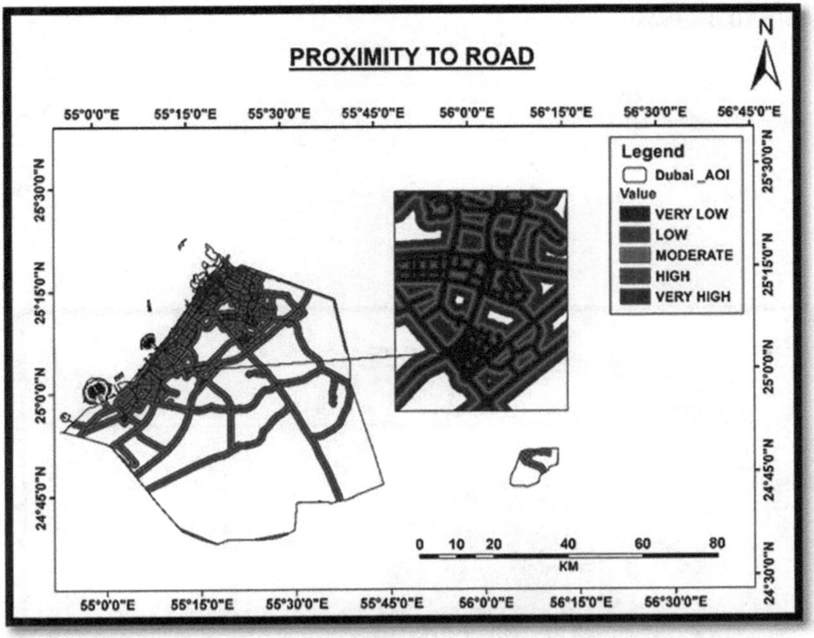

Fig. 10.5 Proximity to road

The Slope layer is categorized into five classes. On the Slope map, it can be seen that most (0–12°) are highly suitable regions; subsequently, moderate sloping areas (slope of 12°–16°), least suitable areas (slope of 16°–20°), steep slope areas (20°–30°) and very steep slope areas (> 30°) are considered to have a smaller slope value it was feared could bring about a landslide particularly when there is downpour or higher water seepage, as shown below in Table 10.8 and Fig. 10.6.

10.4.5 *Proximity to Airport*

Distance is a critical consideration in the placement of landfills since they might draw birds and dust flows that can impede and endanger air traffic (Daneshvar et al., 2005; Monavari et al., 2012). Ideally, landfills should not be situated within 20 kilometres of an airport, although adhering

Table 10.8 Proximity to slope

S. No	*Slope*	*Area %*
1	> 30°	0.41
2	20°–30°	0.85
3	16°–20°	1.12
4	12°–16°	2.99
5	0°–12°	94.60

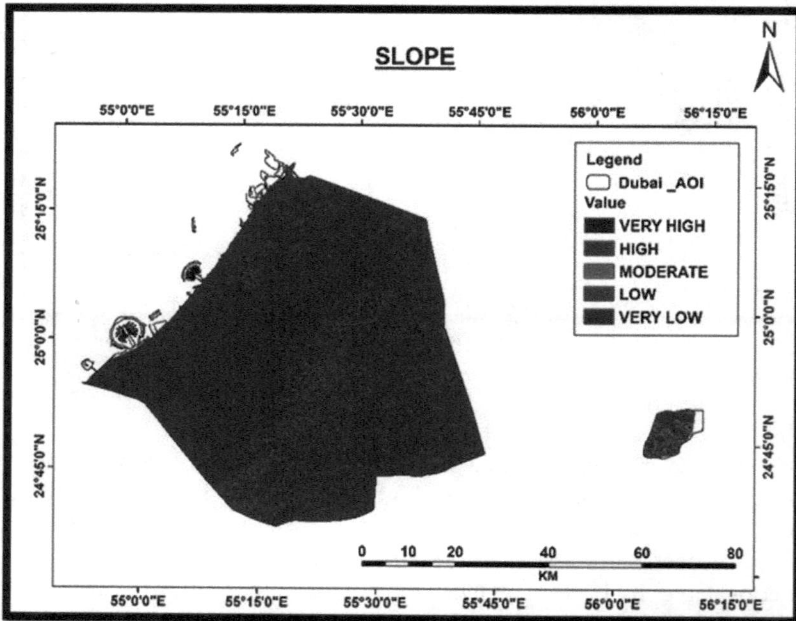

Fig. 10.6 Proximity to slope

to such a distance can be challenging in certain circumstances as shown below in Table 10.9 and Fig. 10.7.

Table 10.9 Proximity to airport

S. No	*Distance*	*Area %*
0	500	11.21
1	1000	5.20
2	2000	14.86
3	3000	21.02
4	5000	52.95

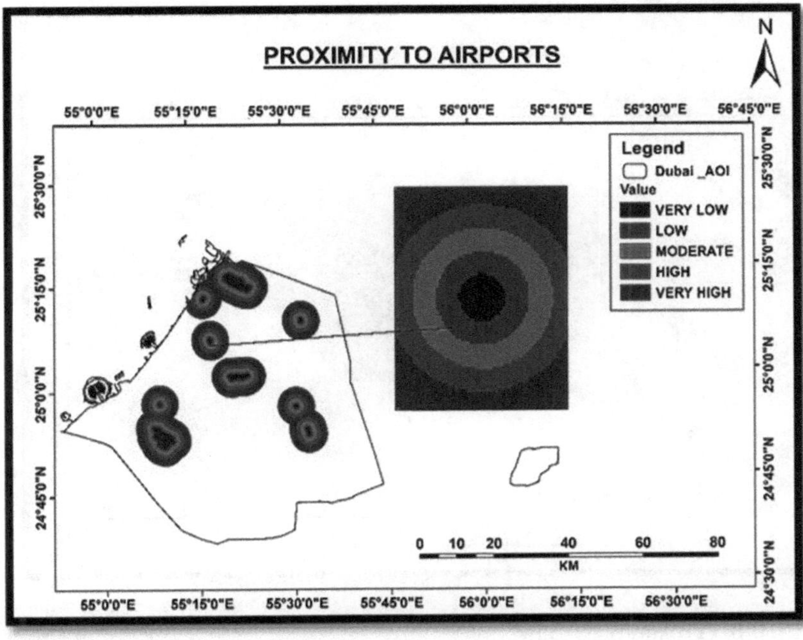

Fig. 10.7 Proximity to airport

10.4.6 Proximity to Railway

55% of the region is at > 500 m, making it convenient for transit and lower logistical and operating expenses. Despite the area's poor rail connection, almost 94% of it is highly appropriate, as shown below in Table 10.10 and Fig. 10.8.

Table 10.10 Proximity to railway

S. No	*Distance*	*Area %*
1	150	15.10
2	300	14.90
3	450	14.97
4	600	15.05
5	1000	39.95

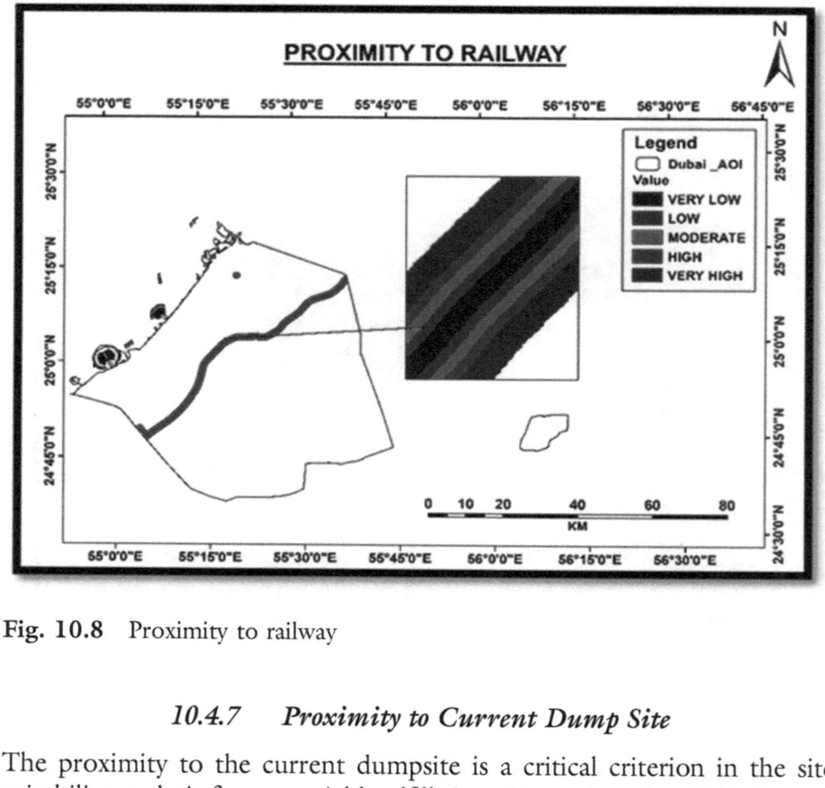

Fig. 10.8 Proximity to railway

10.4.7 *Proximity to Current Dump Site*

The proximity to the current dumpsite is a critical criterion in the site suitability analysis for potential landfill sites. Dumpsites should be located sufficiently far from the current site to avoid possible environmental and health hazards associated with waste accumulation. Proximity to the current dumpsite also impacts logistical considerations, such as transportation costs and access to waste collection and disposal facilities. Therefore, identifying potential landfill sites that are appropriately distanced from the current dumpsite is essential to ensure effective waste management practices and minimize negative impacts on the surrounding environment and communities (Fig. 10.9, Tables 10.11, 10.12).

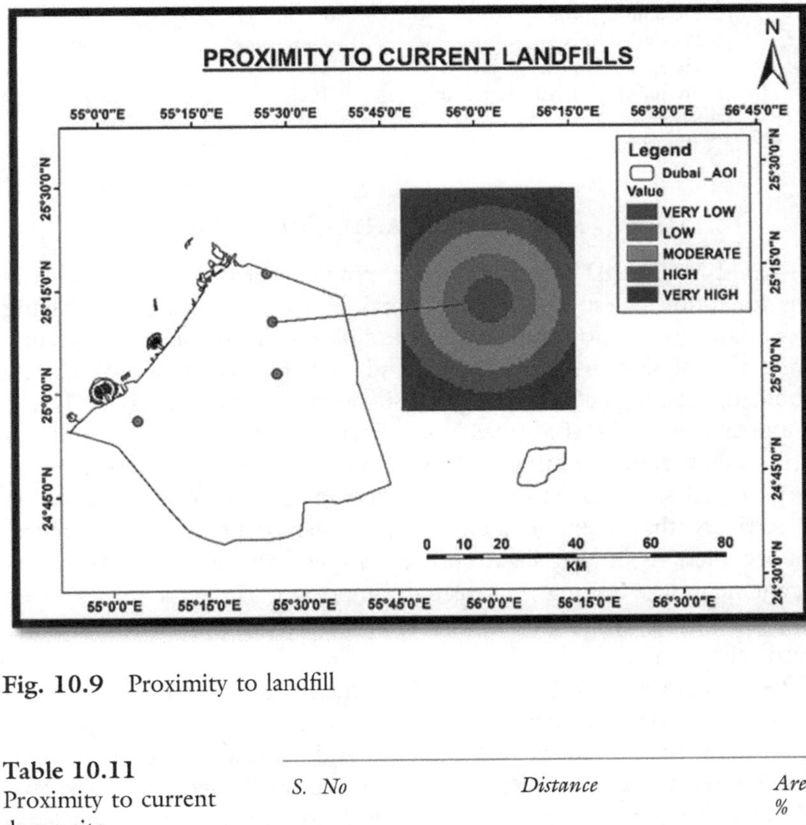

Fig. 10.9 Proximity to landfill

Table 10.11 Proximity to current dump site

S. No	*Distance*	*Area %*
1	250	2.88
2	500	8.66
3	750	14.44
4	1000	19.88
5	1500	54.10

Table 10.12 Preferred suitable site areas

S. No	*Criteria*	*Suitability Class*	*Area in Sq. Km*
1	Land use Land Cover	Bare Land	1625.09
2	Proximity Built-up Area	> 1000 m	674.91
3	Proximity Roads	150 - 600 m	398.78
4	Proximity Railways	150 - 600 m	63.82
5	Proximity Airports	> 3000 m	475.16
6	Proximity Current Dumpsites	> 1000 m	20.1
7	Slope	< 12°	3702.92

10.5 Discussion and Conclusion

GIS-based MCDA-AHP methods were employed to locate landfill locations for municipal solid waste in Dubai. While GIS aids in identifying appropriate sites, it does not serve as a replacement for on-site confirmation. The analysis considered seven standards: land use, Slope, Proximity to built-up, roads, rail, Current dumpsite and the airport (Fig. 10.10).

Approximately 12.40% (493.7 sq. km) of the area was considered highly suitable for locating a landfill site. The study offers alternative potential sites for relocating the existing landfill, selected based on the territory that every location in the zone of greatest appropriateness occupies. As industrialization rises in speed and urbanization, waste management has become increasingly important. However, it is often overlooked in developing countries due to more pressing issues, pushing it into relative unidentified.

The population growth combined with the ongoing drive for economic expansion and development has resulted in a notable rise in the production of solid waste. Recycling, reusing, and cutting waste all help to minimize solid waste problems, but they are insufficient on their own without other management strategies, such as appropriate landfill location. Municipal solid waste (MSW) is frequently disposed of uncontrolled land in developing nations. The process of choosing landfill locations is difficult and typically involves public opposition in addition to considering technical, social, environmental, and financial aspects. Both broad metropolitan regions and cities in the Dubai Region can use the technique and approach described in this study.

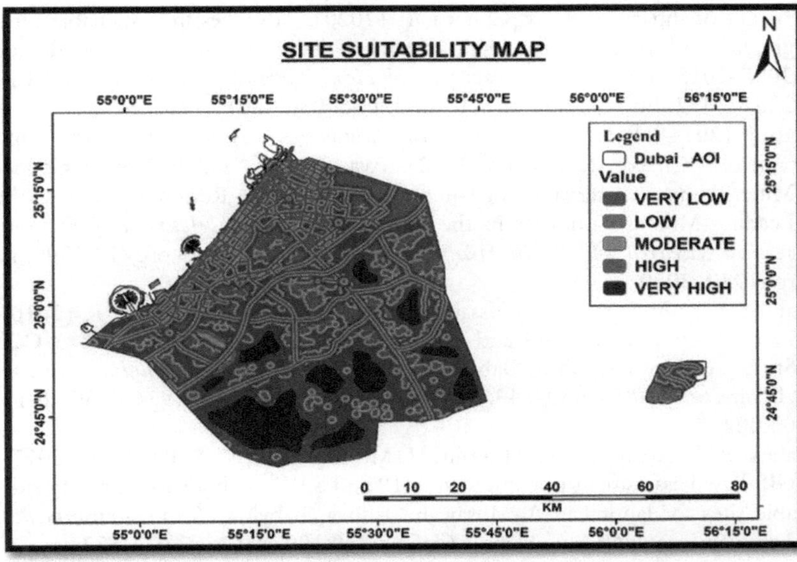

Fig. 10.10 Site suitability map

Acknowledgements The authors wish to express their gratitude to the Department of Geography, the Department of Remote Sensing and GIS Applications, and the Department of West Asian and North African Studies at Aligarh Muslim University. They also express their gratitude to the UAE Ministry of Climate Change and Environment (MOCCAE) for providing important data and information that contributed to this study. Additionally, the authors appreciate the valuable suggestions from the reviewers, which helped enhance the quality of the article.

Declarations

Conflict of Interest The authors declare no conflict of interest.

References

Abu Samah, M. A., Manaf, L. A., Aris, A. Z., & Nor, W. (2006). Solid waste management: Analytical hierarchy process (AHP) application of selecting treatment technology in Sepang Municipal Council, Malaysia. *Current World Environment, 1*(1), 1–16. https://doi.org/10.12944/CWE.6.1.01

Asefi, H., Shahparvari, S., & Chhetri, P. (2020). Advances in sustainable integrated solid waste management systems: Lessons learned over the decade 2007–2018. *Journal of Environmental Planning and Management, 63*(13), 2287–2312. https://doi.org/10.1080/09640568.2019.1702652

Barré, J. (2014). *Waste market in urban Malawi—A way out of poverty?* 19–60.

Cacciuttolo, C., & Atencio, E. (2022). Past, Present, and Future of Copper Mine Tailings Governance in Chile (1905–2022): A Review in One of the Leading Mining Countries in the World. *International Journal of Environmental Research and Public Health, 19*(20), 1. https://doi.org/10.3390/ijerph192013060

Chabuk, A. J., Al-Ansari, N., Hussain, H. M., Knutsson, S., & Pusch, R. (2016). Landfill Siting Using GIS and AHP (Analytical Hierarchy Process): A Case Study Al-Qasim Qadhaa, Babylon, Iraq. *Journal of Civil Engineering and Architecture, 10*(5), 530–543. https://doi.org/10.17265/1934-7359/2016.05.002

Chabuk, A. J., Al-Ansari, N., Hussain, H. M., Knutsson, S., & Pusch, R. (2017). GIS-based assessment of combined AHP and SAW methods for selecting suitable sites for landfill in Al-Musayiab Qadhaa, Babylon. *Iraq. Environmental Earth Sciences, 76*(5), 1. https://doi.org/10.1007/s12665-017-6524-x

Clark, R. M., & Lee, J. C. H. (1976). Systems planning for solid waste collection. *Computers & Operations Research, 3*(2–3), 157–173. https://doi.org/10.1016/0305-0548(76)90026-5

Daneshvar, R., Fernandes, L., Warith, M., & Daneshfar, B. (2005). Customizing arcmap interface to generate a user-friendly landfill site selection, GIS tool. *Journal of Solid Waste Technology and Management, 31*(1), 1–12.

de Souza Pinho, G. C., Calmon, J. L., Medeiros, D. L., Vieira, D., & Bravo, A. (2023). Wood Waste Management from the Furniture Industry: The Environmental Performances of Recycling, Energy Recovery, and Landfill Treatments. *Sustainability, 15*(20), 14944. https://doi.org/10.3390/su152014944

Dolui, S., & Sarkar, S. (2021). Identifying potential landfill sites using multicriteria evaluation modeling and GIS techniques for Kharagpur city of West Bengal. *India. Environmental Challenges, 5*, 1. https://doi.org/10.1016/j.envc.2021.100243

Ebistu, T. A., & Minale, A. S. (2013). Solid waste dumping site suitability analysis using geographic information system (GIS) and remote sensing for Bahir Dar Town, North Western Ethiopia. *African Journal of Environmental Science and Technology, 7*(11), 976–989. https://doi.org/10.5897/AJEST2013.1589

Erkut, E., & Moran, S. R. (1991). Locating obnoxious facilities in the public sector: An application of the analytic hierarchy process to municipal landfill siting decisions. *Socio-Economic Planning Sciences, 25*(2), 89–102. https://doi.org/10.1016/0038-0121(91)90007-E

Ferronato, N., & Torretta, V. (2019). Waste mismanagement in developing countries: A review of global issues. *International Journal of Environmental Research and Public Health, 16*(6), 1. https://doi.org/10.3390/ijerph16061060

Gbanie, S. P., Tengbe, P. B., Momoh, J. S., Medo, J., & Kabba, V. T. S. (2013). Modelling landfill location using Geographic Information Systems (GIS) and Multi-Criteria Decision Analysis (MCDA): Case study Bo, Southern Sierra Leone. *Applied Geography, 36*, 3–12. https://doi.org/10.1016/j.apgeog.2012.06.013

Ghazifard, A., Nikoobakht, S., & Azarafza, M. (2016). Municipal Waste Landfill Site Selection based on Environmental, Geological and Geotechnical Multi-criteria: A Case Study. *Iranian Journal of Environmental Technology, 2*(1), 49–67.

Gunko, M., & Medvedev, A. (2016). "Seasonal suburbanization" in Moscow oblast': Challenges of household waste management. *Geographia Polonica, 89*(4), 473–484. https://doi.org/10.7163/GPol.0069

Jerie, S. (2017). Site Suitability Analysis for Solid Waste Landfill Site Location Using Geographic Information Systems and Remote Sensing: a Case Study of Banket Town Board. *Zimbabwe. Review of Social Sciences, 2*(4), 19–31. https://doi.org/10.18533/rss.v2i4.99

Kalisha, S. M., & Munthali, K. G. (2024). Multi-Factor GIS Modeling for Solid Waste Dumpsite Selection in Lilongwe. *Malawi. Sustainability (Switzerland), 16*(3), 1. https://doi.org/10.3390/su16031202

Karthiheyan, P. N., & Yeshodha, L. (2016). Site Selection for Urban Solid Waste Disposal Using Remote Sensing and Open Source GIS In Krishnagiri District, Tamil Nadu. *International Journal for Innovative Research in Science & Technology, 2*(10), 233–239.

Keeney, R. L., & Raiffa, H. (1976). *Decisions with multiple objectives: Preferences and value trade-offs*. Wiley. https://doi.org/10.1017/CBO9781139174084

Lin, H., & Kao, J. (1999). Enhanced spatial model for landfill siting analysis. *Journal of Environmental Engineering, 125*(9), 845–951. https://doi.org/10.1061/(ASCE)0733-9372

Moeinaddini, M., Khorasani, N., Danehkar, A., Darvishsefat, A. A., & Zienalyan, M. (2010). Siting MSW landfill using weighted linear combination and analytical hierarchy process (AHP) methodology in GIS environment (case study: Karaj). *Waste Management, 30*(5), 912–920. https://doi.org/10.1016/j.wasman.2010.01.015

Mohammedshum, A. A., Gebresilassie, M. A., Rulinda, C. M., Kahsay, G. H., & Tesfay, M. S. (2014). Application of geographic information system and remotesensing in effective solid waste disposal sites selection in Wukro Town, Tigray, Ethiopia. *International Archives of the Photogrammetry, Remote*

Sensing and Spatial Information Sciences - ISPRS Archives, 40(2), 115–119. https://doi.org/10.5194/isprsarchives-XL-2-115-2014

Monavari, S. M., Hoasami, P., Tajziehchi, S., Khorramichokami, N., & Area, A. S. (2012). Study of solid waste landfill suitability using regional screening method and AHP in Rasht City. *International Journal of Environmental, Chemical, Ecological, Geological and Geophysical Engineering, 6*(2), 820–825.

Nascimento, V. F., Sobral, A. C., Andrade, P. R., Ometto, J. P. H. B., & Yesiller, N. (2017). Modeling Environmental Susceptibility of Municipal Solid Waste Disposal Sites: A Case Study in São Paulo State, Brazil. *Journal of Geographic Information System, 09*(01), 8–33. https://doi.org/10.4236/jgis.2017.91002

Ng'ang'a, T., Wachira, P., Wangai, K., Wango, T., & Matheri, N. (2014). Solid waste dumping site selection using GIS and remote sensing for Kajiado County, Kenya. *Journal of Earth Science and Engineering, 4*, 693–702.

Ngwijabagabo, H., Nyandwi, E., & Barifashe, T. (2020). Integrating Local Community Perception and Expert's Knowledge in Spatial Multi-Criteria Evaluation (SMCE) for Landfill Siting in Musanze Secondary City. *Rwanda Journal of Engineering, Science, Technology and Environment, 3*(1), 1. https://doi.org/10.4314/rjeste.v3i1.8s

Özkan, B., Özceylan, E., & Sarıçiçek, İ. (2019). GIS-based MCDM modeling for landfill site suitability analysis: A comprehensive review of the literature. *Environmental Science and Pollution Research, 26*(30), 30711–30730. https://doi.org/10.1007/s11356-019-06298-1

Pheakdey, D. V., Quan, N. V., Khanh, T. D., & Xuan, T. D. (2022). Challenges and Priorities of Municipal Solid Waste Management in Cambodia. *International Journal of Environmental Research and Public Health, 19*(14), 8458. https://doi.org/10.3390/ijerph19148458

Siddiqui, M. Z., Everett, J. W., & Vieux, B. E. (1996). Landfill siting using geographic information systems: A demonstration. *Journal of Environmental Engineering, 122*(6), 515–523. https://doi.org/10.1061/(ASCE)0733-9372

Singh, A. (2019). Remote sensing and GIS applications for municipal waste management. *Journal of Environmental Management, 243*, 22–29. https://doi.org/10.1016/j.jenvman.2019.05.017

Sisay, G., Gebre, S. L., & Getahun, K. (2021). GIS-based potential landfill site selection using MCDM-AHP modeling of Gondar Town, Ethiopia. *African Geographical Review, 40*(2), 105–124. https://doi.org/10.1080/19376812.2020.1770105

Szpilko, D., de la Torre Gallegos, A., Jimenez Naharro, F., Rzepka, A., & Remiszewska, A. (2023). Waste Management in the Smart City: Current Practices and Future Directions. *Resources, 12*(10), 1–25. https://doi.org/10.3390/resources12100115

Turcott Cervantes, D. E., Romero, E. O., & del Consuelo Hernández Berriel, M., Martínez, A. L., del Consuelo Mañón Salas, M., & Lobo, A. (2021). Assessment of some governance aspects in waste management systems: A case study in Mexican municipalities. *Journal of Cleaner Production, 278*, Article 123320. https://doi.org/10.1016/j.jclepro.2020.123320

CHAPTER 11

Industrial Precision Facilities Cost Estimation Using Artificial Neural Network

Ashraf Mishrif, Mahmoud Alsafy, and Mostafa Atia

11.1 Introduction

The manufacturing cost assessment of machining operations for small batch sizes is a critical operation in industrial and technical production facilities (Costabile et al., 2017). Before the products are manufactured, there are several ways to anticipate manufacturing cost; however, each approach has expenses and varies in complexity and requirements (Manuguerra et al., 2023). Traditionally, the estimation of manufacturing costs has required intricate and lengthy calculative procedures (Duffner et al., 2021). These procedures involve detailed assessments of both material costs and machining operation times, which are derived from selected workpiece parameters (Urbanic & Saqib, 2019). The complexity of these calculations reflects the variability in manufacturing costs, which can differ

A. Mishrif (✉) · M. Alsafy
Sultan Qaboos University, Muscat, Sultanate of Oman
e-mail: ashraf.mishrif@gmail.com

M. Atia
AASTMT, Cairo, Egypt

A. Badran and A. Mishrif (eds.), *Shaping the Future of Development in the GCC*, The Political Economy of the Middle East,
https://doi.org/10.1007/978-981-96-7963-8_11

significantly depending on geographic location and the time required for various processes.

Recent research has sought to streamline the cost estimation process, particularly for small and medium enterprises (SMEs), by reducing the reliance on exhaustive calculations (Alami & ElMaraghy, 2021). These studies have introduced methods that aim to simplify and partially decrease the cost estimation associated with machining processes. This has been achieved through the integration of several factors, including workpiece specifications and the judgments of human experts. By leveraging these parameters, the aim is to provide more accessible and efficient cost estimation tools that accommodate the specific needs and constraints of SMEs. These attempts relied on several parameters that are related to workpiece specifications and human experts' judgments (Atia et al., 2022), and could be time consuming, expensive, and require highly skilled technicians that are not often available in most manufacturing facilities.

To address this challenge, this study aims at estimating the total manufacturing cost in traditional industrial facilities, more specifically total manufacturing time (TMT), which is the main component in operational cost in these facilities. Basically, manufacturing cost is determined by several factors including TMT, overheads, and labor cost. The most influential of these factors is TMT that constitutes around 60–70% of the total manufacturing cost of any product. The overarching focus of this study will be on estimating the TMT to determine the total cost of industrial goods. The rationale for focusing on TMT is that it has a significant impact of reliability and validity that does not change with years or places.

Methodologically, this study will use Artificial Neural Network (ANN) and a parametric estimation method to predict the TMT. These parameters will be collected from the top five experts and specialists in manufacture units in Oman. A survey questionnaire is used to collect primary data on the main elements of cost estimation throughout the different stages of fabrication. A sample of 100 cases were collected from the surveyed industrial units. The ANN is used as an estimator model to predict the TMT of the fabricated parts. Selected parameters of the manufacturing process are fed into the model to estimate the desired output with high accuracy. The model will be initially trained and evaluated by data collected from the industrial units under investigation.

The study has theoretical and practical implications, most notably the potential use of Artificial Intelligence (AI) techniques in manufacturing and the ability of this model to reduce the anticipated TMT and cost. It mainly reduces the time needed for the estimation process, which directly affects product prices and company profits. In addition, the high accuracy of the prediction is significantly important for the manufacturer to reduce the pricing error from different places. Successful implementation of this model depends on the highly skilled technicians and specialists in the industrial units, who can accurately estimate the cost of fabricated parts, especially those with complex shapes. The proposed model is adaptable, flexible, and upgradable to accommodate new designs, types of materials and dimensions.

11.2 Literature Review on Cost Estimation and ANN in Industrial Precision Facilities

Manufacturing operations pricing face specific challenges when dealing with small workpiece jobs, which can influence the total cost of the product (Atia et al., 2017). The low number of workpiece that required machining with a certain specification has a significant issue in pricing comparing with a mass production of a consistent product (Tien, 2011). Manufacturers frequently obtain cheaper per-unit costs when producing things in bulk due to savings in material procurement, setup, and manufacturing processes (Manuguerra et al., 2023). With a small number of workpieces, economies of scale are reduced, resulting in higher per-unit costs. Furthermore, setup costs can be a significant portion of the total manufacturing cost, especially for processes like machining (Atia et al., 2022), injection molding, or printing (Vasco et al., 2019). In small jobs, the setup cost is spread over a smaller number of units, making each unit more expensive to produce compared to larger production runs where setup costs are amortized over a greater number of units (Allahverdi et al., 2008). Darmandieu et al. (2022) mentioned that material costs could be higher for small jobs due to less favorable pricing from suppliers. Bulk purchase often comes with discounts or better pricing agreements, which are not available for small quantities. In addition, the labor costs per unit can be higher for small jobs, especially if the processes involved require manual labor or specialized skills. In larger production runs, labor costs can be spread over more units, reducing the per-unit cost (Schaefer & Singleton, 2019).

Moreover, small production of workpieces particularly has a shorter production run that may increase the lead times per product, especially if production schedules are optimized for larger batches. Delays in production can be directly affected on rising the costs due to expedited shipping or rushed manufacturing processes (Betrand & Van Ooijen, 2008). Custom tooling or equipment configurations could be necessary for small operations, but they can be expensive and time consuming to be required. A modest number of units to cover these tooling expenses can have significant impacts on the cost per part (Braun, 2013). Nonetheless, the need of flexibility and agility in manufacturing processes is highly recommended to meet the frequent changes in specifications or orders (Sherehiy & Karwowski, 2014). This flexibility may come at an increase cost, particularly if it necessitates reconfiguring equipment or changing operations (Ajgaonkar et al., 2022). To meet these challenges, small batch manufacturing operations need to prepare cautiously, manage resources efficiently, and occasionally use modern technologies to create a proper solutions associated with reducing the total manufacturing costs without sacrificing quality requirements (Diaz-Chao et al., 2017).

Recent research has highlighted that incorporating such features at a practical cost and with a reasonable degree of accuracy enhances a company's competitiveness and boosts customer satisfaction (Liu, Piplani, & Toro, 2022a, 2022b). Furthermore, it has been confirmed that cost estimation for SMEs in the Middle East is increasingly becoming essential in today's market (Atia et al., 2022).

11.2.1 Cost Estimation Approaches

Cost estimating of small batch size in job shop facilities significantly requires a customized technique that takes into consideration the project's particular qualities and constraints. In this research study classified the cost estimation techniques in SME into six classes. The Analogous Estimation Approach (AEA) is the first class; it uses historical data from a limited number of workpieces as a foundation for cost estimation, requiring genuine data that is less variable in the dataset (Tayefeh Hashemi et al., 2020). It can create a cost estimate by evaluating the job's dimensions, complexity, labor and material requirements, and comparison with previous projects. It is vital to make sure that the previous projects that are being compared are sufficiently related to the current task in a time-efficient manner (Dashti et al., 2022). This methodology's drawbacks include the requirement for human adjustments, the inability to account for variations in any cost factor, complexity compared to parametric approaches, the inability to allow for changes or upgrades, and the accuracy level being dependent on fitting within the available population of data (Pratama and Rasywir, 2018).

The second class is the Parametric Estimation Approach (PEA) using mathematical models to estimate costs based on specific parameters such as size, weight, or complexity. These models are often developed using historical data and statistical analysis (Campi et al., 2021). For small jobs, parametric estimation can provide a quick and relatively accurate estimate by applying cost factors to the project's characteristics. However, it requires excessive study of the cost factors of producing a part (Manuguerra et al., 2023).

The third class is the Expert Judgment Approach (EJA) which is consulting with experienced professionals or subject matter experts to estimate costs based on their knowledge and expertise. This approach is particularly useful for small jobs that involve specialized or niche requirements where historical data may be limited and is convenient with SME (Huang et al., 2012). Experts can provide valuable insights and recommendations to develop a reliable cost estimate.

The fourth class is Software Tools Approach (STA) that includes a various cost estimation software tools are available that facilitate the estimation process by providing templates, databases, and algorithms for calculating costs based on project parameters (Chirra & Reza, 2019). While these tools can streamline the estimation process, they may require customization to suit the specific needs of small jobs (Kumari & Pushkar, 2013).

The fifth class is Risk Analysis Approach (RAA) that contributes to small job shop facilities may be more susceptible to cost overruns due to their inherent uncertainties and limited margins (Gurcanli et al., 2015). Incorporating risk analysis techniques into the cost estimation process can help identify potential risks and their associated costs, allowing for contingency planning and mitigation strategies (Idrus et al., 2011). The last class is the Benchmarking Approach (BA), which compares the cost of the current job with similar projects in the industry to establish a baseline for cost estimation (Parthan et al., 2012). By analyzing industry standards and best practices, you can identify cost-saving opportunities and optimize the project's budget (Disch, 2023). Combining multiple estimation methodologies and leveraging available data and expertise can help develop accurate and reliable cost estimates for small jobs, enabling better project planning and budget management.

11.2.2 Cost Estimation Using Artificial Neural Network

Recently, the development of cost estimating methodologies employing AI and ANN models has been greatly supported by the fourth industrial revolution. ANN is essentially capable of significantly improving costing procedures in a number of ways, including its exceptional ability to identify complicated patterns in data (Gharaibeh et al., 2020). In order to find hidden patterns and connections in cost estimation that human analysts might miss, they might examine historical cost data in conjunction with other project characteristics. Moreover, the traditional cost estimation techniques often assume linear relationships between project parameters and costs. However, real-world relationships are most likely non-linear. This model can deal with non-linear relationships more effectively, allowing for more accurate cost predictions (Li et al., 2021). The adaptability feature of the ANN can improve the model's accuracy; as the amount of datasets increases, the estimator can train and update their models accordingly, resulting in more accurate and up-to-date cost estimates (Dehraj & Sharma, 2021).

Furthermore, the development of this model can automatically extract beneficial features from input datasets, which helps identify the most significant parameters affecting expenses, enabling better resource allocation and emphasis on essential elements (Luo et al., 2020). In addition, the cost estimation inherently involves uncertainty due to various factors such as market fluctuations, unforeseen risks, and changing requirements (Liu et al., 2022a, 2022b). Alsamadony et al. (2023) developed model that can incorporate probabilistic techniques to provide not just point estimates but also confidence intervals or probability distributions, giving stakeholders a clearer understanding of the range of possible costs. Abdolrasol et al. (2021) integrated with other technologies such as data mining, optimization algorithms, and simulation tools to enhance energy demand forecasting and also can optimize project schedules and resource allocations while considering cost constraints in SME.

Compared to other dynamic project contexts, real-time cost estimating is critical for decision-making (Ateş, 2023). ANN utilized systems that continuously track the status of projects and adjust cost projections in real time based on recent data, enabling stakeholders to take prompt and well-informed decisions. Furthermore, biases that result from individual preferences, prior experiences, or organizational pressures may also affect human expert estimators. ANNs' algorithmic nature allows them to slightly offset these biases, producing cost estimates that are more impartial and objective (Hong et al., 2020). The accuracy, effectiveness, and dependability of cost estimating procedures across a range of sectors and domains may be greatly improved by ANNs by utilizing these features.

11.2.3 Artificial Neural Network Design and Structures

The architecture of an ANN refers to its structure, which includes how its constituent components are organized and interconnected. Feedforward neural network (FFNN) is the fundamental explanation of the network architecture, one of the most prevalent forms of artificial neural networks. As indicated in Fig. 11.1(a), the input layers receive the input datasets. Each neuron in the input layer represents one of the input data's features or attributes. The number of neurons in the input layer is dependent on the input data's dimensionality. Hidden layers are then located between the input and output layers to acquire the real computation in the network. Each hidden layer is made up of several neurons or units that apply mathematical operations on the incoming data. The number of hidden layers and neurons in each layer are design decisions that are determined by the complexity of the issue and the network's performance requirements.

The output layer is the last network layer and contains the output prediction. The number of neurons in the output layer is determined by the nature that the network is completing. As seen in Fig. 11.1(b), each neuron in a layer is linked to every neuron in the substance layer via weighted connections. These connections carry signals (activations) from one layer to the next, and the weights assigned to these connections influence the intensity of the signal. During training, these weights are modified via a method known as backpropagation (BP) to reduce the discrepancy between the network's predictions and the actual objectives.

The network can identify complex structures in the data by introducing non-linearities through activation functions. The hyperbolic tangent (tanh), Rectified Linear Unit (ReLU), and SoftMax are instances of common activation functions. Thus, preparing the data set is the first step

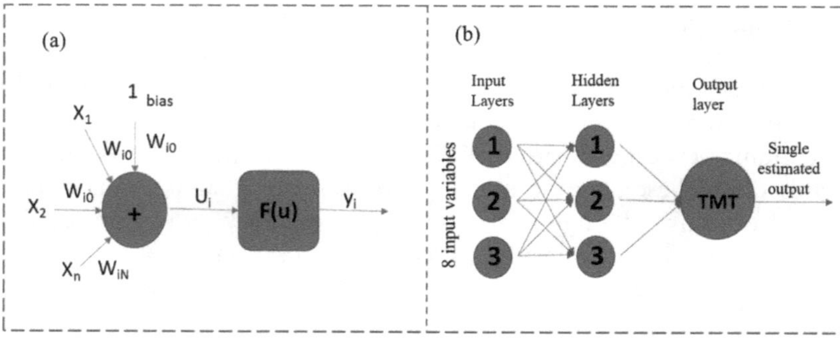

Fig. 11.1 (a) ANN example and (b) Simple feed forward ANN

in the development and training of the model, considering the method previously discussed. Additionally, a different data set is utilized to test and verify network development.

11.3 Methodology

11.3.1 Data Set Preparation

Table 11.1 provides a comprehensive overview of the characteristics of job shop facilities in Muscat. This table includes detailed information such as the location of each facility, the types of work they undertake, the number of employees, the weekly work capacity, the sizes and types of machines, and the specific data collected from each facility. To facilitate robust analysis, efforts were made to ensure a consistent number of workpieces were included in the dataset. The dataset is organized into multiple arrays, each representing inputs and desired outputs for the model used in this study. Specifically, the inputs consist of various relevant machining variables that are instrumental in estimating manufacturing costs, while the output is the expected total machining time required.

The machining variables encompass a broad range of factors related to workpieces, machines, and cutting tools. Given the extensive array of variables that influence machine time, it was necessary to select only those that are most pertinent. To identify these key variables, a survey was conducted involving experts from local manufacturing facilities in Oman. The survey aimed to capture expert opinions on which variables are most relevant for accurate machining time estimation. Table 11.2

Table 11.1 Local facility characteristics

Workshop characteristics	*WS-1*	*WS-2*	*WS-3*	*WS-4*	*WS-5*
Location	Mabella	Ghala	Seeb	Wadi Kabeer	Mutrah
Type of work	Automotive	Automotive	General	Automotive	General
No. of Labors	9	7	5	6	8
Capacity/week	100–130	100–120	50–70	50–90	100–130
Machine type	General Center	Lathe machine			
Machine size	Small & Medium	Small & Medium	Small	Small	Small & Medium
No. of collected Data	20	20	20	20	20

Source Authors' own work

Table 11.2 Input dataset parameters-survey

No	*Variable*	*WS-1*	*WS-2*	*WS-3*	*WS-4*	*WS-5*	*% Importance*
1	Volume	1	1	1	1	1	100
2	Machinability level	1	1	1	1	1	100
3	Hardness	1	1	1	1	1	100
4	Auxiliary tools	0	1	0	1	0	40
5	Surface roughness	0	1	0	1	0	60
6	Turning features	1	1	1	1	1	100
7	Patch size	1	0	1	0	0	60
8	Machine size	0	1	1	0	1	60
9	Tool material	1	0	1	1	0	60

Source Authors' own work

presents the results of this survey, highlighting that nine specific variables were identified as critical for estimating machining time in manufacturing settings. These variables were carefully selected based on their relevance and impact on machining time, ensuring that the analysis remains focused and practical.

11.3.2 Data Input Preparation

The input variables in the model must be normalized values between 0 and 1. However, to achieve the aim of this research, these values should be extracted without going through the details of the operations. As shown in Table 11.3, each variable is categorized into ranges and each range is assigned a value to achieve the model requirements. The specimens employed in this investigation were limited to certain ranges. These ranges are specified by both descriptive criteria, starting with surface roughness, and quantitative measurements, including volume.

Certain parameters, like hardness, have straightforward values, but others, like turning characteristics, involve intricate formulas for determining the associated value. Additionally, the table's normalization functions and some of the variables' calculations are employed. Furthermore, Table 11.3 presents three instances of producing numerical values for the input variables A3, A12, and A7, displayed in Fig. 11.2. The variable (machine size) is fixed in all workpieces obtained from job shops since machine size has no significant effect on machining time, and the bulk of specimens are made on small center lathe machines.

11.3.3 Preparation of Output Data

For each input dataset, there is a corresponding Desired Machining Time (DMT) which represents the anticipated outcome of the operation. This DMT was determined based on expert knowledge and detailed operation sheets, following traditional methods for calculating TMT. The DMT encompasses various time components including direct machining, setup, handling, tool changes, speed and feed adjustments, measurement, and rest periods. In this study, the input datasets comprised 100 workpieces. The actual machining time for these workpieces was recorded, and the TMT was subsequently normalized. This normalization, as described in Eq. 11.1, yields the Normalized Desired Machining Time (NDMT), with a maximum value of one.

Table 11.4 provides a detailed presentation of the prepared data, showcasing seven selected workpieces. This table includes the input parameters for each workpiece, along with the corresponding DMT and NDMT values. By illustrating these samples, Table 11.4 demonstrates how the input parameters relate to the desired machining times and how the normalization process standardizes these values. This approach allows

Table 11.3 Inputs and associated parameters for three specimens

	Input parameters	*Description*	*Range*	*value*	*Normalizing function*	*Examples*					
						value			*Normalized value*		
						A3	*A12*	*A6*	*A3*	*A12*	*A6*
1	Volume	Diameter, mm	10–40	0.25	Dia x L	0.25			0.0625	0.0625	0.125
			40–180	0.5			0.25	0.5			
			180–250	1							
		Length, mm	10–100	0.25							
			100–300	0.5		0.25	0.25	0.25			
2	Machinability level	Heavy	Steel	1		1		1	1		1
			Cast iron	0.9			0.9			0.9	
			Brass	0.6							
		Light	Aluminum	0.4							
			Teflon	0.2							
3	Hardness	Hard		1		1		1	1		1
		Medium		0.5			0.5			0.5	
		Soft		0.25							
4	Auxiliary Tool	3-jaw chuck		1	Σparameters/ 3.1	1	1	1	0.483	0.483	1
		Two centers		0.5		0.5	0.5				
		Movable rest		0.9							

(continued)

Table 11.3 (continued)

	Input parameters	*Description*	*Range*	*value*	*Normalizing function*	*Examples*					
						value			*Normalized value*		
						A3	*A12*	*A6*	*A3*	*A12*	*A6*
		Steady rest		0.7							
5	Surface roughness, Ra	Fine	0.2 - 0.8	1				1	0.5	1	1
		Medium	1.6 – 6.3	0.5		0.5	1				
		Rough	12.5- 50	0.2							
6	Turning features	External	Chamfer	0.2	Σparameters/ 4.7	0.2	0.2	0.2	0.468	0.723	0.276
			Facing	0.3		0.3	0.3	0.3			
			Knurling	0.4		0	0	0.8			
			Grooving	0.7		0	0.7	0			
			Cut off	0.8		0.8	0.8	0			
			Thread	0.9		0.9	0.9	0			
		Internal	Thread	0.9		0	0	0			
			Drilling	0.5		0	0.5	0			
7	Patch size	single	1	0.1		0.6	0.4	0.1	0.6	0.4	0.1
		Medium	2 – 25	0.4							
		large	25 - 50	0.6							
8	Tool material	HSS		0.8	Σparameters/ 1.8	0.8	0.8	0.8	0.444	0.444	1
		Carbide		1				1			

Source Authors' own work

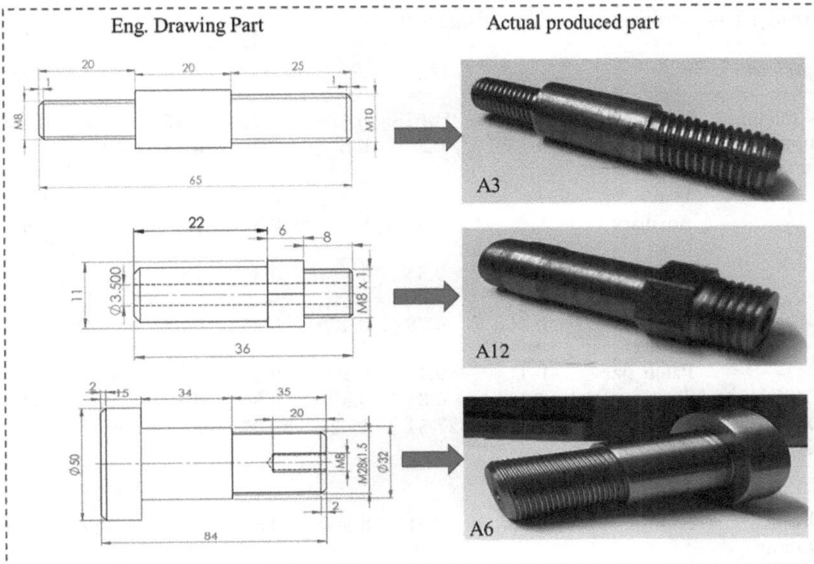

Fig. 11.2 Produced parts of A3, A12 and A6

for a more meaningful comparison and analysis of TMT across different specimens, ultimately supporting the development of more accurate and efficient machining cost estimation models.

$$NDMT = \frac{DMT}{MaximumexpectedTMT(30min)} \tag{11.1}$$

11.3.4 ANN Development Models

The developed ANN's consists of three-layers, feed-forward design is explained in this section using Fig. 11.3 as a desired model. The learning algorithm is backpropagation (BP) with eight input neurons, which is related to the number of input variables associated with single input layer. As illustrated in Fig. 11.3, the input layer is linked to the hidden layers, which are made up of several neurons. During the training phase, the weights are adjusted from 3 to 15 because it was noticed during tuning phase that if it is lower than 3 and above 15, then the learning capability

Table 11.4 Prepared specimens' dataset

Specimens code		*A24*	*A12*	*A9*	*A34*	*A49*	*A87*	*A95*
Normalized Input Variables	Volume	0.0625	0.0625	0.125	0.125	0.25	0.25	0.125
	Machinability level	1	0.8	0.6	0.2	0.2	0.6	1
	Hardness	1	0.5	0.5	0.25	0.25	0.5	1
	Auxiliary tools	0.5	0.5	0	0.5	0.5	0	0.5
	Surface roughness	0.5	0.5	1	0.5	1	0.5	0.5
	Turning features	0.468	0.787	0.489	0.446	0.851	0.574	0.574
	Patch size	0.1	0.4	0.1	0.1	0.1	0.1	0.1
	Tool material	1	0.8	0.8	0.8	0.8	1.8	1.8
Output Parameter	Desired machining time (DMT), min	28.76	27.51	15.28	25.05	10.2	29	17
Normalized Output	NDMT	0.958	0.917	0.509	0.835	0.34	0.966	0.566

Source Authors' own work

of network is weak (Atia et al., 2022). Moreover, the Mean Square Error (MSE) was also high when it was below 3 and above 15.

In this study, the focus was on evaluating a single activation function and a specific training algorithm for the model. The Levenberg–Marquardt algorithm (Trainlm) was chosen as the training function due to its efficiency in updating weights and biases. Trainlm is renowned for being one of the fastest backpropagation algorithms available, which is particularly beneficial for large-scale or complex models (Nassar et al.,

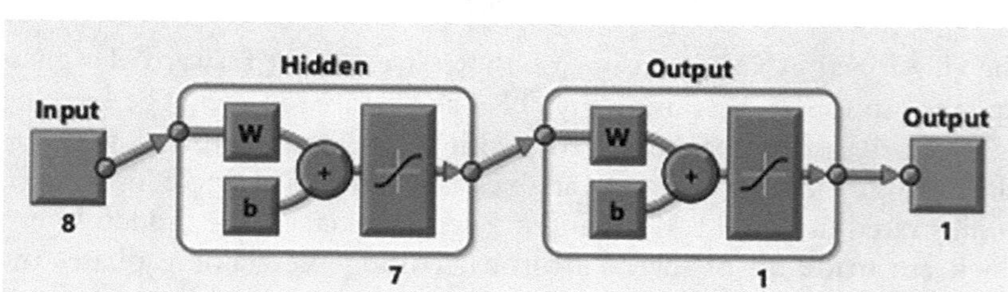

Fig. 11.3 Feedforward neural network with one hidden layer

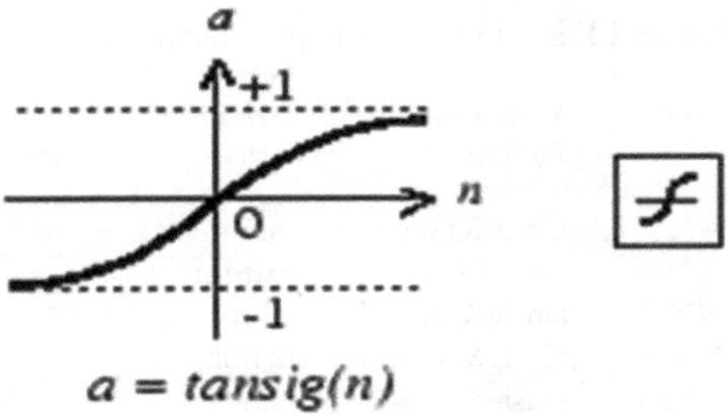

Fig. 11.4 Transfer function symbol and graph of hyperbolic tangent sigmoid

2023). However, it does have higher memory requirements compared to other algorithms, which can be a consideration depending on the computational resources available.

The activation function employed in the model was the hyperbolic tangent sigmoid function (Tansig), which maps input values to an output range between -1 and 1. This function, depicted in Eq. 11.2 and illustrated in Fig. 11.4, is known for its smooth gradient and effectiveness in capturing non-linear relationships. The combination of Trainlm and the tansig function was aimed at optimizing the model's performance by leveraging the strengths of both the training algorithm and the activation function for improved learning and prediction accuracy.

Hyperbolic tangent sigmoid function:

$$a(n) = \frac{2}{1 + \exp(-2n)} - 1 \tag{11.2}$$

.

11.4 Results and Discussions

The number of neurons in the middle layer, the activation function, and the transfer function were the three fundamental design factors that were employed to prepare the generated ANN. After developing more than 50 models with different functions and number of neurons, Table 11.5 displays the six samples that yielded the best design outcomes. The network's performance, including the test, train, and overall regression performance, is significantly impacted by changing the number of neurons in the hidden layer. Because of its greatest regression value, which indicates its best capacity to carry out the necessary estimations, the network number NN-8 was selected compared with the other models.

Table 11.5 Different neural networks

Models	*Transfer Function*	*Activation Function*	*No. of Neurons*	*Test regression*	*Train regression*	*Overall regression*
NN-7	tansig&tansig	trainbr	3	0.86	0.90	0.90
NN-8	**tansig&tansig**	**trainlm**	7	**0.93**	**0.95**	**0.95**
NN-2	tansig&tansig	trainbr	9	0.80	0.96	0.93
NN-1	tansig&tansig	trainbr	10	0.94	0.90	0.92
NN-5	tansig&tansig	trainlm	12	0.85	0.92	0.91
NN-4	tansig&tansig	trainlm	15	0.91	0.94	0.91

Source Authors' own work

The developed model was trained using a dataset sourced from five manufacturing facilities across the country. During the training process, various configurations of neurons in the hidden layer were explored, with the number of neurons ranging from 3 to 15. This approach allowed for an assessment of how different hidden layer sizes impacted the model's performance. For the training phase, 70% of the dataset was utilized to enable the estimator to learn from a substantial amount of data. Training continued iteratively until the model's performance reached the target accuracy, with an error threshold set at 0.001, which corresponds to an equivalent of 0.03 minutes. This error represents the discrepancy between the actual machining time and the time predicted by the ANN, as defined in Eq. 11.3. To validate the model's performance, 15% of the dataset was set aside for validation purposes during the training process. The remaining 15% of the dataset was used exclusively for testing the model's generalization capability. The final step involved identifying and analyzing any errors present at the testing stage to ensure the model's robustness and accuracy in predicting machining times.

$$\text{Error} = \text{Desired}\left(\text{Target}\right)\text{ANN}-\text{Outputs from ANN} \tag{11.3}$$

Figure 11.5 illustrates the decreasing of training error through the iteration mechanism. Start from 0 to 0.0001 with 127 trail number. Figure 11.6 shows the histogram of the error of the selected model. Most of the data are allocated in the middle of graph with -0.00443 errors or 1.329 min, which means the developed model has a good accuracy compared with (Atia et al., 2022). The little number of samples

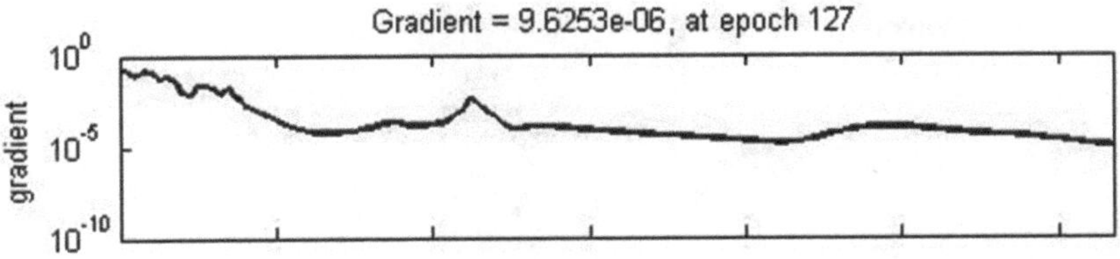

Fig. 11.5 Decreasing of training error with iteration number during trial no

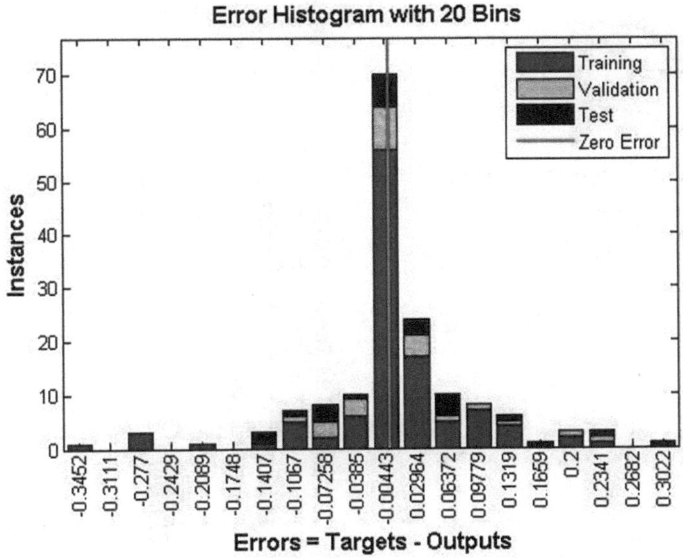

Fig. 11.6 Histogram of error in trial no

allocated to the outer range with high error is explained by the variability in the dataset, which requires additional samples to decrease the error. Figure 11.7 depicts the selected ANN's results collectively with four different regression values including training, testing, validation, and overall performance. It demonstrates the value of the model output versus target output (NDMT) during training with regression value of 0.958, validation with regression value of 0.937, and testing with regression value of 0.9304 with evaluation stages.

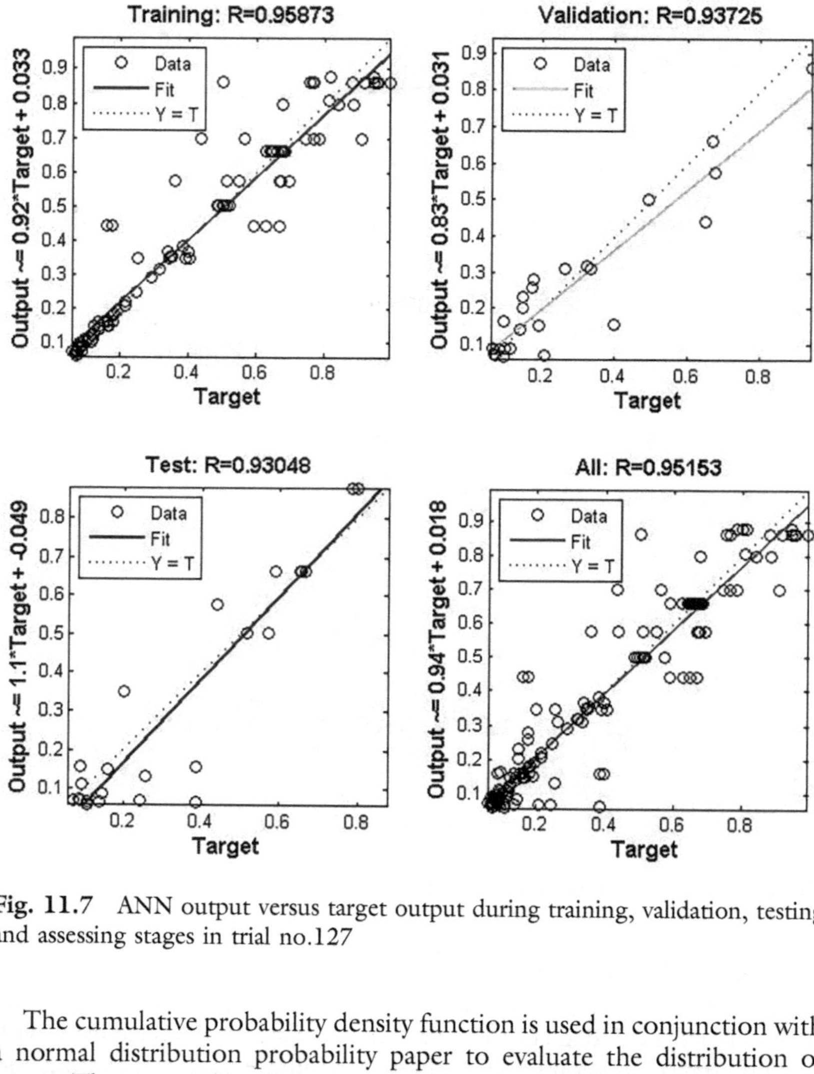

Fig. 11.7 ANN output versus target output during training, validation, testing and assessing stages in trial no.127

The cumulative probability density function is used in conjunction with a normal distribution probability paper to evaluate the distribution of errors. The error is based on the normal distribution. The mean and standard deviation (STD) figures were derived by computing the error of the selected model. The Modified Three-Sigma Test was used to identify 25 samples as outliers. The average value produced from this method, which employs seven neurons in the hidden layer, is 0.034, or 10.2 minutes, with STD of 17.4 minutes. This value is approximately satisfied by experts as a well-designed model that delivers an outstanding estimation in a short time with high accuracy; nevertheless, the dataset size is relatively small in comparison to other studies.

11.5 Conclusion

This research addressed the challenge of estimating manufacturing operating costs in job shop facilities by focusing on Total Machining Time (TMT), which constitutes 60–70% of the total manufacturing cost. The study introduces a novel approach for TMT estimation that generalizes manufacturing time beyond local costing considerations and evaluates time-based data. This method is deemed more effective than traditional techniques because it provides a cost-effective and accurate solution supported by expert opinions.

In this study, a new model for estimating TMT from machining operation data was developed. The model uses eight parameters related to workpieces, equipment, and tools, selected through a survey of manufacturing facilities in Oman. These parameters were categorized into ranges and normalized for the model. The ANN-based estimator was then trained using these normalized values and tested against real-world machining processes.

The results showed that the ANN model could estimate machining time with a mean of 10.2 minutes and a standard deviation of 17.42 minutes, which is acceptable for production environments characterized by variability and uncertainty. The proposed model significantly reduces the time and costs associated with machining time prediction by eliminating the need for detailed operational studies and extensive calculations. It also minimizes the requirement for highly skilled engineers for time estimation tasks.

This methodology proves useful for facilities with limited sizes and can be applied during the product design and development phases. To improve the model's accuracy and generalization, it is essential to increase the number of datasets and their ranges. Overall, the study's approach offers a simplified, efficient, and effective solution for cost estimation in manufacturing settings.

Our findings highlight significant practical implications for the development and application of ANN in estimating manufacturing costs for SMEs. Our research demonstrates that ANN models can enhance the accuracy and efficiency of production time and cost calculations compared to traditional methods. This advancement is particularly beneficial for SMEs aiming to digitize their operations and improve industrial practices, aligning with the United Nations Sustainable Development Goal 9 (SDG-9), which focuses on industrial development, infrastructure improvement, and manufacturing innovation.

The proposed model offers several key advantages for SMEs. Firstly, it provides a faster and more precise calculation of production costs by utilizing a set of parameters related to both the workpiece and the individual cutting operation variables. This model's effectiveness extends to assist SMEs optimize their operations, reduce costs, and boost competitiveness within the industrial sector. However, there are challenges specific to SMEs that must be addressed to effectively implement ANN-based systems. SMEs often face limitations in historical data availability, data quality, and computational resources. Our model, therefore, incorporates simpler neural network architectures with fewer layers and neurons, making it feasible for small-scale manufacturing environments like those in Oman. This design choice reduces computational complexity and training time while maintaining predictive accuracy.

Moreover, SMEs may lack in-house expertise in data science and machine learning. To overcome this, SMEs can collaborate with external experts or use user-friendly AI tools. Additionally, decision-makers might prefer transparent and interpretable models. We address this by incorporating sensitivity analysis and using interpretable techniques alongside ANN, ensuring that the model's decisions are understandable.

Finally, the variability among different types of SMEs necessitates adaptable AI models that can be customized for specific business needs. Our approach includes a continuous improvement framework, where the ANN model is regularly updated based on new data and user feedback, ensuring ongoing relevance and effectiveness. By addressing these factors, SMEs can significantly enhance cost accuracy, improve decision-making, and increase their overall competitiveness in the market.

References

Abdolrasol, M. G. M., et al. (2021). Artificial neural networks based optimization techniques: A review. *Electronics, 10*(21), 2689.

Ajgaonkar, S., Neelam, N. G., & Wiemann, J. (2022). Drivers of workforce agility: A dynamic capability perspective. *International Journal of Organizational Analysis, 30*(4), 951–982.

Alami, D., & ElMaraghy, W. (2021). A cost benefit analysis for industry 4.0 in a job shop environment using a mixed integer linear programming model. *Journal of Manufacturing Systems, 59*, 81–97.

Allahverdi, A., Ng, C. T., Edwin Cheng, T. C., & Kovalyov, M. Y. (2008). A survey of scheduling problems with setup times or costs. *European Journal of Operational Research, 187*(3), 985–1032.

Alsamadony, K., Ibrahim, A. F., Elkatatny, S., & Abdulraheem, A. (2023). Photoelectric factor prediction using automated learning and uncertainty quantification. *Neural Computing and Applications, 35*(30), 22595–22604.

Ateş, K. T. (2023). Estimation of short-term power of wind turbines using Artificial Neural Network (ANN) and Swarm Intelligence. *Sustainability, 15*(18), 13572.

Atia, M., Khalil, J., & Mokhtar, M. (2017). A cost estimation model for machining operations; an ANN parametric approach. *Journal of Al-Azhar University Engineering Sector, 12*(44), 878–885.

Atia, M. R. A., Mokhtar, M., & Khalil, J. (2022). An ANN parametric approach for the estimation of total production operation time. *Ain Shams Engineering Journal, 13*(2), Article 101579. https://doi.org/10.1016/j.asej.2021.09.006

Betrand, J. W. M., & Van Ooijen, H. P. G. (2008). Optimal work order release for make-to-order job shops with customer order lead-time costs, tardiness costs and work-in-process costs. *International Journal of Production Economics, 116*(2), 233–241.

Braun, K. W. (2013). Custom fabric ventures: An instructional resource in job costing for the introductory managerial accounting course. *Journal of Accounting Education, 31*(4), 400–429.

Campi, F., et al. (2021). Parametric cost modelling of components for turbomachines: preliminary study. *Proceedings of the Design Society, 1*, 2379–2388.

Chirra, S. M. R., & Reza, H. (2019). A survey on software cost estimation techniques. *Journal of Software Engineering and Applications, 12*(6), 226.

Costabile, G., et al. (2017). Cost models of additive manufacturing: A literature review. *International Journal of Industrial Engineering Computations, 8*(2), 263–283.

Darmandieu, A., Garcés-Ayerbe, C., Renucci, A., & Rivera-Torres, P. (2022). How does it pay to be circular in production processes? Eco-innovativeness and green jobs as moderators of a cost-efficiency advantage in European small and medium enterprises. *Business Strategy and the Environment, 31*(3), 1184–1203.

Dashti, M., et al. (2022). LEMABE: A novel framework to improve analogy-based software cost estimation using learnable evolution model. *PeerJ Computer Science, 8*, Article e800.

Dehraj, P., & Sharma, A. (2021). A review on architecture and models for autonomic software systems. *The Journal of Supercomputing, 77*(1), 388–417.

Diaz-Chao, A., Ficapal-Cusi, P., & Torrent-Sellens, J. (2017). Did small and medium enterprises maintain better jobs during the early years of the recession? Job quality multidimensional evidence from Spain. *European Management Journal, 35*(3), 396–413.

Disch, M. (2023). Estimating the costs of product development projects based on external data: The new product development cost benchmarking method. *IEEE Transactions on Engineering Management.*

Duffner, F., et al. (2021). Large-scale automotive battery cell manufacturing: Analyzing strategic and operational effects on manufacturing costs. *International Journal of Production Economics, 232*, Article 107982.

Gharaibeh, A., Shaamala, A., Obeidat, R., & Al-Kofahi, S. (2020). Improving land-use change modeling by integrating ANN with cellular automata-Markov chain model. *Heliyon, 6*(9).

Gurcanli, G. E., Bilir, S., & Sevim, M. (2015). Activity based risk assessment and safety cost estimation for residential building construction projects. *Safety Science, 80*, 1–12.

Hong, Y., Bo., Hou, Jiang, H., & Zhang, J. (2020). Machine learning and artificial neural network accelerated computational discoveries in materials science. *Wiley Interdisciplinary Reviews: Computational Molecular Science, 10*(3), Article e1450.

Huang, X. X., Newnes, L. B., & Parry, G. C. (2012). The adaptation of product cost estimation techniques to estimate the cost of service. *International Journal of Computer Integrated Manufacturing, 25*(4–5), 417–431.

Idrus, A., Nuruddin, M. F., Arif, M., & Rohman. (2011). Development of project cost contingency estimation model using risk analysis and fuzzy expert system. *Expert Systems with Applications, 38*(3), 1501–1508.

Kumari, S., & Pushkar, S. (2013). Comparison and analysis of different software cost estimation methods. *International Journal of Advanced Computer Science and Applications, 4*(1).

Li, L., Rong, S., Wang, R., Yu., & Shuili. (2021). Recent advances in artificial intelligence and machine learning for nonlinear relationship analysis and process control in drinking water treatment: A review. *Chemical Engineering Journal, 405*, Article 126673.

Liu, R., Piplani, R., & Toro, C. (2022a). Deep reinforcement learning for dynamic scheduling of a flexible job shop. *International Journal of Production Research, 60*(13), 4049–4069.

Liu, Y., Wang, L., Gu. K., & Li, M. (2022b). Artificial Neural Network (ANN)-Bayesian Probability Framework (BPF) based method of dynamic force reconstruction under multi-source uncertainties. *Knowledge-Based Systems, 237*, Article 107796.

Luo, X. J., et al. (2020). Feature extraction and genetic algorithm enhanced adaptive deep neural network for energy consumption prediction in buildings. *Renewable and Sustainable Energy Reviews, 131*, Article 109980.

Manuguerra, L., Mandolini, M., Germani, M., & Sartini, M. (2023). Machine learning for parametric cost estimation of axisymmetric components. *Proceedings of the Design Society, 3*, 2485–2494.

Nassar, M. M. A., Alzebdeh, K. I., Alsafy, M. M. M., & Piya, S. (2023). Optimizing drilling parameters for minimizing delamination in polypropylene-date palm Fiber bio-composite materials. *Journal of the Brazilian Society of Mechanical Sciences and Engineering, 45*(11), 609. https://doi.org/10.1007/s40430-023-04528-9

Parthan, S. R., Milke, M. W., Wilson, D. C., & Cocks, J. H. (2012). Cost estimation for solid waste management in industrialising regions-precedents, problems and prospects. *Waste Management, 32*(3), 584–594.

Pratama, Y., & Rasywir, E. (2018). Automatic cost estimation analysis on datawarehouse project with modified analogy based method. In *2018 International Conference on Electrical Engineering and Computer Science (ICECOS)*, IEEE, 171–76.

Schaefer, D., & Singleton, C. (2019). Cyclical labor costs within jobs. *European Economic Review, 120*, Article 103317.

Sherehiy, B., & Karwowski, W. (2014). The Relationship between work organization and workforce agility in small manufacturing enterprises. *International Journal of Industrial Ergonomics, 44*(3), 466–473.

Tayefeh, H. S., Ebadati, O. M., & Kaur, H. (2020). Cost estimation and prediction in construction projects: A systematic review on machine learning techniques. *SN Applied Sciences, 2*(10), 1703.

Tien, J. M. (2011). Manufacturing and services: From mass production to mass customization. *Journal of Systems Science and Systems Engineering, 20*(2), 129–154. https://doi.org/10.1007/s11518-011-5166-x

Urbanic, R. J., & Saqib, S. M. (2019). A Manufacturing cost analysis framework to evaluate machining and fused filament fabrication additive manufacturing approaches. *The International Journal of Advanced Manufacturing Technology, 102*, 3091–3108.

Vasco, J., Barreiros, F. M., Nabais, A., & Reis, N. (2019). Additive manufacturing applied to injection moulding: Technical and economic impact. *Rapid Prototyping Journal, 25*(7), 1241–1249.

CHAPTER 12

Comprehensive Supply Chain Performance Estimation with Multi-Output Artificial Neural Networks

Mahmoud Alsafy, Nasr Al Hinai, Sujan Piya, and Ashraf Mishrif

12.1 Introduction

The distinct features of the make-to-order (MTO) production model present a unique set of difficulties for estimating supply chain performance (SCP) (Zhang & Nault, 2023). Lead times for MTO systems might initially differ greatly based on variables including product complexity, raw material availability, and production capacity (Zhai et al., 2023). To guarantee on-time delivery to customers, these differences must be taken

M. Alsafy (✉) · N. Al Hinai · A. Mishrif
Sultan Qaboos University, Muscat, Sultanate of Oman
e-mail: s128777@student.squ.edu.om

A. Mishrif
e-mail: ashraf.mishrif@gmail.com

S. Piya
The University of Sharjah, Sharjah, United Arab Emirates

A. Badran and A. Mishrif (eds.), *Shaping the Future of Development in the GCC*, The Political Economy of the Middle East,
https://doi.org/10.1007/978-981-96-7963-8_12

seriously when estimating SCP. While orders in make-to-stock (MTO) systems are personalized, it can be challenging to predict demand in contrast to MTS systems where demand patterns may be more predictable (Fiems et al., 2020). Thus, scheduling production and maximizing inventory levels depend on precise demand forecasting.

Precise coordination is needed to balance production schedules in MTO systems to reduce the manufacturing cost and achieve customer delivery deadlines in job-shop facilities (Bagheri et al., 2022). Order priority, resource limitations, and production capacity are only a few of the variables that must be considered while optimizing production schedules (Kazemi et al., 2022). To save carrying costs, MTO systems frequently run with lower inventory levels than MTS systems. Sophisticated inventory management techniques are necessary to have the proper amount of goods on hand to fulfill orders without creating stockouts or excess stock, though (Kundu et al., 2022).

To complete customer orders in MTO, suppliers must supply components and raw materials on time. Maintaining efficient communication with suppliers is crucial to avoiding production setbacks and fulfilling expectations from customers (Tanhaie et al., 2020). With the customization inherent in MTO systems, maintaining consistent product quality can be challenging. Implementing robust quality control measures throughout the production process is essential to minimize defects and rework, which can impact SCP (Ben-Ammar et al., 2020).

Furthermore, several comprehensive considerations of production, inventory holding, transportation, and other logistics costs are necessary for the prediction of SCP in MTO systems (Ghasemi et al., 2024). Supply chain managers constantly balance meeting client demands with cost optimization. It is critical for MTO systems to meet customer expectations regarding lead times, product quality, and customization (Liu et al., 2021a, 2021b).

Sato et al. (2023) addressed the client satisfaction needs, and loyalty necessitates recognizing while addressing operational constraints, none of them have specifically addressed it or created a prediction model for the MTO manufacturing system. Thus, many enterprises are frequently transferring from the traditional policies of MTS to MTO to take advantage of the competitive advantage (Piya et al., 2016). However, to maximize performance in MTO, these obstacles must be addressed by integrating efficient planning, coordination, and continuous improvement initiatives throughout the supply chain (Piya & Mahmoud, 2025). Recently, Artificial Neural Network (ANN) technique can facilitate estimation in MTO systems by leveraging their ability to analyze large datasets, recognize patterns, and make accurate predictions (You et al., 2023). By integrating ANN into supply chain management (SCM) processes, organizations can enhance decision-making, improve operational efficiency (Nassar et al., 2023), and ultimately, optimize supply chain performance in MTO environments (Pournader et al., 2021).

The primary contribution of this research study is to create a multi-output prediction model with an ANN-based SCP estimation model that employs the Feed Forward Back Propagation (FFBP) learning technique. To the knowledge of the contributor, this is the first paper to build and analyze SCP measures particularly for an MTO supply chain utilizing the supply chain operation reference framework (SCOR). While developing a model, SCOR incorporates elements of an MTO system found in manufacturing facilities in Oman.

The structure of the paper as follows: The literature on SC management and assessment, including the SCOR® model with SCP systems, is compiled in Sect. 12.2. The details of the ANN model are discussed in Sect. 12.3. The model for estimating SCP, together with the design of the recommended ANN model and the preparation of the data set, is covered in Sect. 12.4. The research outcomes, discussions, data analysis with the model error and validation are covered in Sect. 12.5. Section 12.6 brings the paper to the close and offers some suggestions for further research. Finally, Sect. 7 shows the practical implications of the research work.

12.2 Literature Review

In essence, the SCOR model has a potential advantage in developing the framework of supply chain process in terms of analysis, design, and optimization operations (Zanon et al., 2020). While employing the model into the construction of MTO systems, it provides significant tasks, including supply chain integration (Ikasari et al., 2020), process design (Nicoletti, 2023), analysis, benchmarking, and performance measurements (Pourreza et al., 2022), as well as continuous improvement related to numerous technology integrations (Cerabona et al., 2021). Consequently, the SCOR model offers businesses an analysis of their current MTO manufacturing supply chain procedures (You et al., 2023). This entails comprehending the existing workflow, identifying inefficiencies, and determining where the MTO system needs to be improved (Andia et al., 2021).

The SCOR model enables decision makers in enterprises to benchmark their MTO processes against industry standards and best practices (Cheung et al., 2023). By comparing key performance indicators (KPIs) such as lead times, cycle times, and inventory levels with industry benchmarks, organizations can identify opportunities to enhance their MTO systems.

Employing the SCOR model, enterprises can develop or modify their MTO processes to fit with business goals and consumer demands (Chopra et al., 2022). This includes designing process flows, roles and duties, performance indicators, and technological needs for efficient MTO operations. While SCOR provides a standardized set of measures for measuring MTO system performance across several aspects such as reliability, responsiveness, agility, cost, and asset usage (Delipinar & Kocaoglu, 2016). The company owners can explore the areas for development and evaluate progress over time by comparing performance to established KPIs. Therefore, the SCOR emphasizes the importance of collaboration and integration across supply chain partners (Ricardianto et al., 2022). The model development is able to establish collaborative relationships with suppliers, distributors, and other stakeholders involved in the MTO process, enabling smoother coordination and faster response to customer demand (Wang & Choi, 2020).

SCOR promotes a culture of continuous improvement within the supply chain. Organizations can use the model's framework to identify opportunities for optimization, implement changes, and monitor the impact of initiatives aimed at enhancing MTO system performance over time (Long, 2016). As a part of integrate technology solutions from SCOR model is to support MTO operations, includes enterprise resource planning (ERP) systems, advanced planning, and scheduling (APS) software, and customer relationship management (CRM) systems. By aligning technology investments with SCOR principles, organizations can enhance visibility, automation, and decision-making capabilities within their MTO systems (Sellitto et al., 2015). Generally, the SCOR model is an effective instrument for designing MTO systems because it provides a systematic approach to process analysis, benchmarking, design, performance measurement, collaboration, continuous improvement, and technology integration (Piya & Mahmoud, 2025). Enterprises can use the SCOR architecture to optimize their MTO operations, allowing them to satisfy client needs more efficiently (Lima-Junior & Carpinetti, 2020).

12.2.1 SCOR® Model with ANN

ANN provides significant benefits in various aspects of SCM, particularly with large amounts of data to train efficiently and high quality necessary in the estimate process (Atia et al., 2022); yet they confront obstacles when integrated into the SCOR model (Al-Natour & Turetken, 2020). However, in many supply chains, data can be fragmented, partial, or of less quality. Integrating ANN-based solutions into the SCOR model necessitates addressing data collecting, integration, and cleansing issues to assure input data dependability and accuracy (Lima-Junior & Carpinetti, 2020). ANN models are inherently complicated and can be difficult to interpret and explain, particularly for supply chain practitioners who are used to classical analytical techniques. Integration of ANN-based solutions into the SCOR paradigm may necessitate additional efforts to improve stakeholder knowledge and adoption (Alhumaid et al., 2021).

The main challenge in training ANN requires expertise in machine learning techniques and significant computational resources (Zhang et al., 2020). Additionally, tuning ANN hyperparameters to achieve optimal performance can be time-consuming and resource intensive (Al-Sheheimi et al., 2023). Thus, integrating ANN-based solutions into the SCOR model requires investment in data scientists and computational infrastructure.

The SCOR model encompasses various processes, including plan, source, make, deliver, and return. Integrating ANN-based solutions into each of these processes requires aligning the capabilities of ANNs with specific supply chain activities and objectives (Soori et al., 2023). Customizing ANN architectures and algorithms to address the unique requirements of each SCOR process can be challenging (Ünal & Başçiftçi, 2022). While ANNs can provide valuable insights for supply chain optimization, real-time decision-making capabilities are essential in dynamic supply chain environments (Al-Sheheimi et al., 2023). Integrating ANN-based solutions into the SCOR model requires addressing latency issues and ensuring timely delivery of actionable insights to support decision-making at operational and tactical levels (Ricardianto et al., 2022).

Implementing ANN-based solutions in the SCOR model may necessitate adjustments to existing processes, responsibilities, and organizational structures. Overcoming resistance to change and obtaining stakeholder buy-in are significant obstacles for successfully incorporating ANN-based solutions into the SCOR paradigm (Liu et al., 2021a, 2021b). Because ANN models rely on data-driven algorithms, ethical and legal concerns around data privacy, prejudice, and fairness become more significant (Atia et al., 2017). Ricardianto et al. (2022) confirmed that integrating ANN-based solutions into the SCOR model necessitates resolving these problems to maintain regulatory and ethical compliance.

Most recent research has focused on addressing these challenges, which have a substantial impact on the strategic collaboration of supply chain experts, data scientists, and IT professionals. By overcoming these challenges, enterprises can accomplish digitalization of industrial development in accordance with the fourth industrial revolution, a developed infrastructure system, and the sustainability of supply chain performance in manufacturing facilities.

12.2.2 *Artificial Neural Network (ANN)*

ANN is a model of computation based on the structure and function of the brain of humans. They are made up of interconnected nodes, or neurons, that are grouped into layers. One of the most prevalent types of ANN is the Feedforward (FF) neural network, which is distinguished by information flowing in a single direction, from input to output layer, with no feedback loops. When FF trained using a specific algorithm known as backpropagation (BP), can learn and approximate complex nonlinear functions (Atia et al., 2017). BP is a supervised learning technique that modifies the weights of neural network connections to reduce the error, or discrepancy between expected and actual output. Thus, ANN basically includes input layer, hidden layer and output layer as shown in Fig. 12.1. The input layer is made up of neurons that process input data. Each neuron represents a feature in the incoming data. The hidden layer is positioned between the input and output layers and may consist of one or more layers. These layers alter the incoming data using weighted connections and activation functions (Soori et al., 2023). Followed by the network's final output layer.

The output layer's neuron count varies according on the sort of problem it addresses. Every neuronal connection between neighboring layers is given a weight that indicates how strong it is. These weights are adjusted throughout training to reduce errors. Each layer's neurons

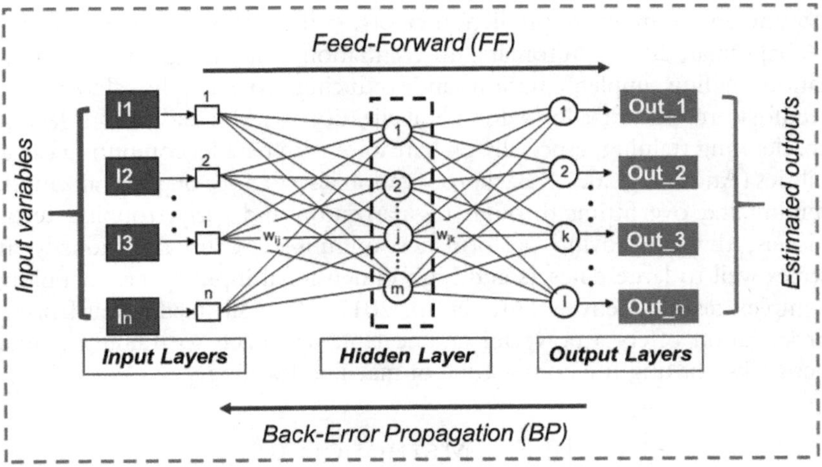

Fig. 12.1 Feed forward back error propagation (FFBP) model

add an activation function to the total of their weighted inputs (Nassar et al., 2023). By employing this process, the network gains non-linearity, which enables it to understand intricate relationships in the data. The network is fed input data during the training phase, and the output it generates is contrasted with the target (actual output). Gradient descent optimization is then utilized to change weight based on the discrepancy between the expected and actual output. Iteratively repeating this approach continues until the network performs satisfactorily on data training (Ünal & Başçiftçi, 2022). FFBP has been successfully applied to various tasks such as classification, regression, pattern recognition, and more. They form the basis of many modern machine learning techniques and are widely used in diverse fields including finance, healthcare, image and speech recognition, and natural language processing (Atia et al., 2022).

FFBP is a widely utilized training algorithm in ANNs due to its versatility and efficiency (Lima-Junior & Carpinetti, 2020; Nassar et al., 2023). It accommodates various network architectures, making it adaptable to diverse tasks from simple classification to complex regression. By updating network parameters through error propagation, it facilitates learning from large datasets in reasonable timeframes, making it suitable for real-world applications. Leveraging gradient-based optimization, it iteratively adjusts parameters to minimize prediction errors, enhancing model performance (Alhaj Omar, 2023). Automatic differentiation simplifies gradient computation, aiding implementation and reducing errors. The algorithm's feedforward nature allows for parallelization within and across layers, accelerating training, especially on hardware with parallel computing capabilities (Atia et al., 2022). Backpropagation also focuses on generalization, minimizing overfitting through regularization and early stopping techniques, thus improving performance on unseen data. Additionally, it scales well to large datasets and high-dimensional input spaces, handling complex tasks effectively (Atia et al., 2017). Overall, feedforward backpropagation offers a powerful and scalable approach to training neural networks, making it a cornerstone of machine learning.

12.3 Methodology

12.3.1 Model Development

This research project utilizes work order sheets collected from five distinct manufacturing facilities situated in Muscat, Sultanate of Oman. These workshops serve as crucial centers for truck engine repair services, addressing a broad spectrum of automotive needs. Each facility services over fifteen different models of truck engines, displaying their expertise in managing diverse repair tasks. Additionally, these workshops handle more than 100 different types and sizes of workpieces monthly, demonstrating their versatile operational capabilities. The layout of these manufacturing facilities is carefully designed to ensure operational efficiency. The configuration supports the required equipment and tools for both manufacturing processes and maintenance tasks. This meticulous design not only optimizes workflow but also enhances productivity, ensuring effective repair and production operations within the manufacturing ecosystem.

12.3.2 Data Set Preparation

In total, 200 product sample work sheets were collected for the purpose of this study. These sheets cover a variety of cylinder head types. The ANN model was trained using the data obtained from these sheets. As demonstrated in Table 12.1, the total cost (price), which is used to determine the total costs of providing goods and services to clients, is the first output performance considered. Resources, capacity planning, inventories, product requirements, client order cost, suppliers, and product demand are the costs that make it up. The order fulfillment cycle time, which is required to calculate the average real cycle time for completing requests, is the second output answer. The receipt of the confirmed order initiates this process, which ends with the customer's acceptance of the order.

The training data set consists of several arrays containing the ANN's inputs and anticipated outputs. As discussed in Fig. 12.1, as two performance attributes, i.e., cost and responsiveness are considered, an integrated model is developed to estimate both outputs. The overall cost to service (price) is the output variable represented by Output_1. The response, which indicates how quickly a SC provides a product to a client,

Table 12.1 Suggested estimation system's metrics with measurement units and description

Variables	*A Brief Explanation*	*Measurement Unit*	*Range*
I1	Assembly and disassembly service costs	Cost (OMR)	10–80
I2	Costs associated with labor and machinery planning for production		10–70
I3	Cost of spare parts as raw materials		20–100
I4	Costs for manufacturing, repairing, and industrial processes		80–250
I5	Costs for order management and fulfillment		30–160
I6	Costs for identifying and evaluating suppliers		30–100
I7	Costs related to product demand management		100–250
Out_1	Total direct and indirect costs for product pricing		200–2000
I8	Duration for source identification and supplier payment processing	time	10:00 -12:00
I9	Time consumed in distribution processes from order to delivery	time	13:00–20:00
I10	Time for acquiring, marketing, and distributing completed products	time	13:30–21:00
Out_2	Time required to fulfill customer requests and achieve satisfaction	Day	1–5

Table 12.2 Applied input variables, and relevant parameters to five sample products

	Cost parameters								*Responsiveness parameters*							
	Input Variables (OMR)							*Output (OMR)*	*Input Variables (time)*			*Output (hrs.)*	*Normalized values of Response model*			
code	*I1*	*I2*	*I3*	*I4*	*I5*	*I6*	*I7*	*Out_1*	*I8*	*I9*	*I10*	*Out_2*	*I8*	*I9*	*I10*	*I2*
F1	70	20	60	0	20	30	0	200	10:00	12:00	13:00	3:00	10	12	1	3.00
F12	50	30	200	240	50	20	0	570	10:00	15:00	15:30	5:30	10	03	3.5	5.50
F13	50	40	180	320	60	20	0	670	10:00	17:00	17:30	7:30	10	05	5.5	7.50
F18	50	40	400	320	80	20	0	910	11:00	18:00	19:00	8:00	11	06	7	8.00
F20	70	50	600	320	130	50	220	1440	10:00	18:00	10:00	24	10	06	10	24.00

is the second output parameter. The three variables for this output estimation are the delivery time (I8, I9, and I10), the due time, and the receipt time.

In this model, output_2 represents the total wait time experienced by the final customer, with Table 12.2 illustrating a sample dataset containing input variables for cost and response. To train the ANN effectively, the response variable must undergo normalization to convert temporal data, such as time, into numerical values. Instances where machining processes or cost of sold product values are absent are denoted by zero values in Table 12.2. As shown in Fig. 12.2, the visually outlines the study's workflow, depicting the sequential process encompassing data collection, preprocessing, ANN training, and result analysis. This schematic provides a clear roadmap of the research methodology employed in analyzing and predicting the total wait time experienced by customers in the manufacturing facility.

12.3.3 *Network Design*

The developed estimator is a FFBP learning algorithm to train the ANN model with three layers for the cost model, as shown in Fig. 12.3. Ten input neurons, one for each input variable, constitute the input layer, as the first layer. The input layer is connected to a hidden layer that is made up of a model design variable that is altered during the design phase. The

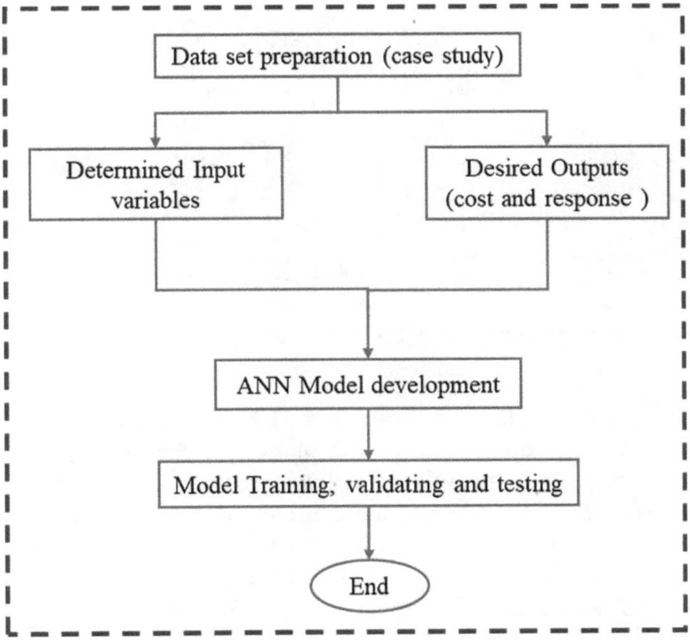

Fig. 12.2 Research flow chart

response efficacy and the total cost to service are provided by two neurons in the output layer. Since this design provides the necessary accuracy in an acceptable amount of time, the number of layers in this network is set to three (Atia et al., 2022).

Weighted connections connect neurons at successive stages. These weights are tuned based on reducing the performance error of the network during the training period. BP is the training algorithm and hyperbolic tangent sigmoid function (tansig) is the transfer function that is used in the model. This is due to the fact that these functions applied to estimate total production time in job-shop facility achieved the best performance with acceptable error (Atia et al., 2022). The function is as shown in Eq. (12.1).

$$A(n) = \frac{2}{1 + \exp(-2n)} - 1 \tag{12.1}$$

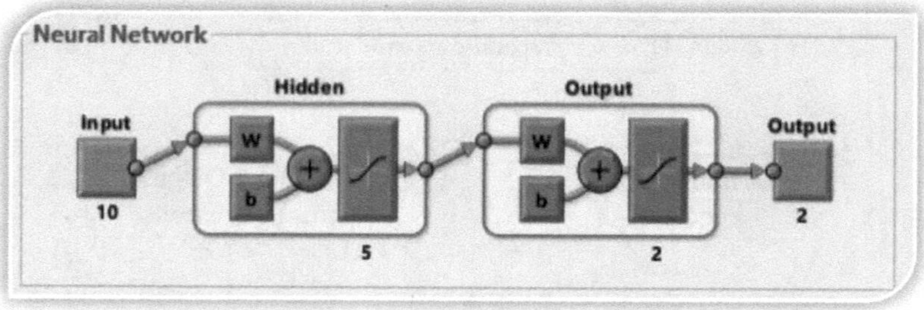

Fig. 12.3 ANN integrated model with hidden layers

The weights are changed from 3 to 10 during the training phase because it was seen during the tuning phase that the network's learning capability was poor if the value was lower than 3 and higher than 15. Furthermore, when the Mean Square Error (MSE) was greater than 10 and less than 3, it was likewise high. In this paper, a single activation function is studied. The "trainlm" method of Levenberg–Marquardt for feed-forward neural networks serves as the training function.

12.4 Results and Discussions

In this multi-output model, the primary design parameters are the activation function and the number of neurons in the hidden layer. The model was developed to estimate cost and customer satisfaction feedback by tuning these parameters using trainlm and trainbr training methods. Table 12.3 displays the top five models based on various criteria including neuron count, overall regression performance, iteration numbers, training duration, and mean square error (MSE), which indicates the effectiveness of the model in reducing network errors. Approximately 70% of the 200 collected data sets were used for training, with the training continuing until the MSE of the network outputs reached the desired targets for each model. The desired value for "trainlm" function is 0.0001 (Atia et al., 2022), which equals OMR 0.278 in the cost output_1 and 0.0024 hours in time with reference to the response output_2. The estimator output error is defined in Eq. 12.2.

$$\text{Error} = \text{Desired (output)} - \text{Estimated Outputs (ANN)} \tag{12.2}$$

15% of the data set was used for testing, and the remaining 15% was used to validate the constructed ANN. The regression value (R) was used to assess the quality of the ANN output, with value equal to 1 or close to 1 meaning that the model has the best estimation between the target value and the output from the network.

12.4.1 Developed Model Analysis

The analysis of the best models is compared with 8 important parameters to justify the optimum model with high accuracy and less time in computing. Table 12.3 shows the regression values for the various estimator designs at each stage of training, validation, and testing for both outputs (1 and 2). The overall regression in the tables represents the entire regression values of training, testing, and validation, indicating that most of the network has the same regression values. As a result, it must focus on the other criteria to justify the differences between networks. It is ready apparent that network NN-2 has the lowest MSE performance (10.18) and gradient training (0.0824). This is due to the network having the most iterations (483), which take longer to train (3:29 minutes) than the other networks. However, the training stage of the optimum network has a long time in this stage, but it improves network efficiency and estimation quality of overall the model.

Figure 12.4, which illustrates the intersection of the three elements training, validation, and testing connected with goal value 0.001 and best performance value as 10.18 after completing 390 rounds, justifies the network's validation performance. Furthermore, as Fig. 12.5 demonstrates, the histogram error provides an additional crucial indication on the optimum model. Following training, it displays the NN-2 model's error histogram. The x- and y-axes, respectively, display the error and sample count. For both answers, most errors appear to cluster around 0.354. Table 12.3 supports the idea that the highly accurate network should be chosen based on the difference in histogram errors.

The comparison between the target and estimated output is presented in Fig. 12.6, as a regression value for training, validation, testing, and overall network performance with values 0.99572, 0.99754, 0.99528, and 0.99584, respectively. All the best network designs as supported in Table 12.3 yielded comparable results. It implies that there is a perfect match between the expected and actual numbers. The usual objective of regression executions is to predict a continuous value. When all data

Table 12.3 Five integrated ANN models with best designs

Network name	*NN-1*		*NN-2*		*NN-3*		*NN-4*		*NN-5*	
Outputs	*Output_1*	*Output_2*	*Output_1*	*Output_2*	*Output_1*	*Output_2*	*Output_1*	*Output_2*	*Output_1*	*Output_2*
Error Histogram	0.691		**0.354**		−1.724		−0.457		0.778	
Gradient (training)	26.3		**0.0824**		152.62		0.721		6.04	
Overall regression	0.91102		**0.99584**		0.91006		0.92303		0.90228	
No. Neurons	15		**5**		10		4		12	
Epoch (iteration)	124		**390**		100		93		100	
Performance (MSE)	104.95		**10.18**		43.18		31.14		17.87	
Train function	trainbr		**Trainlm**		trainbr		trainlm		trainbr	
Time (min)	0:22		**3:29**		1:25		1:27		1:26	

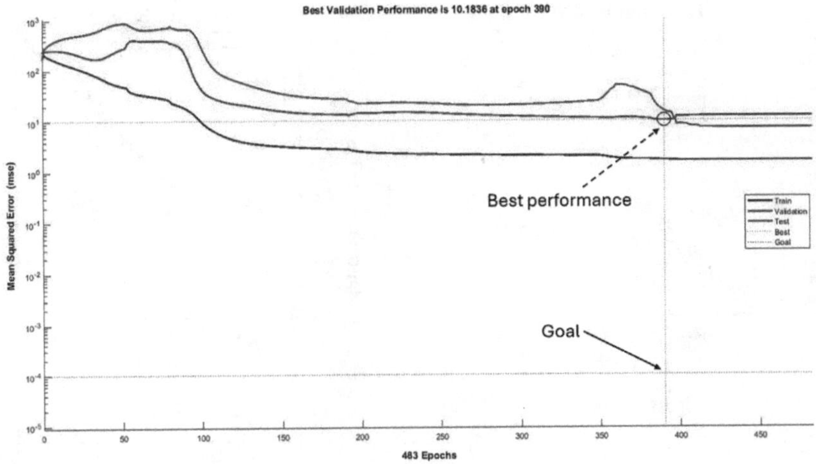

Fig. 12.4 Validation performance of NN-2 model

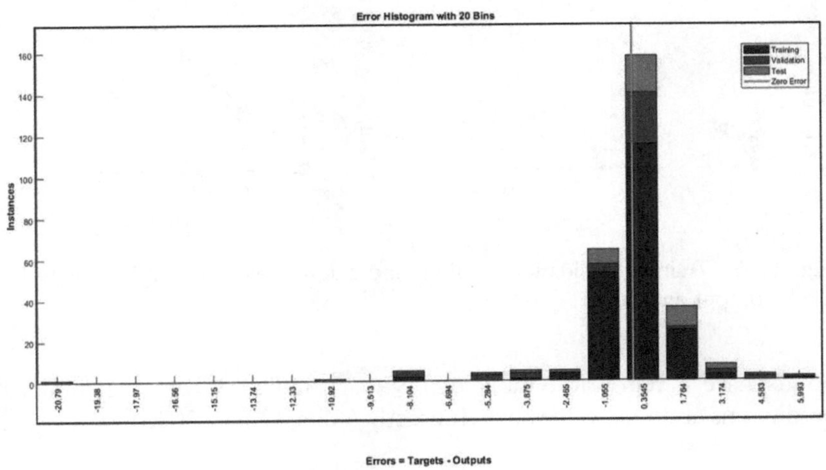

Fig. 12.5 Error histogram of NN-2 model

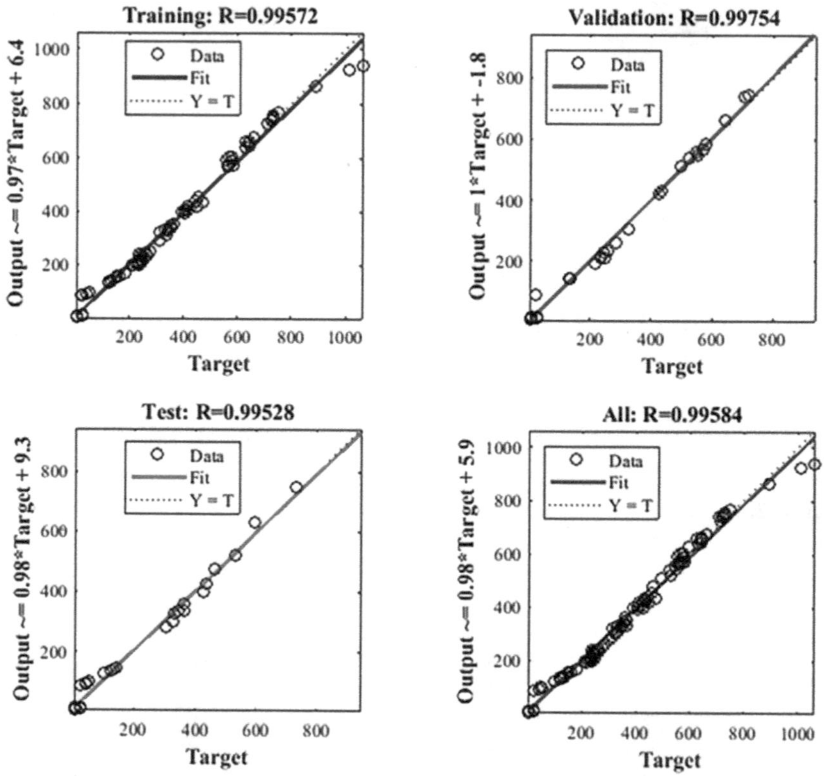

Fig. 12.6 Training, validation, testing, and assessing stages of NN-2 between model output and target

points have a regression value of 0.996, it indicates that the model's predictions and true values match exactly (Alhaj Omar, 2023).

12.4.2 Model Error Analysis

The best five models are compared in terms of different error measurements as average error, percentage average error, standard deviation (STD), and mean square error (MSE), as illustrated in Table 12.4. Network NN-2 shows the lowest percentage error and STD compared with the other networks with 34% and 3.1, respectively. However, MSE is a common loss function used in training ANN for regression tasks because it is a smooth, differentiable function. This property is crucial for training network using techniques like gradient descent, which relies on derivatives to update the model parameters during training and generally behaves well during optimization with easy to compute and interpret. Moreover, MSE penalizes larger errors more heavily than smaller ones. This can be desirable in many regression tasks where large errors are considered more significant and should be minimized (Lima-Junior & Carpinetti, 2020; Nassar et al., 2023). Therefore, we should depend on MSE value as a good indicator of network performance, which shows the model NN-2 has minimum MSE with 10.18.

Based on empirical validation, the most effective design model with the fewest neurons is attained using FFBP coupled with the hyperbolic tangent sigmoid function (tansig) as the transfer function. Moreover, trainlm, aiming to minimize a linear combination of weights and squared errors, is implemented. To further bolster the network's generalization capabilities upon training completion, modifications are introduced to optimize this linear combination. These strategies contribute to refining the network's performance and ensuring robustness in handling diverse data patterns and complexities.

Table 12.4 Average, Standard deviation, and MSE of different models

Network name	*NN-1*		*NN-2*		*NN-3*		*NN-4*		*NN-5*	
Outputs	*Out_1*	*Out_2*	*Out_1*	*Out_2*	*Out_1*	*Out_2*	*Out_1*	*Out_2*	*Out_1*	*Out_2*
Average Error	0.684	0.099	**−0.350**	**0.071**	−1.699	0.216	−0.053	−0.253	−0.269	0.094
%Average Error	68.379	9.850	**−34.954**	**7.143**	−169.945	21.617	−5.255	−25.289	−26.855	9.440
Standard Deviation	10.336	3.521	**3.130**	**0.653**	23.803	2.048	6.622	5.456	12.379	3.421
MSE	10495		**10.18**		43.18		31.14		17.87	

12.5 Conclusion

This study contributes a multi-output model estimation using ANN-based SCP prediction model tailored for a Make-to-Order (MTO) job-shop system. The model estimates two key metrics: the overall cost to serve the customer and the order fulfillment cycle time. The research evaluated various ANN designs, including different activation functions, transfer functions, and hidden layer neuron counts. Results indicated that fewer neurons in the hidden layer generally led to better efficiency. The ANN model was specifically designed to address the adaptation challenges of the SCOR model and fuzzy decision rules, which require frequent human parameter updates. The best ANN configuration achieved an average error percentage of 3.13 and a standard deviation of 0.65 for predicting cost and customer response, with a lowest mean square error (MSE) of 10.18. These results underscore the model's effectiveness as a robust estimator for both cost and fulfillment cycle time.

The findings suggest that this approach can significantly aid managers in making informed, forward-looking decisions by comparing anticipated performance targets with ANN output estimates. Future research could explore alternative learning algorithms for ANN models and develop a user-friendly graphical interface for operators unfamiliar with neural networks and expand the MTO parameters to be suitable for various industries.

12.6 Practical Implications

The main objective of this study is to show the potential of employing ANN in the supply chain performance of manufacturing facilities to improve the SME and raise their profit aligned with the fourth industrial revolution.

The first application is in job-shop facilities, where it can be used to optimize production scheduling by forecasting the time needed to finish different manufacturing jobs based on past performance, the workload at hand, machine capabilities, and other pertinent variables. This can help to cut down on lead times, minimize idle time, and boost overall production effectiveness.

Secondly, by examining sensor data, equipment performance history, and other pertinent factors, the prediction capability in ANN can be used to estimate equipment failures and maintenance requirements in manufacturing plants. By taking a proactive approach to maintenance, one can lower maintenance costs, increase equipment reliability, and avoid unscheduled downtime.

Thirdly, it has a significant impact in optimizing inventory levels in job-shop facilities by forecasting demand, lead times, and production requirements more accurately. This has a direct effect in minimizing excess inventory, reducing carrying costs, and ensuring timely availability of materials and components for production. Furthermore, it is able to analyze production data to predict and detect quality issues in real-time, enabling proactive quality control measures to be implemented. Consequently, it has indirect influence in reducing defects, minimizing rework and scrap, and improving overall product quality and customer satisfaction.

Fourthly, the ANN's ability to analyze production schedules, machine use, and labor availability in order to optimize resource allocation in small manufacturing facilities. This can reduce time wasted, maximize the utilization of resources, and enhance overall efficiency during manufacturing process. By using supplier performance data to forecast lead times, delivery dependability, and quality concerns, the supplier performance prediction can also profit from this technique. By using this data to drive decisions about inventory management, scheduling, and supplier selection, supply chain responsiveness and reliability can be increased. Finally, this method of estimating dynamically prioritizes jobs in SME manufacturing facilities based on parameters such as due dates, client priorities, and available raw material. Although, it can directly assist the decision maker to meet customer deadlines, minimize order lead times, and improve on-time delivery performance.

Overall, the practical applications of ANNs in SME manufacturing facilities include optimizing production scheduling, improving predictive maintenance, improving inventory management, ensuring quality control, optimizing resource allocation, forecasting supplier performance, and dynamically prioritizing jobs to improve supply chain performance and competitiveness.

References

Al-Natour, S., & Turetken, O. (2020). A comparative assessment of sentiment analysis and star ratings for consumer reviews. *International Journal of Information Management, 54*, Article 102132.

Al-Sheheimi, A., Alsafy, M., Al-Hinai, N., & Gultekin, H. (2023). Defining artificial neural network hyperparameters for forecasting nonstationary demand of spare parts. *International Conference on Mechanical, Automotive and Mechatronics Engineering*.

Alhaj Omar, F. (2023). Comparative performance analysis of a feed-forward neural network-based MPPT for rapidly changing climatic conditions. *Konya Journal of Engineering Sciences, 11*, 71–86. https://doi.org/10.36306/konjes.1179030

Alhumaid, K., Habes, M., & Salloum, S. A. (2021). Examining the factors influencing the mobile learning usage during COVID-19 Pandemic: An Integrated SEM-ANN Method. *Ieee Access, 9*, 102567–102578.

Andia, P. L., Camarena, L. G., Campos, G. V., & Merino, J. A. (2021). Model for the optimization of the supply process in a MYPE associated with the consortium of the metalworking sector. *2021 10th International Conference on Industrial Technology and Management (ICITM)*, 56–60.

Atia, M., Khalil, J., & Mokhtar, M. (2017). A cost estimation model for machining operations; an Ann parametric approach. *Journal of Al-Azhar University Engineering Sector, 12*(44), 878–885. https://doi.org/10.21608/auej.2017.19195

Atia, M. R. A., Mokhtar, M., & Khalil, J. (2022). An ANN parametric approach for the estimation of total production operation time. *Ain Shams Engineering Journal, 13*(2), Article 101579. https://doi.org/10.1016/j.asej.2021.09.006

Bagheri, F., Demartini, M., Arezza, A., Tonelli, F., Pacella, M., & Papadia, G. (2022). An agent-based approach for make-to-order master production scheduling. *Processes, 10*(5), 921.

Ben-Ammar, O., Bettayeb, B., & Dolgui, A. (2020). Integrated production planning and quality control for linear production systems under uncertainties of cycle time and finished product quality. *International Journal of Production Research, 58*(4), 1144–1160.

Cerabona, T., Lauras, M., Gitto, J.-P., Montreuil, B., & Benaben, F. (2021). Atomic supply chain modelling for risk management based on SCOR. *Smart and Sustainable Collaborative Networks 4.0: 22nd IFIP WG 5.5 Working Conference on Virtual Enterprises, PRO-VE 2021, Saint-Étienne, France, November 22–24, 2021, Proceedings 22*, 601–610.

Cheung, G. W., Cooper-Thomas, H. D., Lau, R. S., & Wang, L. C. (2023). Reporting reliability, convergent and discriminant validity with structural equation modeling: A review and best-practice recommendations. *Asia Pacific Journal of Management*, 1–39.

Chopra, A., Golwala, D., & Chopra, A. R. (2022). SCOR (Supply Chain Operations Reference) model in textile industry. *Journal of Southwest Jiaotong University, 57*(1).

Delipinar, G. E., & Kocaoglu, B. (2016). Using SCOR model to gain competitive advantage: A Literature review. *Procedia-Social and Behavioral Sciences, 229*, 398–406.

Fiems, D., De Cuypere, E., De Turck, K., & Claeys, D. (2020). Performance analysis of hybrid MTS/MTO systems with stochastic demand and production. *Mathematics, 8*(11), 1925.

Ghasemi, E., Lehoux, N., & Rönnqvist, M. (2024). A multi-level production-inventory-distribution system under mixed make to stock, make to order, and vendor managed inventory strategies: An application in the pulp and paper industry. *International Journal of Production Economics, 271*, Article 109201.

Ikasari, N., Sutopo, W., & Zakaria, R. (2020). Performance measurement in supply chain using SCOR model in the lithium battery factory. *IOP Conference Series: Materials Science and Engineering, 943*(1), 12049.

Kazemi, M., Sadegheih, A., Lotfi, M. M., & Vahdat, M. A. (2022). Developing a bi-objective schedule for an online cellular manufacturing system in an MTO environment. *Soft Computing, 26*(2), 807–828.

Kundu, K., Rossini, M., & Costa, F. (2022). Implementing workload control through lean-based project in MTO-MTS environment. *Journal of Manufacturing Technology Management, 33*(5), 893–912.

Lima-Junior, F. R., & Carpinetti, L. C. R. (2020). An adaptive network-based fuzzy inference system to supply chain performance evaluation based on SCOR® metrics. *Computers and Industrial Engineering, 139*(November 2019), 106191. https://doi.org/10.1016/j.cie.2019.106191

Liu, H., Yang, L., Shen, X., Guo, Q., Sun, H., & Shahidehpour, M. (2021a). A data-driven warm start approach for convex relaxation in optimal gas flow. *IEEE Transactions on Power Systems, 36*(6), 5948–5951.

Liu, S., Yang, L., Chen, B., Yang, S., & Qian, Y. (2021b). Comprehensive energy analysis and integration of coal-based MTO process. *Energy, 214*, Article 119060.

Long, Q. (2016). A novel research methodology for supply network collaboration management. *Information Sciences, 331*, 67–85.

Nassar, M. M. A., Alzebdeh, K. I., Alsafy, M. M. M., & Piya, S. (2023). Optimizing drilling parameters for minimizing delamination in polypropylene-date palm fiber bio-composite materials. *Journal of the Brazilian Society of Mechanical Sciences and Engineering, 45*(11), 609. https://doi.org/10.1007/s40430-023-04528-9

Nicoletti, B. (2023). SCOR Model. In *Supply network 5.0: How to improve human automation in the supply chain* (pp. 19–41). Springer.

Piya, S., Khadem, M. M. R. K., & Shamsuzzoha, A. (2016). Negotiation based decision support system for order acceptance. *Journal of Manufacturing Technology Management, 27*(3), 443–468. https://doi.org/10.1108/JMTM-04-2015-0023

Piya, S., & Mokhtar, M. (2025, August). Supply chain performance rediction model for make-to-rder system using artificial neural network. *Soft Computing, 8*. https://doi.org/10.1007/s00500-025-10553-8

Pournader, M., Ghaderi, H., Hassanzadegan, A., & Fahimnia, B. (2021). Artificial intelligence applications in supply chain management. *International Journal of Production Economics, 241*, Article 108250.

Pourreza, S., Faezipour, M., & Faezipour, M. (2022). Eye-SCOR: A supply chain operations reference-based framework for smart eye status monitoring using system dynamics modeling. *Sustainability, 14*(14), 8876.

Ricardianto, P., Barata, F., Mardiyani, S., Setiawan, E., Subagyo, H., Saribanon, E., & Endri, E. (2022). Supply chain management evaluation in the oil and industry natural gas using SCOR model. *Uncertain Supply Chain Management, 10*(3), 797–806.

Sato, Y. et al. (2023). Switching decisions in a hybrid MTS/MTO production system comprising multiple machines considering setup. *International Journal of Production Economics, 263*, 108877.

Sellitto, M. A., Pereira, G. M., Borchardt, M., Da Silva, R. I., & Viegas, C. V. (2015). A SCOR-based model for supply chain performance measurement: Application in the footwear industry. *International Journal of Production Research, 53*(16), 4917–4926.

Soori, M., Arezoo, B., & Dastres, R. (2023). Artificial neural networks in supply chain management, A review. *Journal of Economy and Technology, 1* 179–196.

Tanhaie, F., Rabbani, M., & Manavizadeh, N. (2020). Applying available-to-promise (ATP) concept in mixed-model assembly line sequencing problems in a Make-To-Order (MTO) environment: Problem extension, model formulation and Lagrangian relaxation algorithm. *Opsearch, 57*, 320–346.

Ünal, H. T., & Başçiftçi, F. (2022). Evolutionary design of neural network architectures: A review of three decades of research. *Artificial Intelligence Review, 55*(3), 1723–1802.

Wang, S. Y., & Choi, S. H. (2020). Pareto-efficient coordination of the contract-based MTO supply chain under flexible cap-and-trade emission constraint. *Journal of Cleaner Production, 250*, Article 119571.

You, X., Yan, G., Al-Masoudy, M. M., Kadimallah, M. A., Alkhalifah, T., Alturise, F., & Ali, H. E. (2023). Application of novel hybrid machine learning approach for estimation of ultimate bond strength between ultra-high performance concrete and reinforced bar. *Advances in Engineering Software, 180*, Article 103442.

Zanon, L. G., Arantes, R. F. M., Calache, L. D. D. R., & Carpinetti, L. C. R. (2020). A decision making model based on fuzzy inference to predict the impact of SCOR® indicators on customer perceived value. *International Journal of Production Economics, 223*, Article 107520.

Zhai, Y., Hua, G., Cheng, M., & Cheng, T. C. E. (2023). Production lead-time hedging and order allocation in an MTO supply chain. *European Journal of Operational Research, 311*(3), 887–905.

Zhang, J., & Nault, B. R. (2023). Information sharing in an MTO supply chain with upstream adjustments. *European Journal of Operational Research, 308*(1), 97–112.

Zhang, S., Zhang, S., Wang, B., & Habetler, T. G. (2020). Deep learning algorithms for bearing fault diagnostics—A comprehensive review. *IEEE Access, 8*, 29857–29881.

CHAPTER 13

Implementation of Artificial Intelligence in Smart Cities of the GCC Region: Comparative Case Studies

Mohammad Osaid Farooq and Tahura Fatima

13.1 Introduction

The urban population has been steadily rising; most of the population resides in the urban area, and this number is expected to grow in the coming years. This rapid transformation is having a negative impact on cities. Researchers have been doing significant research on smart cities, as the concept of smart cities can help the cities grow in a healthy manner. A smart city can be defined as a place equipped with modern and intelligent technology and can effectively handle information in its domain. To enhance the quality of life and to make the environment more sustainable, the concept of smart cities use various technologies (Gracias et al., 2023).

There are multiple features of these smart cities, including introducing technology into buildings, transportation systems, power grids, piping

M. O. Farooq (✉) · T. Fatima
Georgia Institute of Technology, Atlanta, GA, USA
e-mail: osaidfarooq13@gmail.com

A. Badran and A. Mishrif (eds.), *Shaping the Future of Development in the GCC*, The Political Economy of the Middle East,
https://doi.org/10.1007/978-981-96-7963-8_13

networks, healthcare facilities, etc., to improve their efficiency and sustainability. All around the world, countries have been implementing and initiating smart city projects. The internet of things (IoT) is a crucial component of smart cities, it can be defined as the interconnectivity of different things or objects through a common network. The integration of IOT in the fabric of smart cities has revolutionized the face of modern-day cities. (Xia et al., 2012) The implication of IoT can be done through artificial intelligence. The other component is big data. The data collected from various places helps form crucial insights into the city (Hashem et al., 2016).

The revolution brought by artificial intelligence (AI) has transformed the face of cities into various aspects. AI has the potential to be a crucial tool that can provide intelligent solutions to the challenges faced by our cities. Predictive analytic and intelligence models can anticipate population growth, traffic patterns, energy demand changes, potential health hazards, and various other things that could be used to aid the design process, urban planning, and decision-making. It could also streamline energy distribution, waste management, and provide aid and services to citizens.

It has been observed that countries in The Gulf Cooperation Council (GCC) countries, including Bahrain, Kuwait, Oman, Qatar, Saudi Arabia (KSA), and the UAE, have been rapidly expanding in terms of population. As urban population increases in the cities of GCC, the implementation of smart city principles is pivotal for sustainable growth. The GCC is a rapidly growing region in terms of its use of sustainable practices. The issue of rapid urbanization can also be seen in this region, as it is expanding rapidly. According to estimates, by 2050, 9 out of 10 people will be residing in urban cities in this region (Asmyatullin et al., 2020).

There have been several efforts in this region to develop smart cities. There are multiple on-going projects, however, they are restricted to a few countries. It is a well-known fact that by implementing the concept of smart cities, there will be acceleration in automation and efficiency of the systems in the city. This chapter shall investigate the current strategies implemented within the GCC region and provide future directions to implement other strategies to make the system more efficient in the usage of AI. Moreover, this paper has evaluated the role of technologies like machine learning, the internet of things, and data analytics in making cities more sustainable, liveable, and efficient. Further, the benefits of using intelligent systems in the development of cities for the people and the potential of them to alleviate the negative impacts of heavy infrastructure on living standards and day-to-day activities have also been thoroughly discussed. Lastly, as the world is heading towards global warming due to rapid urbanization, the implementation of AI to achieve sustainable strategies was also assessed.

The paper is divided into eight sections, the first being the introduction. Followed by Sect. 13.2 and Sect. 13.3 which has literature review and research methodology. Section 13.4 will deal with case studies, followed by Sect. 13.5 which will be a more detailed comparative study. To highlight the key learning, Sect. 13.6 is prepared to emphasize the lesson. Section 13.7 is a summary of the challenges, and the paper ends with the conclusion and recommendations.

13.2 Literature Review

There is a lot of emerging data on smart cities and AI, which shows a growing interest in technologies to solve urban and architectural problems around the world. This section talks about the existing research around the technologies which power smart cities and how AI is being integrated into smart cities.

13.2.1 Concept and Evolution

Smart cities tend to use technology to create more sustainable, efficient, and livable urban areas. We can tie in the evolution of smart cities to the advancements in information and communication technology (ICT), which have provided real-time data collection and analysis of the data to come up with smart solutions to the problems. Initially, smart city initiatives focused more on the development of infrastructure, while in recent years it has been focusing more on public engagement and delivery of services in the city.

As there is no universal definition of a smart city, and the concept has been explored extensively in academic literature, we can say that a smart city is one which uses technology to enhance the performance of services and infrastructure, and the well-being of humans while reducing the costs and mitigating the consumption of resources. (Hollands, 2008) Further, we can say that smart cities rely on the intelligent use of developing technologies for management of resources and improving the quality of life of its citizens (Batty et al., 2012).

13.2.2 AI Technologies in Urban Development

AI technologies have become an integral part of smart city development, such as IoT (Internet of Things), Machine Learning and data analytics. IoT devices are now present in a lot of infrastructure and objects used by the public daily. This provides a continuous flow of data which guides decision-making and improves the efficiency of services. Machine learning is being used to understand and predict traffic patterns, energy distribution and public health and safety. Data analytics process the raw data that is fed and come up with algorithms and actionable insights that guide the urban planners and policymakers towards a more sustainable and efficient system of doing things.

These predictive algorithms can process vast amounts of data and come up with accurate predictions to guide decision-making. (Goodfellow et al., 2016) For example, traffic systems can predict the flow of traffic during a given period through the city and help in routing the traffic through most efficient routes. Similarly, smart grids use AI to better manage energy distribution according to the requirements and make the supply more efficient with the demands.

13.2.3 Benefits of AI in Smart Cities

AI can offer numerous benefits to the systems of smart cities, these include better resource management, improved public safety and enhanced quality of life for the residents. Predictive analytics can reduce environmental impact by optimizing energy distribution and waste management. Surveillance systems use AI to enhance security by identifying potential threats and responding to them in real time. Also, the use of intelligent systems in transportation can reduce traffic congestion and improve mobility through the roads of the city (Chourabi et al., 2012).

13.3 Research Methodology

The paper critically examines current research on smart cities in the GCC region. This study is essentially conducted by comprehensively assessing and critically analyzing the literature to identify the current areas of interest in the smart city research domain. It is essential to note that despite having focused on recent academic and peer-reviewed literature, news and science magazines might also help to highlight this point due to the novelty of the topic.

To carry out such comprehensive literature evaluation across the world, several bibliographic databases were considered. Several criteria were considered prior to selecting the city. The IMD smart city index was also taken into consideration (Table 13.1).

For instance, Singapore, which was selected because of its Asian slant, small size, yet rich resources, which are under strict control—this central government (still one standing alone) not withstanding its peculiarity of a city/state. Another example would be Helsinki chosen due to being small (sized) without necessarily being high up on the list for smart cities like other places such as those found in the North, among them Finland itself (so not ranked at the highest level within this category), where there are hardly enough means but there're lots of advanced technologies. This study also investigated numerous reports and indices on the GCC cities for data collection.

Table 13.1 List of IMD the IMD smart city index from 2019 to 2023

City	*City HDI*	*Rankings*			
		2019	*2020*	*2021*	*2023*
Zurich	0.989	1	1	1	1
Oslo	0.98	2	2	2	2
Copenhagen	0.967	4	3	5	4
London	0.973	3	10	3	6
Singapore	0.939	10	7	7	7
Helsinki	0.96	6	5	9	8
Geneva	0.966	7	8	6	9
Stockholm	0.972	9	9	11	10
Beijing	0.907	30	22	17	12
Abu Dhabi	0.911	16	14	12	14
Prague	0.96	8	4	10	14
Amsterdam	0.962	11	11	13	15
Seoul	0.952	23	20	18	16
Dubai	0.911	13	19	14	17

13.4 Case Studies

Singapore

Singapore is one of the frontrunners in implementing smart city solutions. AI plays a significant role in this initiative, particularly urban mobility, healthcare and sustainability. AI is used in traffic management systems to optimize the flow and reduce congestion on the roads. AI traffic management systems use sensors and cameras to analyze real-time data and optimize traffic signals and provide traffic information to drivers. Singapore uses AI systems to manage healthcare resources and improve the services provided to patients. The healthcare system uses AI based systems and predictive analytics to identify large scale health risks and optimizes resource allocation to combat that. To balance the demand and supply, renewable energy sources are integrated to smart grids and AI is used. Smart sensors are also used throughout the city for efficient waste management systems, which reduces operational costs and energy consumption (Chan, 2018).

Barcelona

Barcelona is one of the cities that integrated IoT and AI for management of public services to improve the quality of life of the residents. Things like lighting systems, waste and water management systems have had a huge impact due to these technologies. Barcelona has integrated smart systems to their lighting devices that use sensors to analyze real-time conditions to adjust streetlights based on the requirements reducing a lot of unnecessary energy consumption. Barcelona uses AI powered waste management systems which optimize the schedules and waste collection routes. This reduces the operational costs of the service and improves efficiency. The city uses sensors and data analytics in their water management systems to detect leaks and monitor water quality, which ensures a reliable and efficient power supply (Alvarez et al., 2014).

New York City

New York City is a good example of incorporating AI for enhancement of public safety, traffic management and energy efficiency. The city uses

AI systems to monitor public areas and detect potential criminal activities. Real-time data is analyzed for prevention of crime and improving emergency response times. AI powered systems in traffic management optimize traffic flow to reduce congestion. The city uses AI-driven traffic signal control systems which adjust the traffic signals based on real-time data, resulting in improved traffic flow and reduced delays. The city uses AI-driven systems to optimize energy management in smart grids for usage in buildings and also integrates renewable energy sources (Brantingham et al., 2017).

Helsinki

Helsinki is becoming more popular recently since in 2019 it was awarded the title of European Smart Tourism Capital and has one of the best digital twins in the Kalasatama neighborhood. From developing creative ICT technologies for city infrastructure to designing online solutions which would attract tourists to Helsinki archipelago, these are some examples of projects under the IoT program. Within the Smart Mobility initiative, there is a project involving drones with an aim of leading carbon neutrality in logistics, off-site security, and environmental monitoring. At stake are strategies for mitigating the problem of last-mile delivery, such as the usage of drones, self-driving minibuses for municipal transit systems and replacing traditional parcel delivery vehicles by smaller and self-driving cars that use electric energy (Shamsuzzoha et al., 2021).

Dubai

Through the Smart Dubai Initiative, Dubai aims to become the smartest city in the world. AI is a key component for this initiative, which aims to work on transportation, public services and enhance energy systems. Dubai Electricity and Water Authority (DEWA) has used AI in smart grid to monitor and optimize energy distribution according to the requirements in real time. This helps the city to increase their energy efficiency and reduce the operational costs. Also, Dubai's Roads and Transport Authority (RTA) has deployed autonomous transportation systems and AI powered traffic management to improve mobility and reduce travel times (Al Nuaimi et al., 2015).

Riyadh

The city is implementing AI technologies to improve energy efficiency and public transportation systems. King Abdulaziz City for Science and Technology (KACST) is on the forefront of development of AI systems for urban planning and environmental sustainability. The public transportation in Riyadh is being transformed through the use of AI-driven metro system to enhance connectivity and reduce delays while improving the congestion condition on the roads (Al-Kodmany, 2018).

13.5 Comparative Study: The Case Between Manama and Singapore

Manama

Manama, the capital of Bahrain, is a fast-growing city and an important financial hub. According to the 2010 census, the population was 329,510. Due to its small size, it has reached high level of urban development. As the GCC is racing towards smart solutions, the city of Manama holds untapped potential in implementation of AI.

Singapore

Singapore is a small country island in Asia. It has a very extensive market economy despite being one of the densest countries in the world. The smart city initiatives by Singapore are quoted frequently, as a result it is always on the top in the list of smart cities. The success can be attributed to use of extensive technology and citizen focused initiatives.

This paper aims to analyze how Artificial Intelligence (AI) is being integrated into Urban Development. The three aspects in which the comparison will be made, and key learning can be taken are:

i. Environmental Concerns
ii. Healthcare infrastructure
iii. IoT and data analytics

By the means of comparison between the cities of Manama and Singapore, this study gives insight on how the use of AI can improve the quality of life and sustainability of urban areas and giving recommendations for Manama.

13.6 Environmental Concerns

Singapore has been effective in employment of AI into the management strategies of the city. These tackle key problems like air pollution, disposal of waste, and energy efficiency. Use of AI powered systems have enabled the monitoring of current environmental data, optimization of energy distribution and management of waste by the help of predictive analysis. One example is the use of AI to predict energy demands, which allows for better integration of renewable energy sources and also helps to minimize carbon emissions.

Manama is new in the adoption of smart city technologies. Integration of AI systems for use in Urban Development is still under development. To come to the level of advanced cities in this regard, Manama could use AI based environmental monitoring systems like the ones used in Singapore. By using sensors all around the city to track water and air quality, data could be collected and analyzed real time which would lead to fast response from the government in case of any environmental problems. Additionally, AI would help with more effective management of energy consumption and waste disposal. This would decrease the carbon footprint of the city.

13.7 Healthcare Infrastructure

In the case of Singapore, AI is integral to healthcare. AI is used in the enhancement of everything, from predictive analysis which help in forecasting the healthcare trends to diagnostic tools which improve efficiency and accuracy. The role of AI in management of hospitals includes optimization of resources, decreasing waiting times, and improvement to patient care. Predictive analysis models are used to anticipate outbreaks of diseases and patient admissions. All of these facilitate better preparedness and management of resources (Shamsuzzoha et al., 2021).

On the other hand, Manama has not yet integrated AI to utilize its potential in their healthcare system. Use of AI could significantly improve the city's healthcare services. Use of predictive analysis would help the healthcare providers in accessing patients' needs and optimize the resource distribution for maximum efficiency and least wastage on a large scale. Just like in the case of Singapore, AI systems would help in hospital management which could help in reducing wait times and improving the quality of patient care. Also, smart models in medical diagnostics could increase the accuracy of disease detection and improve the treatment which could lead to better outcomes, boosting Manama to the global healthcare standards.

13.8 IoT and Data Analytics

Singapore has been one of the most efficient cities to deploy IoT sensors to optimize the management of urban spaces. The use of these sensors throughout the city has been successful in gathering real-time data on traffic patterns, energy consumption trends, and environmental conditions. AI powered data analysis process this data and enhance a range of public services. Traffic direction and efficiency in energy distribution have been improved. The blending of IoT and AI systems has been the backbone of reducing traffic congestion and improving public transportation throughout the city. These improvements have increased the overall quality of life of the residents.

Manama is currently in the infancy of adopting IoT sensors and implementation of data analytics of the gathered information. To accelerate the development of the framework for smart cities, Manama needs to deploy IoT sensors citywide to monitor the urban parameters. The gathered data would be crucial in analyzing the trends of traffic patterns and energy consumption. This would enable AI systems to help in decision-making in regard to traffic management, public transport systems and energy efficiency. This would help with the overall efficiency of the city and reduce operational costs.

13.9 Key Learning for GCC Region

This study shows the potential of AI to significantly boost the performance of smart cities. Some of the latest advancements in AI are being implemented in GCC regions while there are a lot of possibilities which could be explored further.

13.9.1 Efficiency

With AI, many urban systems have become much more efficient. These include public transportation, energy management, traffic systems and waste disposal to name a few. Through technologies such as predictive analytics, the cities can anticipate public issues before they grow and address the problems with proper counter-measures. This reduces the operational costs as well as enhances energy efficiency.

This is evident in the case of Dubai, where the use of AI in traffic management systems has reduced traffic congestion by 20% and travel times have been improved by 30%. Also, in Riyadh, enhanced public transportation efficiency through AI powered metro systems is projected to reduce dependency on private vehicles which would reduce traffic and lower carbon emissions in the city (Al Nuaimi et al., 2015).

13.9.2 Quality of Life

Smart cities provide their residents with better safety, mobility, and easier access to public services. Implementation of AI in administrative processes makes it easier for the residents to access government services and information.

From the case of Singapore, we can see how AI in healthcare makes it easier for residents to access the services and streamlines their data for seamless use, this is particularly useful for the elderly patients as well as patients with disabilities or chronic illnesses. Also, New York City's safety department has been enhanced using AI which has given a boost to public safety through predictive policing. This has reduced the crime rates while increasing the sense of safety of the residents. (Chan, 2018) (Brantingham et al., 2017) In the GCC region, the UAE has been a success story in terms of implementing AI for the safety of the residents (Batayneh et al., 2021).

Waste management of cities like Barcelona and Seoul can help regulate the waste of the smart cities of the GCC region. Intelligent waste systems, when implemented correctly, can have a positive environmental impact on the city.

13.9.3 *Economy*

Integrating AI into urban systems attracts technology investments and creates high skill jobs in the market which boosts economic development in the region. As the GCC region is growing continuously, with a focus on tourism and urban development, it is in a good position to leverage these opportunities to capitalize on the benefits which AI provides for economic development. Cities like Dubai have attracted numerous startups and technology companies which have significantly diversified the economy and contributed to the overall growth of the region (Al Nuaimi et al., 2015).

13.9.4 *Sustainability*

By optimizing resource usage and wastage management systems, AI has contributed significantly to making smart cities more sustainable. Smart energy grids optimize energy distribution while better transport management lowers carbon emissions. All these elements make an enormous impact on the sustainability of the cities when combined. As seen in the case of Barcelona, AI powered street lighting has lowered the carbon footprint of the city significantly by reducing energy consumption by 30% (Alvarez et al., 2014) (Al Nuaimi et al., 2015).

13.9.5 *Challenges*

Though there are many benefits to AI technologies, there are still some challenges which stand in the way of AI integration across the board. The concerns for data privacy are real, there are some technological barriers and a lack of regulatory frameworks. It is crucial to tackle these issues for the successful implementation of AI in smart city networks.

A large amount of data is collected and processed for the working of AI and data analytics which raise concerns for the privacy and security of citizens. To implement AI systems in the GCC region successfully, there needs to be sufficiently advanced data privacy measures in place and comprehensive data privacy regulations are required to monitor and fight the threats.

To implement proper AI solutions, a lot of skilled personnel are required who have advanced knowledge and technical skills to be able to work with the technology. Also, cities must invest in proper infrastructure for the deployment and upkeep of AI systems. The GCC needs to keep ongoing investment into education and technology.

Due to the rapid development of AI technology and the unpredictable nature of the potential usage of these technologies, there needs to be a focused development of regulatory frameworks that ensure the safe and ethical usage of AI technology. Government should develop policies and standards which guide the implementation of AI systems in smart cities and urban environments. These precautions will make sure of ethical and effective use of AI systems in smart cities.

13.10 Conclusion and Recommendations

Integration of AI into the development and functionality of smart cities has a lot of potential for the GCC region. It can enhance all aspects of everyday life like urban development, better healthcare, efficient public systems, improved quality of life, sustainable solutions, etc. As the cities are progressing towards a smarter future, the inclusion of the cities in GCC is critical for the development of the entire region. Currently, only Abu Dhabi and Dubai (ranked 13th and 17th) are in the top 20 of the smart city index 2023 by the World Competitiveness Center. Innovation can help make the cities smarter, along with adopting existing practices that exist in the modern world. The comparison between Singapore and Manama shows the advancement in AI integration in Singapore. There are a lot of improvements in the quality of life of the residents, particularly in healthcare, environmental management and IoT driven analytics. For Manama, employment of similar technologies would bring about a lot of improvement in urban systems, healthcare infrastructure, energy efficiency, resource management, and reduction of carbon footprint. Through the use of these technologies, Manama can move in the direction of being a smarter and more sustainable city, increasing the overall quality of life of the residents.

13.10.1 Recommendations

- Real-time decision-making and adaptive learning should be incorporated into the urban infrastructure. Sectors like energy management, transportation, healthcare and public services should be prioritized when it comes to integration of intelligent systems to make Manama a smart city (Kandt & Batty, 2021).

- Including the use of AI in governance will help improve the decision-making process and provide more efficient public service delivery which can be achieved by enhancing automated systems and using predictive analytics (Hassan et al., 2021).
- Building collaborations between public and private organizations as well as academic institutions is essential to generating creative ideas and guaranteeing the effective application of AI technology in urban environments.
- AI-driven platforms that involve individuals in planning and decision-making can result in more inclusive and responsive governance. Security, data privacy, and moral issues surrounding the application of AI in public settings should be the main areas of policy change (Khatoun & Zeadally, 2016).
- Enhancing AI literacy and skill development should be incorporated in the curriculum of the educational systems in order to yield a generation equipped with necessary skills to develop, manage and maintain these systems.
- Manama can become to a smart city, if the city starts heavily investing in AI's infrastructure and research and development (R&D) so as to improve urban planning, enhance transportation management, and optimize resource use.

References

Al Nuaimi, E., Al Neyadi, H., Nader, M., & Al-Jaroodi, J. (2015). Applications of big data to smart cities. *Journal of Internet Services and Applications, 6*(1), 25–34.

Al-Kodmany, K. (2018). Smart cities and AI: The future of urban planning. *Journal of Urban Technology, 25*(2), 3–15.

Alvarez, M., Ruiz, M., & Velázquez, G. (2014). Sentilo: An open data sensor platform for smart cities. *Future Generation Computer Systems, 32*, 140–153.

Asmyatullin, R. R., Tyrkba, K. V., & Ruzina, E. I. (2020). Smart cities in GCC: Comparative study of economic dimension. *IOP Conference Series: Earth and Environmental Science, 459*(6), Article 062045. https://doi.org/10.1088/1755-1315/459/6/062045

Bakıcı, T., Almirall, E., & Wareham, J. (2012). A smart city initiative: The case of Barcelona. *Journal of the Knowledge Economy, 4*(2), 135–148. https://doi.org/10.1007/s13132-012-0084-9

Batayneh, R. M. A., Taleb, N., Said, R. A., Alshurideh, M. T., Ghazal, T. M., & Alzoubi, H. M. (2021). IT governance framework and smart services integration for future development of Dubai infrastructure utilizing AI and big data, its reflection on the citizens' standard of living. In *Advances in intelligent systems and computing* (pp. 235–247). https://doi.org/10.1007/978-3-030-76346-6_22

Batty, M., Axhausen, K. W., Giannotti, F., Pozdnoukhov, A., Bazzani, A., Wachowicz, M., & Portugali, Y. (2012). Smart cities of the future. *The European Physical Journal Special Topics, 214*(1), 481–518.

Brantingham, P. J., Valasik, M., & Mohler, G. O. (2017). Does predictive policing lead to biased arrests? Results from a randomized controlled trial. *Journal of Experimental Criminology, 13*(3), 367–390.

Chan, C. (2018). The smart nation initiative: Developing smart cities in Singapore. *IEEE Communications Magazine, 56*(4), 42–47.

Chourabi, H., Nam, T., Walker, S., Gil-Garcia, J. R., Mellouli, S., Nahon, K., & Scholl, H. J. (2012). Understanding smart cities: An integrative framework. *Proceedings of the Annual Hawaii International Conference on System Sciences*, 2289–2297

Goodfellow, I., Bengio, Y., & Courville, A. (2016). *Deep learning*. MIT Press.

Gracias, J. S., Parnell, G. S., Specking, E., Pohl, E. A., & Buchanan, R. (2023). Smart cities: A structured literature review. *Smart Cities, 6*(4), 1719–1743. https://doi.org/10.3390/smartcities6040080

Hashem, I. A. T., Chang, V., Anuar, N. B., Adewole, K., Yaqoob, I., Gani, A., Ahmed, E., & Chiroma, H. (2016). The role of big data in smart city. *International Journal of Information Management, 36*(5), 748–758. https://doi.org/10.1016/j.ijinfomgt.2016.05.002

Hassan, G., Aqib, M., Ahmed, S., Faheem, M., Mehmood, M., Shah, M. A., & Gohar, F. (2021). Towards a smart city framework for smart governance. *Complex & Intelligent Systems, 7*(4), 1869–1882. https://doi.org/10.1007/s40747-021-00318-z

Hollands, R. G. (2008). Will the real smart city please stand up? Intelligent, progressive or entrepreneurial? *City, 12*(3), 303–320.

Kandt, J., & Batty, M. (2021). Smart cities, big data and urban policy: Towards urban analytics for the long run. *Cities, 109*, Article 102992. https://doi.org/10.1016/j.cities.2020.102992

Khatoun, M., & Zeadally, S. (2016). The role of the internet of things (IoT) and AI in smart cities. *IEEE Communications Standards Magazine, 18*(2), 46–61. https://doi.org/10.1109/COMST.2016.2532458

Shamsuzzoha, A., Nieminen, J., Piya, S., & Rutledge, K. (2021). Smart city for sustainable environment: A comparison of participatory strategies from Helsinki. *Singapore and London. Cities, 114*, Article 103194. https://doi.org/10.1016/j.cities.2021.103194

Xia, F., Yang, L. T., Wang, L., & Vinel, A. (2012). Internet of things. *International Journal of Communication Systems, 25*(9), 1101–1102. https://doi.org/10.1002/dac.2417

CHAPTER 14

AI-Driven Transformations: Meteorology and Solar Radiation in the GCC Region

Mohammadu Bello Danbatta and Nasser Al-Azri

14.1 Introduction

As of 2016, renewable energy sources account for 24% of global electricity production, with solar energy making up just 1.2% of that. Many nations are investing in renewable energy projects. The primary challenge with these resources is the unpredictability of their power output, which can lead to overall grid variability. For solar power, this unpredictability is often due to changes in meteorological factors like cloud cover, temperature, and wind speed. Therefore, accurate solar irradiance forecasting is crucial for grid operators. It helps them maintain grid stability, efficiently schedule demand response, manage economic dispatch, and optimize the operations of power plants (Alfadda et al., 2018). Solar energy is a key future renewable energy source. With growing reliance on renewable energy, solar power is receiving increased attention. Data from Solar radiation is crucial for designing and operating solar power

M. B. Danbatta · N. Al-Azri (✉)
Sultan Qaboos University, Muscat, Sultanate of Oman
e-mail: nalazri@squ.edu.om

A. Badran and A. Mishrif (eds.), *Shaping the Future of Development in the GCC*, The Political Economy of the Middle East,
https://doi.org/10.1007/978-981-96-7963-8_14

systems effectively. Accurate prediction of solar radiation at specific locations is essential for maintaining energy stability from solar stations. This prediction is vital for governments, businesses, and energy operators to create optimal strategic plans, especially when integrating multiple energy sources. However, predicting solar radiation accurately is challenging due to the many variables involved, such as weather and topography. To address this, various models have been proposed, including numerical weather prediction (NWP) and artificial intelligence models. The effectiveness of these models depends heavily on selecting a representative set of parameters, or features, to enhance prediction accuracy and reduce the computational cost of real-time prediction systems (Hedar et al., 2021).

Aerosols pose the most significant uncertainty in human-induced climate change, primarily due to the contrasting effects of absorbing and non-absorbing aerosols, along with their indirect influence on clouds. Absorbing aerosols directly alter the climate by modifying the radiation balance and indirectly by impacting cloud nucleation and optical characteristics. Additionally, they exert a semi-direct influence by warming atmospheric layers and diminishing cloud coverage. Hence, studying the global distribution and temporal changes of absorbing aerosols is crucial for understanding climate change (Li et al., 2009).

14.1.1 Air Pollution

Contemporary environmental challenges largely arise from rapid population expansion, industrial advancements, and uneven urban development. Particularly in major urban centers, meteorological elements and atmospheric conditions significantly impact air quality, rendering air pollution a prominent concern in megacities. This is particularly true for cities like Jeddah, where atmospheric pollutants and various climatic conditions impact air quality (Taylan, 2017). The objective of this study is to construct an Adaptive Neuro-Fuzzy Inference System (ANFIS) for assessing the influence of peripheral factors on air quality and pollution, with a specific emphasis on the increasing ozone levels observed in Jeddah. The ANFIS model was employed to monitor ozone concentration levels, and its performance was assessed using data collected from monitoring stations established by the General Authority of Meteorology and Environment Protection of Saudi Arabia. Fuzzy quality charts, based on US-EPA air quality standards, further validated the results.

Findings indicate that the ANFIS model offers a comprehensive and reliable approach for estimating and assessing ozone levels, producing more accurate outcomes (Taylan, 2017).

Similarly, a predictive approach is proposed utilizing a fuzzy-logic model to predict PM_{10} levels in a residential zone in Kuwait, particularly affected by traffic and industrial operations. Seven input variables, comprising four meteorological factors (wind speed, wind direction, relative humidity, and solar radiation) and the ambient concentrations of three gaseous pollutants, were converted into fuzzy sets using a graphical user interface and an artificial intelligence-based method. The model employed trapezoidal membership functions with ten and fifteen levels to define fuzzy subsets for each variable. This prognostic model demonstrated minimal deviations from actual results and exhibited superior predictive performance, achieving a determination coefficient exceeding 0.99(Yetilmezsoy & Abdul-Wahab, 2012).

In Jeddah, Saudi Arabia, a continuous air quality monitoring station was installed to observe multiple air pollutants and meteorological parameters throughout a span of two years (2018–2019) (Rehan & Munir, 2022). Two supervised machine-learning models were devised to analyze the distribution of modeled pollutants, with particular emphasis on key pollutants like NO_2 and O_3, by categorizing their concentrations into distinct quantiles. The study assessed the impact of various pollutants and meteorological variables at each quantile, finding significant variations in the influence of explanatory variables. For example, the coefficients of wind speed for O_3 concentrations varied across different quantiles. The models exhibited correlation coefficients of 0.91 for NO_2 and 0.92 for O_3, with RMSE values of 14.41 and 8.96, indicating satisfactory model performance and valuable insights into the behavior of air pollution.

In Iraq and Kuwait, a unique method to estimate daily $PM_{2.5}$ exposures from 2001–2018 was devised using visibility data collected during regional military operations. This method employed random forest machine learning and a generalized additive mixed model to estimate daily high-resolution visibility, which was then used to infer $PM_{2.5}$ concentrations. The model accounted for meteorological parameters, land use variables, and satellite-derived estimates of surface dust. Cross-validation revealed strong predictive ability ($R^2 = 0.71$), with annual average $PM_{2.5}$ predictions exceeding current U.S. and WHO standards. The study provided long-term estimates of $PM_{2.5}$ exposures, facilitating research on health effects and informing regional environmental policies (Li et al., 2021).

Air pollution is increasing due to heavy traffic, global warming, new industrial facilities, and expanding urbanization. The Air Quality Index (AQI) is crucial for assessing local air quality and addressing public health concerns. Predicting air quality is challenging, but AI techniques have proven effective in handling such complex problems. This study developed an adaptive neurofuzzy logic method to evaluate the impact of various factors on air quality in Jeddah. Data on six environmental pollutants were used to predict the AQI, with different weighting factors assigned to each pollutant. The ANFIS model's performance was evaluated using data from monitoring stations and compared with US-EPA standards, concluding that the model is a comprehensive tool for predicting and assessing air quality (Taylan, 2013).

In regions like Kuwait, where air pollution monitoring networks are scarce, an ensemble machine learning model was developed to predict daily $PM_{2.5}$ concentrations using visibility data. The model, applied to predict $PM_{2.5}$ levels at eight airports in Kuwait and Iraq from 2013 to 2020, achieved a cross-validation R^2 of 0.68. This approach allows for the retrospective estimation of daily $PM_{2.5}$ exposures, which is vital for conducting environmental risk assessments and population health studies in areas with sparse monitoring networks (Li et al., 2022).

During the COVID-19 lockdown in Saudi Arabia, the study investigated the impact on air quality parameters (O_3, NO_2, and PM_{10}) in Makkah using data from five monitoring sites. Two methodologies were employed: comparing measured concentrations during the lockdown in 2019 and 2020 and comparing weather-adjusted concentrations estimated through machine learning with observed concentrations. The research revealed notable changes in air pollutant levels, underscoring the significance of adjusting for meteorological conditions. The increase in O_3 levels was linked to its inverse correlation with NO_2, which decreased during the lockdown (Habeebullah et al., 2022). Additionally, managing the climate of a greenhouse in harsh environments like Qatar is challenging due to extreme temperatures and high humidity. These conditions create significant hurdles for greenhouse climate control strategies, making it difficult to minimize long-term costs effectively (Chen & You, 2021).

14.1.2 *Agriculture*

The growth of the agriculture sector is crucial for Oman's economic development, with effective water use and conservation being key to this advancement. Oman receives some of the highest levels of solar radiation in the world, making it ideal for modernizing and developing sustainable irrigation models. Incorporating modern technology, particularly 4th industrial technologies like AI and the Internet of Things, is essential to addressing these challenges effectively (Adamsab et al., 2019).

A methodology was illustrated through an application to the South Al-Batinah region in Oman, where excessive groundwater withdrawal for irrigation has led to saltwater intrusion in a coastal aquifer. A novel simulation-based water management system efficiently optimizes and assesses various irrigation practices, crop patterns, and abstraction scenarios. Findings from multiple optimizations run underscore the conflicting objectives between profit-oriented agriculture and aquifer sustainability. Consequently, only a multi-objective optimization approach can deliver sustainable water resource management solutions that balance environmental and socio-economic development needs (Grundmann et al., 2012).

The intensification of agriculture has led to groundwater depletion in various parts of the world, with Saudi Arabia being a notable example due to significant agricultural expansion since the 1970s. To grasp the impact of policy interventions on enhanced water resource management, precise data regarding changes in the quantity and size of center-pivot fields are essential. A hybrid machine learning approach was deployed, amalgamating Density-Based Spatial Clustering of Applications with Noise, Convolutional Neural Networks, and Spectral Clustering, to scrutinize annual maximum Normalized Differential Vegetation Index maps derived from Landsat imagery spanning 1990 to 2021. Evaluated against more than 28,000 manually delineated fields, the method attained high accuracies, with a coefficient of determination surpassing 0.97 in comparison to manual delineation. Despite a slight reduction in field acreage from 1990 to 2010, by 2015, the number of fields had surged, encompassing 9310 square kilometers. Recent observations show a return to pre-1990 levels (Li et al., 2023).

In dry regions such as Qatar, ensuring efficient irrigation timing and duration is crucial for sustainable agriculture. A practical AI-based solution was proposed, detailing all phases from design to implementation. Initially, a microcontroller system gathered data on soil moisture, ambient temperature, and solar radiation. Subsequently, a fuzzy logic controller processed these inputs using predefined rules tailored to specific crops, determining the optimal irrigation timing and duration. An in-house ZigBee-based wireless monitoring system was developed to oversee system operation, record sensor data, irrigation schedules, and water usage. Experimental findings demonstrated the system's effectiveness in compensating for water loss due to evapotranspiration, predicted by the Penman–Monteith model adopted from the FAO. The fusion of fuzzy control with wireless monitoring is recognized as a promising advancement in irrigation management and planning (Touati et al., 2012).

A self-powered irrigation system could have a significant and viable impact, especially given Oman's abundance of natural resources. Leveraging online monitoring via IoT mobile applications enhances crop growth by facilitating efficient management of land moisture, humidity, and temperature. Testing the irrigation system within a college campus setting for three cultivation areas yielded satisfactory results. The results demonstrated the system's effectiveness in water resource management, power generation, and monitoring soil parameters, leading to controlled irrigation practices and increased productivity. This study highlights the considerable potential of Industry 4.0 technologies in enhancing falaj systems, solar energy utilization, and agriculture in Oman (Adamsab et al., 2019).

In Qatar, where year-round crop cultivation is essential due to water scarcity, efficient management of indoor greenhouse environments becomes crucial for growing fruits and vegetables such as tomatoes and leafy greens. Temperature, CO2 levels, and humidity play pivotal roles in maintaining the optimal indoor climate for controlled environment agriculture. Precisely regulating indoor temperature within the appropriate range not only enhances tomato production but also safeguards plants from excessive heat or cold stress. Any deviations from the suitable temperature range can negatively impact plant growth, resulting in a significant decrease in crop yield (Chen & You, 2021).

Accurate rainfall predictions are essential for farmers to optimize their crop yields, manage water resources, and plan irrigation. Predicting heavy rainfall and providing information on natural disasters pose significant challenges. Rainfall prediction has historically been a complex issue.

Various methodologies have been employed to estimate rainfall intensity in Saudi Arabia, with data mining (DM) classification approaches proving effective for both numerical and categorical rainfall prediction. By analyzing historical weather data from southern Saudi Arabia, this study evaluated several machine learning (ML) approaches for rainfall forecasting. Accurate crop yield predictions are essential for farmers, and while engineering analysis systems exist, they are underutilized in crop yield forecasting. Predicting the impact of drought on crop yield requires careful consideration of factors such as crop selection, planting timing, harvesting strategy, and storage capacity. The study identified relevant characteristics for predicting precipitation and used an innovative ML approach to classify predicted rainfall as regular or heavy. Performance metrics, including error, accuracy, rates, recall, RMSE, F-measure and MAE, were used to evaluate various methodologies, with Decision Trees (DT) demonstrating the highest accuracy. The Function Fitting Artificial Neural Network classifier (FFANN) achieved an accuracy of 96.1%, surpassing other classifiers in the rainfall database (Baljon & Sharma, 2023).

14.1.3 PV Application

Saudi Arabia aims to reduce its reliance on oil and natural gas by generating 9.5 GW of renewable energy by 2023, with an initial goal of 3.45 GW by 2020. The country's total electricity production is projected to reach about 95 GW by 2023. In desert regions like Saudi Arabia, a notable challenge in implementing solar photovoltaics (PV) is the frequent incidence of dust storms. These storms lead to the accumulation of dust on PV modules, consequently diminishing their overall efficiency. A comprehensive dust assessment, including trajectory analysis, was conducted nationwide to address this issue (Alfadda et al., 2018).

The adoption of solar power faces hurdles like intermittency, grid management challenges, and the complex interplay between weather parameters and solar irradiance. This study focuses on Saudi Arabian weather data, utilizing machine learning and artificial neural network algorithms to enhance the accuracy of solar irradiance predictions. Data sources include PVGIS, KACARE and NREL (Alkhaldi, 2022).

Forecasting electrical load is crucial for effective planning and operation of power systems. This study analyzed meteorological data using various data mining techniques to forecast the electrical load demand of a factory in Riyadh, Saudi Arabia. Hourly records of factory load and meteorological data from 2016 to 2017 were obtained from KACARE and Saudi Electricity Company. Different machine learning algorithms, including ANN and SVR, were employed and compared. The study found that the SVR algorithm utilizing six features was the most accurate predictor for forecasting factory load (Alrashidi & Qamar, 2023).

Efficient optimization of all-photovoltaic hybrid power generation systems within energy-efficient buildings is crucial for attaining net-zero emissions. This study proposed a hybrid approach that integrates conventional solar panels with advanced solar window systems and building-integrated photovoltaic (BIPV) systems. Through meteorological data analysis and simulation models, energy outputs across cities like Riyadh, Sydney, Kuala Lumpur, Toronto, Auckland, Cape Town,, and Kuwait City were forecasted. Despite extended payback periods, the proposed system could fulfill up to 78% of contemporary buildings' energy requirements, with Middle Eastern cities generating roughly 1.2 times more power compared to Toronto. The study highlighted the benefits of integrating intelligent systems to enhance overall energy efficiency (Nur-E-Alam et al., 2024).

Hydrogen, as an energy carrier, can be efficiently produced through various methods, bolstering production while meeting diverse electrical demands. In this study, the integration of meteorological data using HOMER software was explored to identify the optimal solution. The optimal system configuration comprised 270 kW of PV power, a 300-kW wind turbine, a 500 kW electrolyzer, a 100 kg/L hydrogen tank, 70 units of 1 kWh lithium-ion batteries, and a 472 kW converter. This hybrid energy system demonstrated the lowest Levelized Cost of Energy (LCOE), Levelized Cost of Hydrogen (LCOH), and Net Present Cost (NPC), rendering it the most favorable choice for the proposed hydrogen project in Al-Kharj (Okonkwo et al., 2022).

The Middle East and North Africa (MENA) region is ideal for solar energy development due to its abundant solar radiation. Saudi Arabia's Vision 2030 identifies renewable energy as a key economic diversification strategy, aiming to generate 9.5 GW from renewable sources. The NEOM project, envisioning a $500 billion mega-city powered entirely by renewable energy, exemplifies this commitment. Accurate forecasting of solar irradiation is pivotal for optimizing PV system efficiency. This study developed an ANN model to predict monthly average daily solar irradiation in Jeddah, Saudi Arabia, using weather and solar irradiation data from KACARE. The model was validated against experimental measurements, enhancing PV system design and grid management (Alhebshi et al., 2019).

Solar PV plants encounter challenges in energy production owing to the unpredictable nature of solar radiation, chiefly influenced by clouds and aerosol particles. Precise forecasts of PV output are vital for efficient solar energy trading and grid management. This study evaluated a computationally light autoregressive KNN-regression scheme (TSFKNN) for day-ahead forecasts of solar irradiance and energy yield for various PV technologies on an hourly basis, utilizing data from Thuwal, Saudi Arabia. The developed forecasting models, customized for online systems, demonstrated enhanced accuracy and low computational cost, improving predictive accuracy by an average of 10% to 25% (Kamarianakis et al., 2022).

14.1.4 *Solar Radiation Forecast*

Accurate solar irradiance forecasts are crucial for integrating variable solar energy production into the electricity grid. This study introduces the Wrapper Mutual Information Methodology (WMIM) for short-term irradiance prediction, combining mutual information and an Extreme Learning Machine (ELM) for forecasts ranging from 5 minutes to 3 hours ahead. The performance of WMIM was compared to three scenarios of dimensionality reduction: full space (latest 50 variables), partial space (latest 5 variables), and Principal Component Analysis (PCA), using irradiance data from Madina and Tamanrasset. Results showed that reducing the historical input space enhanced forecast accuracy. For example, in Madina, WMIM forecasts surpassed PCA, achieving a coefficient of determination (R2) between 0.927 and 0.967 compared to 0.921 and 0.959 for PCA, and a Mean Absolute Percentage Error (MAPE) of 7.4–10.77 for WMIM versus 8.4–11.55 for PCA. In Tamanrasset, WMIM achieved an R2 between 0.883 and 0.957, better than PCA's 0.873 to 0.910, with a Normalized Mean Squared Error (NMSE) of 0.048–0.128 for WMIM and 0.105–0.130 for PCA. Additionally, the ELM technique demonstrated higher computational efficiency compared to the Multilayer Perceptron (MLP), showing WMIM's potential for superior prediction performance (Bouzgou & Gueymard, 2019).

In Riyadh, Saudi Arabia, a one-hour ahead solar irradiance forecasting model was developed, incorporating Aerosol Optical Depth (AOD) and

Angstrom Exponent data from a ground station. Various data-driven forecasting models, including MLP, SVR, kNN, and decision tree regression, were compared. The MLP model using Saudi Arabian data achieved a RMSE of less than 4% and a forecast skill exceeding 42% for one-hour ahead forecasts. Tested under different feature selection schemes, the MLP model proved highly effective, particularly in desert regions with frequent dust storms and high AOD levels (>0.4) (Alfadda et al., 2018).

Solar power is recognized as a viable renewable energy option due to its abundance and eco-friendly nature, making accurate solar radiation forecasting crucial for predicting power output. This study utilized machine learning techniques to forecast solar radiation in Riyadh, Saudi Arabia. Models including ANN, RF, and linear regression were employed using weather data from KACARE. Results showed that RT had the highest accuracy, achieving 92.86% with an RMSE of 10.32, compared to ANN (91.30%–18.47 RMSE) and linear regression (78.57%–30.41 RMSE) (Alwated & Brahimi, 2021).

A study introduced machine learning techniques to predict sunshine duration across different regions in Saudi Arabia using parameters like maximum possible day length, longitude, altitude, extraterrestrial solar radiation, latitude, and month. Two neural network algorithms, Particle Swarm Optimization and SVM, were used. Employing a leave-one-out strategy, data from 40 stations developed the model, which was then tested on the 41st station. Results showed minimum MAPE of 2.3% and 2.7% at the Al-Madina station using Particle Swarm Optimization and SVM, respectively, while maximum MAPE values of 22.9% and 16.7% were observed et al.-Numas. Higher MAPE values were noted during summer months, with lower values in winter. These findings underscore the effectiveness of the methods for estimating sunshine duration in Saudi Arabia and potentially in similar regions (Mohandes & Rehman, 2013).

The global shift towards environmentally friendly energy sources highlights the importance of accurate solar radiation forecasting for electricity providers. This study analyzed daily global solar radiation data from Najran province, Saudi Arabia, proposing a model for predicting global horizontal irradiance. Weather data from Najran University were used to identify crucial variables. Six machine learning algorithms—CNN, KNN, SVM, logistic regression, RT, and SVC—were employed to forecast GHI. Evaluation metrics included R2, RMSE, MBE, MABE, MAPE, and T-statistic. The study found that the support vector classifier technique was most suitable, delivering precise results based on the evaluation metrics (Alghamdi, 2022).

By combining data from the Terra satellite's moderate resolution imaging spectroradiometer, a radiative transfer model, and machine learning techniques, a study forecasted direct solar irradiance across the Arabian Peninsula. Exploratory data analysis unveiled a correlation between atmospheric aerosols and solar irradiance, particularly evident along the eastern coastlines of the Arabian Gulf and Sea of Oman. Lower solar irradiance was observed during March 2016 and 2017 in central and eastern regions, likely attributed to dust events. The Rub Al Khali desert exhibited high solar irradiance during winter and spring. The study also identified significant dust outbreaks in March 2009 and 2012. The ResNet prediction model demonstrated high accuracy, with a Mean Absolute Error (MAE) of 0.02, Mean Squared Error (MSE) of 0.005, and an R-squared value of 0.99, underscoring the desert's favorable conditions for harnessing solar radiation (Alwadei et al., 2022).

14.1.5 Skin Cancer

The rise in skin cancer cases has underscored the importance of shielding oneself from solar radiation. Consequently, the examination of sun protection behaviors has become a crucial focus in dermatology and pharmacology research. This study aimed to scrutinize public sun protection practices in the Arabian Peninsula regions through a simple random survey. Among various ML algorithms, ANN and SVM were chosen to develop models predicting public sun protection measures based on their prediction accuracy. Model performances were assessed using performance indicators derived from confusion matrices and receiver operating characteristic curves. Results revealed that 51% of respondents exhibited low levels of sun protection practices, while 49% demonstrated high levels. The findings indicated that SVM outperformed ANN significantly in predicting these responses (Sultana, 2022).

To understand and mitigate the harmful effects of Erythemal Ultraviolet Radiation, it's crucial to comprehend its spatial distribution and temporal variations under diverse meteorological conditions. Addressing this concern, a study evaluated the impact of stratospheric ozone and aerosol loading on EUV receipt at six sites across different climatic zones in Saudi Arabia. Sites representing the middle, north, and south of Saudi Arabia were selected. Employing satellite-based measurements from the

Total Ozone Mapping Spectrometer (TOMS) website spanning 1979 to 2005, with a four-year gap from 1993 to 1996, atmospheric data was analyzed intensively. Findings suggest a notable decline in EUV levels despite a significant reduction in stratospheric ozone, particularly during summer months, attributable to increased aerosol loading. However, correlations for other months are less apparent. Overall, the EUV radiation trend remains stable outside of summer months, with only a few exceptions (Al-Mostafa et al., 2015).

In dry regions, primary pollutants play a significant role in the rise of ozone levels, which can adversely affect living organisms. In a study, abductive networks utilizing the group method data handling (GMDH) were investigated for ozone prediction. These models were automatically generated from a dataset containing inputs and outputs. Initially, models were developed for a specific location in the Empty Quarter, Saudi Arabia, using solely meteorological data and its derivatives. The study then explored including NO and NO_2 concentrations and their transformations as additional inputs. Another model predicted ozone levels after 1 hour, primarily using meteorological data, NO, and NO_2 concentrations. Models tailored for specific times of day were found to be simpler compared to generic models. Additionally, an ensemble modeling approach was examined. A time-specific model achieved a MAPE of 3.82%. These proposed models are inherently self-organizing, requiring minimal user intervention, and can be readily implemented by interested practitioners. (Rahman et al., 2012).

14.1.6 Sustainable Buildings

This study focused on regulating the indoor climate of a tomato greenhouse in Qatar, where high temperatures and humidity pose challenges. Using the PKDDRMPC framework, we managed the greenhouse climate effectively, protecting tomatoes from adverse conditions. Uncertainty sets for ambient temperature, absolute humidity, and solar radiation were established using historical weather data. Optimal control inputs were then determined through data-driven optimization at each time step. The performance of PKDDRMPC was compared with rule-based control, CEMPC, RMPC, and SVC-based RMPC. Results indicated that PKDDRMPC reduced total control costs by 14% compared to rule-based control and 4% compared to RMPC. Although CEMPC exhibited the lowest costs, it violated temperature constraints by over 70% and encountered challenges with humidity constraints and CO_2 levels. PKDDRMPC nearly eliminated such violations (Chen & You, 2021).

Kuwait's extreme heat makes air conditioners (ACs) essential, but excessive energy consumption often results from not adjusting the set temperature. This study introduces a Thermal Comfort-based Controller (TCC) that utilizes predicted mean vote (PMV) control to improve comfort and energy efficiency. The TCC system automates rooftop AC units in Kuwaiti homes. Recognizing the significance of mean radiant temperature (MRT) in PMV control, particularly in regions with high solar radiation, machine learning models were devised to estimate MRT without direct measurement. Experimental results revealed that actual MRT averages were 1.5°C higher than air temperature, suggesting potential PMV underestimation. Machine learning models, including linear regression, regression tree, and artificial neural network, were assessed to accurately estimate MRT with minimal data. Simulation outcomes showed these models improved MRT estimation, achieving over a 10% reduction in energy consumption (Park et al., 2021).

The shift towards sustainable buildings has transformed many passive structures into dynamic ones. Mosques, with unique energy usage patterns, have often been overlooked in energy efficiency initiatives due to unpredictable electrical consumption. This study developed a framework for short-term electricity load forecasting for mosques in Riyadh, Saudi Arabia. By analyzing mosque load data and meteorological datasets, four forecasting algorithms were evaluated: ANN and SVR with Radial Basis, Polynomial, and Linear kernels. SVR with a Radial Basis kernel was most effective, yielding the lowest errors with RMSE and MAE, values of 4.207 kW, 2.938 kW, respectively (Alrashidi, 2023).

Mosques hold a special place in the hearts of worshippers and must be maintained in pristine condition. The Prophet's Mosque in Medina, Saudi Arabia, ranks second in importance only to the Sacred Mosque in Mecca. Due to constant overcrowding, ensuring optimal conditions for worshippers is challenging. This paper presents a smart dome model designed to manage air quality and sunlight exposure through artificial intelligence. The model governs dome movements by considering weather conditions and overcrowding levels. Data were sourced from historical weather data of Saudi Arabia and the Shanghai Technology Database. Utilizing Python, a Congested Scene Recognition Network (CSRNet) and fuzzy techniques automated dome operations, facilitating the circulation of fresh air inside the mosque. The model manages dome operations based on real-time data, ensuring optimal air circulation. The system effectively determines the duration domes should remain open each hour, enhancing overall comfort for worshippers (Blasi et al., 2021).

14.1.7 Weather Modeling

Accurately estimating reference evapotranspiration (ETref) is essential for optimizing water use in arid and semiarid regions. In this study, mathematical models for daily reference evapotranspiration (ETref) were developed using gene expression programming (GEP). Eight GEP models (GEP-MOD1–8) were formulated based on different climatic variables, with the Penman–Monteith equation serving as the reference standard. Climatic data from 13 meteorological stations in Saudi Arabia (1980–2010) were used, with 65% for training and 35% for testing. Model accuracy improved with more parameters: R2 ranged from 63.4% (GEP-MOD1) to 95.4% (GEP-MOD8), and RMSE from 3.19 mm/day to 1.14 mm/day. Spatial evaluation showed RMSE from 3.27 mm/day to 1.21 mm/day. GEP-MOD8 had minimal errors across various plant heights, with RMSE values of 0.75 cm and 0.96 cm for 50 cm and 12 cm heights, respectively. Solar radiation had little impact on ETref in hyper-arid conditions, while wind speed and plant height significantly improved accuracy (Alazba et al., 2016).

This research aimed to enhance the accuracy of Fuzzy Logic Systems (FLSs) in predicting next-day solar radiation using a PSO algorithm. Input included outputs from both simulated annealing-based FLS (SA-FLS) and Numerical Weather Prediction (NWP) models, specifically ERA5 from ECMWF. Using data from nine Saudi Arabian stations, results showed that the hybrid model improved predictions for all SA-FLS test samples and performed comparably to the NWP model. The hybrid model achieved RMSE values of 3.8% to 6.7% compared to observed data, indicating high prediction accuracy (Almaraashi, 2023).

Hybrid ML approaches to enhance solar radiation estimation by integrating numerical methods, particularly Weather Research and Forecasting (WRF) models. The goal is to improve predictions by combining machine learning models with numerical methods. Feature selection and dimensionality reduction technique optimized the input features for solar radiation estimation using adaptive memory programming. Classification models then predicted solar radiation classes using these features. Real environmental data from Saudi Arabia were used to assess these methods. Feature selection significantly improved class prediction rates by 8.5% to 15%, depending on the classifier and region. Integrating WRF data into regression models outperformed standalone machine learning and WRF models, with RMSE and mean absolute error improvements up to 5.6% and 8.3%, respectively (Hedar et al., 2021).

14.1.8 Dust Accumulation

The study examines synoptic features and seasonal variations of dust patterns across southwestern Saudi Arabia from 1979 to 2006. Data from TOMS aerosol index, surface station dust observations, and meteorological data NCEP/NCAR reanalysis dataset were analyzed. The seasonal AI distribution shows that about 80% of each year experienced dust events, mainly during warmer months. Surface observations indicate that desert-adjacent stations recorded the most dust, except in summer when Red Sea stations reported more. Synoptic dynamics driving dust events were influenced by high pressure systems (Azores or Siberian) and low-pressure systems (Sudan or Indian) and their interactions. At the 850 hPa level, the systems showed a north–south orientation (anticyclonic-cyclonic) for most of the year, shifting to a west–east orientation in summer and reverting in winter. These interactions are shaped by wind patterns, with anticyclonic winds in winter, cyclonic in spring, northerly/northwesterly in summer, and anticyclonic in autumn. Dust sources varied accordingly: the 'Toker Gap' in Sudan for summer/autumn and the central/eastern Arabian Peninsula for winter/spring (Mashat et al., 2018).

Ground-based measurements from 11 surface stations (1978–2010) examined monthly and seasonal dust variations across northern Saudi Arabia. TOMS AI data and NCEP/NCAR reanalysis datasets were used to study dust synoptic climatology. Dust types were categorized into weak dust and dust storms. Statistical analysis revealed that weak dust events predominate in colder months, while dust storms are more common in hotter months. The distribution of annual dust events revealed fewer occurrences before 1989 and an increase thereafter. Synoptic climate analysis identified two primary wind patterns: anticyclonic and northerly (shamal). Winter and autumn dust events were influenced by the anti-cyclonic pattern, whereas spring and summer events were associated with the shamal pattern. Selected synoptic case studies corroborated these findings, illustrating distinct atmospheric patterns for winter and summer.

These patterns included troughs over the Red Sea and Arabian Gulf and ridges over the eastern Mediterranean during summer, and mid-Arabian Peninsula during winter. Dust storms exhibited pronounced synoptic systems, with the highest pressure/geopotential gradient near the Arabian Peninsula (Mashat et al., 2020).

Four synoptic patterns were identified for extensive dust occurrences in central and eastern Saudi Arabia. These events were categorized based on TOMS AI data. Synoptic regimes were identified through Empirical Orthogonal Function (EOF) analysis of mean sea level pressure (SLP) data from the NCEP/NCAR Reanalysis Project. Variations in SLP for these regimes exhibited meridional distributions for the first two and zonal distributions for the latter two. Surface synoptic analysis of the first two regimes revealed either a robust low-pressure system in the eastern region or a high-pressure system in the western region. The less dominant regimes involved interactions between the northern high-pressure belt and the southern low-pressure belt. Upper synoptic analysis indicated that upper-level systems complemented surface systems. During intense dust activity, surface northerly winds prevailed over the eastern Arabian Peninsula, while southerly winds dominated during weak dust activity (Awad & Mashat, 2014).

14.1.9 Transportation

The transport sector grapples with daily traffic congestion In Kuwait, posing a significant challenge to the economy and impeding the country's development and productivity. Moreover, extreme weather conditions exacerbate road traffic, posing substantial risks to the transportation system. Key weather variables such as temperature, precipitation, wind speed, and visibility play pivotal roles in influencing traffic conditions in Kuwait. Three machine learning approaches fuzzy logic, long short-term memory (LSTM), and decision trees were chosen and applied to a dataset from the Kuwait Control and Meteorological Center for the year 2018. While all three models exhibited good performance accuracy in classifying data based on input features, LSTM demonstrated the most promising results among them (AlKheder & AlOmair, 2022).

14.2 Methodology

The methodology of metrology prediction is outlined in this section.

14.2.1 Classical- Regression Models to Estimate Solar Radiation

Various regression models are employed to estimate global solar radiation based on sunshine hour data. Traditional solar radiation involves methods such as:

14.2.2 Angstrom-Prescott Model

The Angstrom-Prescott model is a widely used empirical model that relates solar radiation to sunshine duration. The equation typically takes the form:

$$H = a + b \cdot n \tag{14.1}$$

where H is the solar radiation, n is the sunshine duration, and a and b are coefficients. This model is simple and effective for estimating solar radiation based on observed sunshine hours.

14.2.3 Hargreaves-Samani Model

The Hargreaves-Samani model estimates solar radiation based on temperature data. It is commonly used in situations where direct solar radiation measurements are not available. The formula is given by:

$$H = \frac{0.0023 \cdot \sqrt{T_{max} - T_{min}} \cdot (T_{AVG} \cdot +17.8) \cdot n}{\sqrt{30}} \tag{14.2}$$

$T(\max)$ and $T(\min)$ are the maximum and minimum temperatures,)$T(\text{avg})$ average temperature, and n the daylight hours. relationship between daily duration of sunshine 'n' and daily total of global solar radiation 'G' is expressed through the following formula:

$$\left({}^{G}/_{Go}\right) = a' + \left(1 - a'\right)\frac{n}{N} \tag{14.3}$$

Here, 'N' represents the maximum sunshine duration, $G0$ represents the daily global radiation under clear-sky conditions, and a' is the mean proportion of radiation received on a completely overcast day. This formula captures the evident correlation between sunshine duration and the solar radiation reaching the Earth's surface. The coefficient a' and the term $(1 - a')Nn$ contribute to the overall estimation of global solar radiation based on the observed sunshine duration.

The other notable regression models used for solar radiation in the literature are: Black et al. model, Macris model, Page model, Rietveld model, Flocas model, Hutchinson et al. model, Chandel model.

14.2.4 *Artificial Neural Network*

In ANN models, neurons are organized into three layers: the input layer, hidden layers, and output layer. These models exhibit the capability to effectively address both linear and nonlinear problems, surpassing the performance of traditional empirical models. The mathematical representation of ANN models can be stated as:

$$y(x) = F\left(\sum_{i=1}^{L} \omega_i \cdot \mathrm{i}(t) \cdot x_i(t) + b\right) \tag{14.4}$$

where: $y(x)$ output, $xi(t)$ input variables, F transfer function for the hidden layer, L number of neurons, $\omega i(t)$ weights, b bias.

ANN models can be classified based on the connection forms between input, hidden, and output layers. These classifications include feedforward, recurrent, and symmetrical connected (Hopfield) neural networks. It's important to note that there is limited research on the application of Hopfield neural networks in predicting solar radiation.

Feedforward Neural Networks (FF-NN) encompass various architectures, with some prominent types being:

- **Multi-Layer Perceptron:** MLP is a simple FF-NN that includes an input layer, one or more hidden layers, and an output layer.
- **Backpropagation Neural Network:** BP-NN is a common FF-NN trained using the backpropagation algorithm.
- **Radial Basis Function Neural Network:** RBF-NN uses radial basis functions in its hidden layer.
- **Extreme Learning Machine:** ELM is an FF-NN with a single hidden layer; it randomly assigns weights to connections and updates only the output weights during training.
- **Convolutional Neural Network:** CNN is a type of FF-NN particularly effective for image-related tasks, with convolutional layers designed to recognize patterns.

- **Adaptive Neuro-Fuzzy Inference System:** ANFIS combines the adaptability of neural networks with the interpretability of fuzzy logic.

ANNs utilize Perceptions to discern dividing lines, planes, or hyperplanes between classes in multi-dimensional spaces. The sigmoid function is applied to input features to adjust their characteristics. ANNs typically consist of input nodes, output nodes, and hidden layers, often with between zero and three hidden layers. Unlike deep neural networks, ANNs forward information and operate in a feedforward manner. The learning process involves adjusting connections between layers. After learning, the output layer generates the desired output. For prediction tasks, a supervised learning approach is employed, assigning a desired output to the network in advance. The backpropagation algorithm (BPA), also known as the extended delta rule, is a widely used learning method for predictions. MSE commonly serves as the cost function in linear regression. The estimates of 'a' and 'b' that best model datasets are typically obtained by minimizing this function. All model-based learning methods share the commonality of minimizing a cost function to discover the best-fitting model for the data. Below are various models utilized to estimate solar radiation using artificial neural networks in literature (Table 14.1).

ANN offer a distinct advantage in efficiently handling highly nonlinear relationships within data, even in cases where the exact nature of such relationships is unknown. The performance evaluation revealed that ANN outperformed regression models. The MAPE values of ANN models were found to be lower compared to regression models, indicating greater accuracy. Additionally, the R values of ANN models exceeded those of regression models, further emphasizing their superior predictive capabilities.

14.2.5 *Support Vector Machine*

Support Vector Machine (SVM) is a binary linear classifier designed to identify an optimal hyperplane that maximizes the margin between two classes of data points. The margin represents the distance between the hyperplane and the closest data points from each class. SVM aims to maximize this margin while minimizing classification errors. This algorithm offers several advantages over other machine learning approaches.

Table 14.1 Solar radiation using ANN

Alawi model	ANN have been utilized to forecast solar radiation in regions where direct measurement instrumentation is lacking. The input parameters for the network typically include location, month, mean pressure, mean temperature, mean vapor pressure, mean relative humidity, mean wind speed, and mean duration of sunshine. The resulting artificial neural network model achieved an impressive accuracy of 93% and a mean absolute percentage error of 7.3 (Al-Alawi & Al-Hinai, 1998)
Mohandes model	The estimation of global solar radiation utilizing an ANN was carried out using data from 41 collection stations across Saudi Arabia. A neural network was trained with data from 31 stations, while the remaining 10 stations were utilized for testing the network. The input parameters for the network comprised latitude, longitude, altitude, and sunshine duration (Mohandes et al., 1998)
Kemmoku model	A multistage artificial neural network was utilized to predict the daily insolation for the following day. The input data for the network encompassed the average atmospheric pressure, which was predicted by another ANN along with various weather data from the preceding day (Kumar et al., 2015)
Kalogirou model	In the first application within this category, the focus lies on predicting the maximum solar radiation. ANN were employed for this task, harnessing their ability to be trained with historical data to provide precise predictions. The input data used in this approach primarily influenced the availability and intensity of solar radiation. Key factors considered included the month, day of the month, Julian day, season, mean ambient temperature, and mean relative humidity(Kumar et al., 2015)
Ouammi model	A specialized ANN model was developed to estimate the monthly solar irradiation for 41 sites across Morocco. The dataset covers the period from 1998 to 2010, with the inputs to the network being normalized values of longitude, latitude, and elevation. The model predicts solar irradiation within the range of 5030 to 6230 W $h/m^2/day$. This application showcases the capability of ANNs in capturing intricate relationships and patterns in solar irradiation data across a diverse set of locations (Kumar et al., 2015)
Yildiz model	Two distinct models, namely ANN-1 and ANN-2, were employed for the estimation of solar radiation in Turkey. The ANN-1 model incorporates latitude, longitude, altitude, month, and meteorological land surface temperature as parameters input. On the other hand, the ANN-2 model utilizes latitude, longitude, altitude, month, and satellite land surface temperature as inputs. During testing, the R-squared values for ANN-1 and ANN-2 are recorded as 80.41% and 82.37%, respectively. This indicates that the ANN-2 model provides a superior estimation compared to the ANN-1 model. The incorporation of satellite land surface temperature enhances the predictive capability of the model, underscoring the significance of input parameters in solar radiation estimation (Kumar et al., 2015)

Notably, it efficiently handles high-dimensional data, demonstrates less susceptibility to overfitting compared to methods like decision trees and neural networks, and is robust in the presence of noisy data and outliers. SVM models can solve regression problems with several kernel functions, which can map low-dimensional data into a high-dimensional feature space.

$$f(x) = \omega\varphi(x) + b \tag{14.5}$$

where $\varphi(x)$ represents the higher-dimensional feature space; ω and b denote the weight vector and bias, respectively. Several kernel functions are used in SVM, including the RBF, polynomial, linear, and sigmoid functions. Among these, the RBF is considered the optimal kernel function due to its high efficiency, simplicity, robustness, and ease of adaptation for optimization. Despite its strengths, SVM has some limitations. Sensitivity to the choice of kernel function and its parameters, along with computational expenses for large datasets, are among the drawbacks. Nonetheless, SVM remains popular and widely used in machine learning due to its solid theoretical foundation and impressive performance across various applications. The Radial Basis Function (RBF) serves as a common kernel function in SVM for both classification and regression tasks. The RBF kernel, a non-linear function, assesses the similarity between two data points in a high-dimensional space. The kernel value decreases as the distance between points increases. The RBF kernel introduces a hyper parameter, gamma, which affects the kernel's width and thus influences the smoothness of the decision boundary. Lower gamma values yield smoother decision boundaries, while higher gamma values result in more complex boundaries that closely fit the data but can lead to overfitting.

$$K(x, y) = \exp\left(-\gamma \|x - y\|^2\right) \tag{14.6}$$

γ hyperparameter controlling the width of the kernel, and $||x - y||$ signifies the Euclidean distance between x and y. Indeed, the RBF kernel is renowned for its capability to capture non-linear relationships in the data while maintaining computational efficiency. Table 14.2 summarizes the benefits and drawbacks of physical, empirical, statistical and ML models.

Table 14.2 Summarizes the benefits and drawbacks of physical, empirical, statistical and ML models

Models		*Advantage*	*Disadvantages*
Physical	Uses meteorological parameters to explore H, sky image based models	Strong physical basis	Complex structure due to the atmosphere conditions
Empirical	Develop regression liner/ nonlinear equations	Ease to deploy/employ operate	Limitation in accuracy
Statistical	Methods like autoregressive moving averages ARMA/ autoregressive integrated moving averages ARIMA developed based on statistical correlation	Higher accuracy that empirical models	Limitation in correlating nonlinear H with other meteorological parameters
Machine learning	Models such as SVM, ANN	Higher accuracy(produce good accuracy in short,medium& long – term forecasting), wider application than Physical, Empirical, statistical	

14.2.6 Data Collection

The crucial stage starts with the process of data acquisition where data is collected. The data can be obtained via 3 commonly channels namely observational Data, Satellite data and reanalyzed data, the inputs are chosen in the feature selection stage after exhaustive analysis on the inputs that have the most significant impact on the models. Afterward, the model is trained after careful consideration of the optimal machine learning model to be used, if the performance of the model is Good the model is deployed otherwise the process is started again at the feature selection stage, Fig. 14.1 showcases a generalized flowchart of how models are trained.

- Observational data: This data is physical measurement from instruments from weather stations. Example Observational data can be retrieved via the NOAA portal.

Fig. 14.1 Generalized methodology

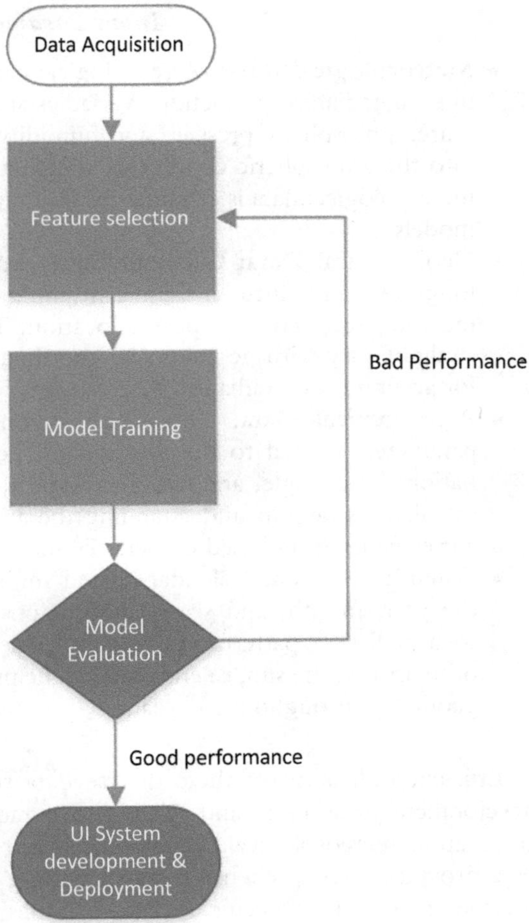

- Satellite data: This data is obtained by processing satellite imagery from various types of Satellite to obtain the desired data, such as LANSAT, MODIS and Sentinel. This data requires preprocessing. Example Satellite Imagery can be obtained from EARTHDATA NASA, SENTINEL HUB and USGS.
- Re-analyzed data: This data is obtained from archived historical numerical weather forecast that has been post analyzed and quality controlled. Example Data obtained from GES DISC NASA.

14.2.7 Input Parameters

- **Meteorological Data:** Meteorological parameters play a crucial role in solar radiation prediction. Variables such as wind speed, temperature, atmospheric pressure and humidity, provide valuable insights into the atmospheric conditions affecting solar radiation. Historical meteorological data is essential for training and validating prediction models.
- **Geographical Data:** Geographical information, including latitude, longitude, and altitude, significantly influences the amount of solar radiation received at a specific location. The angle and duration of sunlight vary with geographical coordinates, making this data vital for accurate solar radiation forecasting.
- **Astronomical Data:** Theoretical astronomical data encompasses parameters related to the position of the sun, such as solar declination, hour angle, and extraterrestrial radiation. These theoretical calculations help in understanding the anticipated solar radiation at a specific location based on celestial movements.
- **Calendrical Data:** Calendar-related information, including day of the year, month, and seasonal variations, is crucial for predicting solar radiation patterns. Considering the Earth's axial tilt and its orbit around the sun, calendrical data helps model the changing solar geometry throughout the year.

Efficient utilization of these diverse data sources contributes to the development of accurate and reliable solar radiation prediction models. Integrating meteorological, geographical, astronomical, and calendrical data provides a comprehensive understanding of the factors influencing solar radiation at a specific location. Tables 14.3 and 14.4 Provides example of commonly used parameters in meteorology and solar radiation forecast.

14.2.8 Evaluation Metrics

The performance of ANN, SVM, RF, and KNN model predictions can be evaluated using assessment metrics such as MAPE, RMSE, and R-squared.

Table 14.3 Geographical, astronomical, calendrical input parameters

Types	*Variables*	
Astronomical	Extraterrestrial Radiation	H_0
	Maximum Sunshine Duration	S_0
	Hour Angle	ω
	Declination Angle	δ
	Solar Zenith Angle	S_z
	Azimuth	A_z
	Inclination	I_n
Geographical	Latitude	L_a
	Longitude	L_0
	Slope	A_L
	Altitude	β
Calendar	Day Of The Year	DOY
	Month Of The Year	MOY
	Hour Of The Year	HOY

- Root Mean Square Error RMSE;

$$RSME = \sqrt{\frac{1}{n}\sum_{i=1}^{n}(H_p - H_a)^2} \tag{14.7}$$

- Mean Absolute Percentage Error MAPE;

$$MAPE = \frac{1}{n}\sum_{i=1}^{n}\left|\frac{(H_P - H_a)}{H_a}\right| \times 100 \tag{14.8}$$

- Absolute Fraction of Variance;

$$R^2 = \frac{\sum_{i=1}^{n}(H_p - H_a)^2}{n\sum_{i=1}^{n}(H_p - \overline{H}_a)^2} \tag{14.9}$$

14.2.9 Selection of Input Parameters

To train the model with the optimum performance, feature selections is important. An in-depth study of how different input parameters interact with each other in comprehensive manner is required and analyzed. The following methods can be utilized and evaluated and compared at each

Table 14.4 Meteorological and air pollution input parameters

Types	*Variables*	
Generalized Metrology	Sunshine Duration Average Temperature Maximum Temperature Minimum Temperature Diurnal Temperature Temperature Ratio Average Relative Humidity Wet-Point Temperature Dew-Point Temperature Maximum Relative Humidity Minimum Relative Humidity Air Pressure Precipitation Rainy Days Water Vapor Pressure Vapor Pressure Deficit Cloud Cover Wind Speed Wind Direction Evaporation Soil Temperature	S T_a T_{max} T_{min} ΔT T_r R_h T_w T_{dew} R_{hmax} R_{hmin} P_r P_t RD W_p V_{pd} CC W_s W_d E_v T_s
Air Pollution	Air Quality Index Particulate Matter < 10 Mic Particulate Matter < 2.5 Mic Sulfur Dioxide Nitrogen Dioxide NO2 Carbon Mono- Oxide Ozone Visibility	AQI PM10 PM2.5 SO_2 NO_2 CO O_3 Visibility

different climate model analyses to choose the right input parameters for each climatic model as illustrated in Fig. 14.2.

The following techniques can be used for the selection of the important parameters:

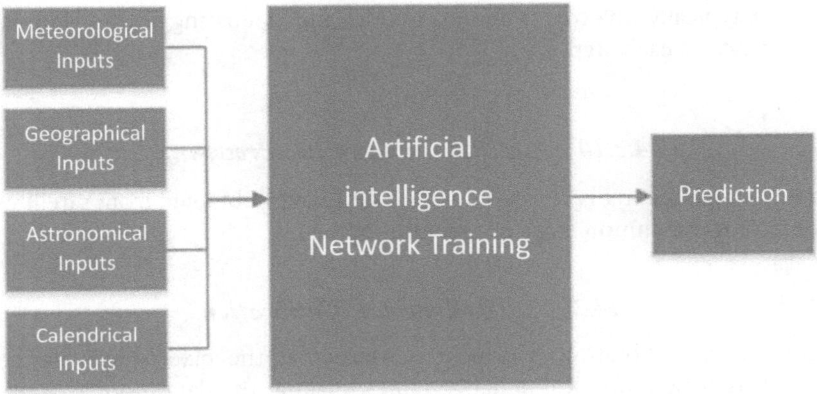

Fig. 14.2 Selection of input parameters

- **Correlation Analysis**: Examine the correlation between each input parameter and the target variable. Parameters with low correlation coefficients may be less important and could potentially be excluded.
- **Principal Component Analysis (PCA)**: A statistical technique that converts the original variables into a new set of uncorrelated variables known as principal components. These principal components are ordered by their variance, allowing to select a subset of components that capture most of the variance in the data while reducing dimensionality.
- **Lasso Regression (L1 Regularization)**: Lasso regression incorporates a penalty term into the regression model, promoting sparse solutions by reducing some regression coefficients to zero. This effectively performs variable selection, as non-zero coefficients indicate important predictors.
- **Random Forest Feature Importance**: a random forest model, can assess the importance of each input variable based on how much it decreases the node impurity across all decision trees in the forest. Variables with higher importance scores are considered more influential.
- **Recursive Feature Elimination (RFE)**: An iterative feature selection method that operates by continuously eliminating the least significant features until the desired number of features is achieved.

It typically involves training a model and evaluating feature importance at each step.

14.2.10 Satellite Imagery Pre-Processing

Data pre-processing is commonly done for images obtained from satellites some of the common steps are mentioned below:

14.2.11 Radiometric Calibration

Radiometric calibration is done to ensure that the pixel values in the images represent physical radiance values, making the data more accurate and comparable across different scenes.

14.2.11.1 Atmospheric Correction

Atmospheric correction is a critical process in remote sensing and image analysis as it compensates for the effects of the Earth's atmosphere on the data captured by sensors. The primary reasons why atmospheric correction is important:

- Quantitative Analysis: Without atmospheric correction, remote sensing data is typically in Top of Atmosphere (TOA) radiance, which may not be directly related to the surface properties of interest. Atmospheric correction allows you to convert TOA data into surface reflectance.
- Comparability: Atmospheric correction makes data collected from different dates, times, or sensors more comparable, as it removes the influence of atmospheric variability. This is crucial for monitoring and analysis over time.
- Enhanced Interpretation: Corrected data provides a more accurate representation of surface properties, making it easier to interpret and analyses. It reduces atmospheric artefacts, such as haze and scattering effects, allowing for a clearer view of the Earth's surface.
- Biophysical Parameters: Surface reflectance obtained through atmospheric correction is essential for deriving biophysical parameters like vegetation indices, land cover classification, and land surface temperature, which require accurate input data.

14.2.12 Thermal Atmospheric Correction

Thermal atmospheric correction is a crucial process in handling thermal infrared data. It eliminates the impact of the Earth's atmosphere on thermal infrared readings, enabling the acquisition of precise land surface temperature (LST) measurements. Without atmospheric correction, the observed thermal radiance will be distorted by atmospheric effects, leading to inaccurate temperature estimates. The key atmospheric effects that thermal atmospheric correction addresses include:

- Atmospheric Absorption: The Earth's atmosphere absorbs thermal radiation at specific wavelengths, particularly by water vapor and carbon dioxide. These absorption bands can affect the radiance observed by the sensor.
- Emissivity Effects: The atmosphere can introduce emissivity effects, which can distort the observed radiance. Emissivity represents the efficiency of a surface to emit thermal radiation, and the atmosphere can influence it.
- Temperature and Humidity Profiles: The atmospheric temperature and humidity profiles can vary with altitude and affect the radiative transfer in the atmosphere, which in turn impacts observed thermal radiance

14.2.12.1 Emissivity Normalization

Emissivity normalization is important in thermal infrared image analysis, particularly when working with data to estimate LST. For accurately estimating LST from thermal infrared data, normalizing emissivity values helps improve the accuracy of LST calculations and values are consistent across different surface types within image.

14.3 Discussion

14.3.1 Advancing Meteorological Precision

In meteorology, AI emerges as a game-changer, propelling forecasting capabilities to unprecedented heights. Machine learning algorithms, fueled by extensive datasets, empower meteorologists to refine predictions with a level of accuracy previously unattainable. The GCC's susceptibility to extreme weather conditions, including heatwaves and occasional storms, underscores the critical importance of advanced meteorological forecasting. AI-driven models not only enhance early-warning systems but also contribute to effective disaster preparedness and response strategies. Beyond traditional weather forecasting, AI enables the identification of subtle climate patterns and trends, providing decision-makers with valuable insights into long-term climate shifts. This proactive approach equips the GCC countries to implement adaptive strategies, fortifying their resilience against the impacts of climate change.

14.3.2 Optimizing Solar Energy Production

AI plays a pivotal role in optimizing solar energy systems. Solar radiation, a cornerstone of renewable energy, becomes more efficiently harness able through AI-driven technologies. By analyzing complex datasets encompassing atmospheric conditions, historical solar radiation patterns, and geographical variations, AI algorithms optimize the placement and performance of solar panels. This results in increased energy yield and more effective utilization of solar resources, aligning with the GCC's commitment to sustainable and renewable energy sources. The integration of AI in solar energy management extends beyond mere optimization. Predictive analytics, enabled by AI, facilitate better planning for energy consumption, storage, and distribution. This foresight ensures a stable and resilient energy grid, reducing dependency on non-renewable sources and contributing to the GCC's broader sustainability goals.

14.3.3 Economic Growth and Innovation

The emergence of AI-driven environmental sciences opens new frontiers for research, development, and employment. Investment in AI technologies fosters a burgeoning ecosystem of skilled professionals, researchers, and entrepreneurs, positioning the GCC countries at the forefront of technological innovation in the environmental sector. Furthermore, the deployment of AI in meteorology and solar energy management cultivates an environment conducive to continuous improvement and innovation. Ongoing research and development initiatives propel the refinement of AI algorithms, ensuring that the GCC remains adaptive to evolving environmental challenges and opportunities.

14.3.4 Challenges

- **High Cost**: Establishing and maintaining observation stations for global solar radiation involves significant costs. The installation of specialized equipment, sensors, and instruments capable of accurately measuring solar radiation can be expensive. Additionally, the costs extend to regular maintenance, calibration, and ensuring the proper functioning of the equipment.
- **Complications in Measuring Techniques, Setup, and Maintenance**: Implementing precise and reliable measuring techniques for global solar radiation is a complex task. Setting up observation stations necessitates meticulous attention to factors like the placement, orientation, and calibration of sensors. Ensuring that the instruments are correctly aligned and regularly maintained is crucial for accurate data collection. Technical complexities may arise in calibrating and adjusting instruments, especially in challenging environmental conditions or remote locations, leading to potential errors in measurements.
- **Inconsistent Reliability of Data**: Observation stations may face challenges in providing consistent reliability of data. Factors such as instrument malfunctions, calibration drifts, and environmental variations can introduce uncertainties into the collected data. In some cases, the reliability of data may be compromised due to issues such as sensor degradation over time or exposure to extreme weather conditions. Inconsistencies in data reliability can impact the accuracy of solar radiation measurements and subsequently affect the quality of forecasts and analyses.

Addressing these problems requires ongoing efforts to invest in advanced technology, implement robust measurement protocols, and ensure regular maintenance and quality control procedures. Overcoming these challenges is essential for obtaining accurate and reliable global solar radiation data from observation stations.

Figure 14.3 highlights the generalized way in which observational data, satellite data and re-analyzed data can be used to develop a robust model utilizing various different types of data.

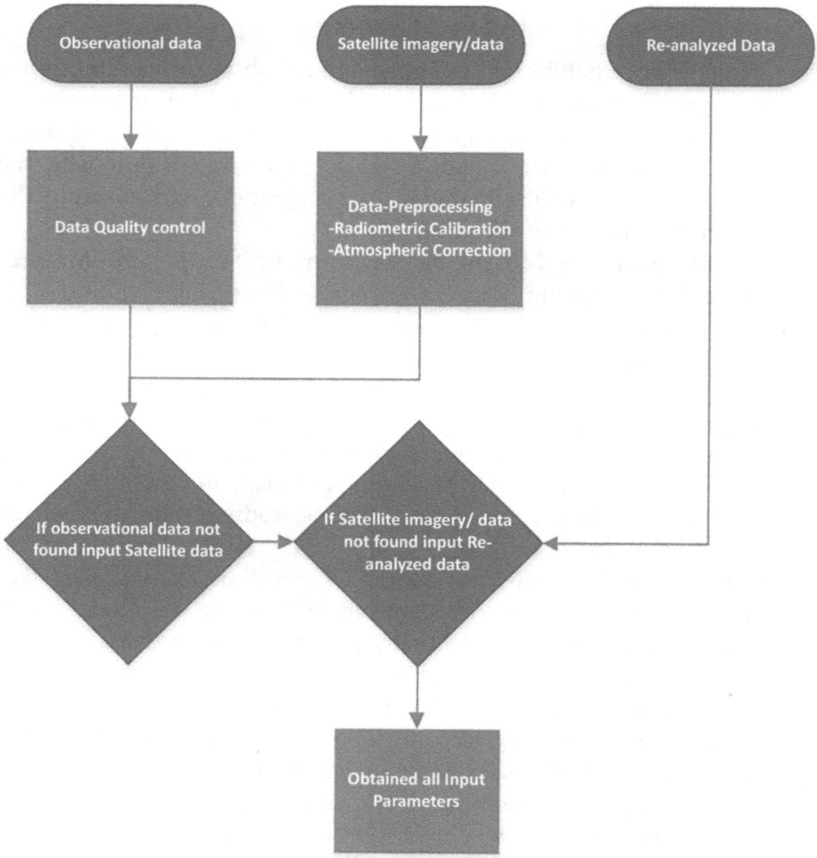

Fig. 14.3 Generalized model development flowchart

14.4 Conclusion

The integration of artificial intelligence (AI) techniques in meteorology and solar radiation estimation presents a paradigm shift in environmental research and sustainable development efforts across the Gulf Cooperation Council (GCC) region. Through a series of innovative studies, researchers have demonstrated the effectiveness of AI-driven methodologies in improving weather prediction accuracy, optimizing renewable energy systems, and enhancing environmental monitoring capabilities.

The findings underscore the significance of leveraging AI to address complex environmental challenges, such as extreme weather events, air pollution, and energy sustainability, in the GCC countries. By harnessing the power of machine learning algorithms, neural networks, and fuzzy logic, researchers have unlocked new opportunities for advancing meteorological science and promoting the adoption of renewable energy technologies. Moving forward, continued investment in AI-driven research and technology development is crucial to furthering our understanding of meteorological phenomena, optimizing energy resource utilization, and fostering sustainable development in the GCC region. Collaborative efforts between academia, industry, and government entities are essential to drive innovation, facilitate knowledge exchange, and translate research findings into actionable solutions that benefit society. In conclusion, the convergence of AI and environmental science holds immense promises for shaping a more resilient, sustainable, and prosperous future for the GCC region. By embracing technological advancements and fostering interdisciplinary collaboration, stakeholders can pave the way for transformative change and accelerate progress towards achieving environmental sustainability goals in the years to come.

References

Adamsab, K., Saif, M., Saif, S., Khamis, I., & Talib, W. (2019). Hybrid powered intelligent irrigation system using Oman Falaj and solar energy. *Materials Today: Proceedings, 41*, 260–264. https://doi.org/10.1016/j.matpr.2020.09.033

Al-Alawi, S. M., & Al-Hinai, H. A. (1998). An ANN-based approach for predicting global radiation in locations with no direct measurement instrumentation. *Renewable Energy, 14*(1), 199–204. https://doi.org/10.1016/S0960-1481(98)00068-8

Alazba, A. A., Yassin, M. A., & Mattar, M. A. (2016). Modeling daily evapotranspiration in hyper-arid environment using gene expression programming. *Arabian Journal of Geosciences, 9*(3). https://doi.org/10.1007/s12517-015-2273-x

Alfadda, A., Rahman, S., & Pipattanasomporn, M. (2018). Solar irradiance forecast using aerosols measurements: A data driven approach. *Solar Energy, 170*, 924–939. https://doi.org/10.1016/j.solener.2018.05.089

Alghamdi, H. A. (2022). A time series forecasting of global horizontal irradiance on geographical data of Najran Saudi Arabia. *Energies, 15*(3). https://doi.org/10.3390/en15030928

Alhebshi, F., Alnabilsi, H., Bensenouci, A., & Brahimi, T. (2019). Using artificial intelligence techniques for solar irradiation forecasting: The case of Saudi Arabia. *Proceedings of the International Conference on Industrial Engineering and Operations Management*, *November*, 926–927. https://www.scopus.com/inward/record.uri?eid=2-s2.0-85080937397&partnerID=40&md5=9673ea9011a6330b7db1fe14fda65036

Alkhaldi, S. M. (2022). Predicting solar irradiance in Saudi Arabia via machine learning & artificial neural networks for efficient grid integration. *2022 Saudi Arabia Smart Grid Conference, SASG 2022.* https://doi.org/10.1109/SASG57022.2022.10200610

AlKheder, S., & AlOmair, A. (2022). Urban traffic prediction using metrological data with fuzzy logic, long short-term memory (LSTM), and decision trees (DTs). *Natural Hazards, 111*(2), 1685–1719. https://doi.org/10.1007/s11069-021-05112-x

Almaraashi, M. (2023). Using particle swarm optimization of fuzzy logic systems as a hybrid soft computing method to enhance solar energy prediction. *Neural Computing and Applications, 35*(29), 21903–21914. https://doi.org/10.1007/s00521-023-08912-3

Al-Mostafa, Z. A., Elminir, H. K., Abulwfa, A., Al-Shehri, S. M., Alshehri, F. A., Al-Rougy, I. M., & Bazyad, A. A. (2015). Evaluation of Erythemal ultraviolet solar radiation over Saudi Arabia. *Solar Energy, 113*, 258–271. https://doi.org/10.1016/j.solener.2015.01.010

Alrashidi, A., & Qamar, A. M. (2023). Data-driven load forecasting using machine learning and meteorological data. *Computer Systems Science and Engineering*, *44*(3), 1973–1988. https://doi.org/10.32604/csse.2023.024633

Alrashidi, M. (2023). Short-Term mosques load forecast using machine learning and meteorological data. *Computer Systems Science and Engineering*, *46*(1), 371–387. https://doi.org/10.32604/csse.2023.034739

Alwadei, S., Farahat, A., Ahmed, M., & Kambezidis, H. D. (2022). Prediction of solar irradiance over the Arabian Peninsula: Satellite data, radiative transfer model, and machine learning integration approach. *Applied Sciences (Switzerland)*, *12*(2). https://doi.org/10.3390/app12020717

Alwated, B., & Brahimi, T. (2021). Solar Radiation Forecasting in Saudi Arabia Using Machine Learning. *Proceedings - 2021 International Conference on Computers and Automation, CompAuto 2021*, 1–6. https://doi.org/10.1109/CompAuto54408.2021.00008

Awad, A., & Mashat, A.-W. (2014). The synoptic patterns associated with spring widespread dusty days in central and eastern Saudi Arabia. *Atmosphere, 5*(4), 889–913. https://doi.org/10.3390/atmos5040889

Baljon, M., & Sharma, S. K. (2023). Rainfall prediction rate in Saudi Arabia using improved machine learning techniques. *Water (Switzerland), 15*(4). https://doi.org/10.3390/w15040826

Blasi, A. H., Lababede, M. A. A., & Alsuwaiket, M. A. (2021). Movement control of smart mosque's domes using CSRNet and Fuzzy logic techniques. *International Journal of Advanced Computer Science and Applications, 12*(3), 301–308. https://doi.org/10.14569/IJACSA.2021.0120337

Bouzgou, H., & Gueymard, C. A. (2019). Fast short-term global solar irradiance forecasting with wrapper mutual information. *Renewable Energy, 133*, 1055–1065. https://doi.org/10.1016/j.renene.2018.10.096

Chen, W.-H., & You, F. (2021). Smart greenhouse control under harsh climate conditions based on data-driven robust model predictive control with principal component analysis and kernel density estimation. *Journal of Process Control, 107*, 103–113. https://doi.org/10.1016/j.jprocont.2021.10.004

Grundmann, J., Schütze, N., Schmitz, G. H., & Al-Shaqsi, S. (2012). Towards an integrated arid zone water management using simulation-based optimisation. *Environmental Earth Sciences, 65*(5), 1381–1394. https://doi.org/10.1007/s12665-011-1253-z

Habeebullah, T. M., Munir, S., Zeb, J., & Morsy, E. A. (2022). Modelling the effect of COVID-19 lockdown on air pollution in Makkah Saudi Arabia with a supervised machine learning approach. *Toxics, 10*(5). https://doi.org/10.3390/toxics10050225

Hedar, A.-R., Almaraashi, M., Abdel-Hakim, A. E., & Abdulrahim, M. (2021). Hybrid machine learning for solar radiation prediction in reduced feature spaces. *Energies, 14*(23). https://doi.org/10.3390/en14237970

Kamarianakis, Y., Pantazis, Y., Kalligiannaki, E., Katsaounis, T. D., Kotsovos, K., Gereige, I., Abdullah, M., Jamal, A., & Tzavaras, A. (2022). Day-ahead forecasting of solar irradiance & PV power output through statistical machine learning methods. *2022 Saudi Arabia Smart Grid Conference, SASG 2022*. https://doi.org/10.1109/SASG57022.2022.10199879

Li, J., Carlson, B. E., & Lacis, A. A. (2009). A study on the temporal and spatial variability of absorbing aerosols using total ozone mapping spectrometer and ozone monitoring instrument Aerosol Index data. *Journal of Geophysical Research Atmospheres, 114*(9), D09213. https://doi.org/10.1029/2008JD011278

Li, J., Garshick, E., Hart, J. E., Li, L., Shi, L., Al-Hemoud, A., Huang, S., & Koutrakis, P. (2021). Estimation of ambient PM2.5 in Iraq and Kuwait from 2001 to 2018 using machine learning and remote sensing. *Environment International, 151*. https://doi.org/10.1016/j.envint.2021.106445

Li, J., Kang, C.-M., Wolfson, J. M., Alahmad, B., Al-Hemoud, A., Garshick, E., & Koutrakis, P. (2022). Estimation of fine particulate matter in an arid area from visibility based on machine learning. *Journal of Exposure Science and*

Environmental Epidemiology, 32(6), 926–931. https://doi.org/10.1038/s41370-022-00480-3

Li, T., López Valencia, O. M., Johansen, K., & McCabe, M. F. (2023). A retrospective analysis of national-scale agricultural development in Saudi Arabia from 1990 to 2021. *Remote Sensing, 15*(3). https://doi.org/10.3390/rs15030731

Mashat, A.-W.S., Alamoudi, A. O., Awad, A. M., & Assiri, M. E. (2018). Seasonal variability and synoptic characteristics of dust cases over southwestern Saudi Arabia. *International Journal of Climatology, 38*(1), 105–124. https://doi.org/10.1002/joc.5164

Mashat, A.-W.S., Awad, A. M., Alamoudi, A. O., & Assiri, M. E. (2020). Monthly and seasonal variability of dust events over northern Saudi Arabia. *International Journal of Climatology, 40*(3), 1607–1629. https://doi.org/10.1002/joc.6290

Mohandes, M., Rehman, S., & Halawani, T. O. (1998). Estimation of global solar radiation using artificial neural networks. *Renewable Energy, 14*(1), 179–184. https://doi.org/10.1016/S0960-1481(98)00065-2

Mohandes, M. A., & Rehman, S. (2013). Estimation of sunshine duration in Saudi Arabia. *Journal of Renewable and Sustainable Energy*, *5*(3). https://doi.org/10.1063/1.4811284

Nur-E-Alam, M., Zehad Mostofa, K., Kar Yap, B., Khairul Basher, M., Aminul Islam, M., Vasiliev, M., Soudagar, M. E. M., Das, N., & Sieh Kiong, T. (2024). Machine learning enhanced all-photovoltaic blended systems for energy-efficient sustainable buildings. *Sustainable Energy Technologies and Assessments, 62*. https://doi.org/10.1016/j.seta.2024.103636

Okonkwo, P. C., Mansir, I. B., Barhoumi, E. M., Emori, W., Radwan, A. B., Shakoor, R. A., Uzoma, P. C., & Pugalenthi, M. R. (2022). Utilization of renewable hybrid energy for refueling station in Al-Kharj, Saudi Arabia. *International Journal of Hydrogen Energy, 47*(53), 22273–22284. https://doi.org/10.1016/j.ijhydene.2022.05.040

Park, J., Choi, H., Kim, D., & Kim, T. (2021). Development of novel PMV-based HVAC control strategies using a mean radiant temperature prediction model by machine learning in Kuwaiti climate. *Building and Environment, 206*. https://doi.org/10.1016/j.buildenv.2021.108357

Rahman, S. M., Khondaker, A. N., & Abdel-Aal, R. (2012). Self-organizing ozone model for Empty Quarter of Saudi Arabia: Group method data handling based modeling approach. *Atmospheric Environment, 59*, 398–407. https://doi.org/10.1016/j.atmosenv.2012.05.008

Rehan, M., & Munir, S. (2022). Analysis and modeling of air pollution in extreme meteorological conditions: A case study of Jeddah, the Kingdom of Saudi Arabia. *Toxics*, *10*(7). https://doi.org/10.3390/toxics10070376

Sultana, N. (2022). Predicting sun protection measures against skin diseases using machine learning approaches. *Journal of Cosmetic Dermatology, 21*(2), 758–769. https://doi.org/10.1111/jocd.14120

Taylan, O. (2013). Prediction of air quality for sustainable environment by artificial intelligent techniques. *Energy Education Science and Technology Part A: Energy Science and Research, 31*(3), 1635–1652. https://www.scopus.com/inward/record.uri?eid=2-s2.0-84892415674&partnerID=40&md5=2efad0e5a6c00be9e8a1f0f57f6dfd40

Taylan, O. (2017). Modelling and analysis of ozone concentration by artificial intelligent techniques for estimating air quality. *Atmospheric Environment, 150*, 356–365. https://doi.org/10.1016/j.atmosenv.2016.11.030

Touati, F., Al-Hitmi, M., & Benhmed, K. (2012). A fuzzy logic based irrigation management system in arid regions applied to the state of qatar. *WIT Transactions on Ecology and the Environment, 168*, 189–199. https://doi.org/10.2495/SI120161

Yetilmezsoy, K., & Abdul-Wahab, S. A. (2012). A prognostic approach based on fuzzy-logic methodology to forecast PM10 levels in Khaldiya residential area. *Kuwait. Aerosol and Air Quality Research, 12*(6), 1217–1236. https://doi.org/10.4209/aaqr.2012.07.0163

CHAPTER 15

The Role of Artificial Intelligence in Shaping the Economic Landscape in the GCC Region

Ahmed Badran and Ashraf Mishrif

15.1 Introduction

In an era when the digital revolution is reshaping the global economy and society, AI is emerging as one of the most prominent tools for strategic transformation, especially in the Gulf Cooperation Council (GCC) countries, which are striving to consolidate their position as regional and global centers for innovation. This book presents a comprehensive analytical journey of the GCC countries' experience in adopting AI technologies, starting from the theoretical and historical foundations, through its applications in vital sectors such as energy, education, health, and security, all the way to its implications for public policy and sustainable

A. Badran (✉)
Department of International Affairs, Qatar University, Doha, Qatar
e-mail: a.badran@qu.edu.qa

A. Mishrif
Sultan Qaboos University, Muscat, Oman
e-mail: ashraf.mishrif@gmail.com

A. Badran and A. Mishrif (eds.), *Shaping the Future of Development in the GCC*, The Political Economy of the Middle East,
https://doi.org/10.1007/978-981-96-7963-8_15

development. Throughout its multiple chapters, the book highlights the unique harmony between Gulf ambitions and emerging technologies, as national visions have been embodied and translated into tangible projects ranging from smart cities to advanced academic laboratories. However, this journey also reveals profound challenges, from digital skills gaps to ethical dilemmas in the use of data and security concerns arising from the expansion of AI applications. The book's chapters also address the social consequences of labor market transformations in this chapter. In conclusion, we review the main threads that wove the fabric of this work and present an integrated vision that combines lessons learned and practical recommendations. It is an attempt to link the past with the future, where policies are formulated not only based on the current reality, but also based on unlimited potential led by technologies capable of redefining the meaning of human progress. Through this synthesis, we aim to present a clear roadmap that contributes to transforming the Gulf countries from consumers of technology to pioneers in shaping the future of AI at the regional and global levels.

15.2 Key Impacts of AI: Summary of the Main Findings and Conclusions

The previous chapters of this book explored the transformative role of AI across various sectors in the Gulf Cooperation Council (GCC) countries. From economic development and employment policies to governance, security, and environmental sustainability, AI has emerged as a pivotal force shaping the region's future. Each chapter provides an in-depth analysis of the opportunities and challenges associated with adopting AI, highlighting its potential to enhance efficiency, drive innovation, and address pressing societal issues. This section aims to summarize the key findings of the book, providing a comprehensive overview of the impact of AI on policy, industry, and governance in the Gulf countries, while identifying key areas that require further attention to maximize the benefits of this technology.

Regarding the status of AI and economic transformation in the Gulf countries, it is becoming increasingly clear that the Gulf countries are adopting ambitious national strategies for AI, such as the UAE Strategy, 2017, which aims to mark the country as a global center for innovation. Studies also predict that the contribution of AI to the gross domestic product of the Gulf countries will reach 34% annually, with a special focus on sectors such as healthcare and education. In addition, the general foundations of AI in the Gulf region highlight its role in economic and social development and emphasize its significant potential.

The governance of AI in the oil and gas industry is also key in pointing out how this technology can be used to improve exploration and production operations, reduce costs, and improve operational efficiency. There is an emphasized need to establish clear regulatory frameworks to ensure the ethical and effective use of AI in this vital sector. An analysis of the oil sector in Oman revealed that 36% of companies have started using AI, especially in the areas of predictive maintenance (21%) and quality control (10%). However, the results indicated a weak regulatory framework, as 70% of companies preferred to form specialized committees to manage ethical risks instead of relying on individuals.

The challenges facing the establishment of AI laboratories in Gulf academic institutions cannot be ignored. Developing these laboratories requires large investments, in addition to the need for international and local cooperation to enhance applied research in this field. In this regard, the experience of the University of Bahrain has brought to light the material and technological difficulties in constructing AI labs, including the high maintenance costs and shortage of skilled workers. In collaboration with global institutions like CERN, the university has managed to create an open-source technology-based infrastructure that facilitates research in fields like Large Language Modelling (LLM).

However, the success within the implementation of AI software is not equal across all industries. The consideration of the performance of AI in summarizing academic texts compared with human summaries is exemplary of the current limitations of AI. AI is characterized by accuracy and speed, but it still lacks deep understanding of academic texts, which requires human intervention to ensure the quality of the outputs. By evaluating the performance of ChatGPT-4 in summarizing academic texts, it is clear that generative models produce concise and readable summaries, but they lack accuracy in conveying precise details and scientific evidence. This highlights the need for the integration of AI with human review to ensure the quality of research vocabulary.

The impact of AI on employment policies in Qatar is thus a crucial discussion. Smart technologies will impact the nature of the labor market, requiring skills development and policy adaptation to ensure maximum benefit from this technology without negatively impacting job opportunities. There is also a disparity in impacts across sectors, with low-skilled jobs expected to be more severely affected, while smart technologies will create new opportunities in areas such as data analysis and cybersecurity. Recommendations also indicated the need to restructure education programs to enhance digital literacy skills among workforces, so employees are better prepared for AI's increasing impact on labor markets.

Regarding public perception of the impact of generative intelligence in the State of Qatar, it has been revealed that surveys in the UAE and Bahrain highlight general optimism about the economic opportunities of AI, particularly in the government services and e-commerce sectors. However, with 45% of respondents expressing concern about job losses, and 60% expressing concerns about privacy and digital security, public perception is clearly mixed. Focusing on Qatari society's attitudes towards AI, the results of Chapter 7 showed that 68% of Qataris believe that AI will enhance economic efficiency, but 55% doubt the ability of current legislation to regulate the use of AI from an ethical perspective. A disparity in acceptance was also observed between age groups, with young people showing greater confidence in the benefits of technology compared to older people.

Like most technological developments, AI does not come without its ethical considerations. These are particularly highlighted in the fields of military and security, focusing on the ethical challenges facing AI applications in the defense industries. One of the most prominent of these challenges is the difficulty of determining responsibility if intelligent systems fail to perform their role. Potential future navigations include the establishment of regional bodies to monitor compliance with international standards and enhancing transparency in the development of military technologies.

The role of AI in waste management is also becoming increasingly important, especially in the context of the United Arab Emirates. Geospatial models and AI can be used to identify optimal waste disposal sites in Dubai, achieving an accuracy of 12.4% in classifying suitable areas. Recommendations also indicated the need to increase recycling projects to reduce the amount of waste by 75% by 2030. Considering the digital transformation in the industrial sector and AI applications, further considerations arise relating to how AI technologies can best be applied to develop operations in the industrial sector. Thusly, neural network models in Oman have proven their ability to reduce manufacturing costs by 14% by improving production planning and supply chain management. These models also have contributed to reducing the time required to estimate costs from ten hours to a few minutes, which enhances the ability of small businesses to compete in smart cities.

As smart city practices are becoming more widespread, the role of AI applications in promoting smart city practices and concepts becomes crucial. There is an important comparison to be made between Manama and Singapore, which demonstrates a gap in the adoption of smart city solutions, despite the high potential of the Gulf. For example, Singapore uses AI in traffic management with an efficiency rate of up to 90%, while similar applications in the Gulf are still in their early stages regarding AI applications in the field of meteorology and energy. Predictive models have also succeeded in Saudi Arabia and Kuwait, improving the accuracy of solar radiation forecasts by 25%, which supports plans to transition towards renewable energy. Machine learning techniques have also contributed to reducing carbon emissions by improving the efficiency of agricultural irrigation systems.

15.3 AI in the GCC Region: Current Reality and Unresolved Challenges

This section provides an overview of the expected future trends of AI in the GCC region based on the findings of this book. Therefore, this section provides a forecast of the future of AI in the region based on the findings of the book, not just theoretical recommendations. Therefore, the success in achieving a promising future for AI in the region depends on transforming challenges such as the skills gap into opportunities through proactive policies and investing in the potential to build a Gulf economy based on innovation.

On the front of digital and research infrastructure, there are clear challenges related to building AI laboratories in Gulf universities, such as the lack of qualified personnel and high maintenance costs. In light of these considerations, a recommendation can be made regarding the establishment of joint regional data centers, benefiting from the University of Bahrain's experience with CERN. At this point, cloud-computing platforms can be developed to support joint research in the fields of climate modeling and industrial robotics. Within the same framework, it is proposed to support open-source technologies, as in the University of Bahrain's experience, where it is recommended to adopt open-source software solutions to reduce costs and increase flexibility.

Regarding the development of legislative and ethical frameworks for AI applications, there is an absence of clear standards for AI governance in sensitive sectors such oil and defense. From this standpoint, a set of recommendations can be presented, foremost among which is the need to issue a Gulf Code of Ethics for AI (Badran, 2021, 2023). This code should include rules for data use and accountability in military systems and privacy protection in smart city applications. In addition, a regional oversight body could also be established, like the AI Authority in the United Arab Emirates, but with powers that include all Gulf countries, to monitor legislation and rules regulating AI. Another potential model involves forming governance committees within oil companies, to act as a regional standard that countries in the region can benefit from in developing this legislative and regulatory framework for AI applications.

With regard to bridging the gap in required skills in the labor market and restructuring education, most of the Gulf workforce is not sufficiently qualified to deal with AI technologies. Therefore, it is proposed to integrate AI into the curricula starting from the secondary school stage, with a focus on programming and data identification. This is based on this book's findings, which emphasize the importance of accuracy in academic outputs using AI applications. In addition, intensive training programs can also be developed for the private sector to train workers on the use of AI in some fields, such as predictive maintenance. In this context, a Gulf AI academy can be launched to unify training standards among the GCC countries in terms of the transition to a circular economy and sustainability.

The use of geospatial models to improve waste management in the United Arab Emirates, and the role of AI in achieving the concept of energy efficiency is also noteworthy. In this context, the discussion presented in these two chapters can be used to develop mechanisms that help convert waste into energy using data analysis algorithms and improving sorting and recycling processes, while achieving the UAE's goal of a 75% waste line. This is a model that can be used in many other Gulf countries. In addition, the discussions presented in this book can also be used to develop smart energy networks that rely on integrating accurate weather forecasts with energy management systems in smart cities, with the aim of achieving a balance between supply and demand regarding leadership in emerging technologies and strategic industries.

In addition to the positive changes in the public's opinion of AI and its uses, the effectiveness of neural networks in lowering manufacturing costs is crucial. With an emphasis on producing robots for the oil and healthcare industries, these findings highlight the need for the GCC area to grow its robotics industry by taking use of Oman's successful industrial models. It may also be possible to create specialized economic zones to draw in new businesses in the blockchain and metaverse industries. This might be made possible by establishing the Gulf Advanced Technologies Fund to fund generative intelligence initiatives.

By enhancing regional cooperation and building global partnerships, there is a gap between smart city applications in the GCC states and some other countries, such as Singapore, which calls for benefiting from international experiences in this field. Therefore, it is proposed at this point to establish joint research initiatives that represent partnerships between Gulf universities to work in areas such as renewable energy. It is also proposed to establish investment alliances that encourage Gulf companies to invest in global emerging companies, similar to what the Emirati Mubadala Company has done in the field of health AI (Reynolds, 2025). The establishment of the Gulf Innovation Forum as an annual platform for exchanging experiences between policymakers and researchers in light of these results and the identified trends could help achieve these trends.

15.4 Towards AI-Powered Smart and Sustainable Future in the GCC Countries: Policy Recommendations

Based on the analysis of the results of the book's main findings and in light of the identified future trends related to enhancing the application of AI in the Gulf Cooperation Council countries, a set of policy recommendations can be formulated. The aim is to support the adoption of AI applications and maximize its economic, social, and security benefits for the countries of the region. In general, the Gulf Cooperation Council countries represent a fertile environment for adopting AI technologies, thanks to their massive investments in digital infrastructure and their ambitious plans for economic transformation. However, achieving the maximum benefit from these technologies requires sound policies that address current challenges and anticipate the future. The following are some recommendations that may help decision-makers in this field develop appropriate regulatory policies for AI.

Firstly, it is necessary to strengthen governance and ethical frameworks specific to AI applications. At this point, we can talk about establishing independent national bodies to supervise AI applications, similar to an AI Ethics Committee, provided that these bodies include representatives from the government, academia, the private sector and civil society institutions. In addition, a comprehensive legislative framework must be established to regulate the use of AI. A basic set of pillars should form the core of such a framework. At the forefront of these pillars comes the need to achieve transparency in the decision-making process that takes place through AI applications, in addition to the need to emphasize the protection of personal data, ensure privacy and apply some standards related to this matter, such as the standards specific to GDPR (Wulf & Seizov, 2024). There is also the aspect related to legal accountability in cases of errors or algorithmic bias (Novelli et al., 2024). Some mechanisms that ensure accountability in the event of any error or bias resulting from the use of AI application algorithms are needed. At this point, we can also discuss the need to enhance regional cooperation with the aim of harmonizing regulatory policies and coordinating between the various entities working to formulate these policies in the Gulf Cooperation Council countries, especially in the areas of cybersecurity and e-commerce (Badran, 2024). Given the rapid pace of development of AI applications, legislative, regulatory, and ethical frameworks must be highly flexible in terms of policy formulation and continuous evaluation of these frameworks. AI policies can be adopted that are flexible and adaptable, so that these frameworks and policies can be changed considering developments in AI technology. National observatories can also be established to monitor the impact of AI, issuing periodic reports on the impact of AI applications on employment and privacy in Gulf societies. Grants can also be used as tax incentives for companies to encourage responsible innovation, adopting ethical practices in developing AI applications.

Secondly, in terms of developing technological and research infrastructure, it can be noted that it is impossible to separate the progress of AI and the provision of the infrastructure that supports benefiting from this progress. Therefore, it is recommended to increase investment in high-performance computing (HPC) centers, as the University of Bahrain has done through partnerships with international research centers to support the training of large models locally. It is also necessary to create open-source platforms to collect the necessary data from various sectors, such as public health or traffic data, while applying encryption technology to protect identity. In addition, it is necessary to link AI with the technologies of the Fourth Industrial Revolution, such as the Internet of Things (IoT), in smart city projects, so that sensors are used, as is the case of Dubai to monitor energy consumption in government buildings.

Thirdly, in terms of reforming the educational system and developing cadres, the results of the chapters that addressed this topic in this book concluded that the Gulf labor market faces a gap in terms of the skills required in the field of AI technologies. Hence, to bridge this gap, it is necessary to integrate AI into educational curricula at all levels, starting from the primary stage through some interactive educational activities that use educational robots with a focus on developing critical thinking towards technology by students. In addition, it is necessary to launch reintegration programs for the current workforce in cooperation with global technology companies to train engineers on machine learning technology and its applications in industry. It is also necessary to encourage precise specializations such as the ethics of AI and data engineering by allocating fully funded scholarships to outstanding students in prestigious universities around the world.

Fourth, regarding stimulating innovation in strategic sectors, we can talk about some measures that would support the process of adopting AI applications in vital sectors such as energy, health, transportation, and the financial insurance services. Regarding the energy sector, we note that at this point AI can bring about a shift in the oil industry through a set of measures. In this context, predictive maintenance is one of the mechanisms that can help, through the application of smart sensors, predict equipment failure before it occurs, which helps in significantly reducing maintenance costs, as previously discussed in the chapters of this book. AI applications can also be used to improve exploration operations by analyzing seismic data using deep learning algorithms, as was done by the Oman Oil Company. In the health sector, AI applications can contribute significantly to the accurate diagnosis of diseases by using models that help analyze medical images to detect diseases such as cancer in their early stages. King Fahad Medical City in Riyadh is currently trying to benefit from this matter. AI applications in the health sector can also be used in the field of crisis management, as smart platforms are being developed to distribute resources during epidemics, such as the ALHOSN app in the UAE during the COVID-19 pandemic (Abu

Sarhan & AlFalasi, 2023). In the financial sector, AI applications can help in specific areas such as combating fraud by using learning algorithms to discover unusual patterns. These applications can also be used in the field of smart insurance, where customized insurance policies are provided based on the analysis of personal data through platforms. With regard to smart cities, AI applications can help develop transportation management, as these applications are used to predict traffic congestion through GPS data and weather data, as implemented in some countries such as the Kingdom of Saudi Arabia. There is also the aspect related to rationalizing consumption, where AI applications, especially smart systems for managing water in homes via Internet of Things devices connected to the electronic cloud, greatly help in rationalizing water use.

Fifth, regarding national security and defense capabilities, it is noticeable that with the increase in electronic threats and drone attacks, there has become a necessity to develop a set of tools that ensure the proper use of AI applications in the security and military fields. In this regard, it is recommended to develop self-defense systems, such as drone systems, in the Gulf Cooperation Council countries, as these armed, autonomous technologies are capable of accurately distinguishing targets, but under human supervision, so that individuals can make the final decisions regarding directing these drones. It is also useful in this regard to establish specialized centers in the field of cybersecurity in partnership with advanced countries in this specialty, in order to train national cadres on how to confront complex electronic attacks. It is also useful to employ AI to protect vital infrastructure, such as desalination plants, through monitoring systems capable of detecting breaches in real time. In all cases, all ethical aspects related to the application of AI in military and security fields must be considered in order to avoid the harm that may result from the expansion of the use of these technologies to individuals.

Sixth, in terms of sustainable development and environmental sustainability, AI can be a pillar of the green transformation in the GCC countries by converting waste into energy by using smart robots to separate waste in landfills, which increases the efficiency of recycling this waste. In addition, in the field of smart agriculture, irrigation systems can be developed that rely on AI to improve water consumption in farms using satellite data. Such technologies will help the GCC countries expand agricultural operations and use the available quantities of water to the maximum possible efficiency to grow crops and achieve food security. In the field of renewable energy, the efficiency of solar panels can be improved through algorithms that predict dust accumulation and direct robots to clean automatically, which helps raise the efficiency of solar energy generation farms. In this context, it is also necessary to work on empowering emerging companies and small projects, as the role of small companies in the AI economy is still limited in the GCC countries. Therefore, it is recommended to launch specialized business incubators with the provision of soft loans for startups in areas such as financial technology or digital health, in addition to the need to simplify regulatory procedures for granting licenses to companies that adopt business models based on AI, while providing testing platforms to experiment with new technologies without legal risks.

To ensure that all segments of society benefit, digital inclusion must be promoted by raising community awareness through media campaigns in multiple languages to explain the benefits of AI and warn of the dangers of electronic impersonation. Smart applications can also be designed to serve people with disabilities, such as sign recognition applications for the deaf, in cooperation with civil society organizations. The digital gap between urban and rural areas can also be bridged by expanding the scope of fifth-generation networks to remote areas. At this point, international cooperation between the GCC countries and countries that have made great strides in the field of AI can help achieve these goals by forming strategic partnerships with global research centers in the field of AI, as well as participating in setting global standards that regulate the work of smart applications. International conferences can also be hosted, such as the World AI Summit to contribute to attracting experts and industry leaders.

15.5 Conclusion

In conclusion, the bottom line is that the GCC states have all the ingredients to become a global hub for AI. They have advanced infrastructure, abundant funding, and political will. However, success requires balanced policies that link innovation and governance with economic growth and social justice. These policies must be data-driven, with the involvement of all stakeholders in society. Only by balancing opportunities with challenges can the Gulf transform from a consumer of technology to a major player in shaping the future.

References

Abu Sarhan, T. M., & AlFalasi, S. J. (2023). United Arab Emirates (UAE) leadership in controlling COVID-19: Practical policy steps and outcomes. *Journal of Global Health Economics and Policy, 3*. https://doi.org/10.52872/001c.117618

Badran, A. (2021). Thoughts and reflections on the case of Qatar: Should AI be regulated? In E. Azar & A. N. Haddad (Eds.), *AI in the Gulf* (pp. 69–92). Springer Singapore. https://doi.org/10.1007/978-981-16-0771-4_5

Badran, A. (2023). AI between government and self-regulation policies: A Theoretical approach. جكامة. https://doi.org/10.31430/IJZH4708

Badran, A. (2024). Regulating cyberspace for children: Reflections on the Qatari case. *British Journal of Cyber Criminology, 3*(1). https://www.pubtexto.com/pdf/?regulating-cyberspace-for-children-reflections-on-the-qatari-case

Novelli, C., Taddeo, M., & Floridi, L. (2024). Accountability in AI: What it is and how it works. *AI & SOCIETY, 39*(4), 1871–1882. https://doi.org/10.1007/s00146-023-01635-y

Reynolds, R. (2025). *Mubadala executive on how AI is reshaping healthcare industry*. The National. https://www.thenationalnews.com/podcasts/recorded/2025/01/24/mubadala-executive-on-how-ai-is-reshaping-healthcare-industry/

Wulf, A. J., & Seizov, O. (2024). "Please understand we cannot provide further information": Evaluating content and transparency of GDPR-mandated AI disclosures. *AI & SOCIETY, 39*(1), 235–256. https://doi.org/10.1007/s00146-022-01424-z

Index

A. Badran and A. Mishrif (eds.), *Shaping the Future of Development in the GCC*, The Political Economy of the Middle East,
https://doi.org/10.1007/978-981-96-7963-8

FSC
www.fsc.org
MIX
Papier | Fördert gute Waldnutzung
FSC® C083411

Kolibri 360 GmbH
Ferdinand-Jühlke-Straße 7
99095 Erfurt, Deutschland
produktsicherheit@kolibri360.de